W9-BNB-424

Christian Worship: Manual

Christian Worship:
Manual

Gary Baumler
and
Kermit Moldenhauer, Editors

NORTHWESTERN PUBLISHING HOUSE
Milwaukee, Wisconsin

Authorized by the
Commission on Worship of the
Wisconsin Evangelical Lutheran Synod

Further copyright information on pages 487-497.

Library of Congress Card 93-84935
Northwestern Publishing House
1250 N. 113th St., Milwaukee, WI 53226-3284
© 1993 by Northwestern Publishing House.
Published 1993
Printed in the United States of America
ISBN 0-8100-0501-8

Acknowledgments

Section Editors:
  Section One: James Tiefel
  Section Two: Wayne Schulz
  Section Three: Harlyn Kuschel
  Section Four: Victor Prange

Copy Editor: Sharon Uekert

Contributors: Ames Anderson, Bruce Backer, Kris Altergott
  Eggers, Kurt Eggert, Michael Engel, Bryan Gerlach,
  Theodore Hartwig, Harlyn Kuschel, Edward Meyer,
  Kermit Moldenhauer, Victor Prange, Wayne Schulz,
  George Tiefel, and James Tiefel

Contents

Introduction

Early in the process of preparing *Christian Worship: A Lutheran Hymnal,* it became evident that if the resources contained in the hymnal were to be fully utilized, a manual of some kind was necessary. Members of the Joint Hymnal Committee time and again commented that a given suggestion belonged "in the manual."

It became essential that a manual be published once the decision was made not to include the Sunday and Festival Propers in the hymnal. The major Lutheran hymnals published in recent years, as well as *The Lutheran Hymnal,* all included the Propers. By publishing the Propers in *Christian Worship: Manual,* considerable space was saved in the hymnal for additional hymns and services. Since the average congregational member does not make use of the Propers, their inclusion in the hymnal was not judged necessary.

This manual is intended especially for all who have responsibility in planning and carrying out the corporate worship of the church: pastors, presiding ministers, accompanists, and choir directors. Others who have a special interest in worship or have a responsibility for worship education in our churches and schools will find much useful information in this manual. Those who are preparing themselves for a life of public ministry in the church will benefit greatly from a careful study of this book.

Christian Worship: Manual has four sections with the chapters numbered consecutively. "Worship in Theology and Practice" is the subject of Section One. Not only will one find a presentation of the history and principles that underlie *Christian Worship,* but also many practical comments with regard to worship space, vestments, congregational outreach, and planning.

Section Two, titled "The Services in Detail and Use," includes commentary on all the services found in *Christian Worship* along with a discussion of items that the services have in common

(Psalm, Verse of the Day, Canticles, Sermon). It offers many helpful suggestions for conducting public worship.

"Music in Christian Worship" is the subject of Section Three. Major articles discuss hymns, organs and other instruments in worship, and choirs. One will find much helpful information and a variety of resources for all facets of music ministry in the church.

The final section of this manual contains the Propers (readings, Psalm of the Day, Prayer of the Day, Verse of the Day, Hymn of the Day, color) for Sundays, Major and Minor Festivals, and Occasions. An introduction gives background information on the origins of the calendar of the Christian year and the Propers. Finally, one will find a variety of indices helpful in worship planning.

St. Paul said of the worship of the Christians in Corinth: "Everything should be done in a fitting and orderly way" (1 Corinthians 14:40). That continues to be one of the goals for ministers of worship today as the people of God come together to glorify him. This manual is intended to be a help in attaining that goal.

SECTION ONE:

WORSHIP IN THEOLOGY AND PRACTICE

CHAPTER 1:

Worship in
the Life of the Church

The Worship of Christians

The central truth of the Christian faith is this: "All have sinned and fall short of the glory of God, and are justified freely by his grace through the redemption that came by Christ Jesus" (Romans 3:23,24). In all of history and in all of creation, no better news exists for human beings than this good news. Through Christ, God frees us from the guilt we have carried and the eternal punishment we have deserved.

The gospel, however, does more than release us from death. It also enlivens a spontaneous outpouring of gratitude and praise, of love and respect for God. This thankful response the Bible calls *worship*. The Apostle Paul wrote: "Therefore, I urge you . . . in view of God's mercy, to offer your bodies as living sacrifices, holy and pleasing to God—this is your spiritual act of worship" (Romans 12:1). Since Christ himself stands as the centerpiece of God's mercy, the believer's thankful response is rightly called *Christian worship.*

Every God-pleasing thought, word, and action a Christian does from a heart of faith is worship, but the best and most necessary worship of God is to *listen as he speaks to us.* Martha loved serving her Lord and was busy in her activity, but it was Mary whom Jesus commended for choosing to listen to what he said. Faith knows its source: "Faith comes from hearing the message, and the message is heard through the word of Christ" (Romans 10:17). Martin Luther wrote, "Since God at first gives faith through the Word, so he thereafter exercises, increases, confirms, and perfects it through the Word. Therefore the worship of God at its best and the finest keeping of the Sabbath consists . . . in dealing with the Word and hearing it."[1]

Every believer finds a two-fold joy in his or her relationship with God. Christians open their hearts to Christ to hear his saving and empowering gospel. At the same time, they come to offer Christ their confidence, their lives, and everything they have. This receiving from God and giving to God is the sum total of the Christian life. It is a never-ending cycle; it begins at baptism and endures into eternity. If we do not receive from God, we cannot have faith. If we do not respond to God, our faith is dead.

The Worship of the Christian Church

Receiving from God and responding to God are not only the sum total of each individual Christian's life, however. They are also the heart and soul of the public worship of the Christian Church. Believers desire to express in public what they believe in private, and they long to share with other Christians what they believe as individuals. In public worship, therefore, God speaks and his people respond. God serves the congregation and the congregation serves God.[2]

This two-fold function of the Christian assembly is apparent throughout the history of God's people. God placed his rainbow in the sky and attached his promise to it. Noah and his family built an altar in grateful response for the protection God gave during the ordeal of the flood and for his promise that he would not send another universal deluge. The people of Israel built a tabernacle in response to God's command, and God filled the place with smoke, the symbol of his presence and promises. The daily sacrifices that God's people brought in the temple showed their confidence in his promise to send a final sacrifice that would supersede the blood of bulls and goats, a sacrifice for sin that Christ would make once and for all. When the first Christians assembled, they not only devoted themselves to the apostles' teaching

---

[1] *What Luther Says,* Ewald Plass, editor, Vol. 3 (St. Louis: Concordia, 1959), p. 1545.

[2] In his excellent volume, *Worship in the Name of Jesus,* (translated by M. H. Bertram and published in St. Louis by Concordia in 1968) author Peter Brunner goes into great detail on just this point on pp. 11-24.

and to the breaking of bread, but they also joined in fellowship to offer prayers in response to Christ's promises.

St. Paul's inspired instruction to the congregation at Colosse lets us know what the Holy Spirit sees as the function of the Christian assembly. Paul wrote, "Let the word of Christ dwell in you richly as you teach and admonish one another with all wisdom, and as you sing psalms, hymns and spiritual songs with gratitude in your hearts to God" (Colossians 3:16). When today's church arranges its public worship to include both God's service to the congregation and the congregation's service to God, it expresses the essential functions of the life of each of its members.

Worship: The Preeminent Activity of the Congregation

Christian congregations understand that public worship is only one part of a church's life. Christians gathered in a visible church also authorize and support the teaching of children, teenagers, and adults. In the name of the congregation, pastors visit the sick and dying and counsel the troubled and erring. Individually and as a group, Christians search for opportunities to proclaim the good news to the lost. Each of these ministries, and many others besides, is important. All are encouraged by the Savior in his Word. All have been carried out by Christians of every age. But none has the same function or value as the public worship of the congregation.

In its public worship more than in any other place, Christian churches look and act like the Holy Christian Church, i.e., the assembly of believers. The true Church is invisible, and its members are known only to God. Yet, when believers who confess Christ gather around the Word and the sacraments and respond to Christ in prayer and praise, we see what the Church is like and how it functions. Peter Brunner wrote, "[The] worship . . . of the Christian congregation . . . is virtually the dominant mode of manifestation of the Church on earth. In such an assembly the epiphany of the Church takes place."[3] Believers gather together in many places and for many reasons. It is in public worship, how-

---

[3] Brunner, *Worship,* pp. 18,19.

ever, that more believers gather than at any other time to do what believers do more than any other thing, that is, to receive from God and to give to God.

This truth by itself makes the congregation's worship its most important activity. But worship holds the church's greatest interest for other reasons as well. Worship affords the best opportunity for believers to encourage each other with the Word. It sets a full banquet of the means of grace and marshals all of God's created gifts for the praise of his grace. Worship repeats for Christians the truths about Christ that are essential for Christian faith, and it sets a pattern and a pace for the Christian life. No other congregational activity affords such a variety or such fullness of receiving and response.

Worship Provides for Mutual Encouragement

Believers understand that they enter into a relationship with God on a personal level. Yet, from the beginning to the end of the Scriptures, the Holy Spirit tells us about individual believers coming together to receive from God and to respond to God as a group. The Old Testament believer David maintained, "I rejoiced with those who said to me, 'Let us go to the house of the LORD'" (Psalm 122:1). If anything, Jesus' followers valued the worship gathering more than their Jewish ancestors did. We have every indication from the New Testament that "congregational meetings for worship were the focal point for the Christian's every thought and act."[4]

Gathering into an assembly is natural for a group that considers itself to be the body of Christ. But there is much more than a theological symbol in this gathering. The members of the church see a very practical reason for coming together in worship. The author of the letter to the Hebrews put his finger on it when he wrote, "Let us not give up meeting together, as some are in the habit of doing, but let us encourage one another—and all the more as you see the Day approaching" (Hebrews 10:25). The encouragement that believers give their brothers and sisters is invaluable. Satan, his evil cohorts in the world, and even the believ-

---

[4] Brunner, *Worship,* p. 17.

er's own sinful self mount daily challenges against individual Christians to undervalue both God's giving and their responding. In contrast, believers of various ages, from various walks of life, living in various situations come together as the church to encourage and to be encouraged in the essentials of the Christian life, i.e., receiving from God and giving to him.

Worship Offers the Fullness of the Means of Grace

God comes to his people in both the Word and the sacraments. Here is another reason why Christians value public worship so highly: the church's regular worship assembly includes the fullest use of the means of grace. Martin Luther was reflecting what had been the church's worship practice since its beginnings when he wrote, "Among Christians the whole service should center on Word and sacrament."[5] As valuable and important as they are, none of the other activities of the congregation offer such a complete use of the means of grace.

Worship Employs the Richness of God's Creation

When God comes to his people, he speaks to their hearts as well as their minds; he addresses the entire person and personality. We cannot understand all the mysteries of how God does this, but we know from the Scriptures that God uses more than just the spoken or read word to communicate his love. He brings the fullness of creation to bear in his effort to solidify and underscore what he tells us in his Word. He uses symbols, pictures, and illustrations. Bread and wine and water carry specific promises in the supper and baptism. The concepts of the prophet, the priest, and the king explain his mission. A compassionate father welcoming home his wayward son illustrates God's love. God speaks with clear language for the sake of our intellect and he speaks with beautiful language for the sake of our emotions. The Holy Spirit uses both clarity and loveliness to carry God's message into the bloodstream of the believer, penetrating bone and marrow and bringing life, health, and joy to the entire person and personality. Better than many contemporary Lutherans, Martin Luther under-

---

[5] Luther's Works, American edition, Vol. 53 (Philadelphia: Fortress Press, 1967), p. 90.

stood how God adds the glories of his creation to his Word to implant the message of love powerfully in the minds and hearts of his people:

> The Book of Psalms is a sweet and delightful song because it sings of and proclaims the Messiah even when a person does not sing the notes but merely recites and pronounces the words. And yet the music, or the notes, which are a wonderful creation and gift of God, help materially in this, especially when the people sing along and reverently participate.[6]

As long as believers have gathered for public worship, they have appreciated the value of adding the arts to worship for the sake of proclaiming the gospel to head and heart. God himself set the standard for this kind of worship when he established the worship of Old Testament Israel. The early Christian church did not lose sight of that example. As soon as the persecutions ended and Christians were able to gather freely, they added beauty and richness to their public worship.

In the centuries which have passed since then, there is hardly a part of God's creation which Christians have not employed at worship: speech in prose and poetry; music in harmony and unison; instruments of wood and metal; architecture with its science and technology; artifacts of stone, wood, fabric, gold, silver, brass, iron, and glass; ritual, symbolism, and ceremony; light and darkness; money and the fruits of the earth—the list is endless.

Today's church ought to understand that God comes to believers at worship not only with the fullness of the means of grace but also with the richness of his creation. At public worship, therefore, all of God's spiritual gifts and all of his created gifts join to proclaim the good news about Jesus. The eternal light in the chancel joins with the Savior's words in John 8:12 ("I am the light of the world") to proclaim the unending and enlightening presence of Christ. The sign of the cross adds image to language to remind believers that "the message of the cross . . . is the power of God" (1 Corinthians 1:18).

---

[6] Luther's Works, American, Vol. 45, p. 273.

Worship Repeats What Is Essential for Faith and Life

Worship brings to the church the fullness and the richness of God's giving, but it does not offer everything that God gives. The congregation's teaching ministries are better suited than its public worship to deepen and expand knowledge of the intricacies of God's will. The pastor's counseling ministry applies law and gospel to specific situations in ways that public worship cannot—and, for the sake of privacy, ought not. Besides the information it presents to us about the purpose of the worship assembly, Scripture speaks often about teaching, witnessing, making disciples, and giving personal exhortation and encouragement.

Nevertheless, when the assembly gathers, God proclaims what is essential if faith is to survive and grow: the promises of Christ in Word and sacrament, God's decree of full forgiveness, the words and works of Christ on which forgiveness is based, the good news that Christians are redeemed from sin, death, and devil and that they are redeemed for unity with Christ and a life of service.

Public worship repeats these themes precisely because they are essential for faith. Here again is why the church finds public worship so valuable. Faith lives on these basic doctrines of Scripture. Cut off from them, faith becomes weak and eventually dies. If faith were just knowledge, if an intellectual awareness of historical facts made one a stronger Christian, then public worship's repetition of the basics would not be nearly as important. But faith is more than intelligence; it is respect, love, and trust in God, which is created, maintained, and strengthened by the gospel. The gospel is the essential gift that God imparts Sunday after Sunday in Christian worship.

Worship Sets the Pattern for Christian Response

The service the church brings to God in its public worship sets the pattern for the service believers bring to God, both as they participate in the public ministry of the gospel and as they carry out their personal and daily ministry. In a certain sense, the church's service to God at worship is a practice session for its total life of worship. The end result almost certainly will imitate the pattern.

9

At public worship believers of all ages, shapes, and sizes join to offer God their mutual response of faith. Worship intends to bring the church together, not to separate it by age groups, financial status, or social circumstances. And the responses these united believers bring cover a multitude of life activities which are common to all. They praise, honor, and glorify God. They confess their sins to him and affirm their faith in him. They pray for themselves, for fellow believers, for the earth, the state, and the creation, and for those who are without faith. They offer to God a portion of the gifts they have received from the riches of his grace. They listen, they eat and drink, and they long for the perfect worship of heaven. In public worship the body of Christ does in summary fashion exactly the same spiritual things that each of its members does on every day of the year.

What would happen were worship to cease? Without the gospel to enliven faith, all congregational activities would quickly come to an end. Church members would not be willing to bring their gifts and offerings at the cost of their earthly wants and desires. Parents would stop caring about the faith of their children and would no longer support Christian education. There would be no motive for witnessing and no interest in mission work. If the congregation's praise of God and its prayers to him are lifeless, cold, and without enthusiasm at public worship, it follows that daily loving, living, working, and witnessing will be lifeless and cold as well. If there is no encouragement from Christian to Christian to give to God at worship, what encouragement can be expected day by day? If Christians get into the habit of giving God only the leftovers of his gifts to them at public worship, it is not likely they will give him any more than leftovers when they are not at worship.

Christian worship focuses on the joyful use and reception of his Word and sacraments, and that encourages the joyful response of the people of God. When congregations, like individual Christians, experience a lack of spiritual energy and enthusiasm, the reason may well lie in their neglect of public worship. With that reality in mind, those who lead public worship find a powerful incentive to make worship the preeminent activity of the congregation and to put their hearts and hands and voices to eager and careful work as they plan, prepare, and pre-side at worship.

Setting Objectives: A Vital Part of Planning for Worship

Studying the purpose of public worship not only supplies an incentive to worship leaders, but also helps them understand how worship is to be planned and arranged. This understanding is a necessary prelude to worship leadership. Without it, public wor-ship may not accomplish the purpose it has in the congregation. In order to gain this understanding, it is necessary not only to dis-cover the function of public worship, but also to know the pur-pose of other activities in the congregation.

The work of the Christian Church is to proclaim the unchang-ing law of God and the saving gospel of his Son, Jesus Christ. This is the church's only ministry. Everything the congregation or groups of congregations do must be a part of this ministry. How-ever, the ministry of the gospel has various forms, and Scripture gives freedom to the church to decide which forms will be carried out in a congregation. While each of these forms of ministry has as its over-arching objective the proclamation of law and gospel, each has a unique objective as well.

When a congregation determines to conduct an evangelism ministry, it sets this objective: those who are designated to evan-gelize want to present the law and the gospel in such a way that the hearer gains a clear understanding of the message of sin and God's love in Christ. Simplicity is essential in this ministry, as is clarity. If the Holy Spirit is to have access to the hearer's heart, the message of law and gospel must be clearly proclaimed. Wis-dom tells us that the simple message of salvation is best pro-claimed in a non-threatening situation and often within the con-text of friendship and familiarity.

When a congregation sets out to teach, it wants to find teachers and teaching tools that will be able to teach the law and the gospel in such a way that the learner comes to learn and love the Savior and his Word to an ever-expanding degree. Teachers will want to understand the basic principles of the teaching/learning process. They will arrange students in groups that are similar in ability and interest. They will use visual aids to promote interest and solidify concepts. They will establish a curriculum so that the knowledge of the students is always growing. Students will be encouraged to participate in the class presentation, to answer questions, to discuss biblical principles with each other, and to take work home for additional study.

When a congregation sees that it must practice Christian discipline in a certain situation, it will instruct those who have been given this ministry to present the law and the gospel in such a way that the weak and erring see their specific sins, hear of God's personal forgiveness, and find God's specific promises that he will supply the power for life-changes. A personal approach is essential in this area of ministry, for the sake of both confrontation and absolution. Since the erring members of the congregation often try to hide from this ministry, discipline calls for determined, consistent, and patient efforts on the part of those who are ministering.

The Christian counselor wants to apply the law and the gospel in such a way that the counselee comes to know how God's will speaks to his situation and that God's love and power can give strength to deal with human problems. Careful listening and patient instruction are part of counseling. Counselors also require an ability to know when a psychological malady needs the assistance of a medical doctor or trained psychologist.

The congregation's public worship also has the objective of proclaiming law and gospel, but it has additional goals as well. Worship means to present a review of those teachings of the Scripture that feed faith and foster the Christian life, and to present that review with all the gifts, both spiritual and physical, that God gives. It also means to give believers a purposeful opportunity to respond to God's gracious promises with all the riches of his blessings to them. The goals of receiving from God and responding to God are met in the context of the encouragement given from Christian to Christian.

Matching Content with Objectives

Our society connects religion almost automatically and almost exclusively with public worship. "I go to church" tends to mean "I attend church services, and, therefore, I belong to a church." Even many church members see public worship as almost the entire ministry of the congregation. It should not be surprising, then, that some Christians expect public worship to "carry the load" of all the congregation's ministries. To some, worship ought to be able to function as evangelism, education, discipline, and counseling. When public worship begins to carry all those responsibilities, its own objectives can hardly be met. It is just as likely that the objectives of the other ministries will not be met, either, when they are placed into the context of worship.

Those who have been called and appointed as leaders of the church are wise to decide which ministries can be assumed by their congregations and then to use the tools, methods, and forms that best meet the objectives of each ministry. A liturgical canticle and a sermon based on a church-year Scripture lesson are excellent forms for worship, given worship's emphasis on the repetition of the life of Christ and its desire to touch both the head and the heart. However, neither are well suited for teaching. A monetary offering and a hymn by Martin Luther are natural parts of worship, considering worship's inclusion of the confessional response of faith, but neither works very well to present the basic concepts of sin and grace to an unchurched person. Overhead projectors and discussion questions are excellent teaching tools, but they intrude into a worship situation. And no one would dream of asking from the pulpit the kind of searching questions that are often essential in counseling.

Public worship stands as the preeminent activity of the Christian congregation, but it is not the only activity, and it ought not be perceived or arranged as though it were. Worship serves the congregation best when it remains what the church's worship has always been: the intellectual and emotional interaction between the Bridegroom and his bride, between Christ and his Church. When public worship matches this objective, it supports in its unique way all other facets of the congregation's ministry.

CHAPTER 2:

The Lutheran Liturgy

Once the church properly determines the objective of its public worship, it needs to choose worship forms that will match that objective. Leaders in the Lutheran church today agree that the form of worship that best allows public worship to be an interaction between Christ and his Church is *liturgical worship*.

The word *liturgical* and its root word *liturgy* have a variety of meanings and uses among Christians. The word comes from two Greek words meaning "people" and "work." In the Bible this word and its derivatives are used for the formal, organized worship of both Christians and non-Christians, as well as for the lifelong worship of believers. As many people understand the word, liturgy is a regular and formal order of worship, and a liturgical church is one that uses such an order of service.

The term liturgical has a narrower focus, however. It describes a kind of worship that is unique among the many orders of service used in Christian churches. *Christian Worship: A Lutheran Hymnal* adopts this more precise meaning and defines liturgical worship as a worship style that is built on the historic Christian liturgy. An order of service that is in keeping with liturgical style includes the historic liturgy's basic progression of the Ordinary (fixed parts) and the Proper (variable parts), its focus on the emphases of the Christian church year, and its regular offering of Holy Communion.

We connect the words liturgical and *style* for good reasons. During the eighteen centuries that have passed since the Christian liturgy first appeared, there have been countless variations on the basic themes. The liturgy has appeared in dozens of languages and endured hundreds of local innovations. However, in the churches that have embraced the emphases of the liturgy, the basic form and primary focus of worship, that is, the liturgical style, have remained in place.

The Roots of the Liturgy

For as long as believers have gathered together, they have naturally included certain elements in their worship of God. Proclamation, acclamation, prayer, and purification had been part of worship since before the time of Moses. From Moses until Christ, God himself set the standards for the worship of the church, especially in the rites of the tabernacle and the temple. The Jewish people crafted additional worship forms and customs for worship in the synagogue.

Since the first Christians were Jewish believers, it was to be expected that some elements of Old Testament worship life would be retained. The early church continued to sing the psalms and pray many of the prayers that had been part of worship in both the temple and the synagogue. We can assume that the believers added rich symbolism (e.g., the use of salt and oil for anointing) to their early baptism rites because they were used to the temple's high ceremony and striking types and pictures. Believers continued to read from the Scriptures, just as they had in the synagogue service; they even retained, more or less, the synagogue's order of service. Jesus himself suggested a prayer for the believers, the Lord's Prayer. The Apostle Paul urged that "requests, prayers, intercession and thanksgiving be made for everyone" (1 Timothy 2:1). He assumed that the words Jesus spoke on Passover night would be repeated whenever the Sacrament was observed, and he also made suggestions about how the church should use its "psalms, hymns and spiritual songs" (Ephesians 5:19 and Colossians 3:16).

St. Luke may be telling us what the first Christian order of service looked like when he wrote, "They devoted themselves to the apostles' teaching [the synagogue order with its lessons] and to the fellowship [perhaps the fellowship meal that was eaten between the Word service and the Sacrament service], to the breaking of bread [the Lord's Supper] and to prayer [perhaps the prayer of thanksgiving]" (Acts 2:42). Less than a generation after Pentecost, St. Paul seems to be quoting early Christian hymns in his letters to the congregations. (e.g., Ephesians 5:14, Philippians 2:6-11)

First and second century Christians faced a variety of problems that they needed to address, and the church composed many of its worship forms as these specific needs arose. Over the span of several centuries the major liturgical songs were added—*Glory be to God; Holy, Holy, Holy; O Christ, Lamb of God*—and choirs began to take the lead in singing them. Over the same span the church calendar came into being, and Christian hymnody flourished. Before many years passed, Gospel and Epistle readings were added to the lessons from the Law and the Prophets. By A.D. 150, the order of service used in Rome looked similar to the liturgy we still use today. By 200, the text of the preface of the communion service had been established:

M: The Lord be with you.
C: And also with you.
M: Lift up your hearts.
C: We have them with the Lord.
M: Let us give thanks unto the Lord.
C: It is meet and right.[1]

By the seventh century after Christ, the church's worship order was in a form it retained until the Reformation.

The Christian worship rite was thoroughly Christ-centered. The early church had arranged its Sunday worship service to emphasize the words and works of Jesus. Besides regularly including the Lord's Supper, it provided that the lessons from the Gospels should be read in sequence, therefore following the story of Jesus' life. The formation of the church calendar followed this progression of lessons. Hymns, psalms, and prayers came to the support of the emphases of the gospel readings and, together with the lessons, became known as the Proper of the service. In addition to the changing themes, the service included a set of unchanging songs called the Ordinary, which repeated the principal truths of Christianity: *Kyrie (Lord, Have Mercy), Gloria in Excelsis (Glory be to God), Sanctus (Holy, Holy, Holy), and Agnus Dei (Lamb of God).* The *Credo* (Nicene Creed) found its regular place in the liturgy around A.D. 1000.

The rite that the early leaders of the Christian church arranged for the church's worship assembly accomplished what the be-

---

[1] Bard Thompson, *Liturgies of the Western Church* (Cleveland, Ohio: 1961), p. 20.

lievers intended. It presented a weekly review of those teachings of Scripture that fed faith and fostered the Christian life, and it presented that review with all the gifts, both spiritual and physical, that God had given. At the same time, it gave the church a purposeful opportunity to respond to God's gracious promises with all the riches of his blessings to them. The goals of receiving from God and responding to God were met in the context of the encouragement that Christians brought to one other. While arranged in freedom, the new rite, like the church it nourished, was "built on the foundation of the apostles and the prophets, with Christ Jesus himself as the chief cornerstone" (Ephesians 2:20).

The Liturgy in Today's Church

The liturgy does today exactly what it did for Christians of ages past: it focuses the attention of worshipers squarely on the words and works of Jesus. It does this by reviewing the principle teachings concerning Christ's work of salvation (the Ordinary) every Sunday and by reviewing Christ's life and ministry (the Proper) every year. It also presents to the believers a regular opportunity to receive the holy sacrament instituted by Christ.

The focus of the Proper is set by a unique calendar called the Christian church year. Beginning in late November or early December each year, the Christian calendar repeats the cycle of Jesus' ministry and mission: his forerunner in Advent, his birth at Christmas, his manifestation in the world during Epiphany, his battles with Satan and evil during Lent, his suffering and death during Holy Week, his resurrection in the Easter season, his Ascension into heaven, and the commissioning of his church on Pentecost. During the months between Pentecost and Advent, the Christian calendar calls to mind the nature and work of the church and its people, as well as the special relationship that exists between Jesus and the believers.

From its beginnings, the Christian church has placed a high value on the holy supper that Jesus gave to his people on Maundy Thursday, the night he was betrayed. Unfortunately, many believers have not rediscovered the kind of love for Holy Communion that the first Christians had. However, the liturgy assumes

17

that such love exists in some hearts and minds in every congregation, and it therefore includes a regular provision for this sacrament.

A service based on the historic Christian rite, the determinative use of the church calendar, and the inclusion of the Sacrament are, then, the marks of the liturgical style of worship. With this understanding, *Christian Worship: A Lutheran Hymnal* speaks of the liturgical lessons, those Scripture readings that are part of the church year's lectionary; liturgical preaching, sermons that are based on one of the liturgical lessons; liturgical chant, the prose hymns that are part of the historic liturgy; liturgical colors, the colors that appear on the paraments for the altar, pulpit, lectern, and vestments; and a liturgical choir, a choir that takes its specified part in the liturgy.

The following chart displays the two versions of the historic Christian liturgy that appear in *Christian Worship: A Lutheran Hymnal:*

The Common Service	*Service of Word and Sacrament*
Hymn	Hymn
Invocation	Greeting
Confession of Sins	Confession of Sins
Lord, Have Mercy	Absolution
Absolution	Lord, Have Mercy
Glory be to God on High	O Lord, Our Lord
Salutation	
Prayer of the Day	Prayer of the Day
First Lesson	First Lesson
Psalm of the Day	Psalm of the Day
Second Lesson	Second Lesson
Verse of the Day	Verse of the Day
Gospel of the Day	Gospel of the Day
Nicene Creed	Hymn of the Day
Hymn of the Day	Sermon
Sermon	Nicene Creed
Offertory (Create in me)	
Offering	Offering
Prayer of the Church	Prayer of the Church

Lord's Prayer	Lord's Prayer
Preface	Preface
Holy, Holy, Holy	Holy, Holy, Holy
Words of Institution	Words of Institution
O Christ, Lamb of God	O Christ, Lamb of God
Distribution	Distribution
Song of Simeon	
Thanksgiving	Thank the Lord
Closing Prayer	Closing Prayer
Blessing	Exhortation and Blessing

Alternate Worship Forms

Christian Worship assumes that every Lutheran congregation will choose to use one or both of the liturgical services it contains. However, most congregations have a need for other worship rites besides the regular Sunday service.

Occasionally some congregations will decide to omit Holy Communion in a Sunday service. They may retain the use of the liturgical service, but without its sacramental rite. *Christian Worship* provides the *Service of the Word* as an alternate service for times when the Sacrament is not offered.

The Christian church has some historical precedent for a service without Holy Communion. A preaching service called *Prone* was common in Europe after the time of Emperor Charlemagne, and German Lutheran congregations were given the option to end the liturgical service before the Preface if there were no communicants at a given service.[2] The preaching service in *Christian Worship* does not follow any of the historical orders of *Prone*. It relies on the regular precommunion progression of the liturgical rite, but offers different prayers and canticles.

Congregations that schedule several services without Holy Communion each month will find the *Service of the Word* to have a good deal of similarity to the full liturgical rites of *Christian Worship*. However, the service contains enough character of its own so that the liturgical services will remain distinctive when

---

[2] Philip Pfatteicher, *Commentary on the Lutheran Book of Worship* (Minneapolis: Augsburg, 1990), pp. 145,449.

19

used. The *Service of the Word* will also find use in new congregations that are experiencing liturgical style for the first time. In these situations, pastors may consider using the simplicity of this service until they have opportunity to teach their members to appreciate the richness of the full liturgical rite.

Although they are not intended to serve as the main services of the congregation, *Christian Worship* includes two additional worship orders, *Morning Praise* and *Evening Prayer.* These orders are contemporary versions of the historic *Matins* and *Vespers,* both of which have their roots in the Daily Office. Daily prayer and praise services were an important part of the spiritual life encouraged by the Old Testament synagogue. The early church inherited this piety and continued the practice of morning, noon, and evening meditations. A full cycle of such services gained maturity in the medieval monastery and included *Matins* and *Lauds* at dawn, *Prime* at the beginning of work, *Terce* at 9:00 a.m., *Sext* at noon, *None* at 3:00 p.m., *Vespers* at the close of the day, and *Compline* before sleep at night. The Lutheran Church saw value in preserving at least some of the services of the Daily Office and used *Matins* and *Vespers* especially in the schools and larger churches.

Christian Worship offers rich variety by including five orders of service for the public worship of the congregation (six by adding the noncommunion version of the *Common Service*). However, it intends that one of the liturgical rites, the *Common Service* or the *Service of Word and Sacrament,* be considered the main order of the worshiping congregation.

CHAPTER 3:

The Principles
of Lutheran Worship

Despite its long history and its Christ-centered content, the liturgical order of service is not the only form of worship that Christian congregations use. Lutherans must be sure to understand that God has not given explicit directions about the form the church's worship should take. The apostles, especially Paul, made it clear that the forms of public worship should remain in the realm of the church's Christian liberty. When Jewish converts tried to insist that Old Testament worship laws should be retained by the Galatian congregations, Paul wrote, "It is for freedom that Christ has set us free. Stand firm, then, and do not let yourselves be burdened again by a yoke of slavery" (Galatians 5:1). The Confessions of the Lutheran church place a high value on this principle. *The Formula of Concord* insists that "the congregation of God of every place and every time has the power, according to its circumstances, to change such ceremonies in such manner as may be most useful and edifying to the congregation of God."[1] Lutherans maintain, therefore, that the forms and rites of our public worship are *adiaphora,* that is, things God has neither commanded nor forbidden in his Word.

The Voice of Martin Luther Concerning Worship

Our Lutheran understanding of adiaphora in worship is a legacy we have received from Martin Luther himself. Luther was interested in the worship life of the Christians in Germany. He incorporated the historic Christian order of service into two ser-

---

[1] *Formula of Concord: Thorough Declaration,* Art. 10:9. Unless otherwise noted, all quotations from the Lutheran Confession are referenced to the *Concordia Triglotta.*

vices: one in Latin, the *Formula Missae,* and another in German, the *Deutsche Messe.*[2] He produced several orders for Holy Baptism and for private and personal confession, and wrote rites for marriage and ordination. Luther was a gifted musician who put music to good use in his services. He also wrote a number of original hymns and rewrote or edited many more.

He was always careful, however, to insist that forms of worship in the church were not more important than the gospel. If forms did not serve the gospel, they were to be eliminated. Concerning his German service, he wrote:

> This or any other order shall be so used that whenever it becomes an abuse, it shall be straightway abolished and replaced by another. . . . For the order must serve the promotion of faith and love and not be detrimental of faith. As soon as they fail to do this, they are invalid, dead and gone.[3]

Luther did not write the Apology of the Augsburg Confession but surely agreed with the author, his coworker Philip Melanchthon:

> But just as the dissimilar length of day and night does not injure the unity of the Church, so we believe that the true unity of the Church is not injured by dissimilar rites instituted by men.[4]

Despite his clear confession of Christian liberty, we should not get the idea from Martin Luther that any form of worship is acceptable among Christians. As he looked into the Scriptures and at the history of the early church, Luther committed himself to the worship style and form we have defined as liturgical. He chose this form of worship for his Lutheran church for doctrinal reasons and on the basis of principles drawn directly from God's Word. Four of these principles are reviewed here in detail.

First Principle: The Predominance of the Gospel

Like the leaders of the early church, Luther was convinced that God's gracious love had to be the predominant voice in public

---

[2] Luther's services, rites, and hymns are found in Luther's Works, American, Vol. 53.

[3] Luther's Works, American, Vol. 53, p. 90.

[4] *Apology,* Art. 7 and 8:33.

worship's divine/human dialog. He wrote: "When God's Word is not preached, one had better neither sing nor read, or even come together."[5] He arranged his services in such a way that the proclamation of the gospel was clearly their primary function. He did not ignore the people's sacrifice of praise; Luther valued that aspect of worship. But in order to maintain the doctrine of justification by faith, he determined that the view of worship that God serves the church with his grace would have to continually oppose the ever-recurring view of worship as humanity's meritorious service to God. Luther wrote, "For among Christians, the whole service should center on Word and sacrament."[6]

Second Principle: The Participation of the Congregation

The church into which Martin Luther was born had removed the response of faith from the members of the congregation and placed it into the hands of the clergy and the clergy choir. That transformation had begun centuries before, when large numbers entered the church with little formal instruction. The choral groups, which had first been formed to assist the congregation, finally came to replace the congregation. The dominant role of the clergy choir likely encouraged the theological system in which it eventually fit perfectly; since the church taught that the people gained merit by simply attending the Mass, there was little need for their participation. Besides, it was accepted doctrine that the people required the intercessory actions of the priest if they were to approach God at all.

Luther attacked both of these teachings. "Every baptized Christian is a priest already, not by appointment or ordination . . . but because Christ himself has begotten him as a priest and has given birth to him in baptism."[7] This was not a devaluation of the pastoral office, but a restatement of what Scripture clearly taught, that by faith in Christ all believers have access to God. Luther understood that Christians should come to God in worship because they could come to him. Since they could come to him in faith, it was clear that no one should think that coming without faith was

---

[5] Luther's Works, American, Vol. 53, p. 11.

[6] Luther's Works, American, Vol. 53, p. 90.

[7] Plass, *What Luther Says,* p. 1139.

acceptable to God. In other words, the act of doing the Mass or watching the Mass gained nothing from God. Philip Melanchthon, Luther's colleague at Wittenberg, wrote in the Apology of the Augsburg Confession:

> Our opponents condemn us for teaching that human traditions do not merit the forgiveness of sins, and they require so-called universal rites as necessary for salvation. Here Paul is our champion; everywhere he insists that these observances neither justify nor are necessary over and above the righteousness of faith.[8]

With a clear understanding of the congregation's role in worship, Luther arranged the new services to include the people's full participation. In the Latin service, he stipulated that the sermon should be preached and the hymns sung in the language of the people, although he retained the other parts of the service in Latin, a language that most educated people used in conversation. In his German service, he replaced the traditional Latin songs of the Ordinary with German paraphrases for the sake of full congregational participation.

Third Principle: The Historic Voice of the Church

Very early in the Reformation years, Luther expressed concern that those who were following him were being considered sectarian and not simply reformed. He discouraged the use of the term "Lutheran" for that very reason. He insisted the churches that followed his lead were teaching what true believers had always taught. In 1524 he wrote: "We teach nothing new. We teach what is old and what the apostles and all godly teachers have taught."[9] He continued to make that point to the end of his life. In one of his last sermons he said, "We can prove that our faith is not new and of unknown origin, but that it is the oldest faith of all, which began and continued from the beginning of the world."[10]

Luther had no desire to separate himself from the purity of the church's past. He understood that the outline and the basic ele-

---

[8] Apology, Art. 15:49-50.

[9] Plass, *What Luther Says,* p. 861.

[10] Plass, *What Luther Says,* p. 860.

ments of the Roman rite had their roots in the early church and were pure; only medieval additions had polluted the service. He was not about to abandon the pure for the sake of the impure.

> The service now in common use everywhere goes back to genuine Christian beginnings, as does the office of preaching. But as the latter has been perverted by the spiritual tyrants, so the former has been corrupted by the hypocrites. As we do not on that account abolish the office of preaching but aim to restore it again to its right and proper place, so it is not our intention to do away with the service, but to restore it again to its rightful use.[11]

If his church was, as Luther believed, the continuity of the Christian church, Lutheranism had a right to the ancient liturgy. In fact, the use of that order was a public confession of the same. Given his concerns that the new church was being perceived as just another sect, we can understand why Luther chose the historic Christian rite for the worship of Lutheran Germany.

Luther felt that much of the existing service proclaimed the gospel. He commended the church fathers for their selection of the Introit psalms, the *Kyrie,* the Epistle and Gospel lessons, the *Gloria in Excelsis,* the graduals and alleluias, the Nicene Creed, the *Sanctus,* the *Agnus Dei,* and the collects. While he wondered if some "lover of works" had chosen the epistle selections for the ancient church, he was satisfied that the church year lessons were witnessing to the gospel. He encouraged pastors to preach on them to ward off any temptation to "preach his own ideas."[12]

Thus, in both the *Formula Missae* and the *Deutsche Messe,* Luther honored the traditions of the Christian church and considered them to be a faithful witness to the voice of the gospel. More than just a conservative nature led him to keep the church's past practices. He carried on the traditions because his congregations, together with those of the early church, were members of "one holy Christian and apostolic Church." A common faith invisibly united them, and Luther intended that they should be united visibly by a common form of public worship:

---

[11] Luther's Works, American, Vol. 53, p. 11.

[12] Luther's Works, American, Vol. 53, p. 78.

It is not now nor ever has been our intention to abolish the liturgical service of God completely, but rather to purify the one that is now in use from the wretched accretions which corrupt it and to point out an evangelical use.[13]

Fourth Principle: God's Gift of Music and the Arts

In Martin Luther, God gave his people a determined champion for the cause of music and the arts. So highly did Luther value music that he wrote:

I most heartily desire that music, that divine and precious gift, be praised and extolled before all people. . . . Experience proves that, next to the Word of God, only music deserves being extolled as the mistress and governess of the feelings of the human heart.[14]

Luther not only believed that the arts had power over the emotions; he also understood that God was the creator of music. From that point of view Luther could call music the "living voice of the gospel" and be convinced that God used music to carry his message to the human heart. He did not consider only music to be valuable. Speaking against the enthusiasts who haughtily considered God's created gifts to be unworthy of carrying the message of the gospel, Luther wrote:

Nor am I of the opinion that the gospel should destroy and blight all the arts, as some of the super-religious claim. But I would like to see all the arts, especially music, be used in the service of him who gave and made it.[15]

Luther valued both the legacy he had received from western civilization and the musical traditions of his native land. He drew from both sources as he brought music into worship. He had a deep sense of artistic appreciation and integrity. He considered it improper, for instance, to force rough German words into the flowing Gregorian chants of the historic liturgy. He would not produce a German service until he had an opportunity to consult

---

[13] Luther's Works, American, Vol. 53, p. 20.

[14] Luther's Works, St. Louis Edition, Vol. 14, p. 428.

[15] Luther's Works, American, Vol. 53, p. 316.

with musicians he considered more skilled than himself.[16] He was loathe to lose the beauty of language and strongly urged that the children learn Latin.[17]

Luther also valued the services of those who created art and music. He was a good friend of Johann Walter, the cantor at the church in Torgau, who in turn offered him sound advice in the area of church music. As a result of this friendship, Walter wrote a great deal of music for the Lutheran service.[18]

Challenges to Luther's Worship Principles

Although Luther's worship principles were firmly grounded in Scripture, patterned after the New Testament church, and defended by the Lutheran Confessions, not all of the churches of the Reformation accepted them or put them to use. The rejection of Luther's principles, and the liturgical form of worship they supported, has occurred several times in the centuries between Luther's day and ours. Today's worship leaders ought to understand the reasons why many denominations—and even some Lutherans—have followed neither Luther's example nor advice.

Challenges from Calvinism

Long before Luther's work came to an end in Germany, voices were sounding in Europe with a theological emphasis that was profoundly different from his. We place these voices into the branch of western Christianity called the Reformed church. While the Reformed churches seem to have much in common with Lutheranism, already Luther understood that they possessed a "different spirit," one that made them as strange to Lutheranism as Catholicism was. The Reformed theologians had a major impact both on the Reformation and on the subsequent history of the Protestant church. They would have a notable influence on Lutheran worship as well.

---

[16] Carl F. Schalk, *Luther on Music: Paradigms of Praise* (St. Louis: Concordia, 1988), p. 27.

[17] *Luther's Works*, American, Vol. 53, p. 63.

[18] Schalk, *Luther on Music*, p. 27.

Ulrich Zwingli, pastor in Zurich, was the first of these voices to speak out against the teachings of Luther. Others soon followed. Martin Bucer, John Knox, and Guillaume Farel eventually carried the Zwinglian perspective to France, England, Scotland, and Switzerland. But by far the most important voice of the Reformed movement was that of John Calvin of Geneva. Because of his influence, the Reformed point of view is often called Calvinism.

To understand the different spirit of the Calvinists, it is necessary to know that the Reformation was more than just a theological upheaval; there were social, political, intellectual, and artistic reforms as well. The Reformation was born while the Renaissance was championing human reason and unbinding personal consciences from the dictates of the medieval church. Since many of the leaders of Calvinism were Renaissance men before they were theologians, they soon established their own reason as the judge not only of the church but of the Scriptures, too.

Calvin's primary and major error was his effort to rationalize God's eternal election. He erred here because he saw Christ as sovereign more than savior. This error led him away from an emphasis on the means of grace and made Reformed worship style decidedly different from that of Lutheranism.

Calvin held to this argument: if God chose some to have faith, it was a reasonable assumption that God chose some to unbelief. To that deduction he added: once believers were chosen, they remained chosen. Calvin incorrectly thought that people were added to the Old Testament Church by God's sovereign choice alone, and not by the means of grace. He deduced that people were added to the New Testament Church in the same way.

With that false presupposition in place, it was natural that Calvin would pattern religious life in Geneva after the Old Testament theocracy. He insisted, for example, that government should impose on all its citizens the dictates of the moral law. He also held that only the Book of Psalms, the "hymnal" of the Old Testament, could be used in worship, and that all images and statues had to be destroyed. Of no surprise, Calvinistic worship had minimal use for music and art. Some even considered them harmful for the believer. Church walls were whitewashed, organs were destroyed, and choral singing and chanting were disallowed.

Calvinistic thought also strongly emphasized personal morality. Luther, too, stressed moral living, but from a totally different perspective. In Luther's understanding, Christian living was the fruit of a Spirit-created and gospel-empowered faith. To the followers of Calvin, faith was an intellectual understanding of the facts of God's salvation, and moral living was the result of an intellectual understanding of God's will. To the Calvinists, both faith and life were part of obedience. The objective of their worship, therefore, was not to receive the gospel, the power of God for salvation, but to be instructed and trained for the sake of gaining the knowledge that brought about right living.

The focal point of Lutheran and Calvinistic disagreement centered on the use and value of the means of grace. Since the Calvinists held that believers became and remained members of God's family only by his sovereign choice, and since faith to them was little more than an intellectual and obedient understanding of God's will, they did not see the means of grace, the gospel in word and sacrament, as that which the Holy Spirit used to create, sustain, and empower faith. God's choice was made without the means of grace, they said, and God's people could live morally without the means of grace.

Calvinists rejected, therefore, the teaching that the gospel in word and baptism could miraculously create faith, and they rejected the teaching that the gospel in word and supper could miraculously strengthen faith. To them the sacraments were nothing more than divine obligations. This explains why their worship service was not patterned after the Christian communion service, but after the medieval preaching service.

Considering their theological emphases, it is easy to understand why Calvinism repudiated the historic liturgy that Luther had retained. For exactly the same reasons Luther valued liturgical worship, the Calvinists repudiated it. The liturgy made the gospel predominant; Calvinists emphasized the law and God's sovereignty. The liturgy encouraged the participation of the people; Calvinism stressed the instruction of the people. The liturgy spoke with the voice of the New Testament church; Calvinists felt closer to the Old Testament church. Because it grew out of the gospel, which calls forth glorious expressions of praise (listen to the songs of heaven in the Revelation), the liturgy valued music and art. Given Calvinism's stress on intellectualism and moral instruction, Calvinists found no reason for music and art. Reformed church leaders allowed organists to play concerts in the churches, but not to play at the service.[19]

The challenges of Calvinism to the worship principles of Martin Luther and to Lutheran liturgical worship were, in reality, challenges to the gospel itself. The differences between the worship of the Reformed and that of our Lutheran churches should not be seen as simply the result of different traditions or emphases, but as a difference in theological spirit and understanding.

Challenges from Pietism

The years that followed Luther's death were not easy ones for the Lutheran church. As Europe's Catholic princes made a determined effort to regain the lands they had lost to the Reformation, some Lutherans began to compromise pure scriptural teaching, either to gain peace by accommodating the demands of Rome or to prepare for war by joining forces with the Calvinists. Faithful Lutherans resisted the compromises and, in 1577, framed the last of the great Lutheran Confessions, The Formula of Concord.

Orthodox Lutheranism remained strong in Germany until it was severely tested by the Thirty Years War. Between 1618 and 1648, Germany was literally a battleground. In many cases, the church suffered as much as the land and the people did. Pastors were killed or driven into exile, churches were burned, and congregations scattered. In many localities, a whole generation of German youth grew up without religious education.

Pastors tried to restore a regular church life after the war ended, but only with great difficulty. Their staunchly orthodox pastoral education had included a great deal of doctrine but very little practical training, as they had been trained to fight the raging doctrinal battles of their day. In many cases, their doctrinal precision must have seemed somewhat superfluous amid the carnage of the battlefield and the sorrow of the cemetery. The congrega-

---

[19] Donald J. Grout, *A History of Western Music* (New York: W.W. Norton, 1980), p. 256.

30

tions that were spared devastation eventually regrouped, often with twice and three times the members. Church discipline became nearly impossible. Some pastors began to allow the government to legislate church and communion attendance. What had been true to some extent already before the war became more common in its wake: church members who lived notably impious lives regularly sat below the pulpit and knelt at the communion rail, not because they cared to, but because they were obligated by the law of the land. One can imagine the confusion that was felt in many pious Lutheran homes.

The gospel had done its work in Germany, and there were thousands of Lutherans who were not satisfied with the state of the church. The man who became the leader of this dissatisfaction was Philip Jacob Spener (1635-1705). Spener was an orthodox Lutheran pastor who wanted to cleanse the Lutheran church. He and his followers encouraged more practical and effective preaching and teaching and promoted Bible reading, personal devotion, and prayer. They stressed the privilege and responsibility of lay activity and encouraged an interest in mission work and social ministries. They made a determined effort to add the warmth of personal faith and love to the cool and objective precision of orthodoxy. These emphases came into the church under the banner of a movement that was eventually called Pietism.

Wherever these emphases were promoted within the parameters of biblical theology, they brought great benefit to the Lutheran church. The hymn writer Paul Gerhardt and the composer Johann Sebastian Bach were both influenced by Pietism. However, Pietism was not always connected to right teaching. It soon became obvious that many Pietists possessed the spirit of Calvin rather than that of Luther. They spoke more often about believers living for Christ than they did about Christ's living for believers. They tended to talk about Christian living without connecting it with the means of grace, which empowered that living, and they gave the impression that the Christian's response to the gospel was a surer guarantee of personal salvation than the promise of the gospel itself.

What had been the strength of Lutheranism, its careful formulation of correct doctrine, was considered by many Pietists to be exactly that which had brought about the need for change. It seemed, at least to them, that proclaiming the objective facts of Scripture had done nothing in Germany but encourage deadness and hypocrisy. The Pietists were correct in their opinion that the church needed reform, but they were tragically wrong when they laid the blame on the Word and the sacraments.

Since the Word and the sacraments were most often in use in church, Pietism first challenged and then abandoned the traditions and the principles of Lutheran liturgical worship. Already Spener had suggested that genuine Christians should meet by themselves, apart from the regular church service. As they struggled for a personal consciousness of their conversion and rebirth, and as their meetings became more subjective and emotional, many Pietists lost all appreciation for the objective facts of the gospel. With that point of view, the Christian liturgy and church year, stressing the words and works of Christ, became irrelevant. The doctrine-filled prayers of the church gave way to *ex corde* meanderings by pastors and laymen. The chorales of the Reformation era as well as the fine hymn texts and melodies that early Pietism had contributed to the hymnody of the Lutheran church were eventually set aside for hymns with highly emotional texts and tunes. Opera-like solos and sentimental songs in the popular, contemporary styles replaced choral music that had so carefully carried biblical texts to Lutheran hearts. And Pietism, more than any other force, devalued the use of Holy Communion among Lutherans.

For all of its weaknesses, the Pietistic movement in Germany had some strengths, and one of these was its interest in missions. The primary focus of Pietism's mission zeal was America. Pietists formed societies for the promotion of missions and the training of missionaries, and soon a steady stream of money and men were traveling across the Atlantic to the United States.

One of the first of the Pietistic missionaries was Henry Melchior Muehlenberg (1711-1787), pastor for many years in Pennsylvania. Muehlenberg had been influenced by Lutheran orthodoxy and had learned to value the liturgical heritage. The liturgy he prepared for his congregations followed sound Lutheran practice. Unfortunately, Muehlenberg had also been influenced by the Pietists and had inherited their lack of concern for correct teaching. Not many years passed after he prepared his liturgy that his failure to provide confessional leadership brought trouble to the worship life of America's Lutherans.

> For the most part, the communion hymns in the New York collection of 1814 [a hymnal prepared by the Lutheran pastor Frederick Quitman] contained nothing that would distinguish them from a Presbyterian or Methodist collection of that time. Hymns or hymn verses offensive to the Socinianism of the times [Socinianism placed reason over Scripture] were omitted. The divinity of Christ . . . often seemed to be kept carefully in the background. Doxologies [praise to Father, Son, and Holy Spirit] were conspicuous by their absence. There were few hymns that could not be sung with satisfaction by a Unitarian. . . .[20]

Samuel S. Schmucker (1799-1873), founder of the Lutheran Seminary at Gettysburg, Pennsylvania, was the author and leading proponent of what he called "American Lutheranism," an idea that Lutheran theology had to be retooled for the new land. He sent out from Gettysburg a generation and more of pastors whom he taught to see five errors in the Augsburg Confession: (1) that it approved of the ceremonies of the Mass, (2) that it approved of private confession and absolution, (3) that it refused to call Sunday the divine replacement for the Sabbath and thus carried with it the Old Testament obligations, (4) that it affirmed baptismal regeneration and (5) that it affirmed the real presence in the Lord's Supper. With those presuppositions, it follows naturally that Schmucker was no defender of Luther's worship principles.

With their roots in Pietism, their emphasis on missions, and their emerging "American Lutheranism," these postcolonial Lutherans were strongly attracted to the Revivalism that swept across the United States during the early years of the nineteenth century.

Challenges from Revivalism

Revivalism is a unique religious phenomenon of America. It has its heritage in the teachings of Jacob Arminius (1560-1609), who rebelled against the doctrines of Calvinism in Holland. Especially

---

[20] *Handbook of Church Music,* Carl Halter and Carl Schalk, editors (St. Louis: Concordia, 1978), p. 85.

33

repulsive to Arminius was Calvin's teaching of double predestination. Calvin found in the Scriptures that God elected his own to eternal life. With his human reason, Calvin assumed that God must, therefore, elect others to eternal death. Arminius could not believe that a gracious God could elect anyone to eternal death. He found in the Scriptures that those without God had rejected him of their own free will. With his human reason Arminius assumed that those with God had chosen him of their own free will.

The Arminians, therefore, taught that conversion occurred through the cooperation of God and the human will. This was a violent departure from Calvinism, and yet these two strains of Reformed theology were not very far apart. Calvinism taught that human beings entered the Church by God's sovereign choice; Arminianism concluded that human beings entered the Church by their own choice. Both denied the scriptural reality that God brings human beings into the Church and keeps them in the Church through the means of grace, the gospel in the Word and the sacraments. Luther expressed this clearly as he explained the Third Article in his Small Catechism:

> I believe that I cannot by my own thinking or choosing believe in Jesus Christ, my Lord, or come to him.

> But the Holy Ghost has called me by the gospel, enlightened me with his gifts, sanctified and kept me in the true faith. In the same way he calls, gathers, enlightens and sanctifies the whole Christian Church on earth, and keeps it with Jesus Christ in the one true faith.

While Arminius's concept of the free human will never found much acceptance on the European continent, it became the heart and soul of John Wesley's (1703-1791) English Methodism. When Methodists joined forces with other Protestants to reclaim the pioneers who were moving to the American frontier, Revivalism was born. Charles Finney (1792-1875) was a leading voice of this new movement, and his own words indicate how he felt about the role of the gospel in conversion: "A revival is not a miracle, or dependent on a miracle in any sense. It is a purely philosophic result of the right use of means."[21]

---

[21] Michael Scott Horton, *Made in America: the Shaping of Modern American Evangelicalism* (Grand Rapids: Baker, 1991), p. 60.

The worship assembly was Revivalism's primary conversion tool, and its leaders approached worship with pure pragmatism: if worship forms succeeded in gaining converts, they were legitimate; if they failed to gain converts, they were discarded. What worked best, in Finney's point of view, were experiential hymns, compelling choir anthems, and fiery preaching ("Start with an earthquake and work up from there"[22]). Since many Revivalists agreed that "in order to move people spiritually it was also necessary to move them physically,"[23]

new techniques were introduced: a mourners' bench for those who desired prayer for their conversion, the sawdust trail for converts to come forward, and a series of bizarre physical expressions, which some . . . relished as signs of true conversion.[24]

Some Lutherans, especially those from the Gettysburg tradition, accepted Revivalism enthusiastically. In 1843 Benjamin Kurtz, the editor of *The Lutheran Observer,* wrote:

If the great object of the anxious bench can be accomplished in some other way, less obnoxious but equally efficient—be it so. But we greatly doubt this. We consider it necessary in many cases, and we believe there are circumstances when no measure equally good can be substituted. Hence we are free to confess that we go for this measure *with all our heart.*[25]

Within 300 years after Luther's death, the majority of American Lutheran congregations had nearly abandoned the worship principles that Martin Luther had established. In many places the liturgy of the historic church, with its emphasis on the words and works of Jesus by means of Ordinary, Proper, and church year, had been replaced by services that included little more than long sermons, lengthy confessions of sin, and subjective hymns. In most congregations Holy Communion was offered no more than

---

[22] Duane Arnold and George Fry, "Weothscrip," *Eternity,* September, 1986.

[23] James F. White, *Protestant Worship: Traditions in Transition* (Louisville: Westminster/John Knox Press, 1989), p. 174.

[24] White, *Protestant Worship,* p. 174.

[25] E. Clifford Nelson, *The Lutherans in North America* (Philadelphia: Fortress, 1980), p. 215.

four times a year. Other than singing the hymns, many Lutherans had little chance to participate in public worship.[26] Not many of the rugged Lutheran chorales that stressed the objective truths of Christ's redemption found their way into Lutheran hymnals. There were some pockets of resistance, and some Lutheran congregations followed Luther's principles more than others, but not often was there found the richness of Christian worship that Luther surely envisioned when he set about to reform the worship life of the Lutheran church.

The deeper tragedy, however, was that this same segment of Lutheranism had lost what was more dear to Luther than any worship style or form, and that was the pure doctrine of the Holy Scriptures. When Calvinism, Pietism, and Revivalism challenged Luther's worship principles, they actually challenged his principles of *by Grace Alone, by Faith Alone,* and *by Scripture Alone.*

The demise of Luther's worship principles in the Lutheran church may not have initiated the false doctrine; the loss of the liturgical service and Lutheran hymnology was a symptom of the problem rather than the cause of it. But once the emphasis of Lutheran worship moved away from Christ and the Scriptures, the stress on human reason and human reaction quickly filled the void. Luther himself saw the logic of this. He wrote, "It must also necessarily follow where faith and the word or promise of God decline or are neglected, that in their place there arise works and a false, presumptuous trust in them."[27] Where such was the focus of Lutheran worship, Lutheranism's worship did much to encourage and further false doctrine.

Efforts to Reclaim Luther's Worship Principles

What actually began to turn the tide of Lutheran worship practice was the three-hundredth anniversary of the Lutheran Reformation, celebrated with much German nationalism in 1817. In an effort to reclaim their heritage, Lutheran pastors began studying

---

[26]The Form I order of service in the Wisconsin Synod's *Book of Hymns* (used between 1920 and 1941) restricted the Confession of Sins, the Apostles' Creed, and the Lord's Prayer for use by the pastor alone.

[27] Luther's Works, American, Vol. 25, p. 92.

Luther again. A few of these noticed that they had become far removed from Reformation thought and theology. They returned to the Lutheran Confessions and began to promote sound Lutheran doctrine and practice. Although small in number, these orthodox pastors exerted a strong influence, first in their own communities and eventually in America.

Their influence reached America by means of scholarly writing and especially by immigration. Lutherans from Saxony established the Missouri colonies under C. F. W. Walther in the 1830s; Wilhelm Loehe sent confessional missionaries to Michigan's Saginaw Valley in the 1840s; Charles Porterfield Krauth led sound Lutherans away from their association with Samuel Schmucker's Gettysburg Seminary. In all three cases, orthodox leaders not only rediscovered Lutheran confessionalism but also reclaimed Luther's worship principles.

The efforts of these three men had direct influence on the formation of *The Common Service* of 1888. This order of service was the first order of service prepared for English-speaking Americans that truly embraced Luther's principles. The *Common Service* entered the churches of the Midwest during the early years of the twentieth century. It was the order of service that was included in *The Lutheran Hymnal*, and it is the direct ancestor of the liturgical rites in *Christian Worship: A Lutheran Hymnal.*

The framers of *The Common Service* maintained that they had based it on "the common consent of the pure Lutheran liturgies of the sixteenth century, and when there was not an entire agreement among them, the consent of the largest number of the greatest weight."[28] The service was actually much more than an order of worship; it also contained English translations of the historic introits, graduals, collects, and creeds, all of which were new to American Lutheran worship.

Many of the forms that found their way into *The Common Service,* as well as many translations of the Lutheran chorales, were gifts to the Lutheran Church from the Church of England. The English Anglicans (and American Episcopalians) were returning

---

[28] Luther D. Reed, *The Lutheran Liturgy* (Philadelphia: Fortress, 1947), p. 195 (Minutes of the General Council, meeting at Zanesville, Ohio, 1879).

to their worship roots at the same time Lutherans were. During the last years of the nineteenth century and the early decades of the twentieth century, Gothic architecture once again became the popular style for churches. Ceremonies long rejected by Protestants reappeared. Anglican choirs raised the Anglican psalm chant to a high art, and the language of the English court, standardized by the King James Version of the Bible, became the language of public worship.

In its language and, to a certain extent, in its music, *The Common Service* was influenced by the character and quality of the Anglican's *Book of Common Prayer*. "They expressed the same churchly feeling in forms of comparable literary value."[29] This English connection turned out to be a mixed blessing for American Lutheran congregations. On the one hand, the American church regained much of the liturgy and many of the hymns that previous generations had disavowed. On the other hand, congregations lost the opportunity to move directly from the language of their native lands to the language Lutherans actually spoke in America. While they lived through the age of the automobile, the age of space, and the age of computers, most Lutherans in America worshiped with the language and music of eighteenth century England.

Conservative, midwestern Lutherans were willing, in most cases, to accept the worship renewal that had dawned. Not all was bright on the horizon, however. *The Common Service* served as the impetus for a determined effort to regain the art, music, ceremony, and liturgical emphases that Calvinism, Pietism, and Revivalism had destroyed. Interested parties formed societies and attended conferences devoted to these concerns. To the Lutheran farmers whose worship roots had been deeply sunk in Pietism, some of these regained "treasures" must have seemed a little much, but given some time, they might have become used to some high ceremony. Even their pastors, often more uncomfortable with liturgical richness than the people, might have tried a chant or a procession. What brought liturgical innovation to a halt in conservative Lutheran circles, however, was the association of the liturgical movement with liberal ecumenical theology. By far

---

[29] Reed, *Liturgy,* p. 195.

the majority of midwestern Lutheran pastors perceived that those most interested in the liturgical worship forms tended to be the same ones who were most interested in encouraging a unity among Lutherans without establishing confessional agreement.

Efforts to regain liturgical fullness in conservative circles would have been difficult even without that association, but the most troublesome hurdle for many midwestern Lutherans was the perception that what some church leaders were calling part of the Lutheran heritage looked a great deal like the customs of Roman Catholicism. The situation at the midpoint of the twentieth century lent itself to anti-Catholic phobia. The Church of Rome during that era was pressing harder than ever its conviction that it is the only true church and that there was no salvation apart from its sacraments and priesthood. One might have hoped that pastors and teachers had been able to impress upon their members that there was a difference between Catholic doctrine, which was decidedly different from Lutheran doctrine, and Catholic customs, which in many cases had been carried into Lutheranism by Luther himself. Unfortunately, this distinction between doctrine and form was not often understood or maintained.

The long-standing and deeply-held fear of liturgical richness and variety, fueled by fears of liberal or Catholic encroachment, hindered efforts to reclaim fully the principles that Martin Luther had established for the Lutheran church. Many of the liturgical practices that seemed decidedly Romish in 1950 (e.g., vestments, chanting, processions) had been decidedly Lutheran before the age of Pietism. Innovations that seemed to come directly out of Rome's Second Vatican Council (e.g., a free-standing altar and an every-Sunday Communion) were suggestions made by Luther himself. The sad fact was that many of the ceremonies and practices that had been cherished by Christians and Lutherans for hundreds of years were rejected as soon as they were suggested.

Finally, and more seriously, some of the same Lutherans who took a strong stand against these ancient and useful rites seemed ready to align themselves with the worship practices of Calvinism, Pietism, and Revivalism. In their efforts to keep out of their congregations practices they supposed were anti-Lutheran, they opposed customs that served the principles and doctrines Luther gave to the church. More than that, many adopted worship forms that not only opposed Luther's principles but actually undermined Lutheran theology.

A review of the worship principles of Martin Luther and the historic challenges these principles faced has value for today's worship leaders in a variety of ways. Such a review allows them to be convinced that Luther's principles stand on a solid scriptural ground and that, therefore, they have enduring relevance. It encourages leaders to strive for a worship life in their congregations that is built on Luther's principles and that includes liturgical fullness. It enables them to understand how the worship attitudes of today's Lutherans were formed and why they themselves sometimes fail to appreciate the forms that *Christian Worship* proposes and endorses. Finally, it prepares them for the challenges that contemporary worship moods and modes continue to mount against Luther's principles and, in reality, against the Scripture's teachings. In fact, the primary challenge to Lutheran worship today comes from the direct descendant of Calvinism, Pietism, and Revivalism, namely, the neo-Evangelical movement.

CHAPTER 4:

Lutheran Worship Principles and *Christian Worship*

Christian Worship: A Lutheran Hymnal intends to mold the worship life of our church so that public worship might be what it has always been in the church: the intellectual and emotional interaction between the Bridegroom and his bride, between Christ and his Church. *Christian Worship* endorses the principles that Martin Luther clearly set forth on the basis of God's Word and that he demonstrated in his own worship reforms and innovations. *Christian Worship* stands with those who are convinced, as Luther was, that the Scripture's objectives for public worship are best met and applied when congregations adopt a liturgical style of worship, i.e., a set of worship forms that are built on the patterns and emphases of the historic liturgy of the western Christian church.

The Predominance of the Gospel

Christian Worship intends that the gospel of Jesus Christ will be predominant in public worship. By making the liturgy its main order of service, *Christian Worship* reviews the saving doctrines of Scripture in the Ordinary, repeats the words and works of Christ in the Proper, and in the Sacrament offers Christ's true body and blood, given and shed for the forgiveness of sins. Especially in its main orders, but also in all its rites and hymns, *Christian Worship* places its focus on *Christ for us,* the heart of the gospel.

The Common Service retains the five historic Ordinary texts: *Kyrie, Gloria in Excelsis*, Nicene Creed, *Sanctus,* and *Agnus Dei.* For centuries the church has valued the gospel content of these texts. The language of the texts in *Christian Worship* is contemporary, although the musical settings are from the 1901 *Choral Service Book.*[1]

The *Service of Word and Sacrament* presents several alternate Ordinary texts, different in some ways from the historic songs, but written in a similar spirit. *Lord, Have Mercy (Kyrie)* reinstates the dialogue arrangement of the historic *Kyrie* and helps worshipers understand for what they are praying as they sing, "Lord, have mercy." The rite's song of praise, *O Lord, Our Lord,* focuses on Christ and his work of salvation perhaps even more pointedly than does *Gloria in Excelsis:*

> O Lord, our Lord, how glorious is your name in all the earth.
> Almighty God, merciful Father, you crown our life with your love.
> You take away our sin;
> you comfort our spirit;
> you make us pure and holy in your sight.
> You did not spare your only Son, but gave him up for us all.
> O Lord, our Lord, how glorious is your name in all the earth.
> O Son of God, eternal Word of the Father,
> you came to live with us;
> you made your Father known;
> you washed us from our sins in your own blood.
> You are the King of Glory, you are the Lord!
> O Lord, our Lord, how glorious is your name in all the earth.
> *(Christian Worship* [CW], pp. 28,29)

The revised text of *Holy, Holy, Holy* includes several phrases from Psalm 118, the great Easter psalm, to replace the historic *Benedictus* ("Blessed is he who comes in the name of the Lord"): "You are my God and I will exalt you. I will give you thanks for you . . . have become my salvation" (Psalm 118:28,21). The phrases point to the saving acts of Christ on which the promises of the Sacrament stand. They also restore the giving of thanks

---

[1] The musical settings of the Ordinary that became well-known to Synodical Conference Lutherans appeared in the *Choral Service Book* prepared by Harry G. Archer and Luther D. Reed in 1901. They found their way into the Missouri Synod through the so-called "Baltimore Hymnal" (tune edition 1906) and the *Evangelical Lutheran Hymnal* (1912). The Wisconsin Synod used portions of this setting in its 1920 *Book of Hymns. The Lutheran Hymnal* (1941) reissued the 1912 setting.

that the historic liturgy invites ("Let us give thanks to the Lord our God") but that the Lutheran liturgy lost when Luther excised the Great Thanksgiving Prayer in his liturgical revisions of the 1520s. *Thank the Lord* is not in any way a part of the historic Ordinary. However, it has value as it encourages worshipers to recall the gracious promises of God as they go into the world with a thankful witness of Christ on their lips and in their lives.[2] The canticle *This Is the Feast of Victory* is included in the Hymns of the Liturgy section and is encouraged as an Easter season alternate for *Glory Be to God* and *O Lord, Our Lord.* As these canticles join the Nicene Creed and *Lamb of God,* they present a clear witness to Christ and thus accomplish the objective of the liturgy's Ordinary.

Christian Worship also provides generous opportunities for a use of the Proper in its services and so encourages the annual review of Christ's life and work and the church's life of faith. A complete set of the various elements of the Proper is included in Section Four of this volume.

The hymnal highlights the Proper in ways that other worship books have not. Its refrain settings of the psalms make the singing of the psalms possible and natural for most congregations. Proper Prefaces and Seasonal Sentences are carefully crafted to fit into the liturgy in a streamlined way.

Christian Worship encourages the choir to become liturgical in its orientation, i.e., to have as its objective not simply to sing an anthem in the service, but to present an anthem based on the Christian calendar and especially to assist the congregation by singing the parts of the Proper that are assigned to the choir. Settings of the Verse of the Day are available for use by soloists, children's choruses, and sections of the choir as well as by the choir itself.

The Hymn of the Day, a hymn chosen from the best hymns of Christendom and selected on the basis of its connection to the lectionary, finds its place after the Gospel of the Day. Congregations

---

[2] The text is by John Arthur (1922-80) and appeared in *Contemporary Worship 2: Services of Holy Communion* prepared by the Inter-Lutheran Commission on Worship in 1970. It appeared subsequently in *Lutheran Book of Worship* and *Lutheran Worship* as the post-communion canticle.

are encouraged to use special settings of the Hymn of the Day that often include the participation of the choir and instruments.

The liturgical rites in *Christian Worship* have been arranged so that even larger congregations can include the celebration of the Sacrament within normal worship times. There is a great deal of evidence from the history of the church that supports an every-Sunday communion in addition to an every-Sunday sermon. That the early Christians received the supper whenever they gathered on the Lord's day is obvious as one reads in the Acts and 1 Corinthians. The Apology of the Augsburg Confession states: "In our churches Mass is celebrated every Sunday and on other festivals, when the Sacrament is offered to those who wish for it."[3] Wilhelm Loehe, one of worship's nineteenth century champions, wrote:

> A morning service on Sundays or festivals without communion is like a broken column. . . . God is rich toward all who seek him, and those who come to his table shall be satisfied with the abundance of his house. Nor ought anyone to say that frequent celebration serves to bring the Sacrament into contempt, for those who are rightly prepared will always hunger for this bread and thirst for this drink; and the more frequent that they commune, the firmer becomes the persuasion that all of the earthly life is only a preparation for the celebration of the great Supper on high. . . . It should not often occur that the Communion is altogether omitted from the morning service.[4]

While it may be true that Christians have never, even in Luther's day, valued the Sacrament as the Savior desires, worship leaders ought to be the first to encourage others, by word and example, to come frequently to the Lord's table. The risk of offending visitors, the consideration of service schedules, and the fear that some might partake unworthily ought not to be more important factors when planning worship than the wonderful blessings the Sacrament offers to Christians.

Christian Worship and its liturgical style serve the gospel of Christ by paying attention to the truth of the Savior's Word. Because Lutherans believe that the Holy Spirit works through the Word to create, maintain, and strengthen faith, they value the

---

[3] Apology, Art. 15, 49-51

[4] Wilhelm Loehe, *Agenda for North American Congregations.*

"pattern of sound teaching," and nowhere is the pattern of sound teaching more important than in the forms of public worship. *Christian Worship,* like orthodox hymnals of the past, views its liturgy and hymns as a precise confession of biblical theology and as the standard that guides the faith and life of the church.

As pastors and congregations think about the benefit of orthodox, gospel-centered worship forms, they will need to consider carefully how they use their freedom to choose orders of service and hymns that are not found in *Christian Worship.* While it is legitimate for believers themselves to decide which forms of worship they want to employ, it is equally proper that they take care in the exercise of that right. It is necessary to ask whether the congregation itself always has the ability to know which forms of public worship best suit its real spiritual needs. Whether old or new, not every religious song found on a list of congregational favorites edifies Christian faith. Some contain doctrinal errors, some encourage faulty perceptions, and some contain no error simply because they contain little theology. And—before melody or musical style—the text is the standard by which worship forms must be judged.

The liturgical orders in *Christian Worship* assure that the generation of Lutherans that uses them will receive benefit from public worship that allows the gospel to predominate. It is noteworthy that none of the orders follow a specific version of a historic Christian service; they do not encourage a mindless traditionalism. Yet they ensure that the strength of the liturgy—its gospel voice—will be proclaimed and heard.

The Participation of the Congregation

Christian Worship intends that believers who gather at public worship will be able to participate in the church's response to the gospel of Jesus Christ. In order for the people to respond, however, there must be opportunity for dialogue; the people as well as the pastor must be involved in activity. If there is to be meaningful and understandable dialogue, the language and music of worship must in some way belong to the people. If the people are to gain lasting benefit from the dialogue, there must be ritual, something that is standard and static, and there must be ceremony, something that touches the believer's eyes as well as his ears, his heart as well as his head.

The Dialogue of Worship

The service of the congregation to God is the second part of the interaction between Christ and his bride that takes place at public worship, and a liturgical style allows the dialogue between God and his people to occur freely and repeatedly. The pastor, God's spokesman at worship, invites the believers to confession, the congregation confesses its sins, and the pastor absolves. The pastor reads the First Lesson, the congregation sings the Psalm of the Day; the pastor reads the Second Lesson, the congregation (or the choir) sings the Verse; the pastor reads the Gospel, the congregation sings the Hymn of the Day; the pastor preaches the sermon, the congregation responds with the Nicene Creed. The pastor greets the people in the Lord, the congregation returns the greeting to its pastor; the pastor invites the believers to lift up their hearts, the congregation resolves to do so to the Lord; the pastor exhorts the congregation concerning the value of giving thanks to God, the congregation agrees that thanksgiving is good and right. Even by speaking its *Amen* ("So let it be"), the congregation takes part in the dialogue of the service. The settings of the Psalms in *Christian Worship,* as well as the arrangement of the Prayers of the Church and the *Lord, Have Mercy (Kyrie)* encourage the activity of the congregation. In the liturgical canticles, it is the congregation that takes its turn to proclaim the truth about the triune God at the same time as it offers praise and adoration.

The Language and Music of the Congregation

In its language and music, *Christian Worship* intends to retain the church's past confessional witness by placing historic forms into contemporary language and style. The language of the liturgy and the prayers, of the psalms and most hymns is the language of America. In most cases the words of Scripture follow the translation of the New International Version of the Bible, although superior translations occasionally replace those of the NIV. At times certain words, terms, and even punctuation occur primarily because worshipers move quickly through hymns and liturgy; they do not have time to study the meaning of a word in its context. Commas are added for ease in speaking, although in some cases their use is not in keeping with standard practice. On the assumption that our modern society more and more defines the word "man" or "men" as having to do with male human beings, *Christian Worship* generally uses the masculine words only when the sense of the text indicates a masculine reference.

Christian Worship is the worship book of the congregation, not a book of hymns and rites for one specific social or age group. Cliches, breezy phrases, and terms liable to become dated are avoided. The book makes no attempt to be clever.

Although it strives for simplicity, *Christian Worship* makes no attempt to avoid the words that are essential for a clear confession of Christian teaching, e.g., justify, sanctify, confess, absolve. It assumes that Christians who gather at public worship will be able to employ a spiritual vocabulary. Nor is an attempt made to avoid allusions or passages from the Bible. While some may be unfamiliar with these references, the inclusion of the Scripture's own words is one of the strengths of a hymnal.

The hymn texts of *Christian Worship* were considered individually as far as language is concerned; there is not an over-arching language guideline. In many cases contemporary words replaced archaic words, but not always. No attempt was made to dramatically alter all English hymns written in an older style (e.g., "My faith looks up to thee, Thou Lamb of Calvary"). There was also a recognition that many Lutherans memorized familiar Christian hymns in their youth. In some cases these texts retained their traditional form.

Christian Worship's concern for contemporary communication is consistent with its commitment to put the forms of worship into the mouths of the people. The liturgy is, by definition, the "work of the people." Since the people are worshiping, they have a responsibility and a right to worship in a language and style that is their own. This helps to make the service of the congregation to God timely and genuine. It also allows the worshipers to understand the words of Scripture in a clear and concise way and then to take those words and doctrines into their hearts.

Ritual and Ceremony

When God's people come to participate with him in worship, they come with "hearts and hands and voices." While the response of the believing heart is always new and fresh, the actions of believing hands and the words of believing voices necessarily repeat themselves. The repeating words of worship we call *ritual:* orders of service, rites, prayers. The repeating actions of worship are *ceremonies:* hands raised in blessing or folded in prayer.

Because they are human creatures, believers require ritual and ceremony. They need these not just in worship but in everyday life. Certain verbal patterns are necessary summaries of deeper feelings: "I love you," "Happy Birthday," "Because I said so!" Nonverbal actions are just as necessary; it is almost impossible to describe the perfect golf swing without arms or a feeling of helplessness without eyes.[5] Christians who come together at worship need a service that can become familiar, a calendar they can remember, a body of hymns they know. They need signs and symbols, motions and movements. *Christian Worship*'s liturgical style helps preserve a meaningful ritual and encourages beneficial ceremonies.

Whenever believers gather regularly for worship, they run the risk that their words may become vain repetition and their actions little more than going through the motions. That risk, however, dare not discourage worship leaders from placing a high value on ritual and ceremony, on words and actions that are a repeating part of the believers' worship. In fact, leaders are wise to help worshipers see the value of ritual and ceremony, to encourage their use, and to continually explain their meaning and significance. When Christians understand why ritual is necessary within the body of believers, when they come to appreciate ceremonies old and new, and when they understand the meaning of the ceremonial symbols, not only are the risks minimized, but the actual use of ritual and ceremony is enhanced.

Ritual and ceremony exist for the sake of stability, something the people of our changing society need. Dr. Luther expressed

---

[5] For an expanded commentary on this issue, cf. Craig D. Erickson, *Participating in Worship* (Louisville: Westminster/John Knox Press, 1989), p. 148 ff.

concerns about the wide variety of worship rituals and cere-monies that could be found in Germany in his day. He feared "everyone parading his talents and confusing the people so that they can neither learn nor retain anything." [6]

C. S. Lewis made a point about the "liturgical fidget" whose continual novelties serve only to set up obstacles to worship. A service, he said, "is a structure of acts and words through which we receive the sacrament, or repent, or supplicate, or adore." As in dancing so in worship, Lewis suggested, one needs to be thor-oughly at home with the form in order to concentrate on the con-tent without distraction: "As long as you notice, and have to count, the steps, you are not dancing, but only learning to dance." The ideal service, he said, "would be one we were almost un-aware of; our attention would have been on God. But every nov-elty prevents this. . . ." He concludes with an entreaty for unifor-mity, and says he could

> make do with almost any kind of service whatever if only it would stay
> put. But if each form is snatched away just when I am beginning to feel
> at home in it, then I can never make any progress in the art of worship.[7]

Closely connected to the matter of stability is the issue of rev-erence at worship. The ritual and ceremonies of *Christian Wor-ship*'s liturgical style also help believers keep in mind the awe that attends an entrance into the courts of the King of kings. It may be that worship leaders are misreading the attitudes of to-day's believers by assuming that people really want worship to be casual. Studies indicate that the opposite may be true.[8] People in our society seem to be looking beyond the materialism of our age toward something more noble and transcendent. The church can best address this longing for reverence with a worship style that expresses a mixture of awe, wonder, and joy at the close en-counter with the living God. The Augsburg Confession speaks as

---

[6] Luther's Works, American, Vol. 53, p. 80.

[7] C. S. Lewis, *Letters to Malcolm: Chiefly on Prayer* (New York: Brace and World, 1973), pp. 4,5.

[8] The January 15, 1990 issue of *U.S. News and World Report* included an article on the amazing growth of liturgical churches. Reporter Jeffrey Sheler concluded, "While no one expects ritualism to replace evangelical traditions, there is a clear recognition that the pendulum has begun to swing in that direction."

vitally today as it did in the sixteenth century: "Nothing contributes so much to the maintenance of dignity in public worship and the cultivation of reverence and devotion among the people as the proper observance of ceremonies in the churches."[9]

In its various services, prayers, and hymns, *Christian Worship* offers a worship ritual for today's church. Within that ritual there is room for a wide variety of ceremonial actions: hands lifted in blessing, extended in greeting, folded for prayer, poised for the sign of the cross; eyes raised in joyful praise and closed for quiet reverence; kneeling for confession, standing for the Gospel of the Day, sitting to hear and sing; processions, recessions, dedications. Liturgical worship does not insist or expect that every congregation will use the worship ritual and ceremonial in lockstep fashion. The liturgy allows variety, and does so purposefully.

Suggestions concerning ceremonies are kept to a minimum in *Christian Worship* because it is recognized that congregational customs will vary. There is as much room in liturgical worship for some "high church" ceremonies as there is for some that are decidedly "low church." The liturgical ritual also allows room for variety. There may be some good reasons to use forms from time to time that have not been tried and tested. There may even be a place for what is avant-garde, esoteric, or elementary. It is precisely so that there might be innovation and individuality in worship that the liturgy offers precision, clarity, and repetition in its unchanging core.

Especially in the church body that properly considers the service of God to the congregation to be the primary benefit of public worship, the leaders will want to take special interest in the congregation's service to God. The gospel of Jesus is surely the power that generates the life of the church, but worship is the proof of the power. In worship the church inhales; it receives forgiveness of sins, life, and salvation given by the Father in the means of grace through the Son in the power of the Holy Spirit. But in worship the church also exhales; it offers its sacrifice of praise to the Father through the Son in the Spirit. *Christian Worship* and its liturgical worship intend to help keep this worshipful breathing in balance.

---

[9] Augsburg Confession, Art. 15:22.

The Historic Voice of the Church

The liturgical rites, the services of *Morning Praise* and *Evening Prayer,* as well as many of the prayers and hymns of *Christian Worship* help today's Lutherans confess that they believe themselves to be the continuity of the one Christian and apostolic Church.

Orthodox Lutherans have always been inclined to respect and repeat the church's historic proclamation. The various authors of the Lutheran Confessions added references and quotations from the fathers of the ancient church in order to show that Lutheran doctrine was nothing other than the historic faith of the church. Generations of Lutherans have imitated that sixteenth century attitude. Because they believe the Lutheran Confessions to be a "true exposition of the Word of God and a correct exhibition of the doctrine of the Evangelical Lutheran Church," our pastors vow without hesitation on the day of their ordination to "perform the duties of [their] office in accordance with these Confessions."[10] In a similar way, today's Christians join their contemporary voices to the Christian witness of the past as they bring their worship to God.

Ours is not, however, a mindless traditionalism. Of course, whatever is carried into the present from the past must be faithful to the Scriptures. Also, a respect for the past does not obligate today's church to use every historic form exactly as it first was used. The tradition of the church always continues to move forward, and new forms of worship come to stand next to the old. Luther's *Deutsche Messe* may be in place at a Reformation festival now and then, but only in the rarest circumstance would that order of worship become the regular liturgy for a contemporary Lutheran congregation. However, today's congregations should take care that they do not begin to feel obligated to be always fresh and new. Peter Brunner understood what the mind of the church ought to be as it scans the history of Christian worship:

---

[10] *The Lutheran Agenda,* authorized by the synods constituting the Evangelical Lutheran Synodical Conference of North America (St. Louis: Concordia, 1951), pp. 106,107.

"What! Did the Word of God originate with you, or are you the only ones it has reached?" (1 Corinthians 14:36 RSV). This critical question of the apostle, which the Enthusiasts in Corinth had to hear, obligates the church of all times to approach with due respect and reverence the traditions of Christendom which do not conflict with Christ's institution and the Word of God. Just because we are aware of the eschatological freedom of the form of worship, just because we are liberated by the Gospel and are free and cannot be enslaved by the power of tradition, we are liberated also for the acceptance of critically tried and tested tradition. To stand in fear of tradition is by no means a sign of freedom. On the critical presupposition and premise that we belong to Christ, all of Christendom's traditions in worship are ours.[11]

In Lutheran worship, twentieth century believers repeat, word for word, forms that were repeated by believers in the second century. At the same time, believers of one visible communion join with unseen and unknown believers throughout the world as well as with the saints and angels in heaven. Today's Lutherans are well served, therefore, when we teach them to view public worship as a conversation between God and his people that has been going on for centuries throughout the cosmos, and that they have joined the conversation only recently and, then, with only limited experience. With that understanding, they will be more inclined to listen awhile before insisting on adding new elements to the worship conversation or deleting traditions that have been part of the church's worship for centuries.

In a purposeful way, *Christian Worship* includes forms of worship from virtually every era and every area of western Christianity. As we have mentioned, the progression of the liturgical rites, as well as that of *Morning Praise* and *Evening Prayer,* actually have their roots in the Old Testament synagogue. The hymns that Luke recorded in his Gospel obviously are included. *Glory be to God* is in *The Common Service,* the *Song of Mary* and the *Song of Simeon* are sung in Evening Prayer. The *Song of Zechariah* is located among the Hymns of the Liturgy in the hymn section. Besides these inspired hymns of praise, the historic *Lamplighter's*

---

[11] Brunner, *Worship,* p. 231.

Hymn (CW, p.54), written in Greek about 150 years after Luke's gospel, appears in *Evening Prayer.* A Latin hymn attributed to Pope Gregory I (A.D. 590-604) is the prelude for *Morning Praise.* The prayers at the close of both *Morning Praise* and *Evening Prayer* (the Prayer for Grace and the Prayer for Peace) have been used in the church since before the eighth century. Martin Luther composed the prayer that is spoken at the end of *The Common Service* ("We give thanks, almighty God").

Alongside worship forms that have accompanied the voice of the church for centuries, are prayers, hymns, and musical styles that are part of the church's 20th-century confession. The translations of the Lord's Prayer and the Nicene Creed are those that are held in common by most English speaking Christian churches. The liturgical songs of the *Service of Word and Sacrament,* as well as the canticles of *Evening Prayer,* have a definite modern sound with their emphasis on rhythm and melody. The refrain style of psalm singing is decidedly contemporary; we have borrowed the concept from the Roman Catholics who first popularized it the 1970s.

The hymn section offers even wider representation than the liturgy section. *Christian Worship* includes hymns from the Greek church of the east as well as from the Latin church of the west. Some hymns were attached to the Daily Office. A number of first millennium hymns are accompanied by the simple plain chant tunes to which they originally were sung. Many of the Martin Luther's hymns are present, along with their rhythmic tunes. Several of the Reformation chorales appear with isometric settings that became common during Bach's era. The best hymns of the Lutheran author Paul Gerhardt are included, together with the well-loved tunes written especially for them by Johann Crueger. Besides the best from the German heritage, *Christian Worship* offers hymn texts and musical styles from virtually every country of Lutheran Europe.

Christians from Great Britain have bequeathed a wonderful legacy of hymns. Our hymnal has many of the grand tunes of Wales and the English cathedrals and outstanding texts by the Congregationalist Isaac Watts, the Presbyterian Horatius Bonar, and the Methodist Charles Wesley. Protestant America has a heritage of its own: the hymns of the colonial era, the refrain hymns of Revivalism, the plaintive tunes of Appalachia, the rhythmic spirituals of the African-American slaves. The last decades of the twentieth century witnessed an explosion of interest in hymn writing, and *Christian Worship* benefits from this era of creativity. The influence of American folk music is apparent in some of the hymn tunes composed after 1960.

The members of the one holy Christian and apostolic Church have confessed the truth of God's Word in various ways and in various places for twenty centuries. *Christian Worship* recognizes the value of their contribution and offers today's believers an opportunity to join believers of other places and other ages in singing a new song to the Lord. Someone once insisted, "When you make that hymnal, make it as different as you can. People should know instantly when they're not in one of our churches!" One wonders to what extreme one should go in this effort. Should we eliminate the Apostles' Creed and the Lord's Prayer? The Roman Catholics are singing *A Mighty Fortress* these days; should we keep that hymn away from our members? Hymnal Committee member Prof. Theodore Hartwig presents an eloquent summary of Lutheran thought on this issue:

> In matters of outward form, past Lutheran practice . . . has avoided the sectarianism of going it alone, being different, striving for the unique. Thus Luther kept with the church year and the general structure of the Mass inherited from the medieval church. . . . Though for confessional reasons, we live in a state of outwardly divided communions, the Christian Church nevertheless remains a single, universal community of believers confessing one Lord, one faith, one baptism, one God and Father of all.

> In this light would anyone want to gainsay that the sameness of outward form . . . has been a heartwarming and compelling witness to the true unity of the Church?[12]

As congregations strive to appreciate the worship legacy of the church, they will have to learn to know the difference between le-

---

[12] Theodore J. Hartwig, "The Creeds in Contemporary English," *Wisconsin Lutheran Quarterly,* Vol. 86, No. 3, p. 203.

gitimate traditions and local customs. Local customs do not become traditions of the church until Christians outside of the immediate locality recognize their value over time. For every hymn the church has accepted into its enduring corpus, it has rejected several hundred others. Hymnologists estimate that hymnal committees have more than 2.5 million hymns from which to choose, but not many hymnals contain more than 600 of them. Some musical styles have found favor across the length and breadth of Christendom; others have flickered and then faded.

Church members display a certain arrogance when they insist that customs ("we've been doing it this way for ten years") ought to have equal standing with traditions that have been part of the life of the whole church for centuries. And they ought not to dismiss automatically worship practices that the wider church has appreciated for hundreds of years, simply because such practices are "not our custom." Perhaps the time has come to make the orthodox traditions of the Christian and Lutheran church more a part of local custom than they have been in the past.

God's Gift of Music and the Arts

Christian Worship is committed to church music and Christian art that proclaims the gospel of Jesus Christ, that allows and encourages the praise of his saints, and that reflects the people's determination to bring to Jesus their best and finest offerings. This commitment retains the attitude that Scripture and the Lutheran fathers hold toward the arts.

Proclaiming the Gospel

God himself is the creator both of beauty and of an appreciation for what is beautiful, and he has given what is beautiful to his creatures to bring them joy and gladness. Since the primary source of joy for Christians is Christ, religious music as well as Christian art needs to have as its primary objective to carry to the heart of the believer the message of what Christ has done.

This does not mean that every artistic expression needs to carry the christological fullness of, say, the Athanasian Creed. Where Christian artists place primary emphasis on Christ, there is room for the proclamation of the providential blessings of the Father and of the empowering gifts of the Holy Spirit. Believers also recognize that music and art serve as symbols and reminders of Christian truth. A cross has no message in and of itself, but it carries a powerful message to a believer who knows that it was on a cross that the Savior gave his life for sinners. Although it has no words and may not even call to mind a familiar hymn text, exalting and exciting organ or instrumental music played on Easter morning brings spiritual joy to believers because it accentuates the joy they feel over the resurrection of Jesus from the dead.

Even in cultures where only a remnant of divine truth can be found, people understand that the arts have a compelling influence on the heart. Psychological studies abound that indicate that music, for instance, more than any other human activity, moves the emotions, affects attitudes, and even influences the activities of human beings.[13]

These observations by themselves would encourage believers to be eager to use the artistic and musical blessings of God for the sake of communicating the gospel. But it is more than psychological observation that brings this encouragement to the church. We would expect that he who created art to affect the mind would speak the same language as those who observe how art affects the mind, and so he does. The fact is, God himself solidified his message of grace in the minds of believers through religious art and music. Consider how the vestments of the Old Testament priests (Exodus 28) or the song of the angelic hosts on Christmas night (Luke 2:14) strikingly reinforced God's gracious proclamation. More than that, God encouraged the church to follow his divine example. The Holy Spirit led David to compose psalms for the church's use and inspired Paul to give the church guidelines for the use of psalms, hymns, and spiritual songs.

Tragically, Satan's temptation affected the arts no less than any other part of God's creation, and sin turned especially music into a force for evil as well as good. That reality does not discourage Lutherans from the use of music and art, as, for instance, it discouraged the early followers of John Calvin. Rather, Lutherans

---

[13]Anne H. Rosenfeld, "Music, the Beautiful Disturber," *Psychology Today,* December, 1985.

take care in the selection of music and in the use of art so that the divine objective is met despite the reality of sin.

Pastors and musicians must recognize that selecting music for worship may be difficult. Much artistic expression purposely communicates ideas and encourages actions that are decidedly anti-Christian. The church needs to be constantly alert so that artistic expression in worship does not obscure the christological focus of the worshipers. This can occur easily when music or art is so lofty that Christians cannot see past it to Christ. It can also happen when the artistic form is so closely attached to a non-Christian message that worshipers cannot see through the form to any religious truth. The musical styles of rhythm and blues or rock and roll may have a legitimate place in the musical legacy of America, but it is doubtful that average Christians, at least those of our era, can disassociate those styles from their past and present use and come to see Christ through them. The same may also be said about some classical music, e.g., Bach's *Toccata and Fugue in D Minor* or Richard Wagner's *Bridal March,* both of which conjure up images that detract from rather than focus on Christ.

Christian artists must also keep in mind that it is not the task of Christian artistic endeavor simply to affect the emotions or to make worshipers happy or sad. For the church, art remains a vehicle that carries something, and that something is the gospel. Christian artists who place their art into the service of the gospel must be determined to know the difference between art that carries Christ to the emotions and that which encourages shallow emotionalism.

It is a mistake, of course, to insist that church music ought to be cold and calculating and emptied of emotional appeal. After all, the primary objective of music is to carry Christ to the heart. As has been mentioned, the Scriptures abound with examples of God's people using the arts to direct the divine message to the emotions. God placed a beautiful rainbow into the sky as a lasting testimony to his faithfulness. So also Christian artists use color, highlight, and texture to solidify in the heart the message of God's grace. The Creator has also enabled Christian musicians to join to basic musical sounds rhythm, dynamics, tempo, timbre, pitch, and style so they may touch the heart as they proclaim the gospel. All óf creation is God's, and God intends it all to be used for his glory and for the edification of his people. Frederick Pratt Green encourages today's church in his hymn *When in Our Music God Is Glorified:*

> Let ev'ry instrument be tuned for praise;
> Let all rejoice who have a voice to raise,
> And may God give us faith to sing always:
> Alleluia! (CW, #248)

Concern about legitimate ecclesiastical art and edifying church music is not by any means a twentieth century phenomenon. Long before the the Reformation addressed the issue, the church struggled in its selection of music. Even Plato and Aristotle had opinions on the emotional power of music for good and ill. Some Lutherans are intrigued these days with studies by men like Manfred Clynes, who has contended that some music by its very nature leads the human emotions toward self and away from Christ.[14]

Today's church must keep in mind that Scripture makes no laws concerning the type and variety of music that believers use in the service of the gospel. Christian artists and Christian theologians must continue to work together to determine whether their music actually communicates Christ. Experience in ministry and good taste help in this effort, but nothing serves the Christian artist better than a continuing study and an increasing love of the gospel and an appreciation of the worship principles Scripture encourages.

Allowing and Encouraging Praise

Lutheran worship leaders who take gospel proclamation seriously may discover that the Lutherans who worship under their guidance do not always appreciate their serious efforts and concerns. Sometimes musicians and pastors deserve to carry the blame here. It is not necessarily a mark of Lutheran orthodoxy when every hymn in the service has its roots in Lutheran Germany. Those who select hymns and choral and organ music will want to keep in mind that the artistic tastes of the average wor-

---

[14] Manfred Clynes, *Sentics* (New York: Anchor Press, 1977).

shiper are usually somewhat less sophisticated than those of their leaders. People like to sing and hear what is familiar. Paul Bunjes, for many years a Lutheran music teacher, composer, and observer, noted that the "people don't know what they like, but they like what they know."

It will not be in the best interest of the church's music or its worship if its musicians hold to a haughty disdain for "schmaltz." Sometimes what is warmly emotional serves the spiritual needs of average Lutherans better than art that is coolly intellectual. This caution is also sounded as we recognize that many Lutheran worshipers do not have a North German lineage. Not only is their heritage different from that of long-time Lutherans; their emotional make-up is different, too. Musicians who serve the congregation must keep this reality in mind as they plan music for worship.

Laypeople have a wide variety of viewpoints concerning art and music, and sometimes those opinions are different from those of the pastor and the church musicians. There are a number of reasons for this. It is true, of course, that Scripture does not identify a preferred artistic style. Add to this the reality that the principles of Christian worship are not well-known or understood by most laypeople. Finally, music and art are a matter of taste, and, as the saying goes, "*de gustibus non disputando est*" (when it comes to taste, there can be no argument).

The leaders of the church have a legitimate obligation to honor the musical tastes and preferences of the worshipers. However, the honor accorded to the laity ought not to be extended without careful thought. The likes and dislikes of the average worshiper are not always tempered by sound theological judgment. Many people determine their favorite hymns not on the basis of the hymn's confessional strength, but because of its emotional appeal. This is especially true of hymns people consider part of that "old-time religion," e.g., *Nearer My God to Thee, The Old Rugged Cross, In the Garden,* and *Blessed Assurance.* When it becomes obvious that the Lutheran church is not always enamored of these old favorites (and some contemporary favorites as well), the reaction is not usually "why is this hymn not doctrinally appropriate for me?" but rather "this hymn is emotionally appropriate for me!"

59

From a certain point of view, it is gratifying that some Christians feel strongly about "feeling good" at worship. That believers desire to rejoice in their status as God's children is good and salutary. Such a feeling is to be encouraged. Too often, however, people are looking to fulfill this desire in something besides the good news about Jesus. There is nothing at all wrong with lilting melodies, syncopated rhythms, uplifting modulations, and easy-to-learn refrains, but these dare not become the source of the good feeling that needs to come from the gospel. Without the everlasting gospel, joy is never lasting. Those who teach the concepts of worship need to remind people that the key to joy is Jesus, not hype. Worship forms may surely be chosen with the people in mind, but when the forms begin to replace the gospel as that which moves the heart, then the church's leadership is failing to meet the true objective of church music.

Leaders in today's Lutheran congregations get little help from other Christian denominations, especially those influenced by Evangelicalism. The twentieth century descendants of Revivalism have not appreciably changed their tune when it comes to the purpose of music and art in worship. They look at worship forms from a purely pragmatic perspective: does the form "work" to generate the emotional response that is an essential evidence of salvation. With that principle in mind, religious publishing houses are producing music without end that has as its purpose nothing else but to elicit a comfortable or enthusiastic frame of mind. Despite its complete lack of interest in Christ or Christian faith, the entertainment industry recognizes a trend when it sees one and floods the market with more of the same. Americans who are content with this form of spirituality are only too happy to keep these publishers in business.

Christian Worship includes musical forms that are strong both in gospel content and emotional appeal. Worshipers will find some old favorites that at one time might have been considered by some to be quite musically "un-Lutheran." Because the content of these hymns meets the Scripture's doctrinal standards, however, our hymnal eagerly includes them for use in our congregations. At the same time, it must be recognized that other hymns, thought by some to be cold and unemotional, can indeed touch the heart and become well-loved as Christians sing them again and again.

The Best and Finest Offerings

In worship believers come together to serve God, and they acknowledge his worth by returning to him the best of his blessings. Week after week, hundreds of Lutheran congregations present their monetary offerings before the Lord as they sing:

> We give thee but thine own,
> Whate'er the gift may be;
> All that we have is thine alone,
> A trust, O Lord, from thee.
>
> May we thy bounties thus
> As stewards true receive
> And gladly, as thou blessest us,
> To thee our firstfruits give. (CW 485:1,2)

What the Scriptures have to say about our offerings of money and goods surely applies also to our music and art.

Obviously, God's call for the firstfruits of our musical and artistic offerings has an enormous impact on the way church musicians prepare and perform in the public service. It should not occur (how could it occur?) that an organist or choir director could offer something to God that is slipshod. Someone has said "Holy shoddy is still shoddy." This advice may be hard for some church musicians to swallow, but it is definitely to the point:

> God knows when a performance is diligently prepared or carelessly "thrown together." That he not only accepts but even desires our imperfect sacrifices of praise is a wonder of his love and grace. We abuse his generosity when we presume that anything we bring to him, regardless of its condition, must be received with gratitude.[15]

It is the church musician's duty before God to practice and perform with the best of his abilities. He ought to do nothing mechanically, by habit, lightly, or casually. Everything in the service ought to be done by decision, with thought and prayer. Not only

---

[15] "The God Who Sings," *Christianity Today*, July 15, 1983, pp. 19-210.

does such service indicate the worth the musician ascribes to the Creator, but it also serves the worshipers. Anything less than excellence is extremely distracting to worship. In his book The Church Musician, Dr. Paul Westermeyer wrote:

> . . . the preacher or lector can stumble over a word here or there, and still the message will have impact. To stumble over a note is much more dangerous; the message's impact will dissipate more quickly when there is a musical error.[16]

Does this observation eliminate all but the most talented artists from the service of the gospel? Not at all. Dr. Westermeyer added:

> . . . the amateur with little time and meager ability can develop the necessary skills just as the professional with much time and many abilities can. For both, continuing practice is mandatory and critical. If skills are matched to responsibilities and situations, each person can do an admirable job. The difference here is simply one of degree, not kind. Neither person is better than the other. The task for both is the same: serve the people and practice sufficiently to be able to do it well.[17]

The point is not that only talented musicians may bring a musical offering to God, but that all musicians ought to bring their best musical offerings to him. The Savior's parable of the talents gives food for thought for all serious and dedicated church musicians.

This principle of Christian worship also speaks to the kind of music the church brings to its public services. Our age is one in which there is a great deal of disagreement about what is musically proper for public worship. Some desire to abandon the old for the new. There is a growing movement these days to abandon the new for the old. But both the "terminally hip and the rigid repristinators"[18] miss the point. The Lutheran Church has never had a problem absorbing a wide variety of musical styles, from Gregorian chant to American gospel.

---

[16] Paul Westermeyer, *The Church Musician* (New York: Harper and Row, 1988), p. 39.

[17] Westermeyer, *The Church Musician*, p. 23.

[18] Carl Schalk, "Church Music in the 90s: Problems and Prognoses," *The Christian Century*, March 21, 1990.

The yardstick by which suitability must be gauged (assuming, of course, that gospel content is consistent across the various styles) is not style but excellence—is the musical form a true, honest, legitimate, and notable representation of its own style? The artist is obligated to determine if the selection is, in fact, good Gregorian chant, good Renaissance motet, good Baroque chorale, good gospel hymn, or good folk song. The same standards of excellence that have been applied to historic music— standards that have eliminated literally millions of hymns through the ages—ought to be applied to contemporary music as well, for God deserves only our best. Musical diversity is a noble goal in the church, composed as it is of people of many ages and cultures, but stewards of the gracious gifts of God ought never be satisfied with musical superficiality.

Once again the Evangelicals often compromise this worship principle, much to the chagrin even of many Evangelicals. The disenchanted Evangelical Franky Schaeffer wrote this before he left the movement for Greek Orthodoxy:

> Today, Christian endeavor in the arts is typified by the contents of your local Christian bookstore-accessory-paraphernalia shop. For the coffee table we have a set of praying hands out of some sort of pressed muck. Christian posters are ready to adorn your walls with suitable Christian graffiti to sanctify them and make them a justifiable expense. Perhaps a little plastic cube with a mustard seed entombed within to boost your understanding of faith. And as if this were not enough, a toothbrush with a Bible verse stamped on its plastic handle, and a comb with a Christian slogan or two impressed on it. On a flimsy rack are stacked a pile of records. You may choose them at random blindfolded, for most of them will be the same idle rehash of acceptable spiritual slogans, endlessly recycled as pablum for the tone-deaf, television-softened brains of our present-day Christians.
>
> In fact, without making the list endless, one could sum up by saying that the modern Christian world and what is known as evangelicalism is marked, in the area of the arts and cultural endeavor, by one outstanding feature, and this is its addiction to mediocrity.[19]

---

[19] Franky Schaeffer, *Addicted to Mediocrity* (Wheaton, IL: Good News Publications, 1980), pp. 22,23.

Schaeffer has been joined by a host of Evangelicals who utter the same laments.[20]

Can excellence be gauged in a world of multi-culturalism and hedonism? Isn't it true that "there has never been a maudlin voluntary that someone has not considered beautiful?" The fact remains that personal likes and private judgments do not render the unbeautiful beautiful. In the subjective land of artistic appreciation, there is a place for objectivity.

When St. Paul wrote, "Finally, brothers, whatever is true, whatever is noble, whatever is right, whatever is pure, whatever is lovely, whatever is admirable—if anything is excellent or praiseworthy—think about such things" (Philippians 4:8), he clearly indicated that he was content to let the valued judgment of human experience decide what was lovely and worthy of praise. He wants Christians to think about what is best in God's creation, both from the divine and from the human perspective. Understanding St. Paul is to know that he will insist that God's perspective comes first. But in matters that God allows to be free, in areas where God does not express his will, then the human perspective counts, too. Paul would surely assent to the contention that anything that is considered worthy of praise in the length and breadth of human experience, anything that human beings tend to agree is lovely, anything that gains a consensus of excellence across a broad human perspective, deserves the attention of and use by the people of God.

The differences between Evangelicalism and Lutheranism are real and in step with the theological emphases of each. Lutheranism considers art to be a part of worship and, therefore, calls for the giving of one's best to God. Whether in language, speech, music, poetry, sculpture, tapestry, or painting; whether in historic or contemporary form, Lutherans bring their art first to

---

[20] Also see . . .

Thomas Howard, *Evangelical Is Not Enough: Worship of God in Liturgy and Sacraments* (San Francisco: Ignatius Press, 1984).

Michael Horton, *Made in America: The Shaping of Modern American Evangelicalism,* (Grand Rapids: Baker, 1991).

Thomas Day, *Why Catholics Can't Sing: The Culture of Catholicism or the Triumph of Bad Taste,* (Crossroads, 1991).

God. But Lutherans also bring their art for the benefit of their fellow believer and employ it in the church to affect intellect and emotion for the strengthening of faith. Thus art glorifies Christ and proclaims Christ at the same time.

Christian artists do not have to invent some convoluted defense for the joy they feel as they pursue art, music, and musical instruments that are lovely and worthy of praise. The church can enjoy and strive for those things that even unbelievers—to say nothing of countless believers—consider to be among the highest forms of artistic expression known to human beings and among the noblest contributions civilization has ever made to society.

Lutherans dare not compromise their stewardship of God's lovely and praiseworthy gifts simply because something less lovely might seem just as effective. This is an appealing temptation in our world. It seems as though everything we do these days has to be cost-efficient and task-effective. In the technological world in which we live, loveliness and nobility don't fare very well, primarily because they don't seem to be either cost-efficient or task-effective. The question comes from all over, even from inside the church, and it usually sounds like this, "Couldn't something else be just as effective—and certainly less expensive?" The question is well-intended, but surely misses the point. Believers pursue loveliness because this is God's will; believers proclaim the love of Jesus because this is God's will. And then believers are confident, as St. Paul was, that as they do both with heart and mind and soul and strength, God will surely bring his blessing, and he will bring it effectively!

Christian Worship: A Lutheran Hymnal presents to Lutheran worshipers countless opportunities to give their best to God and to give their Christ to their neighbor. The orders of worship literally demand music; they encourage the choir, the cantor/soloist, the organ, and other instruments. They seek beauty of language in prayers and hymns, and loveliness in tunes and settings. They encourage respectable designs in architecture, symbolism, and ceremony. The worship point of view espoused in this hymnal allows Lutherans to practice what they preach about art, which is a gift of God, they say, for the glory of God and the edification of his people.

65

The following offers a fitting and memorable reminder for those artists God has given to his church:

1. When you do music, present it as well as you can.

2. Good music, done well, offers a glimpse of creation after the sixth day. God saw that it was very good.

3. Good music, done well, points to the wonders of God's creation that remain to this day.

4. Good music, done well, looks ahead to a new heaven and a new earth that God is preparing for those who long for the Lord's return.[21]

---

[21] These four reminders are presented by Prof. Bruce Backer to his organ students at Dr. Martin Luther College, New Ulm, Minnesota.

CHAPTER 5:

The Worship Space

In their private devotions and meditations, individual Christians can worship God not only in any manner and at any time, but also in any place. They can offer God their prayers and praises on a crowded bus, in a busy emergency ward, or in a quiet bedroom. God can serve individual believers wherever they can open his book and read it. But when Christians, especially many Christians, come together for worship, their service to God and God's service to them demands a worship space, that is, a building, a church. Lutheran congregations which begin plans to provide this space for worship (or to renovate an existing space) need to think about energy conservation and maintenance. Much more, however, they need to study concepts and theories of church design. The congregation's called and elected leaders will want to be determined that their worship space, like their worship rite and their worship music, matches the theological emphases of God's Word and is in step with the worship principles of Lutheranism.

Objectives of the Worship Space

What is our church building for? is an important question, even though it sounds rather obvious. There are right and wrong reasons to erect a building for worship. Although Scripture doesn't call the tower of Babel a church, we do know that the people of Babel began their building program with two wrong objectives: "'Come, let us build ourselves a city, with a tower that reaches into the heavens, so that we may make a name for ourselves and not be scattered over the face of the whole earth'" (Genesis 11:4). King Herod's objective in building the great temple in Jerusalem (20 B.C.) was to placate the Jews and to coerce them into accepting his Idumean monarchy. History makes no effort to hide the truth that much of the cathedral building in medieval Europe was carried out with decidedly commercial rather than spiritual objectives. With these realities in mind, a church planning committee is wise to begin its work by asking the question, "What is our church building for?"

Functional Objectives

A church building is for worship, for the intellectual and emotional interaction between the Bridegroom and his bride, between Christ and his Church. The church comes to worship to serve God, and God is at worship to serve the church. The church comes to pray, confess, sing, listen, and offer. God comes in the Word and the sacraments, in water at baptism and in bread and wine at Holy Communion. The worship space needs to allow believers to do what they do at worship, and it needs to provide space for God to do what he does at worship. Planners must take care that the design of the worship space does not hinder either the believers or God, but that architecture, furnishings, and art encourage the interaction of Christ and the Church.

The church of the first centuries after Christ's ascension thought about church design primarily with this "function" objective in mind. As long as Christians lived under the threat of persecution, they were concerned only with finding a place that allowed them to carry out the most necessary worship activities.

After the civil authorities allowed Christian worship and then even made Christianity the religion of the state (fourth century A.D.), the church's leaders still thought first of function. Rather than erecting new buildings for their worship, Christian congregations took over the large public meeting halls that were found in most Roman communities. The basilica was open and airy, it had a raised central platform that allowed for preaching and reading, it had room for praying and praising, and it allowed people to move for eating and drinking. It invariably had an atrium or vestibule in which Christians could gather before and after the public service and often had a pool at which baptisms could be performed. The design was so perfectly functional for Christian worship that the basilica style remained the preferred church architecture for over a thousand years.

The functional pragmatism of the early church is a good place for church planning committees to begin their work. A list of the various functions that take place in Lutheran worship will help:

1. the pastor *leads;* he preaches, reads, speaks the believers' prayers and intercessions, and takes part in the liturgy's dialogue
2. believers *participate;* they sing, listen, confess, pray, and praise
3. believers *move* for communion, for baptisms, with their offerings, for entry and exit
4. the choir and the organ *assist* the worship of the believers
5. believers *assemble* for concerts of sacred music and for dramatic and artistic programs
6. believers *gather* before and after worship

   (These functions will receive in-depth analysis later in this chapter.)

Once a list of worship functions has been determined, studied, and prioritized, church planners can begin to design a building that will allow the functions to take place easily and naturally. It is a sad reality that too many building committees have failed to address these functional questions, with the result that many church buildings have hindered and sometimes even made impossible important components of Christian worship.

The "form follows function" concept of architectural design has had the dominant voice in church building for almost a century. In their 1989 book on church architecture, James and Susan White agreed that

Christian worship is not an esoteric, devious affair; usually the most simple, direct, utilitarian approach is the best. The finest church buildings in every era have sought to provide the simplest and most useful settings for worship. The Christian community gathers not to admire its building but to use the structure. It is not a community of tourists from afar, viewing something in which it never shares. The Christian community must build simply and directly for its own needs in worship. Anything beyond that is conspicuous consumption and contrary to the essence of Christianity.

Frequently, when Christians take most seriously that which is simple and direct, eschewing the monumental or purely decorative, the resulting building has the greatest aesthetic appeal. The dictum of

69

architect Ludwig Mies van der Rohe, "Less is more," has much to say to church builders.[1]

Symbolic Objectives

One cannot help but wonder how the Whites react when they read of God's obvious approval of Solomon's temple. The point has been made previously that God not only communicates his message directly through the divine word but also reinforces the Word with symbols. Martin Luther understood that art carried Christ to the eyes just as music and speech carried Christ to the ears:

> [The gospel] has been proclaimed richly and clearly; it has been emphasized masterfully and powerfully by the apostles; now it is announced everywhere by word of mouth and with the pen; it is written, sung, pictured, etc.[2]

Again he wrote, "God's Word is presented so powerfully, lucidly, and clearly in preaching, singing, speaking, writing, and painting that they must concede it is the true Word of God."[3]

In the same way that believers cannot judge whether the gospel has greater effect in one place on earth than in another, so they cannot determine absolutely that the gospel has more effect when it is delivered through one medium than through another. The Holy Spirit has his own economy. That reading the Scripture is better in every case for every Christian than singing the Scripture, or that singing the Word is more effective in every case and for every Christian than picturing or symbolizing the Word cannot be known. The truth is that the author of the divine Word has communicated his message to his creatures in various ways and calls upon his followers to do the same.

As believers began to build churches of their own instead of taking over unused Roman basilicas, they thought about arranging wood, stone, iron, and a variety of other materials with the specific

---

[1] James F. and Susan J. White, *Church Architecture: Building and Renovating for Christian Worship* (Nashville: Abingdon Press, 1989), pp. 20,21.

[2] Luther's Works, American, Vol. 24, p. 404.

[3] Luther's Works, American, Vol. 13, p. 168.

objective of proclaiming the divine story in symbolism. The styles of architecture have changed through the centuries, often because of advances in constructional technology, but each succeeding style retained an emphasis on symbolic communication:

- Thick walls, rounded arches, and barrel vaults gave Romanesque churches (eleventh century) a heavy and durable quality that underscored the eternal nature of God.

- The Gothic style appeared a century later in France, with its pointed arches and ribbed vaults. Flying buttresses removed the building's weight load from its walls, and architects filled the space with bright and colorful windows. The height, light, and upward direction of the Gothic style pulled believing eyes to heaven and encouraged medieval souls to live and long for heavenly glories.

- The period of the Renaissance (sixteenth century) wanted to recall the orderliness of the Greek and Roman cultures, and the artistic harmony and classical proportions of Renaissance architecture exalted the orderly creation of God.

- The churches of colonial and pioneer America did not have the splendor of many of Europe's churches and cathedrals, but the durable materials of which these churches were built spoke about God's eternal presence; the spires that reached toward the sky in thousands of towns and cities pointed to the eternal worship of heaven.

The furnishings and artifacts that are inside history's churches have spoken similar symbolic messages. Only God knows how many of his people were strengthened in faith through the centuries as they contemplated gem-studded crucifixes of gold and silver, as they gazed at Bible stories in stained glass windows, or as they thought about Christian symbols on tapestries and paraments. In fact, there have been times in the Church's history when the gospel was proclaimed more often through ecclesiastical art and architecture than it was in sermons.

The Christian church has also intended its buildings to be symbols of the worth its people ascribe to God. Through the centuries believers themselves may have lived in shacks, tenements, or sod houses, but they have built sturdy and beautiful structures where together they might enter the presence of God. Just as they worshiped God in many languages and types of music, so they constructed buildings in various styles and with varying degrees of splendor. But invariably their buildings confessed symbolically that God was greater than they were and that their service to him, to say nothing of his service to them, demanded nobility, beauty, and loveliness.

Building committees are obligated to understand that the structure, that holds the worship space of a Christian congregation, as well as the furnishings and artistry that serve the congregation's worship, are inevitably symbolic of something. Some are convinced that extreme examples of modern architecture and art are intended to be symbols of disorder and chaos and fail to speak a valid and honest message about God. Therefore, while the question of function ought to be the first question a committee asks, it ought not to be the last. How will we proclaim God's story to human eyes as well as to human ears? is a legitimate question for any church that wishes to convey, through every possible medium, the intellectual and emotional interaction between Christ and his bride in worship.

The principle of "form follows function" can be overstated and too simply applied. In fact, an emphasis only on the function of the worship space can rob the church of exactly that which, in some cases, is most beneficial in reinforcing the gospel message on the human heart. Building committees need not choose between function and symbolism; realistic and honest church design includes objectives for both.

When Christians try to follow both objectives, however, voices occasionally insist that architectural symbolism and artistic beauty rob the church of offerings that could be better used for the physically and, especially, the spiritually oppressed. "This money could have been spent for missions" is the often-heard criticism when congregations erect beautiful and symbolically rich church buildings.

The Savior's commission to "make disciples of all nations" was a call both to bring unbelievers to begin the walk with Jesus and to strengthen believers already on the walk with Jesus. A building for worship certainly serves the cause of the church's mission if both parts of the great commission are recalled.

It is also a part of the divine record that Jesus did not disapprove of Mary anointing him with costly perfume (John 12:1-7) and in fact rebuked the disciples, especially Judas, when they criticized her action. In his rebuke ("You will always have the poor among you") Jesus was not negating the value of helping the poor; he was rather exposing the error of setting false alternatives.

The Christian life is not always a matter of doing one thing or the other; it more often involves "doing the one and not leaving the other undone." The Lord himself promises his Church that he is able to supply the necessary gifts that will allow believers to carry out a variety of tasks. It is true enough that the church has a mandate to carry the gospel to the lost, but who can determine to what degree a beautiful church building, rich in its testimony of the gospel, helps to encourage believers to carry out their mission? For that matter, who knows how the Spirit works through such a building to draw the attention and the interest of the unbeliever? Decisions in these matters are part of sanctified Christian judgment and wise Christian stewardship. That tensions are present is often good, for thereby members of the congregation are obligated to reflect on both the mission of the church and on the role of artistry and symbolism in Christian worship.

Theological Objectives

Setting theological objectives for the worship space involves the examination of both functional objectives and the symbolic objectives. Planning committees want worshipers to be able to perform easily and naturally the worship activities that are in line with its theological priorities. They also want the building and its furnishings to symbolize the importance of those priorities. Although there is no inherently Lutheran or Christian style of church architecture, all architecture makes a statement about what a church believes.

> A church is a place where God's people gather together to worship him, and how they worship, as well as what they believe, is either reinforced or undermined by the architecture. Church architecture is

73

therefore first and foremost a matter of theology rather than a matter of style.[4]

Historic examples illustrate the validity of that opinion:

1. The shallow chancels of the early Christian basilicas were deepened only after the Roman Church changed the theology of the Lord's Supper and turned the Sacrament into a sacrifice. The chancel became a separate room reserved for the celebrant and his clergy assistants; the people remained in the outer room (the nave) since their participation was not essential for the sacrifice. Thus, the "two-room" church was born in the false theology of the Roman mass.

2. Catholic churches of the Baroque period (early eighteenth century) resembled opera houses, with their banks of balconies circling the nave. The plan was true to Roman theology, which insisted that its people derived spiritual value simply by seeing the performance of the mass.

3. Leaders of the Reformed community stripped existing churches of everything that had roots in Catholicism and rebuilt church interiors to encourage preaching and hearing. Massive central pulpits towered over insignificant communion tables and carried a strong message about the Reformed theology of the Sacrament.

4. The lack of a pulpit and rows of facing pews in the worship buildings of the Quakers is an obvious indication that among the Quakers subjective expression has more theological significance than objective proclamation.

5. The design of contemporary Evangelical church buildings speaks just as clearly about modern Reformed theology. Worshipers gather in an unthreatening theaterlike atmosphere where it is not necessary (nor possible, really) to move and participate. All the action of worship takes place in an expansive chancel, which enables preachers to wander around, choirs to perform, dramas to be staged, and musical combos to be set up with ease. Thus, church architecture is made to perfectly match the entertainment focus of the church growth movement's style-over-substance theology of worship.

---

[4] Donald J. Bruggink, and Carl H. Droppers, *Christ and Architecture* (Grand Rapids: Eerdmans, 1965), p. 6.

Architectural design, the floor plan, building materials, placement of furnishings, acoustics, and much more, all speak a message about the theological priorities of a Lutheran congregation. It is imperative, therefore, that church building committees study both church design and theology before they embark on a building or renovation program.

Lutheran Church Design

Since Lutheran worship has two primary components—God's service to his people and his people's service to God—it is obvious that a worship space designed for Lutherans will have, in most cases, two primary sections. Throughout the history of Lutheranism, Lutheran churches usually have had a distinctive chancel and a distinctive nave: the chancel where God comes in word, baptism, and supper, and the nave where the people offer prayer, praise, and confession. Since Lutherans believe that there can be no service to God without service from God, the chancel is the center and focal point of Lutheran church design.

Some have insisted that the chancel/nave design fails to give a clear confession about what the Scripture teaches concerning the universal priesthood of all believers and that it rather represents the incorrect Roman Catholic doctrine of the priesthood. Traditional Roman doctrine surely would have insisted upon the two-room church, but the chancel/nave design does not necessarily give a compromised message.

The Lutheran church speaks clearly about the universal priesthood; Luther enunciated the scriptural principles that are still held by most Lutherans today. But the Scripture also speaks about the public ministry of the gospel and calls upon believers to designate certain individuals as their representatives not only at public worship but in other areas of gospel ministry as well. The chancel/nave design is not only very functional as far as movement, sight, and sound are concerned, but it is entirely in keeping with the Scripture's perfectly balanced teachings of the universal priesthood and the public ministry.

The chancel/nave design can also be helpful as a reminder to believers that they can come into the presence of God only through Christ. The writer to the Hebrews wrote, "Therefore, brothers, since we have confidence to enter the Most Holy Place by the blood of Jesus, by a new and living way opened for us through the curtain, that is, his body, and since we have a great priest over the house of God, let us draw near to God with a sincere heart in full assurance of faith, having our hearts sprinkled to cleanse us from a guilty conscience and having our bodies washed with pure water" (Hebrews 10:19-22). This symbol becomes even more striking when the pastor speaks the Confession and Absolution in the nave and then moves—as the representative of the people—into the chancel.

The Altar

A century ago, a study of Lutheran chancel design would not have begun with discussion of the altar. Especially among Lutherans who had their roots in Pietism, the altar was not a notable chancel furnishing. Calvinism refuses to speak about an altar at all, even to this day.[5] The strong reaction against the altar was born in Calvin's determination to rid Reformed churches of everything that smacked of Catholicism; the altar, as much as anything else in church design, was the symbol of Rome's doctrine of the sacrifice of the mass. Pietism was closely aligned with Calvinism, and many Lutheran chancels at the turn of the twentieth century had altars that were in fact tables, and small tables at that, located at the foot of massive pulpits. The altar's size and placement symbolized more than an aversion to Rome's sacrificial theology, however. There was also a statement in that design that the Lord's Supper was neither often celebrated nor highly cherished among Pietists.

Lutherans who retained the worship principles of Martin Luther did not have the same difficulty making the altar the focal point of their chancels and the most lavishly adorned of the chancel's furnishings. That reality does not mean that they held to a sacrificial theology in communion or even that they ranked the

---

[5] Two works previously cited, the one by James and Susan White and the other by Donald Brugginck and Carl Droppers, do not use the term *altar*. White writes about the "altar-table" and Brugginck and Droppers insist that "the table should look like a table!" (*Christ and Architecture*, p. 14)

76

Sacrament above the Word. It simply meant that they were content to follow Luther's example of accepting the tradition of the church unless the tradition clearly violated the Scriptures.

Luther eliminated from Lutheran worship the doctrine of the sacrifice of the mass, but he did not eliminate the basic structure of liturgy that surrounded the sacrifice nor the altar at which it was offered. When Lutheran congregations assumed control of existing Roman Catholic churches, they renovated sparingly; they took over the organ, the windows, and even church names—Luther attended St. Mary's Church in Wittenberg until he died! These Lutherans also retained the elaborate central altar, and when they came to America, they built churches that were copies of what they had known in Germany.

Lutherans maintain a balanced thought concerning the symbolism of the altar. They recognize its Old Testament significance: on the altar, animals were sacrificed. God had designed the sacrificial rites for the nation of Israel to point his people to the truth that "without the shedding of blood there is no forgiveness" (Hebrews 9:22). In the Old Testament worship rites, the altar was a foreshadowing of Christ, who finally "appeared once for all at the end of the ages to do away with sin by the sacrifice of himself" (Hebrews 9:26). For New Testament believers the altar is a visual reminder that there is no forgiveness without the shedding of the blood of Christ.

Just as the ark of the covenant, placed in the temple's Most Holy Place, was the visible symbol of God's presence in the Old Testament, so the altar also symbolizes that God is present with his people in Word and sacrament. When the pastor speaks to the people from the altar in the Words of Institution or in the Blessing, he is speaking as God's ambassador from the foot of God's own throne. When the pastor speaks for the people facing the altar, in prayers and in the confession of sins, he is addressing the throne of God. Of course God is not confined to the altar any more than he was confined to the ark of the covenant. This is symbolism, not reality. But it is symbolism that correctly represents a theological reality, and it is an important reality. Our society has little interest in supernatural revelation, and society's attitudes often influence the thoughts of Christians. The altar helps believers to remember that God is present in a supernatural way whenever the Word and sacrament are used. This is reality.

The altar has an important functional use besides its symbolic purpose. The sacred vessels are placed on the altar in preparation for Holy Communion, and the people gather around the altar to receive Christ's true body and blood in the bread and wine. Even here, however, there is some symbolic value. The fact that the elements are positioned in this special place, usually in a special way, reminds believers that the sacred meal that begins at the altar is a unique meal that has no equal except in heaven, where the church confesses it will "eat of the eternal manna and drink of the river of thy pleasure forevermore."[6] That all the believers receive bread and wine from a single location is also a confession of the truth St. Paul related: "Because there is one loaf, we, who are many, are one body, for we all partake of the one loaf" (1 Corinthians 10:17).

Therefore, by means of the altar that they place in the chancels of their churches, Lutherans symbolize Scripture's theology in three ways: they portray the vicarious sacrifice of Christ as the central theme of God's plan of salvation; they symbolize that God is actually present among his people in the Word and sacrament of Christ; and they show that Holy Communion is a unique meal offered to believers.

Because of the symbolism that Lutherans attach to the altar, they usually place the altar in a dignified and beautiful setting. Often a *reredos,* a backdrop made of wood or stone, stands at the back of the altar, usually containing niches for statues, a crucifix, or another Christian symbol. Some altars are positioned beneath a *triptych,* a set of panels decorated with paintings or carvings. Occasionally Lutheran altars are covered by a *baldechin* (also called a *tester* or *ciborium*), a canopy supported either by pillars or from the wall behind the altar. A popular innovation during the 1950s and 1960s was the dorsal, a large curtain that replaced the reredos as a backdrop for the altar. More recently church designers simply have set the altar against the chancel wall and have decorated the wall with a prominently displayed Christian symbol.

As he conducts the liturgy at the altar, the pastor honors the altar's symbolism (and helps the people understand its symbol-

---

[6] *The Lutheran Liturgy* (St. Louis: Concordia, 1948), p. 290.

78

ism) by his orientation to the altar. He faces the altar when he speaks to God on behalf of the people, and he faces the people when he speaks to them on God's behalf. The idea that pastors should never turn their backs on worshipers is new to the church and seems to be nothing more than trendy advice.

In the *Deutsche Messe,* the German service Luther composed for village parishes, he made this comment as he wrote about the liturgy for communion:

> In the true mass of real Christians, the altar should not remain where it is [i.e., against the wall], and the priest should always face the people as Christ doubtlessly did in the Last Supper. But let that await its own time.[7]

The freestanding altar actually waited for the Roman Catholics, who introduced it during the middle decades of the 20th century. However, the concept concisely matches Lutheran theology, which considers the Words of Institution to be the gospel proclamation of the Sacrament. Whether serving at a wall altar or at a freestanding one, the pastor more properly speaks the words facing the people than facing the altar. Luther purposefully removed the words from the ancient Thanksgiving Prayer so that they would be proclaimed and not prayed.

The freestanding altar has much to commend it, but committees need to take care that the altar is constructed and positioned in such a way that it can serve not only as a place for communion but also as a symbol of Christ's atoning sacrifice and of God's abiding presence. A freestanding altar that retains the three traditional functions of a Lutheran altar invites the pastor to continue to face the altar as he speaks to God and to face the people as he speaks for God. In fact, it is best if the pastor conducts the entire *Service of the Word* in front of the altar, facing the people when he speaks as God's representative and facing the altar when he speaks on behalf of the people.

The altar is *not* a lectern. In no case should the lessons be read from behind the altar. If a lectern is not installed in a church's chancel, the lessons may be read from a position in front of the

---

[7] Luther's Works, American, Vol. 53, p. 69.

altar. This position should not be the same as that used during prayer or liturgical proclamation, however. Traditionally, the lessons are read at the "horns," or corners of the altar: the First and Second Lessons at the right side and the Gospel at the left side (as one faces the altar). Whatever materials are needed by the leader (e.g., a copy of the psalm or the creed) can be placed into the Bible. The leader moves to the other side of the altar to read the Gospel as the choir or congregation sing the Verse.

If the Creed follows the Gospel (as it does in the *Common Service*), it may be spoken by the pastor from the middle of the altar as he faces the people. The pastor moves behind the altar either after the Lord's Prayer (just before the Preface in both the *Common Service* and the *Service of Word and Sacrament*) or during *Holy, Holy, Holy.* He then returns to the front of the altar after the distribution and concludes the service there.

Some Lutheran congregations have noticed that their deep, tiered chancels require uncommon physical activity of pastors who must move frequently and quickly between the wall altar and the communion rail. To minimize the problem, they have installed a communion table on a lower chancel platform and closer to the rail. The communion table may be used as a free-standing altar during the proclamation of the Words of Institution. If there is a desire to conduct the entire communion liturgy around the communion table, the suggestions made in the previous paragraph may be followed.

The Pulpit

Before he ascended into heaven Jesus instructed his followers, "Preach the good news to all creation." Martin Luther wrote, "When God's word is not preached, one had better neither sing nor read, or even come together."[8] The Apology of the Augsburg Confession includes in its German text: "There is nothing that so attaches people to the church as good preaching."[9] Considering what the Scriptures, Luther, and the Lutheran Confessions have to say about the value of preaching, it would be strange indeed if

---

[8] Luther's Works, American, Vol. 53, p. 11.

[9] Apology, Art 24:51.

preaching did not occupy a prominent place in Lutheran worship. It would be equally strange if Lutheran church design did not accentuate the position and artistic significance of the *pulpit.*

Lutherans have usually positioned the pulpits in their churches close to the altar; the symbolism of the centrality of Word and sacrament is obvious. However, pulpits have come in all kinds of sizes and shapes. Some were large and high, reaching above the level of wrap-around balconies that were common in Lutheran churches a century ago. Many were topped by an ornate canopy, a *Schalldeckel,* which served primarily as a sounding board. As public address systems became common (and as some people began to resent pulpits that seemed as though there were "six feet above contradiction"), the canopies were often removed and the pulpits lowered. The church architects of the Victorian era (nineteenth century) tended to value artistic symmetry and often designed pulpits and lecterns that were identical in size and shape.

Some contemporary church architects are beginning to rethink the diminuation of the pulpit. In recent designs pulpits have once again risen above the floor of the chancel and many have had canopies attached overhead. This has been done not for the sake of function, but for symbolic purposes; the massive, towering pulpit speaks a visual message about the authority of the Word. It underscores what the pastor says in the sermon: "What I am saying to you here is what the Lord says in his Word!" As inviting as this idea may be to Lutherans, care must be taken that the pulpit does not again begin to suggest dominance over the altar. The Lord does not rank the means of grace; neither should symbolism.

Building committees must keep several practical concerns in mind. In some way the pulpit must be able to accommodate preachers of various heights; an adjustable book stand helps deal with this situation. The book stand ought to have room for a Bible and the preacher's manuscript if he uses one. A shelf for a glass of water, a handkerkerchief, an additional book, and perhaps even a small tape recorder is desirable. Some preachers want a small clock installed in the pulpit. A good lighting system is important so that the pastor does not preach from the shadows.

Dimming the nave lights (in some churches the nave lights are actually turned off) and training spotlights on the speaker is a practice of doubtful value. The custom tends to isolate the worshipers, who may desire to participate actively as they listen, and makes it more difficult for the preacher to establish eye contact. In fact, it does more to invite dozing than it does to encourage attention.

The Lectern

The *lectern* is the place where the pastor or lector reads the lessons of the day. Usually it stands on the opposite side of the chancel from the pulpit and often is designed with a book stand that accommodates not only the Bible or lectionary but also other materials that are used during the Word section of the service, e.g., the psalm and the creeds.

Although it has been standard chancel furniture in most Lutheran churches for years, some liturgical design consultants wonder if the lectern is really necessary. Especially in small churches the lectern often makes for a crowded chancel; sometimes it needs to be moved before the communion distribution can take place. Also, when the lectern becomes one of the three visual centers in the front of the church, the baptismal font often has to be relegated to a corner of the nave. Some are convinced that the lectern draws too much attention away from the pulpit and inadvertently undervalues the work of preaching.[10] With all this in mind building committees might be wise to ask if money could not be better spent on something more important for worship than the lectern. (The place for the reading of the lessons when there is no lectern has been discussed earlier in this chapter.)

The Font

The sacrament of baptism requires nothing more in Lutheran worship than a bowl of water. However, Christians have invariably placed in their churches elaborate and artistically significant

---

[10] White, *Church Architecture,* p. 4: "To read God's Word from one place (the lectern) and then go elsewhere (the pulpit) to open the Scriptures to our understanding is bad theology and a counterproductive effort."

baptismal fonts. In the medieval churches of Europe and the Near East, the font often stood in a chapel of its own, separated from the main church building. Beautiful fonts of marble and wood grace many churches in both the old world and the new.

The elaborate and obvious baptismal font means to be a symbol of the great value Lutheran theology ascribes to baptism. By far the greatest number of believers in any given congregation enter the church through infant baptism. The reality that baptism initiates the miracle of faith is enough justification for a font of significant character and design.

However, Lutheran theology also maintains that baptism is a lifelong reminder of the believer's daily spiritual struggle and triumph of faith. Luther made the point that confessing sins and receiving forgiveness is nothing else than a reliving of baptism.[11] It was this truth that led the framers of *Christian Worship* to include confession and absolution in the baptism rite. In fact. the rite includes the words of Luther's Small Catechism:

> Baptism means that the sinful nature in us should be drowned by daily sorrow and repentance, and that all its evil deeds and desires be put to death. It also signifies that a new person should daily arise to live before God in righteousness and purity forever (CW, p. 12).

Therefore, the architecturally significant baptismal font serves as a visual reminder to every worshiper of both the initiating and the durative value of Holy Baptism.

The observation that many present-day Lutherans need these truths about baptism underscored in their minds and hearts is sufficient justification for thinking carefully about the design and placement of the baptismal font. A position in the chancel on the opposite side from the pulpit (replacing the lectern) commends itself, as does a place in the center of the main aisle just below the first chancel step. Some contemporary church designs position the font at the entry of the nave, although this requires careful pew placement so that the congregation can be involved in the

---

[11] A lengthy treatise of this point is found in Luther's Large Catechism in the section entitled "Infant Baptism." This section can be found in Theodore Tabbert's edition of the Lutheran Confessions; it is not added in the *Concordia Triglotta*.

83

baptism rite. Beautiful and significant works of art can be attached to the font just as they are to the altar and pulpit.

Chancel Appointments

It is not the objective of this cursory treatment of the worship space to cover in detail all aspects of chancel design. It would be impossible to give an adequate presentation of all the various sacred vessels, lights, paraments, banners, and other appointments that are used in Lutheran worship. However, there are several considerations that apply generally to all the appointments that congregations place into the chancels of their churches.

The first of these considerations has to do with *excellence.* What is placed in the chancel as a gift to God for the visual proclamation of his truth ought to be of high quality. Building project monies need to be reserved for altar ware, communion vessels, and paraments. Since these are used to present to the worshipers the choicest of Christ's gifts, they demand the best his people can give. If a congregation invites individual members to present these items in memory of a family member, the responsible committee will retain the right to designate what will be purchased. The point of view cannot be accepted that "anything will do." Well-meaning members occasionally volunteer to create and produce items for the chancel. The committee ought to know exactly what is being offered and approve designs *before* the gifts are presented. Banners prepared by little children are usually best placed in Sunday school rooms or in the narthex.

Whatever is placed in the chancel ought to *neither replace nor compete with* the altar, pulpit, and font as the focal points of the worshipers. It is possible to have too many floral arrangements and too much greenery. The chancel is not an art museum. Pictures, statues, symbols in brass or wood, and tapestries must be chosen carefully. Altar candles, paschal resurrection, or Christ candles, and eternal lights ought to be included judiciously, or they do nothing but clutter the chancel and obstruct both the worshiper's view and attention. Fewer adornments of good quality do more to accentuate Christian truth than many appointments of questionable value.

Committees must also take care that the appointments (cross and candlesticks) that are placed on a freestanding altar are actually designed for a freestanding altar. The elaborately tall appointments that are so fitting on a more traditional altar are out of place (to say nothing of being in the way) on a freestanding altar.

The chancel appointments ought to carry a clear and distinctive *theological message,* and the worshipers ought to be able to know what the message is. The chancel or altar cross can be so "common" that it fails to draw attention to the centrality of the cross in Christian teaching. Although some insist that an empty cross is a symbol of the resurrected Christ, it is to be remembered that some denominations display a plain cross precisely to overcome the implications of the Savior's vicarious atonement of blood. Committees are wise to consider a crucifix, i.e., a cross with the *corpus,* either depicting the suffering Christ or the exalted Christ dressed in his high-priestly vestments.

Congregations do not, however, need to eliminate every chancel appointment that has carried an imprecise meaning in other Christian churches. Both the eternal light and the altar candlesticks have been defined by Roman Catholics as symbolizing the presence of the living host in the church, i.e., the bread placed in the altar tabernacle that remains the body of Christ even after the communion. Lutherans can use these lights in freedom as long as they carefully explain what the lights truly symbolize.

Some churches like to include the national, Christian, and denominational flags in the chancel. While many Lutheran congregations have displayed flags of one sort or another, building committees ought to carefully analyze this tradition. Altar, pulpit, and font "all point to Christ," while national flags "speak not of Christ, but of the nation."[12] Especially in an age when so many Christian churches confuse the separate roles of church and state, it may be wise to place national flags in the narthex rather than in the chancel. The use of the Christian flag may promote an imprecise view of the church and a false ecumenism besides. Denominational loyalty is important in a congregation, but recent history seems to indicate that it is better to teach loyalty to the Scriptures

---

[12] Brugginck and Droppers, *Christ and Architecture,* pp. 250ff.

that cannot err than to denominations that can. The important work of the church body can surely be emphasized in better ways than with a flag.

There are many books and tracts available from Lutheran publishers that give more specific and detailed information concerning the appointments, paraments, sacred vessels, etc., that Lutheran congregations may desire to place in their church chancels. Paul H. D. Lang's book, *What An Altar Guild Should Know,*[13] remains an invaluable resource.

The Nave

The Lutheran church understands that the service of the congregation to God is the second purpose of public worship, and it rightly defines worship as an *interaction* between Christ and his bride. Therefore, participation is the key word as church building committees think about the design of the *nave,* the place for the worship of the people. Two considerations ought to be studied: where will the people stay and how will the people move?

For the most part Lutherans remain in one place, usually in *pews,* while they worship. Church furniture companies offer a variety of pew designs that can serve almost any congregation. Committees will have to decide whether they want pews to be padded and how they will include places for hymnals and Bibles. Often pews need to hold visitor welcome cards, communion registration cards, and even used individual communion glasses. Some church planning committees have replaced pews with dignified and well-constructed chairs, usually made of wood. Movable seating commends itself for several reasons. By removing a chair or two, wheelchairs can be located in any place in the nave and still be kept out of the aisles. Chairs can be rearranged for smaller worship gatherings (e.g., weddings and funerals) or for organ and instrumental recitals. The use of chairs also eliminates the problem of crowding too many people into a church pew.

---

[13] Paul H. D. Lang, *What An Altar Guild Should Know* (St. Louis: Concordia, 1964).

More important than the kind of seating is the placement of pews and chairs within the nave. The traditional two-room rectangular church that Lutherans inherited from Roman Catholics after the Reformation was designed primarily for hearing—and especially for seeing—rather than for participating. Lutheran worship theology that emphasizes the participation of the congregation is not well-served, it seems, by row after row of pews flanking a long central aisle. Not only do worshipers have difficulty seeing the focal point of worship, i.e., the chancel, in such a design, they also find it impossible to see anything but the backs of other worshipers. Such a situation hardly encourages mutual edification.

A nave design that accentuates width instead of length, that gathers worshipers closer to and around the chancel, and that allows worshipers to see one another seems to be far more suitable for Lutheran worship than the traditional rectangular concept. The modern idea that human response has equal value with divine revelation needs to be rejected, of course. Church planners are wise to retain a notable accent on the chancel at the same time that they maximize opportunities for congregational participation in the nave.

Some attention should be paid to the space where the congregation assembles to receive the Sacrament. The *communion rail,* a traditional feature in most Lutheran chancels, is another of the furnishings that Lutherans inherited from Roman Catholics. Lutherans have used the rail in good conscience,[14] although its history is rooted in the false theology that the members of the priesthood were of better spiritual character than laypeople. The rail is a convenient, obvious, and reverent place for the distribution; even a large group of people knows where to go and what to do when they get there. Some Lutherans have used the rail for in-

---

[14] This is not true of all Lutherans. The author served a congregation in which many members had been taught that the communion rail was decidedly papistic. After a rail was installed, several older members steadfastly refused to kneel. Since he arrived after the installation controversy, the author assumed for years that these "standing" members had bad knees. After he expressed some sympathy to one of these "crippled" souls, he was unceremoniously informed of the actual situation!

dividual absolution, for opening and closing prayers,[15] and during the confirmation rite.

The communion rail is not without its detractors, however. In some older churches the rail allows only a few people to gather at a time, resulting in lengthy communion services. Elderly people have real problems using the steps to get to a rail located in the chancel, and many would rather endure the pain that comes with kneeling than the embarrassment that comes with standing. Some surely refrain from attending the Sacrament to avoid both kinds of pain. Many pastors feel that communing people who are kneeling is difficult. The communicants' mouths often are hard to see. Then, too, shorter pastors may find it awkward to serve taller people when they are standing. Nevertheless, both worshipers and their pastors may be happier if the Sacrament is distributed to people while they are standing at a designated place on the main floor in front of the chancel.

Lutheran worship expects that worshipers will occasionally move: people move to receive the Lord's Supper, to bring their children for baptism, to present their offerings, and, of course, to enter and exit the nave. Because such movement occurs, church planners need to think about the *space between the pews* as well as the *aisles*. Not everyone attends communion every time it is offered, and communicants who leave their pews to attend ought to be able to walk easily past someone who remains seated.

Aisles need to be wide enough for a row of chairs when there is an overflow attendance, for caskets to be carried to and from the chancel entrance, and for brides and fathers of brides. The aisle between the first row of pews and the chancel steps should be designed with the consideration that visiting concert choirs (and occasionally the congregation's own choirs) may need space for a piano and instruments. It stands to reason that aisles made of rough brick or uneven tiles, while perhaps beautiful, are

---

[15] Many Scandinavian Lutherans assembled at the rail twice during a communion service: once for confession\absolution and again for the communion. The liturgy composed for Danish and Norwegian Lutherans by Johannes Bugenhagen began and ended with a prayer, which the pastor or the song leader spoke while kneeling either at the altar or the rail.

impractical and actually dangerous for the people who must walk on them.

The Balcony

The *balcony,* standing a story above the nave and usually at the back of the church, has often been called the *choir loft* or the *organ gallery.* Both optional titles identify the traditional function of the balcony.

Many Christian denominations place the organ and choir in the chancel, in front and in the view of the congregation, rather than in back and out of sight of the worshipers. Lutherans occasionally ask about the traditional Lutheran practice and wonder why the choir could not be brought to the front of the church. The answer has to do with the Lutheran understanding of worship and the corresponding function of the choir and organ.

The main participants in Lutheran worship are God and the congregation. The music of worship is the servant of both, assisting God in his service to the congregation and assisting the congregation in its service to God. The organist and the choir have a similar function to that of the worship leader. Just as the pastor is a servant of God as he proclaims the Word and administers the sacraments, so the congregation's musicians are servants of God as they proclaim the Word in music. Just as the pastor directs and guides the congregation's prayers, so the musicians assist the congregation in the singing of the liturgy and hymns. It is vital that the pastor, the congregation, and the musicians themselves understand this role of the choir and organist.

The placement of the choir and organ behind the congregation is, to a certain extent, symbolic; one might say that music "stands behind and pushes" as the congregation brings its praise to God. The two poles of the building may be thought of as representing the two components of worship: God serving the congregation is symbolized at the front of the church by altar, pulpit, and font, and the people serving God are symbolized at the back of the building by the choir loft and organ case. Just as pastoral vestments symbolize that the person of the pastor is less important than his function, so a position in the balcony is a reminder that the function of the music is more important than the musicians themselves.

However, the placement of musicians in the balcony has much more to do with practicality than with symbolism. If the choir is to assist the congregation in its corporate praise of God, the sound of the choir's voices must be directed toward the worshipers and be above the heads of the worshipers. If the choir is able to gather easily and quickly on the chancel steps, this objective will be able to be met. But it would hardly be possible for the choir to be up and down on the steps every time it was to function, and this will occur if the choir is involved in more than an anthem (particularly when the Lutheran choir participates in the hymns and the liturgy as well).

Some make the case that permanent chancel seating solves this problem. However, another matter needs to be mentioned. Neither church choirs nor church organists memorize the music that they present during a Sunday service. They have music to put away, music to get ready, and pages to turn. Musicians must often begin their preparations while other things are happening in the service (e.g., prayers or recitation of the creed). Instrumentalists occasionally need to make tuning adjustments and clean out their instruments. The members of bell choirs must pull on gloves and make quick moves from one bell to another. When they are arranged in the sight of worshipers, the musicians' completely necessary activities become distractions. Unexpected events during the service cause more problems. They often require a "mad dash" to the music cabinet or a "quick grab" for something left in the wrong place.

There are occasions, of course, when musicians may appear in the front of the congregation without these disadvantages. Recitalists often memorize the music they perform; at the very least they rehearse page turning as faithfully as they practice notes. Our college and high school choirs (and church choirs, too, for special song services) prepare concert programs with the understanding that they will be seen as well as heard. Finally, seeing the enthusiasm of children at a Christmas service can be as edifying as hearing the music itself.

The balcony is usually the place where the organ is located, and committees need to take care in the placement of both electronic and pipe organs. An electronic instrument requires less space than a pipe organ does, although the electronic one does demand thoughtful placement of speakers. A pipe organ needs room in the balcony. The romantic organs of a half century ago hid their pipes in chambers and produced a sound that often was unable to encourage enthusiastic singing. The organs that are built today, usually patterned after the great instruments of Lutheran Germany, are able to support our hymns and liturgical music with far greater capability. This is true for several reasons, one of which is that the pipes of these organs are mounted in a freestanding wooden organ case. These pipes are able to speak without the impedances of walls and grill cloth; the case actually serves as a sounding board to amplify the organ's tone. A smaller organ of this design is able to support singing much better than a larger romantic instrument. In any case, building committees still need to design the balcony with the organ in mind. Congregations are often left with very few options when committees have waited until after the church is completed to think about the placement of the organ.

Should a balcony be impossible or undesirable in a building's design, a raised platform (with at least three levels of seating) located in a back of the church serves as an adequate replacement.

Acoustics in the Worship Space

Lutheran worship accentuates sight and sound, and sound is the more important ingredient. Worship does not involve much more than speaking and singing by pastor, congregation, choir, and organ. It is imperative, therefore, that the building committees give genuine and serious attention to the subject of acoustics in the worship space. A noted acoustical expert has written:

> A desirable acoustical setting is a matter of good design and planning. It means making decisions regarding the nature of a space, its shape, dimensions, materials, furnishings, and construction. A great amount of money does not have to be spent to "purchase" good acoustics. A good acoustical environment is a result of proper planning, of selecting and using the components of a space in proper relationship and proportion. A good acoustical environment must be planned early, with clear goals and sensitivity to its importance always in mind.[16]

---

[16] Scott R. Riedel, *Acoustics in the Worship Space* (St. Louis: Concordia, 1986), p. 8. Much of the technical data in the section on acoustics is drawn from Mr. Riedel's excellent pamphlet.

All participants in public worship ought to be able to speak and sing and be heard. This is true first of the pastor. The words of the sermon and the liturgy must be audible and understandable, and the pastor's voice must be clear and articulate, whether it is naturally or electronically amplified. For the sake of precise speech, planners must take care to control unwanted noise from the street or from the building's air conditioning and heating units.

It is equally important that the voices of the worshipers be heard. It is essential that a church building have live acoustics. Live acoustics give music a certain reverberation period so that the music can move from one worshiper to another. In most cases, a two-second reverberation period suits both singing and speech very well. Dry acoustics, that is, where there is little or no reverberation, often give worshipers the feeling that they are singing alone. Nothing discourages singing in worship more than dry acoustics.

There are other acoustical concerns that demand the assistance of an expert. Money spent to secure the services of an acoustical engineer invariably will bring a rich return. Under no circumstances should a building committee rely exclusively on the acoustical advice of an organ or sound system salesperson. Many reputable companies employ sales personnel who are knowledgeable and trustworthy, but not many of these have expertise in the matter of acoustics. Add the reality that always a few people involved in sales are interested solely in selling.

Committees should consider the following points as they discuss the issue of acoustics:

1. Where can worshipers, speakers, and musicians best be located for optimal hearing and sight?

2. What building materials, components, and furnishings encourage good acoustics? What materials discourage this? For example, acoustical tile, draperies, unpainted concrete block, plywood paneling, and especially carpeting should be assiduously avoided. As the saying goes, "Carpet bedrooms, not churches." Brick, plaster, drywall, terrazzo, and glazed tile are excellent materials for promoting good acoustics.

3. What kind of electronic sound reinforcement is best for this building?

It may be that acoustics, even more than pew position, choir and organ placement, or nave design, encourage the active participation of the worshiping congregation. It is imperative that decisions on these issues be made with theology and not just maintenance in mind.

The Narthex

When the social center of most Lutheran congregations was the neighborhood or the school gymnasium, the need for a carefully designed narthex was not very pressing. Hundreds of churches have been designed with only a tiny and insignificant space for gathering. What was true of Lutheran sociology a century ago is not true today, however, and most church members find their prime opportunities for social interaction before and after worship. Congregations that worship in older churches have gone to great lengths (and occasionally into great debt) to enlarge the gathering space of their buildings. Those who are planning a new building have a decided advantage as they design an area for gathering.

The primary objective of the gathering space is to provide opportunities for members to visit with one another. Some churches have a narthex with small tables surrounded by chairs. Often included is a small kitchen for the preparation of coffee, punch, and light snacks. The narthex might well be carpeted and have a low-ceiling; its casual atmosphere means to say, "Come early and stay later." Rest rooms, cloak rooms, and the church nursery ought to be nearby, if possible. In any case, there ought to be clear directions as to where these facilities are located. Occasionally a gathering space may be located outside and decorated with trees and shrubbery.

Those who oversee the worship of the congregation need some space in the narthex. Controls for the sound system are usually best located in a place where they can be adjusted while the leader is functioning. A place to store chairs for overflow seating, a cabinet for offering plates and medical supplies, and a stand for the guest or communion register all need to be included.

Smaller congregations that lack the facilities of a large educational wing or school building may need to use the narthex for

Bible classes and meetings. Study tables and chairs will have to be available for easy set-up and will also have to be stored. Service folders, bulletins, newsletters, and other printed material for members usually need a place in the narthex. Planning committees need to think about where the Christian book and supply shop and the church library will be located to meet the needs of both members and volunteers.

Also the needs of the handicapped ought to be respected and met as the narthex is designed. City building codes invariably dictate this consideration. Christians ought not limit themselves to the letter of the local building codes but plan in the spirit of Christ as they make provisions to allow all of God's people to worship.

CHAPTER 6:

The Vestments
of the Pastor

Since at least the fifth century after Christ, the men who have been chosen to lead the Christian worship assembly have invariably worn a ceremonial vestment of one sort or another. Although customs have varied somewhat in the several strains of Christianity, the basic vestment of the clergy has remained the same in most liturgical churches throughout 1500 years of history.

With a knowledge of the history and purpose of clerical garb, today's pastor is able to understand that the vestments he wears at worship are not simply a matter of personal preference. When he serves at public worship, the pastor is the representative of the people. In the same way that the members of a congregation have the prerogative to determine which rites and ceremonies will be used in worship, so the pastor and the people work together when decisions are made about pastoral vestments. These decisions are not made, however, without guidance. Just as principles shape our use of the Christian service, so there is also a rationale for pastoral vestments. Consequently, pastors help believers learn how Lutheran pastors are vested and why these customs exist in the Lutheran church, just as they teach their people to understand the way Lutherans worship.

The Types of Vestments
Alb and Surplice

The garment that has become the standard vestment of the Christian clergy is the *alb*. In the Roman world the alb was the regular attire of everyday life. It is the garment Jesus had in mind when he said in the Sermon on the Mount, "And if someone wants to sue you and take your *tunic,* let him have your cloak as well" (Matthew 5:40). The alb was the seamless garment the soldiers cast lots for at the crucifixion site (John 19:23). The albs of today are very similar to those worn in Rome: white, collarless, and with narrow sleeves; they reach to the ankles and usually are made of linen. The alb is often worn with a belt of rope or cloth called a *cincture.*

During the first four centuries after Christ, pastors did not have the custom of wearing special clothes for worship. The church father Jerome (died [d.] A.D. 420) instructed only that the clergy should wear "a special suit of clean clothing"[1] The alb became the customary worship vestment only as public worship became more formal and ceremonial, sometime around the fifth century. The pastors were imitating the royal court when they adopted the conservative attire of a by-gone era as a symbol for their worship-leading responsibilities.[2]

The *surplice* is a stylized version of the alb. The alb was worn over a close-fitting undergarment, the *cassock;* the surplice was designed with billowy sleeves and a wider girth so it could be worn over the bulky cassocks that were necessary in the northern climates of Europe. Like the alb, the surplice is white and reaches to the ankles. The combination of close-fitting cassock and loose-fitting surplice has its roots in nineteenth century Anglicanism and was not part of the wider experience of the Christian tradition.

Cassock and Academic Robe

Neither the alb nor the surplice would have been worn on the street after the fifth century; it had become the unique worship vestment of the Christian church. The garment the medieval pastor would have worn when he came to church was the street attire of his own era, the *cassock.* Just like the cassocks of today those of previous centuries were usually black, had narrow sleeves, fit close to the body, and reached to the wearer's ankles.

---

[1] *The New Westminster Dictionary of Liturgy and Worship,* J. G. Davies, editor (Philadelphia: Westminster Press, 1979), p. 523.

[2] The practice of adopting conservative attire of a by-gone era was not unique to the ancient church. John W. Brenner, president of the Wisconsin Synod (1933-1953) and pastor at the large St. John's Church in Milwaukee (1908-1958), wore his Prince Albert coat for weddings and funerals until he retired. In fact, he was buried in the suit.

Since the clergy were also the teachers at the schools and universities, the cassock was what teachers and professors wore when they taught. One might compare the cassock to our modern sport jacket and slacks, or to a pinstripe suit.

Cassocks did not always fit snugly, however. Because school classrooms in northern Europe were cold in winter, the cassocks designed for those locations soon featured heavy sleeves, collars, and fur lining. Thus the slender cassock and the flowing academic robe (the so-called "Geneva" robe) are part of the same tradition. Both were worn by the clergy to church and in school. It is important to note, however, that throughout most of Christian history, neither the cassock nor the academic robe was used for worship. Only under the influence of the Reformed (who rejected almost all of the church's historic worship legacy) did the "Geneva" or academic robe come to replace the alb as the worship vestment. Lutheran pastors of Reformation Germany would have been as reluctant to conduct the liturgical service in an academic robe as today's pastor is to lead the service dressed only in his suit.

Stole

The stole is a colored scarf worn over the alb. Although its origin is somewhat obscure, it is thought to have been a kerchief worn by Roman politicians and soldiers as a sign of rank.[3] Stoles carry the liturgical colors and are usually prepared to match the paraments as far as fabric and symbolism are concerned. Two types of stoles are common. One design is about two inches wide at the back of the neck and three or four inches wide at the bottom. This version of the stole is usually worn over a surplice or Geneva robe and extends down the sides of the vestment to about the knees. Stoles that are designed specifically for today's albs are wider and longer. Most are about five to six inches wide overall and hang to about the same length as the alb itself. It is proper to wear the stole that matches the style of the vestment.

The stole is traditionally reserved for those who hold the office of the pastoral ministry and is worn primarily at the main Sunday communion service.

---

[3] *New Westminster Dictionary*, p. 525.

Chasuble

As the alb traces its history to the indoor tunic of ancient Rome, the *chasuble* has its roots in the outdoor cloak. Paul had this garment in mind when he asked Timothy to bring his cloak to Rome (2 Timothy 4:13).

The chasuble is usually thought to be the principle vestment for the main Christian service. It is a poncho-shaped garment that slips over the head and hangs from the shoulders to about the knees. The chasuble has no actual sleeves; the sides of the garment are not as long as its front and the back, since the wearer must have his arms free to carry out his duties at the service. The color of the chasuble usually matches the liturgical color of the season. Often decorative *orphreys* (strips of specially embroidered cloth) are attached to form a Y or Latin cross in the front and back of the vestment. Where congregations take special pride and care of pastoral vestments, the chasuble is invariably made of the finest and most expensive fabrics.

While many Lutheran congregations have reclaimed the use of the alb and stole and have grown to appreciate them as the historic vestments of Christian worship, the chasuble has not become as common.

The Purpose of Pastoral Vestments

There are principally three reasons why Lutheran congregations have come to expect their pastors to be vested for worship. The first reason concerns the pastor's call into the ministry. The second has to do with his function in the congregation's worship. The third involves the historic practice of the church.

A Symbol of the Pastoral Office

God has graciously allowed the Lutheran church to maintain a beneficial distinction and careful balance between the pastoral office and the universal priesthood. Lutherans believe that the Keys have been given by Christ to all believers, and that Christians may exercise their right to use the Keys in their dealings with their fellow human beings. Lutherans believe that a body of Christians may designate one or more individuals from among their assembly to function in a representative ministry, that is, to use the Keys on behalf of a group of believers gathered in one specific place. Lutherans believe that Christ himself commands the church to call such ministers, and that some of the representative ministers may be given the office of the *overseer or pastor.*

Peter spoke to these overseers about their ministry when he wrote: "Be shepherds of God's flock that is *under your care,* serving as overseers . . . not lording it over those *entrusted to you* . . ." (1 Peter 5:2,3). That these men are called by God himself as well as by the Christian congregation is clear from the prayer the Christians spoke as they called Matthias to replace Judas. "'Lord, you know everyone's heart. Show us which of these two you have chosen'" (Acts 1:24).

The Scripture calls upon Christians to give love and respect to these leaders. "Obey your leaders and submit to their authority. They keep watch over you as men who must give an account. Obey them so that their work will be a joy, not a burden, for that would be of no advantage to you" (Hebrews 13:17). "The elders who direct the affairs of the church well are worthy of double honor, especially those whose work is preaching and teaching" (1 Timothy 5:17).

The pastor's vestments identify him as the called spiritual leader of the congregation. To contend that the custom of a vested clergy places the pastor on a different level than his people is to overlook the importance God has attached to the pastoral office. Although all people, pastor and members alike, are equally guilty before God and are equal receivers of his grace, God also commands the church to designate some men as leaders in the church. Although pastoral authority is derived only from the church and not from some intrinsic quality in the pastor, the Scripture also teaches that the church is to hold its leaders in love and offer them even double honor. Though perhaps only in a small way, worship vestments do help today's church speak a clear message about the value of the pastoral office.

Congregations need not hesitate to ask lay assistants, lectors, and vicars to wear vestments of some sort. However, it seems wise that the vestment of a nonpastoral assistant be different in some way from that of the pastor. It would be usual, for instance, that a lay assistant or vicar might wear an alb but not a stole or chasuble.

The Function of the Leader

Not only does the vestment serve as a symbol of the pastoral office, but it also helps the believers (and the pastor, for that matter) understand the pastor's function as he leads the worship of the congregation. As the designated leader of worship, he serves as God's representative. The pastor proclaims the gospel "as a called servant of Christ and by his authority"; he does not speak on his own behalf. The vestment places onto the pastor's appearance the truth, "It is not I who speak, but God who speaks." The vestment hides the man and accentuates the ministry. A noted liturgical observer has written that vestments are really a discipline for the pastor to control his ego. "Vestments . . . dress us down, not up."[4]

Occasionally someone maintains (sometimes quite emphatically) that the traditional vestments of the clergy encourage ostentation. In some minds a vested pastor is nothing more than a "beribboned dandy." These voices forget that the pastor serves as the representative of the people when he approaches the throne of God at worship. At public worship there is a purposeful formality and a deliberate dignity as the people of God come into the presence of God. Their awe at such an encounter becomes obvious in their words and actions and is symbolized by, among others things, the vestments of their leader. C. S. Lewis offers a reminder that the pastor is actually serving the congregation as he wears the liturgical vestments, since he represents the dignity and propriety Christians ought to feel as they come before God. Speaking to pastors, he wrote:

> Above all, you must be rid of the hideous idea, fruit of a widespread inferiority complex, that pomp on the proper occasions has any connection with vanity or self-conceit. A celebrant approaching the altar, the princess led out by a king to dance a minuet, a general officer on ceremonial parade . . . all these wear unusual clothes and

---

[4] Paul Westermeyer, "Tradition, Liturgy, and the Visitor," *Word and World,* Vol. 13, No. 1, Winter 1993.

move with calculated dignity. This does not mean they are vain, but that they are obedient; they are obeying the *hoc age* which presides over every solemnity.[5]

The man who leads the public worship of God's people with a laissez-faire casualness does not serve God's people well, for he confuses them about the seriousness of both God's service to them and their service to God. His folksy leadership may do more to distract worshipers from the real purpose of worship than the ceremonial vestments he shuns because of their supposed ostentation.

Vestments serve their purpose when they remind the congregation that its pastor serves as God's representative. In addition, the vestments of the pastor, as well as the paraments that hang from the altar, pulpit, and lectern, help to establish for believers the mood of the various seasons of the church year. Science has long recognized that colors carry different moods and feelings. Christians notice the different colors of paraments and vestments, and they should be taught to understand their meaning. Explanations of the colors are appended here.

The Liturgical Colors

White   Color of the godhead and eternity; color of the robe of the glorified Christ and of the angels and saints in heaven; color of perfection, joy, purity.

Black   The absence of color; symbolic of death.

Red   Color of fire, fervor, blood, martyrdom, victorious truth of Christian teaching based on the blood of Christ.

Green   The color of life and nourishment; the basic color of nature.

Purple   The color of royal mourning and repentance.

Blue   The color of the sky and of hope.

Gold   The color of royalty, riches, and victory.[6]

---

[5] C. S. Lewis, *A Preface to Paradise Lost*, p. 17. *Hoc age* might be roughly translated "proper procedure."

[6] Some of the explanatory material offered here is taken from Paul H. D. Lang's *What An Altar Guild Should Know*, p.106.

The proper liturgical colors for the various festivals and seasons are included with The Christian Church Year in *Christian Worship*'s pew edition, page 157.

The Practice of the Church

As compelling a defense as any of the historic vestments of worship is the traditional use of vestments in the Christian church. The Lutheran understanding of the traditions of the church has been sufficiently expounded elsewhere in this volume, and there is no need to review it again with any degree of thoroughness. Let it be said, however, that orthodox Lutherans have agreed that the historic witness of the church holds value in every subsequent age unless that voice denies or compromises the clear teachings of Scripture. In the same way that Christians preserve the liturgy in part because of its ancient roots, so believers value the vestments of worship because the tradition of vestments is part of the legacy of the church.

This was certainly the opinion held by Luther and the authors of the Lutheran Confessions. In his Latin service of 1523, Luther wrote, "We think about these [vestments] as we do about other forms. We permit them to be used in freedom."[7]

Johannes Bugenhagen, pastor at the town church in Wittenberg and Luther's own pastor, wrote about those who wanted to eliminate the traditional vestments:

> There is a two-fold doctrine on chasubles . . . one is the truth, namely, that chasubles can be used; this does not give scandal to those who are accustomed to hearing the Gospel. The other is a Satanic lie out of the doctrine of devils, namely, that it is never lawful to use chasubles; this gives scandal to the people where they hear and believe such lies from ministers.[8]

The Apology of the Augsburg Confession maintains that the Lutheran Church gladly retained the historic liturgy and then continues, "And the usual public ceremonies are observed, the series of lessons, of prayers, vestments, and other like things."[9]

---

[7] Luther's Works, American, Vol 53, p. 31.

[8] Arthur C. Piepkorn, *The Survival of the Historic Vestments in the Lutheran Church after 1555* (St. Louis: Concordia Seminary, 1972), p. 368.

[9] Apology, Art. 24:1.

The careful studies of Guenther Stiller[10] and Dr. Arthur Carl Piepkorn help us to know that the traditional vestments—alb, chasuble, and stole—were used in German Lutheran congregations well into the eighteenth century. In fact, Piepkorn maintains that

> the alb, the cincture, the surplice, and the chasuble have never passed wholly out of use in the Church of the Augsburg Confession. . . . Numbered among their [vestments] doughtiest defenders [are] some of the most impeccably orthodox doctors of the Church of the Augsburg Confession.[11]

It becomes clear, as honest history is perused, that those Lutherans who most carefully maintained the worship principles of Martin Luther thought about vestments as they did about the liturgy. Both were the legacy of the church and, while in and of themselves they were *adiaphora,* they were to be used and maintained as long as they did not obscure the doctrine of justification.

Those who rejected the historic worship vestments, first in Germany and later in America, were aligned more often with the Calvinists, Pietists, and Rationalists than they were with the orthodox Lutherans. As we have seen, Calvinism rejected almost all of the traditions connected to the Roman Church. The Pietists were determined to deemphasize the distinction between laity and clergy. The Rationalists were decidedly anti-authoritarian. For many reasons those who walked within this strain of Protestantism rejected all vestments. Their clergy dressed in the black academic robe not because it was a worship vestment, but because it was not a worship vestment. Like many Protestants today, they wore the everyday professional garb of the medieval scholar and the modern magistrate, the Geneva gown.

While it is incorrect to speak of the academic robe as "the Luther tradition," many Lutherans in Germany and America have come to understand the black robe as being a part of their own history, at least over the span of the last several hundred years. Therefore, the Geneva robe can be said to have taken on a legiti-

---

[10] Stiller's excellent book, *Johann Sebastian Bach and the Liturgical Life in Leipzig* (St. Louis: Concordia, 1984), has pertinent information on pp. 107,108.

[11] Piepkorn, *Historic Vestments,* pp. 119,120.

mate worship tradition of its own among Protestants and some Lutherans. This is more than can be said of many of the so-called "pulpit robes" offered for sale in church supply catalogues.

In Conclusion

In all aspects of the church's life of worship, artistic propriety and legitimate tradition must take second place to the proclamation of the gospel and the gospel's glorious freedom. In the final analysis the Lord Jesus will not be so concerned about either the type of vestments or the kind of liturgy Christians use. He is concerned only that we worship the Father "in spirit and truth" (John 4:23).

None of this disallows our right and our responsibility to employ all of God's many gifts as we proclaim his gospel and as we praise his grace. The Lutheran pastor Wilhelm Loehe said:

> The Church remains what she is even without a Liturgy, she remains a queen even in beggars' rags. It is better to give up everything else and to hold only the pure doctrine than to go about in the pomp and glory of splendid services which are without light and life because the doctrine has become impure. Yet it is not necessary to let the Church go in beggars' rags. Much better it is that her prayers, her hymns, her sacred order, the holy thoughts of her Liturgy, should be impressed upon the people.[12]

Such can surely also be said of the vestments with which the church adorns her worship leaders.

---

[12] Wilhelm Loehe, *Three Books Concerning the Church,* translated by Edward T. Horn (Reading, PA: Pilger, 1908), pp. 198,199.

CHAPTER 7:

Worship for Evangelism and Outreach

There was a time in the history of the Lutheran church when advice about planning for evangelism would not have been included in a book about worship. Christianity did not consider the public worship of God's people to be the place for the initiation of the unchurched. From earliest times, witnessing for Christ, as well as instruction in basic Christian teaching and living, was carried out apart from worship. Werner Elert wrote:

> Admission [to the worship assembly] was not for everyone. . . . The gathering for worship in the early church was not a public but a closed assembly, while the celebration of the Eucharist was reserved for the saints with the utmost strictness.[1]

It ought to be noted that this point of view was held by Christians during the most highly evangelistic era in the history of the church.

Evangelism and Worship in Contemporary Protestantism

What changed the relationship between evangelism and worship was American Revivalism (cf. Section One, chapter 3, pp. 33-36). Initially, Revivalism was a zealous attempt to reclaim pioneer Protestants who became detached from organized religion during the national expansion of the nineteenth century. Efforts by Revivalists like Charles Finney were so successful, however, that the mainline churches eventually invited the Revivalists to reclaim the spiritual deadwood of their congregations, too. Success after success (along with a variety of other factors) helped to

---

[1] Werner Elert, *Eucharist and Church Fellowship in the First Four Centuries* (St. Louis: Concordia, 1966), pp. 75,76.

solidify revivalistic worship principles and practices on the American scene. Many of the churches that are a part of the neo-Evangelical movement as well as those that subscribe to the tenets of the Church Growth Movement consider worship to be the preeminent assembly for evangelization and growth.

The obvious successes of American Revivalism have not gone unnoticed by Lutherans. With a deep interest in reaching the lost, many of America's Lutherans have wondered if the worship style of the Evangelical churches might have some application among Lutherans. A fair share of Lutheran congregations have adopted Finney's pragmatic approach to Sunday morning worship: if the liturgical service helps convince the unchurched to come to church again, retain it; if visitors are put off by the liturgy, change it. With a determination to gain the "seeker" and with hopes of growth, many Lutherans in the United States have discarded the liturgical order, their core of orthodox hymns, vestments, organs, and even a regular celebration of Holy Communion. They have replaced liturgical style with a non-threatening Bible class format, hymnody with contemporary Christian anthems, the organ with a piano or pop ensemble, and vestments with a business suit. Some have moved the celebration of the Sacrament to a weeknight for those who are members of the congregation. Sermons are conversational, usually topical, and rarely based on one of the lessons from the lectionary. Some congregations have retained the liturgical rite for one of the morning services and scheduled a "seeker service" at another Sunday morning hour.

The presupposition many Lutherans hold is that visitors tend to be put off by the way Lutherans "package" their message of law and gospel. They rightly insist that if the package interferes with the gospel, it ought to be discarded. However, what may actually be keeping most visitors away from conservative Lutheran churches is the message of law and gospel itself. Guilt and grace, the essential ingredients of biblical theology, are not a part of natural religion, nor, for that matter, is sin or the bondage of the human will. What may actually appeal to the unchurched in contemporary Protestant worship is not only the style of the worship, but its substance as well. Most American church shoppers are looking for a religion that makes them feel good about themselves: they want to be comfortable with their own persona, they want to feel warm toward their neighbors and happy with their lot in life, they want to achieve personal successes and accomplishments, they want to make their own choices. They do not want to face up to personal guilt, the necessity of a vicarious and bloody substitution, or the total dependency of faith on the means of grace.

A Lutheran analyst described the situation among contemporary Americans like this:

> Truth is measured by what is frequently called "expressive individualism." The ability to express myself, to be in touch with my feelings, to find my own voice, in sum—To Be Me—this is what matters, this is substance.[2]

Lutherans who try to copy the style of the fast-growing megachurches in order to attract these seekers may find themselves in a predicament. As Lutherans they believe that sin damns all people and that only Christ can cover guilt and offer forgiveness. They confess that faith alone receives the benefits of Jesus' life and death. They acknowledge that only the Holy Spirit can convert the human heart and that he does so only through the means of grace. They proclaim the law and the gospel, and they baptize so that the Spirit might work faith and bring souls into the family of God. But if these Lutherans want to provide what the seekers are really seeking, they will have to change much more than their style; they will have to change their substance, too, which, they believe, is what alone can convert the lost.

Those Lutherans who are not willing to sell their inheritance and who want to retain the substance of God's plan of salvation, but are tempted to change their liturgical style of worship, are wise to rethink the value of the gospel-proclaiming content of the Lutheran liturgy. It may be true that American humanists feel neither the guilt of sin nor the need of spiritual healing and that many of these will not be attracted to Lutheran worship. But additional thousands of souls in our land do feel such guilt. The only thing that can offer them help and salvation is the

---

[2] Richard Neuhaus, "The Lutheran Difference," *Lutheran Forum,* Reformation, 1990.

gospel, which is, as we have observed, the preeminent focus of the liturgy.

Pastors and evangelism committees also ought to understand that growth and liturgical worship are not incompatible. In the present scientific and materialistic age, as many Americans may be looking for something beyond the earthly, something transcendent, as are looking for warmth and self-fulfillment. Lutheran worship may not hold much for the humanists, but it may well attract those who are seeking a worship that expresses a mixture of awe, wonder, and joy at the close encounter with the living God. With their liturgical worship, Lutherans are especially equipped to address this perceived need for transcendence as they communicate a fresh and clear understanding of the depth and beauty of their worship tradition.[3] Those who have taken more than a superficial look at the contemporary American scene will likely be compelled to agree with a noted congregational consultant who insisted that liturgical churches can attract people and can grow. He also added, however, that liturgical churches must do their liturgical worship extremely well.[4]

The Witness of Liturgical Worship

Lutherans should not need a consultant to tell them that. It stands to reason that God and their neighbor should receive the best that Lutherans have at worship. For one reason or another, however, too many Lutheran congregations have taken their inherited liturgical style and treated it like some embarrassing old antique: they don't like it, they don't know what to do with it, but they're stuck with it. It is not inability that compromises the liturgy, but poor preparation and poor performance. More than one observer has noticed this problem:

> Lutherans have generally not done a great job utilizing the resources for worship their liturgical forms provide. It is a sad truth that much

---

[3] Dr. John Brug expanded on this idea in an article entitled "Perceived Needs" in the *Wisconsin Lutheran Quarterly,* Vol. 85, No. 4, pp. 303,304.

[4] The consultant was Lyle Schaller whose comments were quoted in an essay by Larry Peters, "Lutheran Worship and Church Growth" prepared for and distributed by the Commission on Worship of the Lutheran Church—Missouri Synod.

Lutheran worship is dull, boring, and seemingly irrelevant. This is an abuse of the liturgical form and not a proper use of it.[5]

Years ago Martin Marty complained, "More junk, more tawdriness, more slip-shodhood, more mediocrity is peddled in church circles than in many others. Yet are we not supposed to give God our best gifts?"[6] When someone insists that visitors are "turned off" by liturgical worship, pastors and evangelism committees must first ask if it is the liturgy or the way the liturgy is done that offends. If the charge that some have failed to put their best efforts into worship has any validity, we have come to a serious matter. If Christians give less than their best in worship, they offend God, for they take advantage of his gracious offer to receive their praise. But even more they offend visitors, because they give them the impression that it is permissible to take advantage of God's grace. Pastors need to lead the way as congregations strive to place into the service of the King of kings that which is an offering worthy of his attention.

In truth, worship that is shabbily prepared and presented is as much of an offense to the churched as it is to the unchurched.[7] On the other hand, many pastors and evangelism committees have come to agree that the public worship of God that attracts and spiritually benefits members will also attract and spiritually benefit non-members.

In his *Parish Renewal: Theses and Implications,* Pastor Paul Kelm enunciated the objectives the Lutheran church ought to keep in mind as its leaders plan and prepare worship that benefits both the churched and the unchurched:

> Worship must be what the church does best, for in our worship we minister to the greatest number of our members and introduce visitors to our Lord. Our worship is still the most apparent statement of the "worth" we ascribe to our God. The challenge for Lutherans today is to combine the best of our tradition with contemporary communica-

---

[5] Larry Peters, "Lutheran Worship and Church Growth," p. 11.

[6] Martin Marty, in *Context,* July 1, 1975, p. 3.

[7] It is interesting to note that, in the experience of a number of conservative Lutheran congregations, the members of the congregation are attracted to the "seeker service" more often than visitors. This supports the contention that members may also be put off by worship that is badly prepared and led.

tion, to be both faithful to Scripture and relevant to contemporary life, to touch head and heart with the message of sin and grace in an age of anti-Christian philosophy, to lift refugees from a jaded generation in praise to their God.

Lutherans must strive for the best preaching possible. That is the product of quality time spent in text study and sermon preparation. Preachers need continuing education in homiletics. Those whose dominant gifts lie in other areas of ministry can benefit from published sermon studies. We need to be both open to the Lord as we study his Word and open to improvement in our crafting and delivery of the message.

Lutheran worship should have clear liturgical progression and a "freshness" each week that is combined with familiarity. That requires easy-to-follow orders of worship, a "personal" tone by the officiant and his conviction that corporate worship is much more than sandwiching a sermon.

Lutherans will want to offer the best instrumental and choral music possible. That will mean training opportunities for church musicians and the availability of music appropriate to a variety of abilities, occasions and preferences. That may mean more than one choir where possible, with varied musical styles. That may mean more than one musical instrument.

Lutheran worship should combine warmth and reverence, avoiding the extremes of cold ritual and trivial fads. That means attention to detail so that slip-ups don't distract our focus. That means also a style of leading worship that reflects God's love for people.

The Lord's Supper should have deep significance and a clear focus on God's grace. Churches may need to find better ways to prepare communicants for the sacrament than the sign-up sheets that have replaced the confessional service and personal "communion announcements" of an earlier generation.[8]

Assisting Guests at Worship

Pastors and congregations surely ought to consider the needs of visitors. While the format of *Christian Worship* makes follow-

---

[8] Paul Kelm, *Parish Renewal: Theses and Implications,* a document available through the Wisconsin Synod's Commission on Adult Education.

ing the order of service fairly easy for member and visitor alike, some congregations may want to reprint the entire service in a service bulletin. This becomes an expensive project (and runs into some copyright problems) but may be helpful in certain situations. At the very least, pastors will speak a word of welcome before the opening hymn and advise the worshipers of the place and progression of the service.

Members of the congregation want to remember that the visitors are watching the members as closely as they are the pastor. The Apostle Paul's encouragement to be "living epistles" has application in worship; members will want to participate with eagerness and enthusiasm. Visitors surely will wonder what benefit Christianity can have for them if those who already espouse the faith respond to Christ meagerly and apathetically.

Common sense dictates that certain other concerns be kept in mind. Visitors may not notice neat landscaping, a clean church, or an easy-to-read announcement board, but they will notice a lack of these. Congregations might consider designating a set of parking spaces near the main entrance of the church not only for the handicapped but also for visitors. Directional signs are helpful, especially those that indicate rest rooms and the church nursery. The service bulletin ought to be neatly typed and kept clean of in-house jargon or negative barbs. Ushers and greeters ought to be ready to offer a low-key but warm welcome and to answer questions and concerns that visitors might have. Many congregations have found that a staffed nursery is much appreciated by members and non-members alike.

While it is altogether possible to attract visitors through the public worship, it may be wise that the congregation not place its entire evangelism emphasis on worship. Evangelism committees will be sure that all visitors receive some sort of response within a day or two after the Sunday service. And for some seekers, side-door entry to the message of the gospel may actually be better than the front-door entry of worship. Side-door approaches to evangelism are those that are not worship but which may attract the interest of the people in the community. Side-door approaches may be molded with both actual spiritual needs or perceived needs in mind. Bible studies that focus on family problems and personal issues may attract the congregation's neighbors. Some feel that day care may be the preeminent side-door approach of this generation. A commitment to find a variety of ways to reach the unchurched demands extra work, a degree of creativity, and even, perhaps, a willingness to challenge a few preconceived notions.

Finally, it remains true that the best evangelism opportunities exist when individual believers, trained and encouraged to "always be prepared to give an answer to everyone who asks you to give the reason for the hope that you have" (1 Peter 3:15), witness for Jesus among their own relatives, friends, and neighbors.

The Gospel in Lutheran Worship

Despite everything they know about the slow working of the Word, the Spirit's own timetable, and God's planting and watering promises, Lutherans want their churches to grow. Ours is a growth-oriented society, and, sometimes, even the church gives the impression that success is gauged by numbers. Church members are only being consistent with their culture when they fret about growth.

"It is required that those who have been given a trust must prove faithful" (1 Corinthians 4:2). God calls pastors and lay leaders to faithfully proclaim Christ through the means of grace. God calls them to faithfully bring him their worship and to lead others to do the same. Faithfulness is faithfulness, whether God grants visible success or whether he does not. God has not asked us to grow the Church. This task he has assumed for himself. He has asked us to be faithful and promised that, in his own way, he will be fruitful.

Lutherans can be faithful in both their proclamation and their praise through the style of worship called liturgical worship, a worship style that retains the core of the historic Christian liturgy, employs the church year, and emphasizes the Sacrament. In fact, the final accounting of the history of the Church may show that the liturgy, carefully prepared and pastorally led, has contributed as much to the growth of disciples inside and outside the church as anything the church has ever done. This is true because the liturgy showcases that which the Holy Spirit uses to make disciples: Word and Sacrament. Harold Senkbeil defends the Lutheran liturgical style like this:

> The Lutheran church has a rich legacy to offer in its worship. Here is reality, not symbolism. Here we have real contact with God; not as we come to him, but as he comes to us. He meets us in the proclamation of the Word. Here the Son of God distributes his actual body and blood for the forgiveness of sins. Here the people of God gather to offer him their thanks, their praise and their prayers. This is the real thing.
>
> It's time for a new initiative in worship. People are longing for God. Where are they going to find him? In the shifting sands of their inner life or on the solid rock of his gospel? How are they to offer him their thanks and praise? With trivial methods borrowed from the entertainment industry or in worship forms which focus on the praise of God's gracious glory? This is the kind of worship which lifts the heart while it exults Christ. And this is what Lutheran worship does.[9]

---

[9] Harold Senkbeil, *Sanctification* (Milwaukee: Northwestern Publishing House, 1988), p. 182.

113

CHAPTER 8:

Planning for Worship

This chapter is about planning for worship. Not many people find planning to be an appealing prospect. A pastor, choir director, or organist who plans ahead must spend time sitting at a desk, a piano, or an organ (perhaps on a beautiful day), pouring over books and music. Usually the services being planned are weeks or months in the future.

While planning is going on, there are no people in the pews and no music in the air. Planning has none of the excitement of performing. In many cases the people who receive the most benefit from worship planning are not even aware that it has occurred. Church members are often surprised when they hear how many hours the pastor spends preparing his sermon or how much time the organist spends rehearsing. Even some of the direct beneficiaries of planning do not care that it takes place. Some organists will continue to practice the hymns on Sunday morning even though the hymns were chosen weeks before. Finally, some in our churches wish that worship would be much less planned than it is and that their Sunday morning experience could include much more that is spontaneous.

Spontaneity in Worship

It cannot be denied that there is something wonderfully appealing about spontaneity in public worship. It isn't likely that Mary had rehearsed the *Magnificat* before her visit to Elizabeth. Peter's prayer on the day Matthias was selected to succeed Judas was most likely an *ex corde* prayer, and his sermon on Pentecost was certainly "off the cuff." Hymns and prayers that flow unplanned and unprogrammed from the mouths of believers carry a certain genuineness and vibrancy.

Lutheran worship has room for spontaneity. The worshiper sings the closing hymn with the kind of fervor he had not thought to be "in him" when he walked into church. The pastor comes up with a "zinger" of a sermon conclusion that just "popped into his head" while he was preaching part three. The organist is surprised to hear the congregation singing with unusual enthusiasm and all of a sudden decides to add the trumpet stop on the last stanza of the hymn.

Countless worshipers can recall how spontaneous and unplanned events offered a special, unexpected thrill. More than a few members of a large Michigan congregation will never forget an Easter sunrise service that began on a dark and overcast March morning. All at once, just as the day's preacher was emphatically pointing to the empty tomb pictured in the church's large resurrection window, the sun broke through the clouds. Streams of sunshine burst through the window and flooded the nave with light. Some worshipers gasped out loud, and there were smiles on almost every face.

Unfortunately, spontaneity in worship cannot be planned. Nor can a desire for spontaneity become an excuse for a failure to plan. The chapters in this volume have carefully reviewed the objectives and values of Lutheran liturgical worship. By its very nature Lutheran worship intends to include a planned review of God's gifts and a planned response of God's people. Both the review and the response require evangelical emphases and confessional accuracy. Both need to edify and serve the people who have gathered for worship, and these are people who come from various backgrounds and situations. Lutheran worship desires to call upon voices from the church's past and present as witnesses to the gospel and wants to put into God's service the best of music and artistry. All of these goals necessitate planning. When the leaders of the church come to understand the presuppositions of Lutheran liturgical worship and the implications they hold, they begin to realize how important it is to plan for worship.

It needs to be added that there is no scriptural basis for the idea that spontaneity in worship is somehow more genuine and vital than proclamation and response that is planned and rehearsed. Nor ought anyone to suppose that planning necessarily stifles spontaneity or that it inevitably leads to response that is counterfeit and insincere. Church history places opinions of this kind un-

115

der the label of enthusiasm, and orthodox Lutheran teachers have repeatedly pointed out the fallacy of this viewpoint. Spontaneity is a fruit of faith that the Holy Spirit effects through the means of grace, and like the sudden appearing of the sun, it is neither to be expected in every Christian nor can it be programmed. Although he was speaking more generally of sanctified living, a wise seminary professor wrote years ago:

> . . . we have been speaking about the unexpected, an acting without being asked, a soaring above expected heights. In an age which makes much ado about planning and programming and organization and systematizing we are apt to ask "Isn't there something that we can do to produce more spontaneous sanctification?" The answer is No. Our interference would only stifle spontaneity. We must plant and water. We must pasture Christ's sheep. Beyond that we can only watch and wait.[1]

Planning and Faithfulness in Ministry

Spontaneity cannot be planned, but the use of the means of grace (which build faith and which may, in fact, effect spontaneity) can and must be planned. Any successful farmer will agree that, while the amount of the harvest cannot be mathematically anticipated, the planting, watering, and pasturing need to be planned with care, wisdom, and precision. What is true about the farmer's efforts with the soil is just as true when it comes to worship leaders' efforts with Christian souls in public worship.

The Scriptures do not place planning for proclamation and the fruits of proclamation into a cause and effect relationship. Jesus told the parable of the farmer who "scatters seed on the ground. Night and day, whether he sleeps or gets up, the seed sprouts and grows, though he does not know how. All by itself the soil produces grain—first the stalk, then the head, then the full kernel in the head" (Mark 4:26-28). Worship leaders ought not suppose that by their superior planning and programming, God is going to accomplish greater things in worship than he would have without their planning.

---

[1] Irwin J. Habeck, "Spontaneous Sanctification," *Wisconsin Lutheran Quarterly*, Vol. 76, No. 4 (October 1979), pp. 318,319.

Planning for worship does indicate, however, the value that a congregation's leaders place on public worship. Careful and thoughtful preparation of the lessons and the sermon, of the anthem and the choir's proper songs, of the prelude and postlude, yes, even of the service folder and the communion vessels, usually indicate that the worship participants are taking seriously the role they have been assigned in worship. On the other hand, a consistent pattern of last-hour rehearsing surely betrays an attitude that does not view public worship as having great value and may even give evidence of unfaithful management of God's blessings. Paul's reminder to the Christians in Corinth carries weight for those involved in all of the church's ministries, "Now it is required that those who have been given a trust must prove faithful" (1 Corinthians 4:2).

There are times, of course, when impossible schedules or emergencies make last-minute preparations an unfortunate necessity, and these situations need not be considered a part of laziness or apathy. The exception justifies no rules, however. The fact that public worship can take place even without adequate preparation should not discourage dedicated Christian men and women from putting their best efforts into planning and preparation. We paraphrase advice the preeminent church musician Eric Routley gave his students:

> It is your duty, your contribution to the service, to interpret as well as to play. Do nothing mechanically, by habit, or lightly, or casually. Do all by decision. Do all after thought or prayer. And may the beauty of the Lord our God be upon us, and may he prosper our handiwork.

People Involved in Planning

It is important that all those who have responsibilities in the public worship of the congregation have a part in the planning process. Obviously, the work begins with the pastor who, as overseer of the parish's ministry, initiates the planning. The adult choir director and the primary organist are indispensable participants. The directors of other choirs (youth choir, children's choir, Sunday school children, parish school classrooms, etc.) as well as the assistant organists need to be included someplace in the strategy. Not as obvious but almost as important are the chairperson

117

of the Altar Guild, the head usher, the custodian, and especially the church secretary or whoever prepares the service folder. The congregation's worshipers count on all of these people to carry out their responsibilities so that public worship may take place without distraction and with the highest quality. All of these will serve with eagerness, enthusiasm, and the best of their abilities if they know in advance what is expected of them on any given Sunday or during any given season.

The Worship Committee

Many congregations have found that a worship committee can be of great assistance to those who share leadership responsibilities. In some cases the committee is made up simply of those who share the worship duties: the pastor, organist, choir director, etc. In other situations the leaders are ex officio members of the committee; lay people are appointed or elected to serve as the committee members. Some congregations have found it advantageous to have the chairman of the committee be a member of the church council or the board of elders.

The worship committee does not serve the congregation best if it has the responsibility to actually plan the services. In almost all cases, the pastor and the church musicians have the knowledge, doctrinal expertise, and artistic sensitivities to do this work capably. However, the committee can serve as a sounding board for the ideas and plans of leadership. Its members can provide loving, non-threatening critique of worship efforts. When they have been trained to understand the liturgical presuppositions of Lutheran worship, they can serve to support the pastor and the musicians among the members of the congregation. When major decisions need to be made concerning worship, the worship committee can bring formal recommendations to the voters assembly or church council, with a rationale that has been carefully prepared and discussed.

Congregations that are considering the formation of a worship committee may find assistance by studying the goals and objectives of such a committee in a medium-sized Lutheran congregation:

> The purpose of the Worship Committee at Grace Lutheran Church is
> to assist the worship leaders (pastor, organist, choir director, etc.) in

carrying out the congregation's objective, "We want to praise God and enrich our souls with the gospel in Word and Sacrament." To accomplish this purpose the Worship Committee has the followings goals:

1. To study the principles of Christian and Lutheran worship as they are established by the Scriptures and the Lutheran Confessions and applied in the history of the Church.

2. To provide the worship leaders with response and reaction concerning the planning and leadership of worship services.

3. To assist the congregation's worship leaders in promoting the congregation's various worship opportunities.

4. To support the worship leaders as they strive to maintain appropriate forms and styles of worship.

5. To assist the worship leaders as they introduce new forms into the congregation's worship life.

6. To encourage and promote the use of rehearsing groups which will serve the congregation's worship (e.g., the choir, vocal ensembles, soloists, instrumentalists, etc.) and to assist the music leaders in the discovery of such talent within the congregation.

7. To help assure that the congregation's worship activities are carried out in a "fitting and orderly way."

8. To monitor and support an Usher Corps, an Altar Guild (care of communion ware, candles, paraments, banners), Flower Committee, and Greeters.

9. To work with the Board of Trustees (Property Committee) to ensure the proper maintenance and care of the worship instruments and to promote a good acoustical space for worship.[2]

Planning guides

Before any planning can be done, those involved in worship leadership will want to adopt a *Service Planning Guide* of one

---

[2] This model was adopted by the Church Council of Grace Lutheran Church, Milwaukee, Wisconsin, and edited by the author, a member of Grace, who served as the committee's first chairman.

sort or another. The guide is simply an outline that allows planners to fill in specific parts of the service, e.g., lessons, hymns, prayers, etc. A sample planning guide is shown on the following page and may be reproduced. An additional guide for organists and choir directors is found on page 122. A detailed analysis of each of the parts of the service is found in Section Two. The Propers for the Sundays and festivals of the church year are listed in Section Four. Additional helps for service planning may be found in Section Three, chapter 17, "Selecting Hymns for Worship," pages 279-287 and in *Planning Christian Worship*.

The planning guides suggested in this manual are quite detailed and may be too involved for some congregations. Worship leaders are encouraged to adapt these suggestions for practical use in their congregations.

Service Planning Guide

Date _____ Sunday or Festival _____

First Lesson and Emphasis _____

Second Lesson and Emphasis _____

Gospel of the Day and Emphasis _____

Sermon Text _____

Focus of the service _____

Prayer of the Day _____

Psalm of the Day _____

Congregational participation _____

Verse of the Day _____

Congregational participation _____

Song of Praise _____

Choir Anthem _____

Hymn of the Day _____

Opening Hymn _____

Sermon Hymn
   (or Distribution Hymn) _____

Closing Hymn _____

Festival Treatment of a Hymn _____

	8:00 a.m.	10:30 a.m.
Order of Service	_____	_____
	_____	_____
Choir	_____	_____
Organist	_____	_____
Communion assistants	_____	_____
	_____	_____
Ushers	_____	_____
	_____	_____
Greeters	_____	_____
Special Additions	_____	_____
	_____	_____
Liturgical Color	_____	

Planning Guide for Musicians

Date _____ Sunday or Festival _____

Psalm of the Day   _____

   Manner of performance   _____

Verse of the Day   _____

   Manner of performance   _____

Choir Anthem   _____

Hymn of the Day   _____

Opening Hymn   _____

   Intonation (Prelude)   _____

   Variations   _____

   Festival setting   _____

Sermon Hymn
   (or Distribution Hymn)   _____

   Intonation (Prelude)   _____

   Variations   _____

   Festival setting   _____

Closing Hymn   _____

   Intonation (Prelude)   _____

   Variations   _____

   Festival setting   _____

Preservice music   _____

                                              _____

                                              _____

Music during the Offering   _____

                                              _____

                                              _____

Postservice music   _____

                                              _____

                                              _____

The Pastor

The actual work of planning the service begins with the pastor. As the one called by the congregation to be the leader of public worship, he has received the training that enables him to initiate the planning process. There is, of course, work that comes with planning. For this reason, many pastors have found that worship planning is best completed during the summer months when the schedule is somewhat less hectic.

The first step in planning is to peruse the secular calendar to determine where the major festivals fall. At this point the pastor will want to insert into the calendar the special days that are important in his congregation, e.g., Mission Festival, Christian Education Sunday, etc. Some pastors may look over the calendar of Minor Festivals; a minor festival that falls on a Sunday may be a good replacement for a regular lectionary focus. For example, if the Festival of St. Matthias, Apostle (February 24) falls on a Sunday, a pastor may decide to focus worship on the emphasis of this minor festival. He may feel that a review on the divine call would be beneficial for his members.

After the calendar for the year has been set, and the Sundays, festivals, and special days have been put in place, the pastor consults the lectionary and adds the appointed lessons for each day. Especially choir directors will appreciate the addition of a brief summary of the three lessons. Some pastors may study the lessons on their own and determine the summaries. Others will consult *Planning Christian Worship* and peruse the summaries that manual offers. The planning guide also gives a focus to each set of lessons, and the pastor will want to add either that focus or one of his own choosing.

The pastor's next step is to determine which of the three lessons will serve as his sermon text. Many pastors have found it wise to preach on the various lessons by season: First Lessons in Advent, Second Lessons over the festivals and Sundays of Christmas, Gospels during Epiphany, First Lessons during Lent, etc. Some follow a Sunday by Sunday pattern of First Lesson, Second Lesson, Gospel. It may be wiser to use one of these progressions than to preach on the First Lessons or the Gospels for the entire year.

123

Once the lessons have been chosen and studied, the pastor begins to choose the hymns for the service. Hymn selection becomes a little easier for the pastor who begins with the *Christian Worship* Hymn of the Day list. These lectionary-based hymns have been chosen with an eye not only for excellence but also for familiarity. When one or another Hymn of the Day has seemed likely to challenge the average congregation, an alternate has been offered. If a pastor feels that even the alternate will be unfamiliar to his members, he may opt to choose another hymn in this position. He may also decide to plan ahead so that the choirs may begin to familiarize the congregation with the appointed hymn in advance of its designated Sunday.

Planning Christian Worship offers suggestions for the other hymns of the service besides the Hymn of the Day. Pastors who enjoy choosing hymns on their own will continue to do so, of course, but they will keep in mind that hymns have various functions in the service. The Opening Hymn intends to set the mood and theme of the day. It ought not be too long, and should be relatively familiar to the congregation. The Sermon Hymn does not precede but follows the sermon. This hymn also ought to be well-known to the congregation. It might also be the hymn with the most emotional content. The Closing Hymn, customary in some congregations, ought to be short and to the point. Several stanzas of a longer hymn work very well as the closing hymn.

As he studies the Hymn of the Day and searches for an Opening and Closing Hymn, the pastor may find a hymn that fits naturally as the Sermon Hymn, e.g., *Jesus, Savior, Pilot Me* for the sermon based on Matthew 8:23-27, the record of Jesus quieting the storm. However, the pastor may want to choose this hymn after he has translated and studied the text and found a sermon theme and outline. Even the most planning-conscious musicians will be so pleased to have received at least two hymns in advance that they will not begrudge the pastor the right to save this selection for the week before worship.

When the Sacrament is offered in worship, the Sermon Hymn will usually be sung during the distribution. In this position it may replace the traditional communion hymn. Some may wonder if this substitution is wise. Several generations ago most

Lutheran congregations offered the Sacrament only several times a year. Sermon references to the Lord's Supper were usually limited to the special confessional addresses which preceded the celebration of the Sacrament. Since the Sacrament was so rarely used or mentioned, it was natural that the hymn during the distribution would focus on what was taking place. Today most congregations offer the Supper at least once a month, and many more often. Most pastors mention the value of Holy Communion regularly in their sermons. While a hymn about communion may be beneficial from time to time and may even be added as a second distribution hymn, pastors need not feel pangs of conscience if they replace the communion hymn with the sermon hymn during the distribution.

If a congregation's musicians have studied the principles of Lutheran worship, a pastor may decide to rely on their assistance in the selection of the Opening and Closing Hymns. While he would likely want to retain the right of final approval, he may find that others have more ability and interest in selecting hymns than he does. Sharing this responsibility also gives the congregation's musicians a sense of participation and ownership in worship planning, and therefore encourages more diligent and faithful efforts.

After he has added references to the Prayer of the Day and the Psalm of the Day on the Service Planning Guide, the pastor has completed his individual planning. He places the Sunday planning guides into a three-ring binder (or perhaps makes copies so that the musicians have sets of their own) and makes them available for all who have a part in the planning process.

Pastor and Musicians Together

Before the congregation's musicians can get busy with their individual work, however, it will be wise for the pastor and the musicians to meet together. While this need not be a formal, scheduled meeting, some worship matters do require mutual input, and the result of such work will likely be an enriched worship life for the members of the congregation. Following are some questions that might to be addressed:

On which Sundays (and in which services) will a choir sing the Verse of the Day? Are there settings of the Verse available so that children's choirs and soloists can provide the Verse of the Day. When will the congregation be singing the General Verse? When will the pastor need to be prepared to read the Verse of the Day?

How will the Psalm of the Day be sung? Will the same groups that sing the Verse of the Day be able to perform the psalm? Since variety is the spice of life, how may the psalms be sung in various ways so that the congregation will not tire of one or another manner of presentation? Can this variety be added seasonally? Might the congregation speak the psalms at times? Ought the psalm (and perhaps even the First Lesson) be eliminated in a service with communion?

Are there festival settings of hymns that could be used? Many choral concertatos, based on a wide variety of hymns, are available from music publishers; on which Sundays or festivals might these be used? Are there instrumentalists in the congregation who have the ability to play for public worship?

Which new and/or unfamiliar hymns from *Christian Worship* could be carefully introduced during the coming year? Can a set of such hymns be developed, can these hymns be rehearsed by the choirs, and then presented as choir anthems?

Will a congregational rehearsal be necessary or can new hymns be practiced in Bible classes and church organizations? Could the choir replace its annual concert with a hymn festival designed for teaching new hymns?

Could the choir sing an alternate setting of *Glory be to God* during one season of the church year? Could the congregation be taught that alternate? How can the choir assist? Could the choir help the congregation learn to sing *This Is the Feast of Victory* (CW 265) as a replacement for the main canticle during the Easter season?

Could the choir sing alternate stanzas of the hymn during the communion distribution? Could the choir sing *O Christ, Lamb of God* at the beginning of the distribution instead of the congregation?

Which orders of service will the congregation want to begin using during the year ahead? Is there any value in a careful introduction of Morning Praise or Evening Prayer? Could the choirs begin a study of Service of Word and Sacrament? Could they substitute the canticles from that service for parts of the more familiar Common Service (e.g., *Holy, Holy Holy* from Service of Word and Sacrament as a replacement for the *Sanctus* in the Common Service)?

Obviously, there are many ways in which the choir and the organist can enrich worship, but not all the ways need to be used at the same time. If the choir and the congregation are not accustomed to having the choir function within the context of the liturgy, it may be wise to proceed slowly. If the congregation is not used to brass instruments played at worship, trumpets and trombones should be used sparingly. It is best to introduce one or two new ideas during one year and then several more ideas in the following year.

It is vital that the pastor be involved in this stage of planning. He may want to encourage more reluctant musicians and caution those who are more daring. It is just as important that the musicians be active in these decisions. In most cases they will understand the congregation's musical resources better than the pastor does. They will also know their personal strengths and limitations. Although it takes time, this joint planning is vital in almost every congregation. Not much is gained if the pastor's optimistic plans are beyond the reach of those who work with him in leading the congregation's worship. Nor is much accomplished if the innovations of the congregation's musicians are met by an unsupportive pastor.

The Choir Director

The first planning step for the choir director is to set up a choir schedule for the entire year. There may be eventual changes in the schedule, of course, but these can be made as the year progresses. If a choir takes seriously its role to sing the psalm and the verse in the service and is expected, therefore, to be present in almost every service, the schedule may include dates for sections of the choir or soloists from the choir. When more than one choir regularly takes part in public worship (e.g., a children's choir or classroom choruses), the directors of those groups must receive a copy of the service planning guides for the services at which their choirs are scheduled to sing.

Most experienced choir directors will agree that selecting music is their most difficult task. *Christian Worship* includes a set of psalms for worship, but many choir directors will want to go beyond that basic set to more interesting and sophisticated arrangements of the psalms. There are several complete sets of the Verse of the Day. Especially the Lutheran publishing companies are producing seasonal sets of the Verse. Choir directors will want to keep an eye out for these settings and teach them to their choirs.

A more difficult task is to locate and choose festival settings of hymns (choral concertatos) and appropriate anthems. This work becomes easier if choir directors get their names attached to the mailing lists of religious music publishers. One has to be selective here. Search for publishers concerned with music for worship, and especially those who feature music for liturgical worship. At the present time the best of these are Northwestern Publishing House (Milwaukee), Concordia (St. Louis), Augsburg-Fortress (Minneapolis, but also regional offices), and Morning Star (St. Louis). Gregorian Institute of America (GIA, Chicago) also features excellent music for Lutheran liturgical choirs. All of these offer liturgical music, festival hymn settings, and anthems that match the emphases of the lectionary. Many publishers offer a subscription service that allows choir directors to purchase perusal copies of new music at a reduced cost. Choir directors are wise to enroll in several of these services.

Another way to find new materials is to attend choral reading sessions sponsored by music publishers and retailers. Those that are most valuable are usually connected to a conference or workshop dealing with worship. The pastor can sometimes help the choir director discover where these workshops are being scheduled.

Not everything the choir sings needs to be new. Choir directors need not hesitate to sing music that has been sung in previous years. Balance is the key. While a choir spends four or five weeks learning a new anthem, it can still take its regular turn in the service by singing older music.

There are several questions that choir directors may ask as they search for appropriate music:

> What are the lectionary themes for a particular season? (Since this is the first and most important question, it may be best to select music for one season at a time. It is easier to remember five or six themes than it is to keep 52 themes in mind!)

128

Which choral concertatos and anthems match the themes? (Directors who discover new anthems that beg to be sung will want to search the lectionary themes for an appropriate match. When a match has been found it may be an easy matter to adjust the choir schedule so that the new anthem can be sung on the day its theme matched the lectionary.)

When choosing anthems this question must be asked: Does the text of the anthem contain false or unclear theology? Special care must be taken when music from non-Lutheran sources is considered. The pastor can (and probably should) help here.

When choosing concertatos this question must be asked: Does the text of the concertato match the text of the hymn in *Christian Worship?* It would be embarrassing and confusing if the choir's sopranos sang a descant on the final stanza with a different text from what the people were singing. The texts in choir music may be slightly altered if a difference is found.

Will the choir find the music interesting and enjoyable to sing? Is the level of difficulty beyond the ability of the choir? Is the accompaniment beyond the ability of the accompanist? It is better to sing something easy and to sing it well than to sing something difficult that cannot be mastered.

If the music is scored for instruments, does the congregation have people who can play? Can the number be performed without instruments if necessary? Is there a member of a sister congregation who might be "borrowed" for a Sunday?

If the anthem is based on a new hymn, can it be repeated several times during a season to acquaint the congregation with the hymn? Can the congregation be invited to sing the hymn at some point?

It is wise for the choir director to keep the perusal copies that are not used. These scores can be added to a useful file of materials that can serve as the first source of music for the next choir year and for the year after. As mentioned previously, the director ought not overlook the existing choral library. There may be something in the files that will fit perfectly into the lectionary focus.

Although the focus of this chapter is advance planning, choir directors ought not overlook the necessity of planning each individual choir rehearsal. Several books and manuals are available that can help in this area of planning.

The Organist

The most important planning for a church organist has nothing to do with the service planning guides prepared by the pastor. The organist's planning begins with a filing system. It is perhaps easiest to file organ music alphabetically by the name of the title of the piece or the collection: *Wood Winds* by Dale Wood is filed under "W" and Bach's *Little Organ Book* under "L." Another system files music by name of composer or editor. Any system will do, as long as the organist understands how it works. Since most organ music used in worship is based on hymn tunes, the organist will want a file that references hymn tunes to the alphabetical file, such as follows:

> Ein Feste Burg   *Laudamus*, p. 3.
> Ein Feste Burg   *The Organist's Golden Treasury*, Vol. 1, p. 62.
> Ein Feste Burg   *Pachelbel Organ Works*, Vol. 3, p. 19.

An organist with a smaller collection of music can place references directly into a regularly-used hymnal. Those with larger collections will find the computer to be a perfect help in the referencing process. The initial work of setting up a system may take some time, but once completed, the effort will be a wonderful time-saver. The filing system can be printed on regular pages and placed into a three-ring binder near the music library. When a congregation owns a collection of organ music, a similar system ought to be adopted.

With a filing system in place, the organist can use the service planning guides with ease: a look at the planning guides identifies the hymns; a look into the hymnal identifies the tunes; a look into the filing system locates the organ pieces based on the tunes. While it is a more difficult task to find non-hymn-based music that matches the mood and theme of the day, the filing system gets the organist at the organ for practice much more quickly.

Another part of the organist's work that does not directly interact with planning the service is to build a collection of appropriate organ music. The same Lutheran publishing companies that are most beneficial to the choir director will serve the organist: Northwestern Publishing House, Concordia, Augsburg-

Fortress, and Morning Star. Organists will want to get their names on the mailing lists of these publishers. Workshops and seminars are available for organists just as they are for choir directors.

The congregation will need to recognize that organ music is expensive, and the organist ought to be given some sort of allowance for the purchase of new music. The congregation itself may decide to purchase larger collections like the Concordia Hymn Prelude Series. This set of 42 volumes of easy-to-medium organ preludes, almost all based on hymns contained in *Christian Worship,* comes close to being a "must" for Lutheran congregations and their organists. The Concordia set has a reference index of its own; other new music can be added to the reference library of the organist. (See other information in this manual in Section Three, chapter 22. The Suggested Basic Organ Repertoire will be helpful.)

The service planning guides become very helpful for the organist who wants to take time to learn new music for one Sunday or another. A chorale prelude from Bach's *Little Organ Book* may not be able to be mastered during the course of one week, but it may be learned over the course of a month. Organists with average skills will appreciate the additional time the service planning guide affords so that the organ score of a choral concertato can be learned. Some organists may simply need the extra time to learn hymns they have never played before.

Once the music for the service has been chosen and recorded on the *Planning Guide for Musicians* (see p. 122 in this chapter), the organist is ready to consider the little "extras" that organists add to worship: an intonation (a short prelude) for the Sermon Hymn, an alternate setting of one of the hymns, the accompaniment for the Psalm of the Day. Practice is the final stage of planning and leads the organist to the service itself, ready and eager to assist in the proclamation of the gospel and in the praise of Christ's people.

Others

It is probably unnecessary to give complete copies of the service planning guides to the Altar Guild, ushers, custodian, and church secretary. However, all of these worship assistants ought to know about special services and when certain seasons begin: the Altar Guild will need some direction for the liturgical colors and the church secretary needs to know when a special service will require more time to prepare the service bulletin. Sunday school and Lutheran elementary school teachers ought to know where the service planning guides are kept so they can refer to them when they plan the music their students are to sing.

Long-range Planning

Planning is work and it takes time, but it has wonderful value for a congregation's worship life. Working together, a pastor, choir director, organist, and all other participants endeavor to proclaim the grace of God and to lead God's people in joyful response.

Not all the congregation's worship planning efforts focus on the specific public worship opportunities. Some of the planning needs to look into the more distant future, and some of it has to do with education, evangelism, and church architecture. The pastor will usually provide the leadership for long-range planning, but he will surely be assisted by the congregation's various boards and committees.

Planning for Education

There is much talk in the church about worship renewal. There is also some confusion about how to achieve it. During the formative days of *Christian Worship: A Lutheran Hymnal*, Pastor Bryan Gerlach interviewed the well-known worship expert Robert Webber. After the interview, Gerlach wrote:

> Some of us have tried to achieve worship renewal by adding variety to our worship services. But as we strive for variety, we must also be able to articulate the pitfalls that come with having too much variety or with using inept variety. Webber made the point which is easily overlooked: "Variety, per se, is not that helpful. . . . Rather, rediscover what the liturgy does. If the people are dead, they'll be dead in variety, too." If people don't know what the liturgy does and what their role in the liturgy is, then variety may function as nothing

more than a pious diversion. Webber wrote, "I have talked with ministers and church leaders who have made slight changes in their order and practice of worship and who, because of these changes, feel they have entered into worship renewal. . . . Worship renewal is not primarily changing the order of worship, introducing new elements, or even celebrating the Eucharist more frequently." What is worship renewal? It is leading people to understand that at worship they come into the presence of the living Christ, it is encouraging them to participate with joy and eagerness in their prayers and praises, it is helping them to lift up their hearts to the Lord in a new, faith-filled song.[3]

Gerlach's point makes it obvious why worship education is so vital in a Lutheran congregation. Even though Lutherans worship more often than they do any other spiritual thing, Lutheran leaders generally have not trained their members to understand how Lutherans worship and why they worship as they do. If the members of Lutheran congregations are to be renewed in their worship, they must learn the answers to the hows and the whys.

Pastors may want to include a unit on worship in their instruction classes for adults and children. Bible study courses on worship can be included in an annual adult education curriculum. The teachers in the Sunday school and the Lutheran elementary school need to explain the purpose and the parts of public worship in their classrooms. Portions of the video tape Bible study *The Way Lutherans Worship*[4] can serve a variety of congregational needs.

Pastors may notice that not only the members of the congregation need to be trained to understand worship, but even the leadership assistants need such training. *Christian Worship: Manual* might be an excellent tool for helping choir directors and organists understand Lutheran concepts of public worship. Other re-

---

[3] Bryan Gerlach, "Advice for Lutherans from an Evangelical," *Focus on Worship,* Fall, 1992, p. 9.

[4] Prepared by the author and produced in 1992 as part of *Christian Worship*'s introduction program, the twelve-part video presentation is general enough to have application in various educational settings. (Produced by Northwestern Publishing House, Milwaukee.)

133

sources are available.[5] Perhaps study meetings could be scheduled every other month. Pastor and musicians might come to the meetings having read various sections in advance. Questions might be advanced that dig more deeply into the concepts. Another meeting on an already busy schedule might not seem like an inviting prospect, but a congregation that sees the need to train Sunday school teachers and lay evangelists ought to be as concerned that those who function in a representative ministry in worship are well-equipped for their tasks.

In some congregations a strategic plan may have to be established to teach the members a wider variety of hymns and liturgical materials. A number of planning steps will be helpful:

Decide which new items will be least likely to cause immediate dislike. Will responsive prayers arouse less opposition than chanted psalms? Will certain hymns be immediately popular? Begin with what the people will probably enjoy, and they will be more likely to be content with additional training.

Plan to introduce new forms by seasons. Several Lenten hymns might be taught during the Lenten season. Several hymns about Christian love might be used during the fall.

Decide which new forms will be introduced; don't add others on the spur of the moment. It is better to teach a few things thoroughly than to frustrate people by teaching too much too quickly.

Once the forms for the year have been chosen, marshal the congregation's resources. Teach the hymn to the choirs and the children. Let each take a turn to sing the hymn in church. Practice the hymn in the Bible classes and the church organizations.

On the Sunday the new hymn is to be sung, have a five-minute practice session before the service begins. Make sure that the service does

---

[5] Training Christians for Ministry, an in-depth course for training Christian lay leaders, has a study track for those involved in worship leadership. The course is available through Northwestern Publishing House.

Many excellent materials have been prepared by the LCMS Concordia Publishing House. Two volumes that may be especially helpful for training organists and choir directors are *A Handbook of Church Music and Key Words in Church Music*, the former edited by Carl Halter and Carl Schalk and the latter by Schalk alone.

not become five minutes longer! Shorten the lessons, the sermon, and the other hymns so that the people can practice and still be out of church at the usual time.

An option to this idea is a Hymn-of-the-Month plan. Choose twelve hymns in advance of their use. Have choirs rehearse a hymn of the month for performance on the first Sunday of the month. Use the hymn in various positions over the next three weeks. By the fourth week the congregation will be able to sing the hymn with some degree of ability.

Obviously a great deal more planning will be necessary to introduce a complete service. This task can be accomplished well only over several months. On the other hand, the introduction of responsive prayers or the choir's performance of the Verse of the Day may take very little educating. Good judgment and a pastoral heart are the guiding factors in any time of change.

Planning for Musical Leadership

It would be impossible to count how many of the organists and choir directors who have served Lutheran congregations through the years were pressed into service out of emergency or necessity. Usually these faithful men and women are the first to admit that they lacked the training for the task they were assigned. They accepted the congregation's call because "it had to be done and there was no one else to do it." God is glorified when his people reach beyond their abilities and, with great sacrifice of time and energy, supply what God's people need for worship. Many Lutheran congregations owe these willing servants a sincere debt of love.

These same congregations also owe their willing volunteers a careful long-range plan which includes the securing of a trained church musician. For the sake of those who respond to emergency situations, the emergency should not become the accepted status quo. To perpetuate a situation that was intended to be temporary does a disservice both to the volunteer and to the congregation. While a congregation may not have the means or the manpower to quickly solve an emergency situation, it does have the ability to establish a plan that will eventually address the problem and replace the temporary solution with something more permanent.

The most obvious solution to a musical emergency may not involve securing the services of a new musician at all. Many musical volunteers would be more than happy to serve on a more permanent basis if they were able to secure more advanced training. The congregation can help by being willing to pay the expenses of organ and choral workshops offered by the synod's Commission on Worship. The church council might also express its willingness to make monies available that would cover the cost of organ lessons or a course in choral conducting at a local college. Our church colleges offer summer school courses related to worship; the congregation might cover the cost of the musician's enrollment. The worship committee might find it possible to secure child care so that the organist-mom might have time for adequate practice without spending her own money.

Another possible focus of long-range planning is a position of staff minister in music. Larger congregations, especially those with a Lutheran elementary school or a very active Sunday school, would not find it difficult to create a job description that would justify a full-time position. Two-thirds of the service playing in a busy congregation (including funerals and weddings), directing the adult choir, youth choir, children's choir, classroom choirs, handbell choir, brass quartet, planning, administering, and rehearsing would more than fill the hours of a week.

Smaller congregations should not automatically eliminate the idea of such a staff minister just because their congregation is small and their music program limited. Especially the younger musicians of our church body might be more than willing to serve as the congregation's music minister on a part-time basis while also holding secular employment of some kind. Usually the church council can be active in guaranteeing that the combination of the church-paid salary, the wages from the secular job, and the housing situation are an adequate remuneration for the individual who has been called.

Another option for smaller congregations is a staff ministry position that includes work in music and in another area, e.g., family education, evangelism, or church administration. Many qualified church musicians possess the gifts to become proficient in other areas of ministry as well, and congregations may be able to guide these people to a staff ministry training course that will allow them to serve the church in ways besides music.

A long-range plan that is really not an option for a confessional Lutheran church is to secure the services of a musician who is a member of a non-confessional denomination. The church musician is a representative minister, appointed by the congregation to proclaim the gospel and to encourage the praise of God's people. An organist playing the Lord's Prayer or a choir director leading the singing of the Lord's Prayer is not doing something different from a pastor leading the speaking of the Lord's Prayer. Confessional Lutherans who would not dream of appointing a person from a different denomination to lead the Lord's Prayer from the altar ought not appoint a person from a different denomination to lead the Lord's Prayer from the balcony.[6] It must also be noted that a musician who is brought in from a non-Lutheran denomination will surely not be able to communicate Lutheran theology through music. One can imagine how sensitive, loyal Lutherans might feel were the organist to play a setting of *Ave Maria* during the offering or if the choir were to sing the *Battle Hymn of the Republic.*

Some have tried to justify the decision to secure the services of a musician from another denomination with the argument that the pastor will teach the members of the congregation to view the musician as just another technician, like the plumber or the piano tuner. It must be granted that this explanation is possible. It must

---

[6] Some critics of this scriptural understanding of the doctrine of fellowship contend that playing the organ or directing the choir is not leadership. Therefore, an organist or choir director can be a member of another church body.

This is their argument: Since confessional Lutheran churches allow women to hold these positions, the roles of organist and choir director must not be leadership roles. If they were leadership positions, a woman could not be an organist or choir director.

The critics misunderstand the biblical principle concerning the role of women in the church. The Scriptures do not forbid a woman to be involved in leadership. What God forbids is a woman usurping leadership from the men of the congregation or binding the will of the men. A woman organist or choir director may indeed participate in leadership as long as she does not seek to usurp the authority of the God-appointed heads of the congregation.

A clear understanding of the Scriptures shows that there is no inconsistency here.

also be admitted, however, that a congregation so trained will not likely come to value the purpose of music and art in worship nor will it likely strive to improve and expand its music ministry.

Pastors who accept this justification can also expect to have a difficult time leading their members to a God-pleasing understanding of the value of the doctrine of church fellowship. They can also anticipate that brother pastors and neighboring sister congregations may be confused and offended. Finally, this action may solidify in the mind of the guest organist or choir director the point of view that is prevalent in many Christian denominations, that "it doesn't make any difference what you believe, as long as you believe." Whatever might be gained musically through the securing of a church musician from another fellowship is more than offset by what may be lost spiritually.

A music ministry that is conducted by untrained volunteers will probably not improve unless one of two things occurs: either an outstanding musician will join the congregation, or the congregation will plan to improve the situation. Since congregations cannot anticipate the former, they are wise to do the latter.

One last question ought to be addressed: Will the congregation's long-range plan to replace an untrained volunteer lead to hurt feelings? Feelings can be hurt in a number of ways. If a congregation asks someone to serve without making it clear that it anticipates the service to be temporary, and if, all at once, the servant is replaced without warning, feelings may well be hurt—and the calling body must shoulder the blame. If an individual has served capably, put personal monies and energy into that service, and then is summarily dismissed, feelings will be hurt—and again, the calling body must shoulder the blame. However, if the long-range plan is set before a volunteer clearly and carefully, if the volunteer does not wish to take advantage of the congregation's offer for self-improvement and advanced training, then hurt feelings are the result of pride and not the fault of the congregation.

Congregational leaders are always struggling to know the difference between hurt feelings and wounded pride. Are the feelings of the retiring pastor hurt—or is his ego wounded—when his congregation eagerly anticipates the arrival of its young seminary graduate pastor? Are the feelings of the Sunday school teacher hurt—or is her pride stung—when the congregation votes to begin a Lutheran elementary school? Congregations must take care not to become the cause of hurt feelings, but progress in ministry cannot be stifled by wounded pride.

In Conclusion

Long-range planning has many applications in the area of the public worship of the church. Many of these applications have been treated elsewhere in this manual: the planning of the worship space, the purchase of a worship-leading instrument, the use of a new order of service, etc. But long-range planning never is an end unto itself. It always has as its purpose to encourage the most zealous proclamation of the gospel of Jesus Christ and the most noble praise from his people.

It is for those very reasons that *Christian Worship: A Lutheran Hymnal* has been offered to our beloved Lutheran church. This worship book and all its satellite publications exist so that Christ might be both proclaimed among his people and praised by his people. With such purpose believers have gathered to worship during all the millennia of the world's history. Believers throughout the ages have been determined that, at public worship, God might serve his people and that his people might serve God. This is the center and core of Christian worship.

> Come, let us sing for joy to the LORD; let us shout aloud to the Rock of our salvation. Let us come before him with thanksgiving and extol him with music and song. For the LORD is the great God, the great King above all gods. In his hand are the depths of the earth, and the mountain peaks belong to him. The sea is his, for he made it, and his hands formed the dry land. Come, let us bow down in worship, let us kneel before the LORD our Maker; for he is our God and we are the people of his pasture, the flock under his care (Psalm 95:1-7).

SECTION TWO:

THE SERVICES
IN DETAIL
AND USE

CHAPTER 9:

General Introduction

Yesterday, Today, and Tomorrow

Christian worship operates in the three dimensions of the past, present, and future because the God whom we worship is the same yesterday, today, and forever. He is the God of Abraham, Moses, David, Paul, and Luther. He is our God, always present with us in our worship. He has said to us, "Surely I am with you always, to the very end of the age" (Matthew 28:20). He is with us: to bless us, to speak to us in the steady course and cadence of his Word, to come to us in the satisfying gift of his sacraments, and to promise that he will come again and receive us to himself in heaven.

Our weekly worship reinforces these truths and becomes a real "Sunday meeting" with God. Worship is an external witness that God has served and is serving his people with his gifts. As such, it is the center of life for us Christians.

Worship renews us to be lights of Christ, the light of the world. In worship, God reaches down, informs us of his redemptive love for us in Christ, and lifts us up for growth and service. The worship service, rich and potent in the Word of Christ, builds up our lives and our words in Christ so that we give "thanks to God the Father through him" (Colossians 3:17). It virtually begs us to invite others to come also and receive the gifts of salvation.

Weekly worship is the high and holy task of the New Testament church, one that dare not be relegated to dusty storage rooms or to electronic wizardry. The Church of God must sing! "Let the word of Christ dwell in you richly as you teach and admonish one another with all wisdom, and as you sing psalms, hymns and spiritual songs with gratitude in your hearts to God" (Colossians 3:16).

We speak and sing our prayers and praises today. But, each time, our orders of worship translate us into yesterday, into the life and times of Jesus and beyond. They also point us to tomorrow, to the end time and our final glory. So, liturgies are much more than paths of worship. They are timeless proclamations of God's will and way. They express the conflict of sin and grace, law and gospel. In absolution, in gospel declaration, in sacraments, they convey the good resolve of God's forgiveness in Christ. The richness of Scripture, which is embodied in their texts, makes liturgies powerful faith-builders for believers and excellent instruments for outreach to those who are searching for spiritual help. Worship structures are worthy of our study and our use.

Christian Worship: A Complete Book of Worship

Christian Worship: A Lutheran Hymnal, like our Bible, is a book filled with the story of God's love and the joyful praises of his people.

Our hymnal paints a full spectrum of Christian worship. To study its hymns and liturgies is to see a sevenfold panorama of doctrine, history, liturgy, poetry, music, prayer and praise, and the Christian church year. Each of these merits commentary, but our focus in this section of the manual is on the uses of the various orders of worship of *Christian Worship.* They include

The Common Service—a revision of the historic Sunday liturgy of the church; may be used for communion services or non-communion services;

Service of Word and Sacrament—a parallel or alternate service of Holy Communion, following the historic structure and elements of Lutheran worship but with new musical settings;

Service of the Word—a service for worship when there is no Holy Communion;

Morning Praise—a revision of Matins;

Evening Prayer—a quiet, meditative service with the historic structure of Vespers but with new music and updated texts; includes two beginnings with the opportunity to use the ancient Service of Light;

Three Devotions—morning, evening, and general devotions as brief services for church organizations, committees, schools, conferences, workshops, and families; and

144

Holy Baptism, Christian Marriage, Christian Funeral—rites crafted for participation by congregations.

Looking Ahead

The orders of worship of *Christian Worship* give full room for both Word and Sacrament to bless us and work in us a genuine response of faith, praise, and thanksgiving. They make provision for the church year Propers, which over the centuries have enriched Christian worship with a yearly emphasis on the life of Christ and our life in him.

At a time when Lutherans are beset with strong pressures to agree that liturgical worship is outworn and unequal to the task of drawing people to Christ and nourishing their faith, we need to keep asserting that the power of God to bring and keep people in his Church lies ever and only in the gospel of Jesus Christ. That saving and transforming gospel is embedded in the texts of the services of *Christian Worship.*

The inclusion of two Communion orders of worship, namely, The Common Service and the *Service of Word and Sacrament,* should encourage use of these adaptations of the historic liturgy and serve as a norm for congregations in their worship. The goal is that *Christian Worship* will restore a semblance of the worship uniformity enjoyed for fifty years with *The Lutheran Hymnal.*

From the age of the apostles to the time of Luther, the Sunday service included the Sacrament. It was only with the coming of Pietism and Rationalism—those twin destroyers of liturgy, doctrinal hymnody, and sacramental life—that the Communion service ceased to be normative. We are still suffering some effects of these movements of the eighteenth and nineteenth centuries.

A further hope, therefore, is that the use of *The Common Service* and the *Service of Word and Sacrament* may result in an increasing appreciation for the unique character of Holy Communion. Christians will always want to be growing in understanding and partaking of the blessings of forgiveness of sins, life, and salvation that are offered and given in the sharing of Jesus' true body and blood.

145

May the Holy Spirit use the liturgies of *Christian Worship* to guide and encourage us and our churches through the murky darkness and dissonant din of this earth until that steady and distant triumph song of heaven becomes our own.

CHAPTER 10:

Items the Services Have in Common

Psalm Use and Performance

The Psalm

A special feature of *Christian Worship* is the inclusion of fifty-nine psalms or selected psalm verses set to music for choir and congregation. Though *The Lutheran Hymnal* contained ninety-three psalms, they were not arranged for singing, nor was there a place in the Sunday liturgy for them to be sung. Except for the fragments of the psalms in the Introits and Graduals, the Psalms were restricted to the *Matins* and *Vespers* and often omitted there. In *Christian Worship* the Psalms, one to a page, are arranged for responsorial singing. The choir or cantor (solo singer) sings the verses of the Psalm, and the congregation sings the refrain. The Psalm is sung in the Sunday liturgies as a response to the First Lesson. The Psalm is also an integral part of *Morning Praise* and *Evening Prayer.*

Brief History of Psalmody

The story of the Psalms leading up to their use in *Christian Worship* is a story worth knowing as told by Luther D. Reed in his classic treatise on the Lutheran liturgy:

> The common recitation of the Psalter united the Jews scattered throughout many lands in their synagogue worship and in the temple services in Jerusalem upon the great feasts. The early church incorporated the Psalter bodily into its worship. It became the first hymnbook of the Christians. The medieval church used large portions of the Psalter in its liturgical and musical enrichment of the Mass. As it developed the hour services into a great system, it arranged that the Psalter be recited in its entirety once a week,

because it regarded the book of Psalms an inexhaustible mine of devotion. . . .

The musical rendition of the Psalter in monasteries, cathedrals, and college churches became a noteworthy feature. The entire Psalter was chanted antiphonally during the course of the week to nine psalm tones, or melodies, eight regular and one irregular (*Tonus Peregrinus*). These were called the Gregorian Tones. They differed widely in character, being in different modes or scales and having different inflections or cadences at the end of their respective reciting notes. Each tone also had a variety of "finals," some for ferial (daily) and others for festival use. An antiphon, consisting of a separate psalm verse sung to a proper melody of its own, introduced and concluded the chanting of each psalm on festivals. . . . The chanting of the Latin Psalter to these fine melodies for a millennium or more is one of the most impressive features in the liturgical and musical history of the church.

The Lutheran Reformers made every effort to retain the chanting of the Psalms and their historic melodies. Where Matins and Vespers were continued as daily services, Psalms 1-109 were assigned to Matins and Psalms 110-150 to Vespers. . . . The great development of vernacular hymnody, however, the dissolution of the monastic communities, and discontinuance of corporate clerical worship, eventually caused the chanting of the psalms and the use of the traditional psalm tones to disappear almost entirely from Lutheran worship. The Anglican Church, with its greater emphasis on Morning Prayer and Evening Prayer and its continuance of the ancient choir system in cathedrals and college chapels, retained the chanting of the psalms much more generally. The Prayer Book provided for the chanting or the reading of the entire Psalter once a month. After the Restoration a new type of chanting was introduced, and hundreds of so-called "Anglican chants" supplemented the ancient Gregorian tones.[1]

The Psalms in Christian Worship

The Psalm section in *Christian Worship* contains fifty-nine psalms carefully selected from the 150 in the Psalter. Why such a relatively small number? The intent was to sing the best of the psalms into the minds and hearts of people. Those chosen were fa-

---

[1] *The Lutheran Liturgy* Rev., (Philadelphia: Muhlenberg Press, 1947), p. 393.

vorite psalms, Messianic Psalms, and those most edifying for corporate worship. They were also selected to fit the Sundays and festivals of the three-year lectionary. It was thought more desirable to have a smaller number of the psalms learned and loved by people than a larger number that would be sung once a year or less.

In most cases, selected verses of psalms were chosen rather than entire psalms. The principle here is the same as that involved in shortening hymns. Many psalms are simply too long to sing in their entirety. Moreover, careful selection of the key verses results in a more focused content. The psalm becomes more understandable and more memorable.

Singing the Psalms

Music may not be quite as important for psalms as for hymns, since the psalms are prose. However, they are highly rhythmic prose, poetic in form, and, like hymns, designed to be sung. One advantage of chanting the psalm verses is that the text goes by a little more slowly than in choral reading, allowing the words to imprint themselves on the mind for better understanding. Often our congregational reading is too fast to allow much thinking, e.g., the Lord's Prayer and Nicene Creed.

Introducing Psalm Singing to the Congregation

Where the congregation has not been singing psalms, the following simple procedure is suggested:

1. Have the choir or a solo singer sing the psalm for several times so that the congregation can listen.

2. Begin congregational involvement by having it sing the refrain. A cantor or choir sings the verses.

3. After several weeks, suggest that the worshipers join the choir in the *Glory Be to the Father.*

4. If and when it seems desirable, have the congregation sing all the verses.

Psalm Performance

Basic information on singing the psalms is found in the hymnal on page 63. Read this page for help in interpreting the markings

149

in the music. A standard method for performing the psalms is outlined. However, there are a number of ways to enhance the presentation. After the psalms have been sung for some time according to a basic pattern, worship leaders may wish to vary the performance to avoid monotony for the choir or congregation.

The Refrain

The refrains in *Christian Worship* are short, metrical (hymnlike), easy, and fun to sing after they have been learned. Thirtyone different refrains allow for some repetition. The texts of the refrains are sometimes drawn from the psalms themselves, but more often from elsewhere. The words are chosen to relate closely to the content and mood of the psalm.

Normally the refrain is simply sung with organ accompaniment as written. But the refrain, too, can be enhanced. One might, for instance, use a trumpet or other instrument to augment the melody. Or, when the choir sings the refrain alone, it could do so in four-part harmony, using the arrangement in the organist's edition of the hymnal.

The Psalm Verses

Christian Worship offers sixteen new melodic formulas for the verses of the psalms. The intent is that normally the choir or cantor sings the verses and the congregation responds with a refrain.

The verses can be kept interesting by using alternating groups or individuals. For instance, the men and women of the choir can alternate by full or half verses. Or the men and women may alternate by groups of verses. Or a solo singer may alternate with the rest of the choir. If no cantor or choir is available, the verses may be spoken responsively (half-verse or verse) by the pastor and the congregation with the congregation singing the refrain as usual. The choir director and pastor may attempt still other variations.

It should be stressed, especially for smaller congregations, that the choir may be of any number. Two or more people will work. Also, a cantor (solo singer), who may be the pastor or another person, may sing the verses. If there is a parish school, use the children! They learn very quickly with enthusiastic leading, and generally enjoy singing the psalm verses.

150

Sing to the Lord a New Song

There is a remarkable resurgence of interest in the psalms and, especially, in singing the psalms. The interest in the hymnbook of the Old Testament exists not only in Lutheran churches, but also in other Christian denominations. Fresh translations, attention to the poetic form of the Hebrew psalms, and the metrical settings of the refrains have spurred this interest. Psalm singing is a helpful addition to the musical participation of the congregation in worship.

The psalms have long been one of the great poetic treasures of the Church. Their inspired content, their portrayal of life as it really is, and their ability to lift people from the depths and restore faith, trust, and joy account for their favored place in the lives of Christians. The progress made in the authentic presentation of the psalms in today's English, along with the attractive musical settings, predict a growing place for them in corporate worship as well as in the hearts of today's worshipers.

Verse of the Day

Its Use

The Verse of the Day (listed in Section Four of this manual) is a familiar or significant Scripture text framed with alleluias. It is a proper, that is, its text changes each Sunday or festival. For this reason it is to be sung by a choir (a *choral* proper), since the congregation is not able to rehearse the changing text each week. The Verse echoes or reinforces the theme or tone of the day or season of the church year. Some of the verses are taken from the Old Testament, but most are from the New Testament. A number of them are taken from one of the four Gospels, sometimes from the day's Gospel itself. Below are two examples of the Verse of the Day:

Text: John 6:68 for Epiphany 6
Verse: Alleluia! Lord, to whom shall we go? You have the words of eternal life. Alleluia!

Text: Luke 2:11 for Christmas Eve
Verse: Alleluia! Today in the town of David a Savior has been born to you; he is Christ the Lord. Alleluia!

The First Lesson (Old Testament or from the Acts) and the Psalm have been restored to the church in the Sunday liturgies of *Christian Worship*. The Verse is sung between the Second Lesson and the Gospel. It is a major proper that is in tune with the day's Gospel or the thought of which is consonant with some other Gospel expression. As such, it looks forward to and welcomes the reading of the Gospel.

Its History

The history of the Verse is a bit complicated. In a sense its roots go back to the Jewish synagogue worship where a psalm was read between the Scripture lessons. We might also identify it with the Gradual, an important proper that grew out of the Mass. It consisted of a liturgical arrangement of psalm verses together with the Alleluia. The Verse, then, seems to be as old as the readings themselves.

Originally there were three readings: Old Testament, Epistle, and Gospel. The Gradual was sung after the Old Testament Reading, and the Alleluia was sung after the Epistle. When in the Middle Ages the Old Testament Reading disappeared as a lesson, the Gradual and the Alleluia were reunited.

Its Performance

The Verse is a choral proper, so it is best sung by a choir, even a choir of two or more (for small church settings). Parish school children or a junior choir also may take part in the liturgical worship by singing this proper. The idea and ideal is always to have the Verse sung, be it by choir, pastor, cantor, or children.

A general verse has been provided in the text of all three Sunday liturgies of *Christian Worship*. This is to be sung by the congregation when no group or person is available to sing the proper Verse of the Day. Though the general verse may serve nicely as a prelude to the reading of the Gospel, it does not serve distinctively as a special verse that strengthens the theme of that particular Sunday or festival.

Various publishers carry full sets of verses for the church year. They print the verses in booklets covering one or more seasons. The music department of Northwestern Publishing House can assist and make recommendations.

152

Canticles and Hymns of the Liturgy

The definition of *Canticle* is somewhat elastic. Webster defines it as coming from the Latin *canticulum,* literally, a "little song." It is further defined as "song, poem, or hymn," or, more specifically, "one of the biblical hymns or songs of praise (as the *Benedictus, Magnificat,* and the *Nunc Dimittis*) used in church services."

In common usage, we might describe it as a liturgical song with a biblical prose text (but not usually from the psalms). It differs from what we ordinarily call a hymn because it is not arranged in stanzas with regular meter or rhyme. Musically, the canticle is usually through-composed or set to some type of chant formula.

Canticles in Christian Worship

Christian Worship includes the following canticles in its five major liturgies:

The Common Service
    Glory Be to God (Gloria In Excelsis)
    Create in Me
    Holy, Holy, Holy (Sanctus)
    O Christ, Lamb of God (Agnus Dei)
    Song of Simeon (Nunc Dimittis)

Service of Word and Sacrament
    O Lord, Our Lord (Song Of Praise)
    Holy, Holy, Holy (Sanctus)
    O Christ, Lamb of God (Agnus Dei)
    Thank The Lord

Service of the Word
    Oh, Taste And See

Morning Praise
    Oh, Come, Let Us Sing to the Lord (Venite)
    We Praise You, O God (Te Deum)

Evening Prayer
    Song of Mary (Magnificat)
    Song of Simeon (Nunc Dimittis)

Four canticles are included in the hymn section titled *Hymns of the Liturgy* (Hymns 262-278):

> *Glory Be to the Father (Gloria Patri)*
> *This Is the Feast of Victory* (Canticle: *Worthy Is Christ*)
> *Create in Me*
> *Blest Be the God of Israel (Song of Zechariah, Benedictus)*

Using the Canticles

Ideally, the congregation should learn to know and sing all the canticles in the liturgies of *Christian Worship* and their metrical versions as well. If the congregation is not acquainted with them, it is best to start with the canticles included in the orders of worship and to learn them one at a time. It is important to focus first on the text. Otherwise, the music in these Scripture-rich texts may draw most of the congregation's attention. So it may be beneficial for the congregation to speak the canticles before adding the music.

Comments on the canticle text in the service folder will also help. The canticle can be used as a sermon text or as a text for Bible study while the congregation is working with it. Many Lutheran Christians may never have looked at or thought about the words of even the most common canticles.

Small congregations with limited numbers of musical resources should not think that they cannot learn the canticles. Some of them, in fact, do an excellent job of it. An organist who plays only the soprano and bass can do well in leading the congregation in singing. Some small churches utilize a cantor (lead singer) who leads the singing by example.

Using Alternate Versions of the Canticles

When a canticle has become very familiar to a congregation and there is a desire for modest variety, another canticle can be substituted for the usual one. Or the hymn (metrical) version of the canticle can be sung for a time. Either alternative would be positive, since it not only provides freshness and variation but also helps the congregation learn liturgical songs that might otherwise be ignored year after year.

For example, *This Is the Feast of Victory* (CW 265) during the Easter season in place of the *Glory Be to God,* the *O Lord, Our*

Lord, or the *Oh, Taste and See.* This not only provides variety, but is an excellent way to sing out the resurrection theme through all the Sundays of Easter.

Martin Luther wrote or provided for hymn settings of the basic chants of the Ordinaries (*Kyrie, Gloria, Credo, Sanctus,* and *Agnus Dei*), so that the congregation would be able to sing these important songs. The chant settings sung by the choirs were, of course, not available for the people. Today we have prose canticles of these liturgical songs which include English texts and singable music for the congregation. The exception here is the creeds. We generally speak them instead of using the metrical versions of *We All Believe in One True God.*

Occasionally, however, it is an interesting and welcome change to sing the creeds.

A list of the alternate versions of the canticles of *Christian Worship* follows (Suggestions for use are found at the end of each of these hymns):

Hymns of the Liturgy in Christian Worship

Canticles	*Hymn Version*
Lord, Have Mercy	*Kyrie, God Father in Heaven Above* (CW 266)
Glory Be to God	*All Glory Be to God on High* (CW 263) *All Glory Be to God Alone* (CW 262) *Glory Be to God in Heaven* (CW 264)
Nicene Creed	*We All Believe in One True God* (CW 271)
Apostles' Creed	*We All Believe in One True God* (CW 270
Holy, Holy, Holy	*Isaiah, Mighty Seer in Days of Old* (CW 267)
O Christ, Lamb of God	*Lamb of God, Pure and Holy* (CW 268)
Song of Simeon	*In Peace and Joy I Now Depart* (CW 269)
Song of Zechariah	*Blest Be the God of Israel* (CW 275)
We Praise You, O God	*God, We Praise You* (CW 277) *Holy God, We Praise Your Name* (CW 278)
Song of Mary	*My Soul Now Magnifies the Lord* (CW 274)

155

A number of the liturgical hymns in *Christian Worship* are easy to sing. The Reformation-age hymns are more of a challenge, however. With careful preparation, assistance by a choir, school children, or a cantor, these hymns can be learned and should be sung for a special Reformation service, for a season of the church year, or for a hymn festival when Christians gather together to sing the great hymns of the church.

The Sermon in Worship

There are a number of things a sermon ought not to be, but there is one thing the sermon ought always to be: the Word of God, proclaiming the living voice of the gospel to God's redeemed people. The preacher is the appointed representative who illuminates the Scripture for the congregation's members and applies it to their contemporary situation. He is neither lecturer nor entertainer, but a link through whom the Holy Spirit brings law and gospel to bear upon the hearts and minds of the worshipers and enlivens their faith and life. With his sermon the pastor enhances the dialogue in the liturgy between God and the congregation. His presentation of the sermon, together with the lessons, stands alongside the Sacrament of Holy Communion as one of the twin peaks in the liturgy, one of the two vital parts of our worship.

Brief History

The roots of the sermon go back to Judaism, where commentaries followed the readings. The sermon was also part of the worship of the Christian community from the very beginning. Homilies on the lessons were part of virtually every gathering of believers. In the medieval period, however, the sermon was increasingly omitted, and in Luther's early days was eliminated most of the time. On those occasions when the sermon was preached, it consisted mostly of anecdotes on the lives of the saints or, as Luther put it, "discourses on blue ducks." One of the most important of Luther's reforms was the restoration of the sermon with true gospel preaching, exposition of biblical texts, and applications to the congregation.

In the period of Pietism, the sermon became detached from the liturgy as one liturgical part after the other was peeled away.

Gradually the sermon stood alone as the most important part of the worship. In the time of Rationalism, with the liturgy abolished, the sermon was elevated to the position of highest honor and importance. Unfortunately, the sermons generally consisted of ponderous philosophical or scientific lectures with no relevancy to spiritual life.

The Place of the Sermon in the Liturgy

Sometimes pastors as well as people in the pew characterize the sermon as something independent of the rest of the service. However, the sermon functions best when it serves as an integral part of the order of worship. Its historical function has been to serve as the pinnacle of the Lessons. It is ordinarily based on one of the three Lessons. All the parts of the Propers (Psalm, Verse, Hymn, and Prayer of the Day) are influenced by the thrust of the Gospel of the Day. If the sermon is based on the Gospel or even one of the other lessons of the day, the Propers and Sermon tend to inter-relate, undergird, and reinforce one another. In the *Service of the Word* and the *Service of Word and Sacrament* in *Christian Worship* the Creed is placed after the Sermon, thus moving the Sermon closer to the Lessons. (In *The Common Service* the Creed is placed after the Gospel and before the Sermon.) The Word section of the *Service of the Word* and the *Service of Word and Sacrament* have the following order:

First Lesson
    Psalm of the Day
Second Lesson
    Verse of the Day
Gospel of the Day
    (Possible placement of choral selection based on the Gospel of
    the Day or the season of the church year)
Hymn of the Day
Sermon
Creed

The Pluses of Lectionary Preaching

Most pastors preach on free texts occasionally, perhaps for a topical series on the Lord's Prayer or the Ten Commandments, in response to happenings in our world, on special needs of the

157

congregation, or simply according to personal desire. Some pastors also like to preach other series of pericopes from time to time, although the three-year lectionary and the revised one-year traditional series (printed in this manual and listed in *Christian Worship*) provide for considerable variety and richness in preaching.

There will be times when a free text is necessary. Ordinarily, however, both the pastor and the congregation will be better served if the sermons are based on one of the appointed lessons.

Using free texts instead of the appointed texts for the day creates or has the following disadvantages:

1. It tempts worship leaders to ignore careful liturgical planning.

2. It creates a dilemma. Shall the hymns, the Hymn of the Day, Psalm, Verse, Lessons, and choral music fit the sermon, or shall the sermon stand alone with the Propers proceeding in another direction? It might seem more desirable to change the Propers to fit the sermon, but this can be done only with considerable effort. What generally happens is that the hymns may fit the sermon, but little else in the service will fit the sermon.

3. It becomes more difficult to preach in harmony with the church year. It strips away the seasonal emphasis (e.g., eliminating the seven-week theme of the Sundays of Easter).

Preaching in harmony with the church year Propers, and based on the Gospel of the Day has the following advantages:

1. It saves the pastor time and anxiety spent in looking for or deciding on a text for his purpose.

2. It presents opportunity to comment on one or more of the Propers in the Sermon and use them to echo or reinforce thoughts in the text.

3. It provides for general uniformity in the theme or seasonal emphasis of the service, something which most worshipers appreciate. The service is most satisfying when the Sermon, hymns, Psalm, Verse, and choir selections fit together.

4. It tends to assure that the whole counsel of God will be preached over an interval of time. It is a wholesome discipline to preach on subjects which one might not otherwise choose.

158

5. It saves the embarrassment of preaching on a free text and then discovering it two weeks later as the appointed pericope.

6. It is the kind and thoughtful thing to do for organists and choir directors. It encourages efforts by musicians to plan liturgically.

Suggestions

There are no formal rubrics in *Christian Worship* governing the opening and closing of the Sermon. However, the following suggestions may be considered:

1. To minimize the number of times for standing or sitting in the service, the congregation may be taught not to stand for the reading of the text.

2. When the sermon text is read as one of the Lessons, it is not necessary to repeat it at the beginning of the Sermon. When reading the appropriate Lesson, merely announce that the reading will also serve as the sermon text.

3. In *The Common Service* the preacher may speak the Votum after the Sermon, since that serves as a pastoral blessing to the congregation at the conclusion of the Word Section of the liturgy. In the *Service of the Word* and the *Service of Word and Sacrament* the congregation will be invited to stand at the end of the sermon to speak the Creed, which ends the Word Section of those two orders of worship.

Stand! Be Seated! Amen!

In *Christian Worship* there is an effort to strive for some uniformity in the practice of standing and sitting at various parts of the services and to reduce the number of times the congregation stands or sits in rapid succession. In *Christian Marriage* and *Christian Funeral* there are no rubrics for standing or sitting, leaving the choice to be determined by local customs or desire. In the other orders of worship, in general, the assembly stands for the Confession of Sins (or kneels if there are kneelers), the prayers (the normal posture for praying in the Old Testament), the reading of the Gospel, the recitation of the Creeds, the singing of the major Canticles, and the receiving of the closing Blessing.

159

In this matter, Christian freedom does not prescribe one way as being the only way. Whether to stand or be seated may always remain a question that refuses to allow an easy or uniform answer.

Another concern that deserves attention is the use of the *Amen* at the end of a prayer. Should it be sung or spoken as a congregational response to a prayer? A one-word response, sung or spoken, creates the problem of possibly sounding disjointed or even showing disinterest on the part of the worshipers. In *Christian Funeral* there is one prayer early in the service where the minister speaks the *Amen* at the end of prayer. Nevertheless, throughout the rest of *Christian Worship* there is a determined effort to place the *Amen* on the lips of the worshipers to show that this is their prayer, too, even though the minister is the one who reads or speaks it.

There is no uniform practice in regard to spoken or sung *Amens*. Generally, if a prayer is chanted, the congregational *Amen* should be chanted or sung. If a prayer is spoken, the congregational response should be spoken. There are places, however, in the traditional worship orders of our church (i.e., the Prayer of the Day) where a spoken prayer is followed by a sung *Amen*. The committee chose to follow the long-standing practice in those places. A sung *Amen* remains.

In other places (i.e., *Morning Praise* and *Evening Prayer,* where there are a number of prescribed short prayers), the congregation will speak the *Amen* after the spoken prayer. It will be profitable for congregations to pay attention to the familiar christological or trinitarian ending of these prayers so that a firm and unified spoken *Amen* will become the natural way to respond.

Introducing Any Order of Worship

When introducing a service, it may be wise at first to speak more and sing less. The longer songs or canticles may be sung by the choir or by a cantor (soloist who leads others in singing) for a while. Or the congregation may speak the texts or omit some of the larger canticles. The point is to learn one canticle at a time. This may be done just before the beginning of the worship service. Four or five minutes of practice, with the choir or cantor singing a small section and the congregation repeating it (preferably twice), is one good way to proceed.

If there is no choir or cantor, the organ can take their place and play each part, alone first, and then with the congregation. While the congregation is learning a song, the organist should play the melody in octaves. The harmonic accompaniment may be added when the congregation is reasonably familiar with the song. What was taught on Sunday may be reviewed and rehearsed again during the devotional period of congregational meetings during the week.

The Essence of Planning for Worship

The introduction of any liturgy in a congregation is a task that requires special planning and preparation by the worship leaders. Simply putting a new liturgy in the hands of the people without comment, encouragement, or any kind of rehearsal will almost guarantee a negative reaction. Plan exactly what will happen each Sunday, especially in the first few weeks. Decide who will do what. Encourage one another and seek the Lord's help in the venture.

Ask Critical Questions

For the planning process, ask some *critical questions:*

- Why this hymn? Why this hymn at this place in the service? Is the Hymn of the Day being used? If so, what will make it special? Is a new hymn being introduced? If so, how? Will a cantor be used?

- Are the organ preludes performances, or do they match the service and the hymn themes? Does the organ music repeat and reinforce the themes spoken and sung in the service so that this music, too, becomes a tool of the Spirit that touches the spiritual hearts of the people? Has the organist studied the text of each hymn in order to be able to play its tune with great sensitivity to the text?

- Is the choir's role meaningful, or will it just be performance? Are the words of the choir's text printed out to be read by the worshiper? Are people of all ages encouraged to join one of the

161

choirs knowing that the music sung will be in step with the narrative and doctrines of the Holy Scriptures?

- Does the service shout out with the flavor of the season of the church year? What are the Lessons that will be read? Have they been studied and prepared for understandable reading and to avoid shoddiness? How do the arts (displays of art and images; symbols, logos, and graphics in service folders; paraments; banners; candles; floral arrangements) enhance the theme of the day or season?

- Which Psalm will be used? How? Will it be sung?

- Does the Sermon flow from or relate to one of the Sunday's three Lessons? Does it present the Christ as the "main thing," the *Christus pro nobis* (Christ for us), the Christ the Victor theme of Christianity and the meaning of baptismal faith and life? How does it apply to the lives of those who have come to worship?

- Which prayers and special prayers will be used? Are the prayers "praying," or are they overfilled with dogmatical theses? How will the congregation be involved in the prayers? Is there an allowance for meaningful silence so that worshipers may dwell on the profound mystery of God's presence, his righteousness, his redeeming love, and the needs of their neighbors on earth?

- How will the actions of the worship leaders reflect the theme of the service and the joy of the resurrection of Christ? Will there be a joyful spirit in the celebration of the Sacrament where the Lord comes to forgive, to make people spiritually whole, to unite them to himself?

- How will the stranger be genuinely welcomed before the service, in the service folder, and in verbal announcements? How will the service encourage God's holy people in their sometimes difficult struggles in life? Is the peace and the missionary character of the Blessing and dismissal recognized so that the people will go forth in song, in love, in joy, and in the Word?

Know that Doxology Must Continue

All of the above and many more, are elements that should be considered when planning a service. These critical questions ought to indicate how important it should be for worship leaders to be prepared for the hour of worship. They should indicate that worship leaders and musicians ought to be in Bible study and theology together, to know the parts of an order of worship and what they mean, to cultivate their spiritual and cultural heritage, and to work in unison toward educating the young in the joy and meaning of worship as a witness to the beating heart of Christianity and the steady cadence of God's marching orders to his Church.

Worship leaders will study together and communicate with each other as they strive to lead God's saints to look longingly to God and say, "We will worship!" They will move ever more boldly forward in the crisp confidence that "Christ's love compels us, because we are convinced that one died for all, and therefore all died. And he died for all, that those who live should no longer live for themselves but for him who died for them and was raised again" (2 Corinthians 5:14,15).

They will be God's servants who pass through the gates, who prepare the way for the people, who build up the highway, who remove the stones, who raise a banner for the nations, and who "Say to the daughter of Zion, 'See, your Savior comes! See, his reward is with him, and his recompense accompanies him.' They will be called the Holy People, the Redeemed of the LORD . . ." (Isaiah 62:11,12).

They will know that DOXOLOGY MUST CONTINUE in worship, in all levels of Christian education for service to the Lord and his people, in outreach work, in home and world mission expansion, until the "I am coming soon!" of Jesus Christ stands fulfilled.

In all planning, participation, and performance of plans, Christ is to be glorified. Worship is the center of life. It opens the door for God's mighty deeds of salvation in Christ to be heard. The Christ who saves also loves to be praised and thanked. He deserves quality and excellence. Love him with all your heart, soul, strength, and mind (Luke 10:27). That is reason enough for detailed planning of the service.

A pastor should arrive early to prepare spiritually, to make certain that everything (paraments, vestments, banners, hymn numbers, and other items essential to orderly worship) is ready for the service, and to think through the words and meaning of each part of the service. It is a time to focus, to stand back and view the service from a distance, and to fine tune so that there are no awkward moments in the service. God expects his best. So do the hungry souls who have come to hear God's message of the cross of Christ through him.

When the time for worship has arrived, there ought to be concentration on the spirit and flow of the service. If unified planning preceded the service, that will be evident to the discerning worshiper as the service unfolds. The order of worship will not draw attention to itself but to him for whom it has been prepared. To the stranger and the guest it will also be a living and inviting witness of the identity of the true God and his people gathered around the Word and sacraments.

CHAPTER 11:

Rationale and Explanation of Each of the Orders

Holy Baptism

Background

Within the past fifty years, we have normally baptized both infants and adults in church as part of the Sunday worship. In earlier years, however, baptisms were often performed at the home of the parents or in a private service or in a separate building called the baptistery. The orders of baptism inherited from our church fathers bear witness to those earlier practices: the orders included all liturgical forms deemed essential for a complete, self-sufficient service.

When these orders were used in corporate worship, repetition of liturgical forms was bound to occur, and placement of baptisms within the regular Sunday liturgy was bound to vary. Even newly developed orders of baptism failed to resolve all of these matters satisfactorily. The order of *Holy Baptism* in *Christian Worship* was designed to join the baptism with the regular order of service in a manner that would achieve a satisfactory integration of the baptism with the liturgies of corporate worship.

Today's custom of including baptism in our services of public worship helps edify the people of God. It reminds Christians of the manner in which they too were rescued from the kingdom of Satan and enrolled into the kingdom of Christ. It also informs the assembled worshipers that the one baptized has become a member of the body of Christ and the congregation and, therefore, a member to be prayed for, to be cherished, and to be encouraged.

Not only does God receive as his own the person being baptized, but he continues to assure all believers that they too have been clothed with Christ by baptism. Thus baptism, together with confession and absolution, is also a sacrament of preservation. Not only once, but throughout life, it works forgiveness of sins, delivers from death and the devil, and gives eternal salvation to all who believe, as the Word of God declares.

This means that whenever we are sorry for our sins and ask the heavenly Father to forgive us, we are returning to our baptism and making use of it. We are resting our confidence in the security of our baptism, which neither Satan nor sin can tear away from us. As Luther writes in the Large Catechism: "If you live in repentance, therefore, you are walking in Baptism, which not only announces this new life but also produces, begins, and promotes it. In Baptism we are given the grace, Spirit, and power to suppress the old sinful nature so that the new may come forth and grow strong. Therefore Baptism remains forever."[1]

Placement of Baptism

The order of *Holy Baptism* in *Christian Worship* has been designed to serve the Christian church in all the ways just described. It is placed at the beginning of worship in *The Common Service,* the *Service of Word and Sacrament,* and the *Service of the Word* because it replaces the regular Confession of Sins and because in and through it the baptized is received into Christ's Church.

Confession of Sins

In the baptism liturgy, the Confession of Sins at the beginning accentuates, in the words of both minister and congregation, the continuing benefit of baptism throughout Christian life. The paragraph from Luther's Small Catechism will be familiar to all who have committed this text to memory from childhood. The confession spoken by the congregation is identical to that in the communion services. The minister's absolution, also identical to that in the communion services, seals to hearers the precious and permanent blessings of their baptism.

---

[1] *Large Catechism,* 4:75-77.

Sacrament of Baptism

In the rite of baptism which follows, everything essential for Christian baptism of children or adults is present. The full texts of the Apostles' Creed and Lord's Prayer are not included because they appear elsewhere in this integrated service. When making the sign of the cross, a single motion of the hand vertically from forehead to breast and horizontally from shoulder to shoulder seems most natural. The water is applied so that it may be seen by as many as possible. At the conclusion of the baptism the minister states what God has done through this baptism and bestows God's blessing and peace on the one baptized.

Exhortation and Prayer

The Exhortation is addressed to the entire worshiping congregation. The one baptized is now a member of the holy Christian Church. Church members contemplate the cleansing power of God, rejoice at this new life in baptism, and, together with parents and sponsors, are reminded of their responsibility to nurture the tender faith of this baptized child of God until death. If parents and sponsors stand at the font, the minister's words are easily revised as being spoken directly to them in this manner: ". . . Christian love urges all of us, especially you the parents and sponsors, to assist. . . ."

A prayer ends the Exhortation and the baptism. In this prayer (as well as in baptismal hymns) the minister should note that *he*/*him* are written in italics as a reminder to substitute *she*/*her* for a girl and *they*/*them* for multiple baptisms.

At the end of the baptism, the minister will have to indicate clearly to the congregation where the liturgical service continues. For this purpose, an appropriate rubric for direction in each of the three services is included after the prayer on page 14 of *Christian Worship*.

Emergency Baptism

There is a brief form for Emergency Baptism on the bottom of page 14 in the hymnal. All who are present for baptisms at worship will readily see it. Those who teach baptism and its application should also refer to it.

The Common Service

Background

The note at the beginning of *The Common Service* (CW p. 15) in *Christian Worship* reads: "'The Common Service' is a version of the historic liturgy of the Christian Church. It became the service commonly used by English-speaking Lutherans in America and appeared as 'The Order of Holy Communion' in The Lutheran Hymnal. The present version may be used either with or without the Sacrament."

We need to remain in touch with this liturgy that most strongly emphasizes our roots and connection with Christian history and worship practices. This is a strong service, filled with biblical teaching, praise, and prayer. Possible substitutions need to be weighed and carefully compared with it, not only on the basis of music but as to their Christ-centered nature, their scriptural content, and their integration with the traditional church year.

Look at The Common Service

The minutes before the start of the service warrant attention to details. Preservice instrumental music (organ, piano, duets, brass, strings) should be well planned and take into account and relate to the season of the church year and the theme of the day. Its purpose is to prepare the worshiper for what's coming, through chorale preludes (based on hymn tunes) and free preludes (expressing the mood of the service: i.e., joy, comfort, confession of sins, trust). Whenever possible, include in the service folder the titles of the preservice music. The musical references together with a special paragraph on the Sunday's relationship to the church year can help the worshiper become more focused toward active participation in the service.

Something similar can be said for the minister's preservice greeting, welcome to members and guests, and introduction to the forthcoming hour of worship. Let it serve as a help in establishing the understanding, spirit, and tone of the particular Sunday of the church year. Let it express joy and gladness that people have gathered to worship under the cross of Christ.

Hymn

The opening hymn may be one of invocation or of praise to the triune God. It's purpose is to knit together and bring to a focus the thoughts of God's saints who have come from various places and backgrounds to worship the Lord. This hymn is not just an attention-getter for a typical assembly of people, like the "coming attractions" segment in movies. This is the entrance hymn of the "holy nation, the royal priesthood" of the Lord Jesus. It is a sign, too, that God has entered the place where the faithful have gathered in his name. The church is his temple, humble though it may be, dedicated to his glory. The worshipers enter it with a sense of awe at the presence of God, who has found his way into human hearts. God who loves to be worshiped is present, and the singers love to worship him. Thus, the hymn serves as an *Introit,* an entry to the hour of worship, a clarion call to keynote the agenda and create a focus for an important meeting with God.

In the Name of . . .

The trinitarian invocation expressly reminds the worshipers that the God they will meet here is the true God: Father, Son, and Holy Spirit, who is to be worshiped here and now. The invocation also warmly calls to mind the words through which believers have been baptized into Christ and made members of his Church. The faithful respond, "Amen!" "Yes, God is here to bless. Yes, we have arrived to worship him. Yes, it is good to be here."

Confession of Sins

God's people live in daily repentance. Now, when they gather in the presence of God, the minister invites them together to draw near, to confess their inherited and actual sins, and to ask God to grant them forgiveness because of Jesus' perfect life and innocent death. Standing or kneeling, each person joins with every other person and says, "I confess. . . ."

In *The Common Service,* the people conclude their confession of sins by singing the threefold plea to the triune God: "Lord . . . , Christ . . . , Lord, have mercy on us." In the *Service of Word and Sacrament,* on the other hand, the *Kyrie* is used as a congre-

169

gational prayer for the needs of all people. Both uses of the *Kyrie* have historical precedence.

Absolution

In the absolution the pastor announces forgiveness to the penitent congregation. He appeals to the atoning sacrifice of Jesus Christ as the basis for forgiveness.

The pastor has the right to forgive sins on the authority of the risen Savior who gave the ministry of the keys to the disciples and the New Testament church. The congregation has called the pastor to carry out the ministry of the keys publicly in its midst.

Members of the congregation listen to the announcement of the good news of God's forgiveness and respond affirmatively with a sung *Amen*. They affirm, thereby, that their confessed and forgiven sins on earth are also pardoned before God in heaven.

Prayer and Praise

The announcement of Jesus' forgiveness establishes peace in the heart. Peace-filled hearts long to praise the God who forgives. The minister, therefore, leads the congregation into a song of praise with the words, "In the peace of forgiveness, let us praise the Lord."

Glory Be to God (Gloria in Excelsis)

The congregation's song in response reflects the joy of the angels at the birth of the Savior. It gives the triune God glory, praise, and thanks. It uses a form of the *Kyrie* in intercession for others in need of God's mercy in Christ. Luther said that this ancient song "did not grow, nor was it made, but it came from heaven."

Glory Be to God may be sung on Sundays and festivals. It should be used especially on Christmas Day and the Sundays through the Epiphany season. *Christian Worship* includes metrical versions of this hymn (*All Glory Be to God Alone* and *All Glory Be to God on High*), which may also be used. During the Easter season, the hymn, *This Is the Feast of Victory,* may serve as a substitute. (Please refer to pp. 153-156 in this section of the manual for more information on the use of canticles and their alternates.)

170

Prayer of the Day

The minister extends his hands toward the members of the congregation when he greets them with words of blessing: "The Lord be with you." The congregation returns the blessing: "And also with you," declaring its unity with the minister as they conclude the initial part of worship, move through the service together, and prepare to pray.

After inviting the congregation to prayer, "Let us pray," the minister turns toward the altar and pauses a few moments so that there is real concentration on the words of the important prayer that follows. This short prayer is the first part of the liturgy that varies (Proper) from Sunday to Sunday. It is a concisely-worded request for a single blessing. The Prayers of the Day are printed in Section Four of *Christian Worship: Manual.*

The Prayers of the Day end with a formula easily recognized by the congregation: ". . . through Jesus Christ, our Lord, who lives and reigns with you [the Father] and the Holy Spirit, one God, now and forever." Do not read these words too quickly or without emphasis. It is good, for instance, to highlight with an inflection or slight pause the words "who lives." These words refer to the resurrection of Christ, the reason for our worship and our prayers. The point is not that Christ lives with the Holy Spirit. The point is that he LIVES!

The congregation responds to the prayer with a sung *Amen.* This Hebrew word shows that the congregation is involved with the prayer, has taken ownership of it, and proclaims, "This is our prayer, too."

The Word

What follows is not the uncertain word of untrustworthy human beings. It is the Word of God, centered in Christ, that has also gathered people to Christ. This is the Word of God that people have come to hear, a high point in the worship service. This section establishes a pattern which, except for the placement of the Creed, is followed also in the *Service of the Word* and the *Service of Word and Sacrament:*

First Lesson
Psalm of the Day

4

Second Lesson
Verse of the Day
Gospel
Gospel Acclamation
Creed
Hymn of the Day
Sermon

First Lesson

In the three-year lectionary series of Lessons (see Section Four for listings), the First Lesson is normally a reading from the Old Testament (except in the Sundays of Easter when the First Lessons are from the Book of Acts). The minister announces the reading by saying, e.g., "This is the first Sunday in Advent. The First Lesson is from the 63rd and 64th chapters of Isaiah." Information on the specific verse numbers can be placed in the worship folder.

It is best not to give long, oral explanations of each of the readings. These often become complicated and add to the length of the service. It is better to print introductions and explanations in the service folder, to make reference to the readings where possible in the Sermon, or to discuss them in the Bible class. If a verbal introduction is used, it should be short and concise, one that leads quickly into the reading.

At the end of the First and Second Lessons the minister says very simply, "This is the Word of the Lord." This sentence is more preferable than "Here ends the reading." The congregation knows that the reading has come to an end. What the congregation must remember is that this is the Word of the Lord.

Psalm of the Day

A listing of the proper Psalms of the Day is printed in Section Four of this book. That list refers only to the psalm portions (six or seven selected verses) that have been prepared for use in *Christian Worship*. The Psalm of the Day serves as a response to the First Lesson. It will normally be sung. (Please review additional information on the singing of the Psalms in *Christian Worship,* p. 63, and in this manual on pp. 149-151, Section Two).

172

The pattern for singing the psalms is to have the organist or choir introduce the refrain. The congregation then joins to sing it once at the beginning of the Psalm and whenever "Refrain" is printed in the selected psalm verses. The pastor, the cantor, or the choir may chant the verses of the Psalm. The congregation may join the minister, cantor, or choir and sing the chant line of the *Glory Be to the Father* at the end of the Psalm. The *Glory Be to the Father* unites the Old Testament with the New Testament and with the fulfillment in the coming of Jesus Christ.

At times the congregation and pastor may read the Psalm, alternating by verses or by half verses. That method enlists participatory worship. Congregations will find, however, that a psalm that is sung will lend a special flavor of worship in the service. Historically, reflecting the Old Testament custom, the Psalms were sung in the church.

Second Lesson

The Second Lesson is one from the New Testament letters of Paul or another apostle, or from the Revelation to St. John. It stresses Christian faith and Christian living as a response to the Gospel of Jesus Christ. At the end of the reading the minister looks up and says, "This is the Word of the Lord."

Verse of the Day

Refer to chapter 10 (pp. 151, 152) of this section for definitive information about the Verse of the Day, which mirrors the day or season of the church year and forms a bridge between the Second Lesson and the Gospel. By preparing to sing the Verse, as well as the Psalm, the choir has a weekly opportunity to be involved in the service. If, in the absence of a choir, the minister speaks the Verse, the congregation sings the threefold Alleluia (CW p.18), except in Lent when the Alleluia may be omitted.

Gospel

The congregation stands for the reading of the Gospel. In the past soldiers put down their weapons and kings removed their crowns when the Gospel was read. Christ—his life, his words of law and gospel, his suffering, his death, his resurrection, his ascension, his assignment to his Church, his promise to return—is the center of the Gospel. The faithful have waited for this moment, this reading. They stand in reverence.

The minister reads the holy Gospel carefully, joyfully. When finished, he pauses, looks to the congregation, and says, "This is the Gospel of the Lord." The congregation, refreshed spiritually by the Gospel, responds in praise and joyful acclamation, "Praise be to you, O Christ!"

Creed

After listening to the reading of the Gospel, the congregation remains standing and confesses its faith in the triune God. In services without the Sacrament, the more personal confession, the Apostles' Creed, is used. In services with Holy Communion, the Nicene Creed is the standard. The Nicene Creed is a corporate confession of the church in defense of the pure teachings of the Scriptures on the triune God, with special emphasis given to the personhood of Jesus Christ: "God from God, Light from Light, true God from true God." In the words of the Creed, the gathered church declares to the world, "We believe. . . ."

Hymn of the Day

Lists of the Hymns of the Day are prepared and printed in Section Four so that worship planners will use them and not neglect the truly great hymns of the church. This hymn can be given special treatment with choir and congregation or men and women or the right and left sides of the assembly singing in alternation. Occasionally the Hymn of the Day may receive a more elaborate concertato treatment (a festive setting of the hymn involving choir, congregation, and instruments). An accomplished organist may prepare special settings for accompaniment of the hymn. Let there be a joyous singing of this prominent hymn of the church.

Sermon

Preaching based on the lectionary, with its balanced diet of law and gospel and the primary doctrines of Christianity, is to be encouraged. The sermon will then normally be based on the text of one of the readings of the day, preferably the Gospel. If it is not on the Gospel, it will nevertheless be influenced by the emphasis of the Gospel of the Day. All the parts of the Propers (Psalm and Verse of the Day, Hymn and Prayer of the Day) point to the key concept of the Gospel, and, therefore, all influence the message of the sermon. (Additional information on the Sermon in worship is found on pp. 156-159 and 186, 187 of this section.)

After the Sermon, the pastor may invite the congregation to stand as he speaks the words of the blessing (the Votum), "The peace of God, which transcends all understanding, will guard your hearts and your minds in Christ Jesus" (Philippians 4:7). The Votum serves well as a pastoral blessing at the end of the section on the Word.

Create in Me a Clean Heart, O God

Following the Sermon and the blessing, the congregation stands to sing this short canticle, which, in the words of the Psalmist (Psalm 51:10-12), prays for a clean heart and a renewed spirit in response to God's gift of grace. *Create in Me* looks back to the Lessons and the Sermon. But it especially looks ahead to the reception of the Lord's Supper and the strength to be received there for renewed Christian life.

Offering

As a response of faith, gifts of money are received and presented to the Lord. Believers know that God's work must be done. God's Word of salvation, the Word just heard in worship, must be proclaimed to the ends of the earth. Now is the time to bring an offering in the courts of the Lord!

During this time the believers think about the message for the day, its personal application to their lives, and the forward march of God's Church. The musical selections chosen for this part of the service should reflect the spirit of the message of the day.

Prayer of the Church

Following the Offering, the congregation stands for this prayer. Samples of Prayers of the Church with spoken congregational responses and places for silence and special intercessions are printed on pages 123-131 of *Christian Worship*. They may be used ex-

175

actly as printed. They may also serve as examples for those who wish to write their own prayers based on the message and needs of the week in the local congregation, the nation, and the church at large in the world. Such efforts require allowing adequate time for careful crafting. They must take into account the needs of all the people for whom the Scriptures invite us to pray.

Lord's Prayer

The Lord's Prayer follows, printed in two different translations so that congregations can choose which one they wish to use. Those who are accustomed to using *The Common Service* in *The Lutheran Hymnal* will note that the Lord's Prayer has been relocated from its spot after the Words of Institution to the end of the Prayer of the Church.

(When there is no Communion, the service continues with a hymn, short prayer, and the Blessing on page 25.)

The Sacrament

Preface and Holy, Holy, Holy (Sanctus)

When the Lord's Supper is celebrated, the service continues with the Preface. The words of dialogue between the minister and the congregation are the least changed liturgical text of the Christian church. They are known to have existed already by the year A.D. 200. They are to be spoken as joyous words that anticipate the forthcoming reception of the means of grace.

The Preface and seasonal sentences lead the congregation into the *Holy, Holy, Holy (Sanctus)*, the seraphim's song from Isaiah 6:3, the words of heavenly worship (Revelation 4:8), the awesome yet distant triumph song of the saints and angels standing in the presence of God. "Blessed is he who comes in the name of the Lord! . . . Hosanna in the highest" (Psalm 118:26; Mark 11:9,10), are the words of the *Sanctus* that bring the entire Preface to its mighty conclusion.

Words of Institution

Following historical custom (1 Corinthians 10:16), the minister directs attention to the earthly elements of bread and wine and, with the Lord's words of institution, consecrates or sets them aside for sacred use in the Sacrament. The words are not a magic formula that brings about a change in the elements. The presence of Jesus' body and blood comes with the Sacrament through the gracious working of the Lord, whose promise is connected with these words.

Holy Communion is the New Covenant in his blood. It centers in Jesus' sacrifice and the forgiveness that sacrifice procured. In the Sacrament he offers and imparts to believers all the blessings of his redemptive activity.

The Peace

After the Words of Institution the minister turns to the people and extends to them the comforting words, "The peace of the Lord be with you always." In the peace of Christ's rest, earthly frustration, envy, hatred, and discontent are put aside. The people respond with a sung *Amen,* the word of faith.

O Christ, Lamb of God (Agnus Dei)

In this ancient song of the church, believers think of their Old Testament counterparts and their Passover celebration. They come to Christ as spiritual beggars. Seeing their own emptiness, they seek fullness and satisfaction only in the *Christ, the Lamb of God* who takes away the sin of the world. With this canticle (based on John 1:29, Isaiah 53:7, and Revelation 5:6ff.) the poor in spirit plead for Jesus' mercy and peace. A slower musical pace helps to portray the heartfelt meaning of these words.

Distribution

All is in readiness. The communicants step forward to receive the Lord Jesus and his blessings. The minister and those who assist him speak those blessings as they distribute the bread and wine.

In deciding what to say during the distribution, we do well to follow the advice of the paragraph in *The Shepherd under Christ* (NPH, 1974, p. 92): "The positive assertion, 'Take, eat, this is the true body, etc.,' expresses the conviction of the Lutheran faith in the real presence. Any wording which could raise doubt about this is unacceptable. After the union of the Lutheran and Reformed churches in Germany in the last century, the wording was changed to read, 'Take and eat, Christ says, This is my body, etc.' The intent clearly was to allow each communicant to interpret the words to his liking. The words spoken during the distribution must, however, be an unambiguous confession."[2]

It is best, therefore, to establish a definite pattern in what is to be said. At this crucial point, only these words should be spoken. Let the communicant concentrate solely on Christ and the gift of his body and blood in the Sacrament. Included below are three sets of possible standard sentences:

Set #1

Take, eat; this is the true body of our Lord and Savior Jesus Christ, given into death for your sins.

Take, drink; this is the true blood of our Lord and Savior Jesus Christ, poured out for you for the forgiveness of your sins.

Set #2

Take, eat; this is the true body of Christ, given for you.

Take, drink; this is the true blood of Christ, poured out for you.

Set #3

(spoken to each communicant)

The body of Christ, given for you.

The blood of Christ, poured out for you.

The bread may be placed either on the communicant's tongue or in his or her hand.

The cup, too, whether the common or individual cup, may be served to the individual by the officiant or taken by the communicant to drink.

During the Distribution, it is good for the congregation to have opportunity to sing hymns relating to the church year or to Holy Communion.

Thanksgiving

After the Sacrament the people sing the canticle *Song of Simeon;* its metrical version, *In Peace and Joy I Now Depart* (CW

---

[2] Armin W. Schuetze and Irwin J. Habeck, *The Shepherd under Christ* (Northwestern Publishing House: 1974), p. 92.

269); or another hymn of thanksgiving. The responsive use of the Psalm verse, "O give thanks to the Lord, for he is good. And his mercy endures forever," expresses heartfelt thanks to God for the gift just received in the Sacrament.

Prayer and Blessing

There is a choice of two post-Communion prayers followed by the sung *Amen*. The pastor turns to the holy people of God and extends to them the favor of the Lord in the words of the Aaronic Blessing. This draws the service to a close. Nothing more is necessary. Some congregations demand a hymn. Let it be short or just a stanza.

Announcements

If there are postservice announcements, let them be few, short, enthusiastic, well-prepared, encouraging, and not distracting. Let them display the joy of the Christian life of service. There are other ways to publicize events. The people, guests included, have come to be blessed and encouraged. Let them depart in the afterglow of God's favor. Give them opportunities to display their Christian concern and love for each other, to walk and speak in tune with the glorious melody of the eternal music of God.

Service of Word and Sacrament

Background and Use

The *Service of Word and Sacrament* (CW pp. 26-37) is not a revision of any previous liturgy. The text is new, but based on an ancient and firm foundation. It can be described as an updated version that builds on the heritage of the ancient rite of the Western Church. It includes the historic liturgy's basic progression of the ordinary and the proper, espouses regular use of the Word and sacraments, emphasizes the church year and its festivals, permits opportunities for necessary variety, provides for the full use of liturgical arts and colors, and moves forward with the concept of interaction between Christ and his people. Its primary focus is "Christus pro nobis," the Christ who is for us. Therefore, it exudes a joyous spirit of thanksgiving as it leads believers to the benefits of God's Word and sacrament and then dismisses them in

179

the peace of Christ to serve the Lord with gladness and to tell everyone what he has done.

The *Service of Word and Sacrament* may be used as a congregation's normal service of Holy Communion or as an alternate to *The Common Service* whenever Holy Communion is celebrated. Whereas *The Common Service* allows for a conclusion without communion, the *Service of Word and Sacrament* is not intended for use when there is no celebration of the Sacrament. This is not to say that the main service of the church is incomplete without the Sacrament. But it does demonstrate an awareness that much in both history and theology favors an every Sunday opportunity for both Word and sacrament.

Preservice

The subject of preservice music is discussed on page 204 of this section and also in Section Three of this manual. It should mirror the theme and mood of the season and the day. Let it lead the worshiper toward the thoughts of the day's worship. If a new hymn is to be used in the service, let its tune be heard before the start of the service when people wait, listen, and prepare.

Word of Welcome

The custom of an informal preservice pastoral greeting to the congregation and its guests and visitors can be beneficial if it is not too long, complex, or too folksy. The welcome may express joy that Christ's resurrection makes Christian worship both possible and essential, and appreciation that God's holy people have gathered as believers under the cross of Christ to pray, praise, and learn. Its objective is to set the tone and make the worshipers glad that they have come. It will include a brief word about the theme of the day's service and its place in the church year, what liturgical resources will be used and where they can be found, and any unusual events or features of the service. The words of welcome may be spoken from the lectern, another place beside the altar, or directly in front of the seats in small gatherings. The welcome should be spoken sincerely and precisely so that it serves as a help to those who come to worship.

Hymn and Greeting

The entrance hymn draws the thoughts of busy minds from their secular concerns and directs them to the transcendent majesty of the triune God. It serves as a unifier and a reminder of the special meaning of being in the presence of God. "Christ is here!" it announces boldly. This hymn may be joyful, somber, or meditative, matching the theme and message of the season of the church year, or calling on the Holy Spirit to bless this hour of worship and all who are a part of it. At times, to add variety and to emphasize the majestic presence of God, the congregation may stand while singing this hymn or its final stanza.

After the hymn the congregation stands (or kneels if there are kneelers), and the minister begins the service (patterned after the Western Rite) with the apostolic greeting or blessing of the triune God. The congregation returns the blessing ("And also with you"), and thereby expresses its unity with the minister in recognition of their mutual need for God's blessings at the beginning of corporate worship.

Confession of Sins and Absolution

The text of the confession and absolution (CW p. 26) is the same as that in the Common Service. The confession emphasizes the themes of original and actual sins and the overriding need for the Lord's mercy. The absolution stresses the substitutionary atonement of Jesus Christ for the sins of the world and utilizes God's gift of the ministry of the keys to his Church. The congregation verbalizes its faith and assents to this good news of the absolution by saying Amen.

Lord, Have Mercy

The *Lord, Have Mercy (Kyrie)* begins this section. Historically, the *Kyrie* has been used in the two different ways that are evident in the liturgies of *Christian Worship*. In *The Common Service,* it is inserted to be used penitentially and to be sung by the congregation as an integral part of the Confession of Sins. Here, in the *Service of Word and Sacrament,* it follows the pattern most commonly used for the *Kyrie* in the centuries of Christian worship. It serves as an organized form of intercession to God for the needs and conditions of all people. Each petition is followed by a congregational response. In this type of prayer, the words "Lord, have mercy" are an acclamation that may mean "Lord, help us" or "Lord, hear our prayer." These sung responses are easily learned and should not pose difficulties for congregations.

When there is a baptism, the Greeting, the Confession of Sins, and the *Lord, Have Mercy* are omitted and replaced by the rite for Holy Baptism (CW p. 12), which includes the Confession of Sins.

O Lord, Our Lord

After the Absolution and the *Lord, Have Mercy,* the minister faces the congregation and says, "The works of the Lord are great and glorious; his name is worthy of praise." These words lead into the canticle, which gleams as a vibrant song of praise and provides an outlet of thanksgiving to God for all he has accomplished for us through Christ: "O Lord, our Lord, how glorious is your name in all the earth."

This canticle with its text and music is the most challenging of the songs in this service. It should be introduced with the help of a choir or cantor (soloist) and with a sufficient amount of rehearsal time. After hearing the tune a few times and working with it for several weeks, the congregation will discover that it is strong, memorable, and one that people will not tire of singing.

The rubric states that another hymn of praise may be sung in place of *O Lord, Our Lord.* Alternates might be the *Glory Be to God* (CW p. 16, an elaboration of the song of the angels) during the Christmas season, *Oh Taste and See* (CW p. 39), *This Is the Feast of Victory* (CW 265) during the Easter season, or a significant hymn that accentuates the particular season of the church year. Worship leaders should also refer to the Hymns of the Liturgy section (CW 262-278 and pp. 155, 156 of this section) for alternates to the songs and canticles of this and other orders of worship.

Prayer of the Day

After the canticle, the minister looks to the congregation and says, "Let us pray." It is good to wait a few seconds thereafter so that people can collect their thoughts to concentrate on these prayers, which say so much in one short sentence. The Prayers of the Day are printed in Section Four of this manual. All of them are printed with the full trinitarian ending of the New Testament church, "Through your Son, Jesus Christ our Lord, who lives and reigns with you and the Holy Spirit, one God, now and forever." The congregation shows its ownership of the prayer with the sung *Amen.*

God's Witness through the Word

God has not deserted his people. He gives witness to his presence through his Word. He speaks through the powerful word of his law, sharper than any two-edged sword, and cuts through the shells of sin-scarred people. He also speaks through the gospel of Jesus Christ, prophesied in the Old Testament, fulfilled in the coming and the work of Christ as described in the New Testament, and proclaimed here for the life of the world. "Come to me . . . and I will give you rest" (Matthew 11:28). "I am the resurrection and the life. . . . Whoever lives and believes in me will never die" (John 11:25,26). Believers have come as spiritual beggars to hear these words and to apply them to life. This is the time for hearing, meditating, reflecting, strengthening; for forgiveness, instruction, and response.

This section, except for the placement of the Creed, is similar to its counterparts in *The Common Service* and the *Service of the Word:* First Lesson (usually from the Old Testament), Psalm of the Day (as a response), Second Lesson (usually from the Epistles in the New Testament), Verse of the Day (sung by the choir), Gospel, Gospel Acclamation (sung by the congregation), Hymn of the Day, Sermon, and Creed. (A three-year and a one-year series of readings, psalms, and verses are printed in Section Four of this manual.)

A lectionary listing of lessons is one of the hallmarks of the Lutheran church. It provides the church with balance, discipline, direction, and freshness. It gives worship leaders, teachers, and congregation members a tool for group or personal devotions and permits them to look ahead and prepare their thoughts for active participation in the worship service. (Please refer to Section Four of this manual for details on the lectionary.)

Announcing and Concluding the Lessons

The text of the minister's announcement of the Lessons is not given in *Christian Worship*. The announcement should be short since the verse indicators of the lessons (and explanations) will normally be printed in the service folder. This is an example of an announcement of a lesson: "Today is the first Sunday in Advent. The First Lesson is from the 63rd chapter of Isaiah." At the end of the First and Second Lessons the minister says, "This is the Word of the Lord." At the end of the reading of the Gospel the minister says, "This is the Gospel of the Lord."

Explanations

There are many opinions relative to spoken introductions or explanations of the Lessons. They are often a part of the weekly worship folder. In many churches the explanations are repeated verbally from the lectern. Lengthy introductions and explanations tend to serve as the kind of verbiage that can interrupt the flow of the liturgy and add to the length of the service. If there are to be introductions, let them be precise and brief. Fuller explanations can find their way into the service folder, the sermon, or the Bible class.

Read the Word

The reading of the Lessons is a highlight of the service. Those charged with the responsibility of reading should not take it lightly. Public reading is an art that needs to be rehearsed so that proper emphases, inflections, pronunciations, and pauses will be evident. The power is in the Word, of course. The reader, however, will do his best to avoid shoddiness and to keep anything from coming between the listener and the Word. The spiritually hungry have come to be fed and nurtured, and to drink from the water of life. The listeners, knowing that "Faith comes from hearing," sit quietly and wait to be blessed in the hearing of the Word. Their attention is aroused. The readings are for them. Lesson readers must be prepared.

Sing the Psalms

Psalms, Index to the Psalms, and a section on singing the Psalms are located on pages 62-122 of *Christian Worship*. A listing of the Psalms of the Day is printed in Section Three of this manual. In recent years there has been a resurging interest in the singing of the Psalms. In earlier years, *they were always sung.*

Christian Worship includes a section of selected psalm verses (usually six or seven verses from each of the printed psalms) with chanting tones for the minister, a cantor (soloist), or a choir of any size, and with musical refrains that will delight the ears of the singing congregation. Pastors, cantors, small or large choirs, and congregations are urged to sing the Psalms. Of course, the Psalms can also be read by the minister alone or responsively with the congregation. But much is added to the tone and spirit of worship when they are sung. (Instructions on different ways of performing psalmody are found on pp. 149-151 of this section of the manual.)

Sing the Verse

After the reading of the Second Lesson the minister says, "This is the word of the Lord." The choir or cantor is ready to sing the Verse of the Day. (Many choral arrangements are available.) The Verse of the Day is in reality a Gospel verse that in many cases serves as a prelude to the reading of the Gospel, as a reflector of the season of the church year, or as a bridge between the Second Lesson and the Gospel. If one of the choirs does not sing the Verse of the Day, the congregation sings the general verse (p. 30), which leads into the Christ-centered and faith-building reading of the Gospel.

Because Alleluias are found at the beginning and end of the general verse, that verse may be omitted during Lent. Omission of the Alleluias during Lent is a historical Lutheran practice to emphasize the penitential nature of this season and the agony Christ endured in his suffering and dying.

The Gospel

The congregation stands for the reading of the Gospel of the Lord. The Gospel should always be read at this point, even if it serves as the sermon text. Believers have come for this moment. Here Christ speaks in sharp rebuke of human sin and goes by way of perfect life, innocent death, and resurrection grave to procure

185

salvation for the world. Here Christ lives, reorders Christian lives, and promises to return. Here is the empty cross, the resurrection grave, the power of God that brings salvation, the old news that is always new and good and refreshing. The minister will remember that and read the Gospel with the amazement of one who has heard it for the first time and with the thrill of one eager to share it with others. When finished he will look up and say, "This is the Gospel of the Lord!"

Gospel Acclamation

After hearing the Gospel, the congregation responds with the song of Gospel Acclamation, "Praise be to you, O Christ!" The Spirit has touched hearts through the Gospel. The response is a short burst of praise to Christ.

Hymn of the Day

The congregation is seated for this major hymn of the service, usually the Hymn of the Day, one that is representative of the best of hymnody in the Christian church. Listings of the Hymn of the Day can be found in Section Four of this manual. Suggestions relative to the performance of this hymn are given in Section Three.

This hymn can be chosen well in advance of the Sunday. Special music, even concertatos, might be provided. It can be embellished by choir and/or instruments, and by antiphonal singing of some of the stanzas. This hymn needs the special attention of all worship leaders.

Sermon

The Sermon will ordinarily be based on one of the Lessons for the Sunday or festival. (See comments on pp. 156-159 of this section.) The entire text need not be repeated if it was read previously. Repeating a short portion of it for emphasis, however, can be beneficial. To keep the congregation from standing and sitting unnecessarily, the minister may encourage members not to stand at the beginning of the Sermon.

In the Sermon the preacher will want to be at his best as he unfolds the meaning of the text for the minds, the hearts, and the lives of those who have come to hear and to be fed. He will not

186

sidestep the gospel. He will present it, not just talk about it. He will remember that some who listen are spiritual infants, who need the care of the vivid and refreshing words of the water of life. He will recall that those who have come with all the baggage of their lives are also the baptized and redeemed of the Lord, "Christ's holy people," whose daily sins need forgiveness, whose deep wounds need the healing power of the love of Christ, whose lives need to be redirected and refocused according to the will and purpose of God.

The Lord's cross and resurrection grave is the reason the preacher is in the pulpit. Christ's word, "Because I live, you also will live" (John 14:19), will be a part of each sermon as encouragement for the people of God walking through the difficult journey of life to paradise. The Sermon is not a lecture; it is a proclamation of the power and counsel of God.

The Sermon is a powerful tool for those who have been called to nurture and shepherd God's chosen generation. It should not be too long, for the Sermon is just one of the many parts of the *Service of Word and Sacrament,* which reveals God's Word of salvation and sends people on their journey and mission in life. Neither should it be too short, for Satan loves it when the message of God's complete redemption in Christ is not clearly spelled out, and people go home spiritually hungry.

As a blessing to God's people the pastor may speak the Votum. Then, from the pulpit he will lead the congregation in the recitation of the Creed, which summarizes and concludes the central message of God's Word.

Creed

The congregation stands for the confession of its faith in the words of the Nicene Creed, the final item in the section of the Word. The Creed is a summary and profession of the Christian faith. "We believe" is the striking reminder that this is a confession of the whole Christian Church on earth concerning the teachings of Scripture and especially about the person of Christ. False teachings relative to the God of our salvation will not prevail. Believers join their voices with one another and the whole Christian Church on earth to speak out God's truth. They declare confidently that Jesus is "God from God, Light from Light, true God from true God."

Offering

After hearing God's holy Word, the congregation is seated to gather its thankofferings. It places them on the Lord's altar to be used for his work in the community through the local congregation and in the world through the church at large. The organist or other instrumentalists may utilize music that reviews the Hymn of the Day, reinforces the message of the season of the church year, or serves as a prelude to the hymn that will follow. This is a planned lull in the service, a time for the believer to contemplate and to make a personal application of the message of the Lessons of the day.

Prayer of the Church and the Lord's Prayer

The prayer crafted for this service is to be read responsively. It includes a place for special intercessions where the prayers of the congregation are requested. And, it allows for a time of silence so that each individual will have opportunity to bring before the throne of God personal requests for himself or others. At first, the time for silence may seem somewhat awkward to those who are not accustomed to it. However, after a little experimentation, most congregations grow to appreciate the custom.

(Additional Prayers of the Church are printed on pages 123-131 of *Christian Worship*. For more detailed information on praying in the church, see pages 196, 197 in this section of the manual.)

At the conclusion of the Prayer of the Church the congregation joins in praying the Lord's Prayer. The traditional and contemporary versions are included so that the congregation has a choice.

The Sacrament

In this holy supper we receive Jesus' true body and blood for the forgiveness of sins and the strengthening of our faith. Here we celebrate the gift of his redemption, bear witness to the fellowship we share as confessors of the truth, and proclaim his death until he returns.

People flee to the Sacrament with their burdens to be united with Christ and to receive his forgiving gift. The risen and victorious Savior is there to forgive and to strengthen. Emphasize the great and joyous nature of this feast.

Preface

The Preface sets the tone. Speak the words of this ancient preparatory text with joy and a smile: "The Lord be with you. . . . Lift up your hearts (UP with your hearts!). . . . Let us give thanks to the Lord our God." The congregation's musical responses are easily learned. They are sublime tunes that echo a joyous anticipation of the spiritual benefits about to be received.

Seasonal Sentences

These texts were crafted especially for this service and should be carefully read. They highlight important events and truths in the holy Gospels. They enhance the church year's spirit and flavor.

Holy, Holy, Holy (Sanctus)

After the seasonal sentences, the minister introduces the Sanctus with the words: "Now have come the salvation and the power and the kingdom of our God and the authority of his Christ. To him who sits on the throne and to the Lamb be praise and thanks and honor and glory for ever and ever."

Christ destroyed death and demolished the bonds of Satan. Now the congregation has opportunity to join the thousands of angels and all Christians who have died in faith and sing their song of praise to God who loves to be worshiped. This canticle is an integral part of the service and should not be dropped. The melody line is easily learned. Let it soar in the church as worshipers share in the joy of this glimpse of a heavenly scene.

Words of Institution

Another high point in the service has arrived. All is in readiness for the celebration of the feast of God's forgiveness. The earthly elements of bread and wine are prepared. The minister reads or recites the words of the institution of this holy feast. He faces the people and extends to them the peace of Christ: "The

189

peace of the Lord be with you always." In the comfort of peace-filled faith the people respond by singing the *Amen*. In Christ all things are ready. Now it is time to come to the altar of the Lord.

O Christ, Lamb of God (Agnus Dei)

Here is another of the ancient texts of the church. Believers come as spiritual beggars and cry out to Christ, the Lamb of God (cf. John 1:29): "Have mercy on us." They know that they will be filled. So, grant them peace, Lord!

The melody fits the mood of the text. Let it be sung with feeling, and not too quickly. Let thinking accompany the singing of the pleas of repentant hearts.

Distribution

During the Distribution, the congregation may sing one or more hymns. Hymns need not be selected from the Holy Communion section every time the Sacrament is celebrated. In the Sacrament there is a renewed sense of eschatological hope. Hymns of exaltation and resurrection are in place. Let congregational singing soar! Seasonal church year hymns are always appropriate. So are hymns that characterize the theme of the Sermon.

When more than one hymn is sung during the Distribution, the organist does well to pause for a short time between them. Silence is part of worship, too. Observing the action at the altar, listening to the Words of Distribution, and witnessing the personal reception ("Take, eat. This is the true body. . . given into death for your sins. . . .") are also important ingredients in the worship experience. (Necessary information relative to the Words of Distribution is found on pp. 177, 178 of this section.)

The choir should consider participating in the singing at this moment in the service. A hymn could be sung in alternation with the congregation. The choir might introduce a new hymn to the congregation. Or, appropriate choral works could be presented without adding time to the service.

Thanksgiving and Prayer

The intonation of the organ invites the congregation to stand and sing *Thank the Lord*. This canticle, with its strong and lively tune, soars with eucharistic praise and shouts of thanksgiving to the throne of God, who leads his people forth in joy. It encourages worshipers to bear witness to their renewed life in Christ by telling everyone what he has done. It leads believers from the hour of worship to the mission characteristic of their every-day lives. Because of its Alleluias, it need not be sung during Lent. In Lent the first stanza of the mighty hymn of doxology, *O Lord, We Praise You,* (CW 317), may be used.

Here We Are! Send Us!

After a closing prayer that capsulizes what God accomplished through this service and that seeks his guidance through life to eternity, the congregation is dismissed with the Blessing of Aaron. The brothers and sisters in Christ, having sensed the awesomeness of the Lord, having tasted and seen that he is good, are prepared to go out in peace, to live in harmony with one another, and to serve the Lord with gladness. They have a mission from God. They sing "Amen, Amen, Amen" to affirm the blessing and their intentions.

The Liturgy Ends

The liturgy has come to a close. No additional hymn is necessary (although some traditions may expect it). Local customs relative to announcements will prevail. Keep them short and positive. The saints have come to worship and to be encouraged. Let them go out in peace to fellowship with one another, to encourage one another, and to face the world as God's salt and light.

Service of the Word

Background

The roots of the *Service of the Word* can be found in the historic service called *Prone.* Medieval parish priests, sensing that the members of their congregations received little spiritual training from the Latin mass, inserted after the reading of the Gospel a section which included the church year Lessons, several hymns and some prayers all in the vernacular. Often a sermon was added. The *Prone* became so popular among the lay people that it began to exist apart from the mass as a preaching service. The concept of a separate service of the Word has also been used in Lutheran Churches that do not have an every-Sunday communion practice.

Purposes and Use

The *Service of the Word* in *Christian Worship* was designed to serve as an order of service for congregational worship when there is no Holy Communion and when congregations wish to have variety outside of the order of *The Common Service*. It mirrors the spirit, the parts, and the flow of *The Common Service* and the *Service of Word and Sacrament*. Some of the liturgical portions, however, have been shortened or reduced. Thus congregations should become comfortable with the service more easily. The *Service of the Word* may also be used for afternoon and evening services as an alternate to *Evening Prayer*.

This service may be ideal for infant and mission congregations to expose newer Christians to the understanding and appreciation of Lutheran worship. Simple and understandable in format, it can whet the appetite for the learning of the other liturgies that may be somewhat more challenging and that include all the parts of the historic communion service.

The *Service of the Word* makes room for the full scope of preaching and teaching God's Word in sermon and hymns. Some variety has been introduced with a confession of sins different from that of *The Common Service* and *Service of Word and Sacrament,* and with a song of praise formed of selected verses from Psalms 34 and 119.

The essential structure of the *Service of the Word* follows the general pattern that has become traditional in the Lutheran church: confession, praise, reading and exposition of God's Word in Scripture lessons, sermon and creed, then prayer and blessing—and all of these parts interspersed with hymnody. This sameness of pattern is wholesome and needful for congregational worship. Constant liturgical variation Sunday after Sunday wears thin in the long run. More critically, constant variation robs Christians of the security and sense of identity that comes when, by steady use, a form of worship imprints itself into minds and souls, and when sister congregations share common and familiar forms of worship with one another. As stated in our

Confessions, "We like it when universal rites are observed for the sake of tranquility"; and again, "We gladly keep the old traditions set up in the church because they are useful and promote tranquility."[3]

Christians have the freedom to devise new forms of worship. This may also be desirable for special and unusual occasions in congregational life. But for the steady diet, a few standard liturgies should suffice. So it is vital that these liturgies have proved their excellence through the test of extensive use. Therefore, the major liturgies in *Christian Worship* were made to conform in a general way to the traditional pattern. This pattern for worship has been weighed and found eminently worthy in the crucible of long and satisfactory service through the centuries.

Welcome

Before the opening hymn, pastors may welcome members and guests of the congregation, explain briefly the day's worship focus and pattern, and express the joy and the privilege of worship under the cross of Jesus Christ. This is best done from the lectern, or, in small gatherings, directly in front of the seats.

Hymn

The *Service of the Word* begins with a hymn. This hymn may match the theme and message for the day or season of the church year. It leads into the Confession and Absolution, or it lets the worshiper contemplate the awesome sense of the presence of God.

This hymn is important for believers who long for the sense of the supernatural and the awesome feeling of standing in the presence of the holy God. It leads believers to echo the song of the angels, "Holy, holy, holy is the LORD Almighty; the whole earth is full of his glory" (Isaiah 6:3); to cry out in confession with Isaiah, "Woe to me! . . . I am ruined! For I am a man of unclean lips . . ." (Isaiah 6:5); and to hear joyfully God's word of pardon: "Your guilt is taken away and your sin atoned for" (Isaiah 6:7).

---

[3] Apology, 7-8:33; 15:38.

The entrance hymn thus gathers together the wandering thoughts of all the worshipers, turns them to the God of their salvation, and establishes the pace and spirit of the entire service that follows.

Confession of Sins

After the dialogue of blessing between the congregation and the minister, using the words of the Apostolic greeting, the minister leads the people into the Confession of Sins. The placement of the Confession of Sins and the Absolution remains the same as in *The Common Service* and *Service of Word and Sacrament*. Its wording, though somewhat shorter in this service, emphasizes the scriptural themes of original and actual sin, and Jesus' perfect life and innocent death to remove the guilt of sin forever. "You are his own dear child" is the joyous word of the gospel of Jesus Christ to the repentant sinner.

The congregation responds to the spoken absolution with a spoken *Amen*. With a little instruction and patient practice, the custom of letting the congregation speak the *Amen* after the Absolution and after prayers soon will become natural, firm, and automatic. By speaking the *Amen,* the congregation is assenting in faith to the words of the Absolution. By speaking the *Amen* after a prayer, the congregation takes ownership of it and says, in essence, "This is our prayer, too."

Praise and Prayer

After hearing the announcement of forgiveness, there is every reason for relief, joy, and thanksgiving to find its way into the believer's heart, joy that wishes to express itself positively to God. Let the minister reflect that spirit when he says to the congregation, "In the peace of forgiveness, let us praise the Lord."

The worshipers, considering how good God is in Christ and how firm are the promises of his eternal Word, break into the song, *Oh, Taste and See.* Since the first and last two scores of this song of praise are identical in words and music, there should be no great difficulty in learning it. A choir could introduce the canticle by singing it twice and then inviting the congregation to join in the singing the third time through. The tune reflects the joy and the strength of the words of the text (Psalm 34:8 and Psalm 119:89). It should be sung joyfully and firmly, not too fast and not too slowly. The thoughts of the canticle also lead naturally into the Word section of the service.

The rubric indicates that another hymn of praise may be sung in place of *Oh, Taste and See,* for example, *Glory Be to God* (CW p. 16) during the Christmas season, *This Is the Feast of Victory* (CW 262) during the Easter season, *O Lord, Our Lord* (CW p. 28) during the Lenten season, or a significant hymn for the particular season of the church year. Worship leaders should refer to the Hymns of the Liturgy section of Christian Worship (CW 262-278) for alternates to the songs and canticles of the various orders of worship. (Other information relating to the canticles is found in chapter 10 of this section.)

The usual pattern for the Prayer of the Day concludes this section. The minister should pause for a few seconds after saying "Let us pray." When hushed silence has arrived, the timing is right for thoughtful praying. (The Prayers of the Day are found in Section Four of this manual.)

The Word

This section is identical to its counterpart in the Service of Word and Sacrament: First Lesson, Psalm of the Day, Second Lesson, Verse of the Day, Gospel, Gospel Acclamation, Hymn of the Day, Sermon, Votum, and Creed. The only difference is that the Apostles' Creed, a more personal confession of baptismal faith, replaces the Service of Word and Sacrament's Nicene Creed, a corporate confession of the church. Historically, the Creed stands at the end of the section on the Word and serves as the faithful's solid response to the reading and preaching of God's Word.

Since the three-year lectionary includes so many readings that are composed of selected verses of a Bible section, it is proper for the minister to announce only the book and chapter of each lesson, e.g., "The First Lesson is written in the fourth chapter of the Book of Isaiah." The First Lesson is not always from the Old Testament, nor is the Second Lesson always from one of the epistles. Therefore, the terms "First Lesson," "Second Lesson," and

195

"Gospel" are to be used. (For assistance on this section of the Word please refer to additional comments on pp. 171-176 and 183-188 in Section Two of this manual.)

This is the heart and the high point of the *Service of the Word*. It deserves the pastor's best in planning, in reading, in sermon preparation and delivery. It merits the choir's involvement in the selection and performance of the Psalm, Verse, and Hymn of the Day. Musicians and pastors can work in concert to plan this section long in advance so that organists and choirs can highlight the focus of the week in the church year.

Thanksgiving

After the Creed, the congregation gathers its offerings of thanks to the Lord and places them on his altar for his work. For this moment, a lull in the service, the organist may consider using selections that review the Hymn of the Day or that introduce the tune of the hymn that follows the prayers. The worshiper can use this time to reflect on the personal meaning and application of the Lessons of the day.

Prayer of the Church and the Lord's Prayer

The Lord invites our prayers and asks that Christians pray for many people and circumstances. The prayer included in the *Service of the Word* is to be read responsively by minister and congregation. Those who pray this prayer can hardly remain passive through this exercise and through these words. The printed prayer (CW p. 42) includes a place for special intercessory requests and a time for silence so that each worshiper can pray silently for someone or something that is a personal concern. The Lord's Prayer, in two versions, concludes the prayer section.

Additional Prayers of the Church are located on pages 123-131 of *Christian Worship*. Here is a natural and necessary place for variety in the weekly worship format.

At times a shorter prayer is in order, or the minister may choose to write his own prayer based on a particular point of the sermon. Those who do this should not neglect praying for others and the needs of contemporary life in North America and the world. Such prayers may mirror the church year themes and the thoughts and images of the Scriptures, but they ought not to be long doctrinal dissertations. Let prayers echo and reinforce theology, not teach all the fine points of theology.

Congregational responses, if used, should not be too long or complicated. Repeated responses (as in litanies: "Lord, have mercy;" "Hear our prayer, O Lord.") can serve the noble purpose of enlisting congregational and personal involvement. It has been said that those responses are "cries from the belly of the church," for in such well-known expressions from the community of believers, individual thoughts, requests, and deep and unexpressed needs are ascending to God's throne of mercy. Repetition of phrases also helps to make things memorable so that believers may repeat the phrases in their personal praying during the week.

Praise and thanksgiving are a part of praying, but not the only part. God asks that we also make our requests known to him for the needs of the Church universal, the concerns of the local congregation, the welfare of the nation and the world, the success of worthy institutions of society, and the support of those beset by special needs. Words of prayers will relate to the joy of salvation, the foundation of our being in Christ, and the God-given goals for the respective journeys through life to paradise.

Those who choose to write their own Prayers of the Church or to do so *ex corde* will realize that public praying involves the hearts and lives of many people. Much time and careful crafting is mandatory. A rambling prayer, a long monologue, or a prayer that startles and draws attention to itself or its clever writer is a detriment and disturbance to those who have gathered to pray.

Hymn

This is the hymn that will normally capture the essence or reinforce the main theme of the Sermon and the Sunday of the church year. In many cases this hymn will be the last one to be chosen. If the other hymns are presented to the organist with sufficient advance time, most organists will understand that the choice of the hymn at this place may need to be made after the outlining or writing of the Sermon.

Prayer and Blessing

There is the choice of two prayers in the style of the old Collects. The second is a rendition of a closing prayer in the Bugenhagen liturgy, which is familiar and dear to the people of the Evangelical Lutheran Synod.

The closing benediction with its introduction is a twin of the one in the *Service of the Word and Sacrament.* The blessing with its three-fold *Amen* closes the service. Local customs and traditions relative to postservice announcements may decide what follows prior to the postlude.

Brief Historical Background
to Morning Praise and Evening Prayer

The early Christians continued to observe some of the prayer times of their counterparts in the Old Testament. The third, sixth, and ninth hours of the day were set aside as hours of prayer. In the fourth century, when Christianity was recognized by the state, public services began to be held at times that corresponded to the hours set aside for private prayer. In some areas daily congregational services were standard.

Monastic communities increased the number of these prayer hours and elaborated on their forms. They developed a series of seven hours (eight services) known as *canonical hours.* Recitation of the Psalmody was the heart of these services. Everything else in the service was developed to clothe the Psalmody.

The canonical services spread from the religious communities to cathedrals and university chapels where groups of clergy assembled for worship. The services, scheduled mostly for the monks and the clergy, became known as the *Divine Office.* The laity occasionally attended the morning and evening hours of worship. Those services, accordingly, became more embellished and complex.

Luther approved of *Matins, Vespers,* and *Compline* (late evening) as containing nothing but the words of Scripture. The orders, however, remained chiefly the possession of schools, with large portions of the services being sung in Latin. The orders were almost lost through lack of use.

198

The work surrounding the production of *The Common Service* of 1888 restored portions of the *Divine Office* (worship forms for *Matins* and *Vespers*) to Lutheranism in America. *Christian Worship,* in following the forms and the sequence of the traditional *Matins (Morning Praise)* and *Vespers (Evening Prayer),* is not attempting to preserve the monastic routine nor fulfilling any obligation to keep the tradition. It is, rather, emulating the church of the past, the monastic routine included, that through decades and centuries of trial and experiment, settled on these forms and sequences as embodying the essentials of worship and employing the finest forms available, namely, the Scripture's own book of prayer and the prayer and praise gems (canticles) found elsewhere in Scripture.

This remains true in our age. The worship forms and sequences adequately serve the church today. They furnish an excellent introduction to worship, provide an opportunity to use the Bible's hymnody (the Psalms), and make room for the reading and exposition of the Scriptures. They give the church gems of worship (*Te Deum, Magnificat, Nunc Dimittis, Kyrie,* Short Prayers, Lord's Prayer), and they provide a fitting close (Benediction). It is difficult to improve on this.

Chanting in Morning Praise and Evening Prayer

Morning Praise and *Evening Prayer* with their short versicles may be a good place to introduce the practice of chanting. The minister's chant line is accompanied as noted in the organist's manual. More experienced singers may not require the accompaniment. The beginner, on the other hand, may feel more comfortable if accompanied by the organ or other instruments.

Common usage is that if the minister sings his line, the congregation sings its response; if he speaks his line, the congregation speaks its response. The latter would be fitting especially for use in small groups. The practice of having the congregation respond in song to the minister's spoken words may appear to be odd to people of a deep liturgical tradition. However, since it is part of the custom and culture of the congregations of our synod that the minister speak a verse and the congregation sing a response, it is not out of place to continue that way.

199

Local customs may dictate the pattern to be followed. Education in worship principles and enlarging the practices of worship, however, should be an ongoing process in all congregations as they take care of their rich heritage of Lutheran worship. (See Section Three, chapter 15, for more information on music of the chant.)

Morning Praise

Worship in the Morning

The service called *Morning Praise* in *Christian Worship* is a revision of the historic Order of *Matins*. *Matins* (from the Latin *matutinus* meaning "of the morning") was the monastic service marking the beginning of the new day. This revision of *Matins* seeks to emphasize the morning nature of worship. Joined to Christ our risen Lord, we glorify God as we rise to the activities of the new day. In Christ we face the day unafraid, knowing that the Lord's "compassions never fail. They are new every morning . . ." (Lamentations 3:22,23). Morning is a necessary and natural time for praying, praising, and giving thanks.

Morning Praise is not intended to serve as a substitute for the main Sunday service. It should be useful, instead, as a weekday morning form of worship for congregations, schools, conferences, and other meetings. It may also be adapted for use with small groups and in the home.

Morning Hymn, Sentences, and Canticle

The opening ordinary hymn, *Father, We Praise You, Now the Night Is Over*, also called *Morning Hymn*, is a Latin hymn usually ascribed to Gregory the Great. It praises the Holy Trinity and prays for the joys of salvation. Prior to the singing of the hymn, the minister may speak a word of welcome to the worshipers and invite them to stand.

The opening sentences resemble the urgent prayers of those who are threatened by enemies (Psalm 70:1). They verbalize the heartfelt needs of all who have gathered to worship the God of justice, truth, and mercy. With these words the gathered believers call for the Lord's help and thus begin their worship.

The worship leader may either speak or sing his sentences in the service. The melody line for the minister has been provided in the hymnal with an accompaniment in the organist's edition.

Familiar sentences for the various seasons of the church year have been provided to introduce the song *Oh, Come, Let Us Sing to the Lord,* a song called the *Venite* because of its opening word in Latin. With these words from Psalm 95, the worshiper makes a joyful noise in praise of the maker of heaven and earth.

Psalm

The second Psalm in this service (the first being the *Venite*) is one chosen by the worship leader. (See CW pp. 64-122 for the 59 Psalms.) This Psalm may be sung or spoken, or a combination of the two. (Instructions for singing the Psalms are found on p. 63 of *Christian Worship.* Further suggestions for the performance of the Psalms are given on pp. 149-151 of this manual.) The Psalm selected may be one suitable for the season of the church year or one that relates to the lesson for that service. A table of Psalms useful for Psalm-selection is printed on page 62 of *Christian Worship.*

The Psalm concludes with the *Glory Be to the Father.* The *Glory Be to The Father (Gloria Patri)* is the familiar ascription of praise that points us to the triune God and to eternal life. It connects the Old and New Testaments and serves as useful and unifying repetition in Christian worship.

Lesson and Seasonal Response

For this service it is normal that one Lesson be read. In selecting the Lesson, the worship leader is urged to pay attention to the church year calendar (CW pp. 157-160). (Suggested lessons as well as additional helps for all of the days listed in the calendar [cf. the Daily Lectionary] are printed in Section Four of this book.)

Following the reading of the Lesson, the Seasonal Response may be sung or spoken. Musical settings for these Seasonal Responses are available from Northwestern Publishing House. They are ideal for cantors or children or adult choirs of any size. It is not recommended that the congregation sing these responses. Instead, during the singing, the worshipers will have opportunity to think about the meaning of the appropriate season of the church year.

Hymn

The major hymn of this service follows the Lesson. The hymn should be chosen with care, for it builds on the Lesson and the season of the church year. Several indices are provided in *Christian Worship*. A topical index of the hymns is found at the end of this book.

Sermon

There may be times when a sermon will not be a part of *Morning Praise*. Normally, however, and if time permits, the Sermon will follow the singing of the hymn. The worship leader should consider using all or part of the Lesson as the sermon text. When there is no Sermon, the hymn at the bottom of page 47 may also be omitted.

We Praise You, O God

The congregation's sung response to the Sermon may be one of three variations. The first, *We Praise You, O God (Te Deum)* is an ancient and majestic canticle of the Christian church, a confession of faith, a mighty hymn of praise to God. Luther loved the *Te Deum* and referred to it as a fine symbol or creed. People have grown fond of the chanted version printed in this service. Metrical versions of the same are the hymns *God, We Praise You* (CW 277) and *Holy God, We Praise Your Name* (CW 278). The second option is the *Song of Zechariah* (CW 275 or 276). The third option is a hymn selected by the worship leader.

It is suggested that the worshipers stand as they sing. After the hymn and depending on the setting of this service, a thankoffering may be received.

Lord, Have Mercy

The prayer section begins with a cry for mercy to the Lord *(Kyrie)* in the morning hour. The first prayer is the one our Lord taught his church to pray. Two English translations of this prayer are printed. Additional brief prayers may follow the Lord's Prayer. The historic Prayer for Grace brings the prayers to a conclusion.

Blessing and Close

The service ends with a mutual exchange between pastor and congregation in expression of thanksgiving to God. Then the worshiper receives the blessing of the triune God and responds by singing the *Amen.*

Evening Prayer

Worship at Evening

As daylight disappears, it is natural for Christians to desire to thank God for the blessings of the day. It is also important for them to recall the presence and peace of Christ, the light of the world, to combat the haunting elements of darkness and the thoughts it sometimes evokes.

The Scriptures speak of the need for this emphasis: "You will not fear the terror of night . . . nor the pestilence that stalks in the darkness . . ." (Psalm 91:5,6); "From the rising of the sun to the place where it sets, the name of the LORD is to be praised" (Psalm 113:3); "Though I sit in darkness, the LORD will be my light" (Micah 7:8); "You, O LORD, keep my lamp burning; my God turns my darkness into light" (Psalm 18:28).

These scriptural themes, found in *Vespers* and *Compline,* are reflected in *Christian Worship*'s revised *Vespers* called *Evening Prayer.* (See pp. 198, 199 for the historical background to *Evening Prayer.*) This is a meaningful order of worship for all who have interrupted their busy routines to join with one another in quiet reflection on the triune God. Its mood or tone is one of sublime joy, yet somewhat subdued, humbly grateful, and definitely prayerful. Its purpose is to portray the comforting and ever-present light of Christ as daylight disappears and to give Christians a form to raise their voices in thankful prayer and praise.

Evening Prayer

Evening Prayer, as it appears in *Christian Worship*, updates the language and the music of the basic components of the historic *Vespers* (music, psalms, Scripture, canticles, and a series of brief prayers). It is suitable for worship in late afternoons or evenings on Sundays, weekdays, or festivals in churches, schools, and on special occasions. One might also use certain portions of it for

203

brief meditational or devotional use. The *Service of Light*, for instance, could serve as a thought-provoking worship format for a small group gathered around God's Word.

Preservice

Those responsible for preservice music should remember that *Evening Prayer* carries a somewhat subdued, meditative spirit and tone. Many thoughts have wandered through busy minds during the daylight hours. Now it is time to turn and focus on the one thing that is needed in life. Let the music chosen assist in that process. Worship leaders might even consider eliminating the preservice music, especially when the *Service of Light* is used.

Before the service begins, the worship leader may speak a word of welcome and give brief instructions concerning the theme of the service and where to find it in the hymnal. The basic purpose of this is to set the tone and to show an understanding for the needs of those who have come to worship.

The minister will take care not to rush through *Evening Prayer.* This does not mean slow or lethargic speaking and reading. It does mean, however, the judicial placement of pauses that will permit reflective and meditative prayer at eventide.

The Traditional Opening

The traditional or historic opening (CW pp.52,53) to begin *Evening Prayer* starts with a hymn that invokes God's presence or mirrors the spirit of the church year or the evening. This hymn unites the believer with the worshiping family in its address to God.

The congregation stands for the opening verses in which the worshipers plead to God for help and mercy. The minister may sing or speak his parts.

Salutation and Prayer

The opening verses that beseech the Lord's presence are followed by the minister's blessing to the congregation, "The Lord be with you," and the congregation's corresponding response, "And also with you." The minister then leads the congregation in a brief prayer that includes thoughts appropriate for the start of worship. This is the first in a series of short prayers in this service. The prayer concludes with the typical tribute to the living Christ who reigns forever with the life-giving Holy Spirit, thus incorporating the thought of the triune God.

Speak the Amen

The congregation responds to the spoken prayer with a spoken *Amen.* By the *Amen* the congregation is saying, "This is our prayer, too." The pastor may want the congregation to practice speaking the *Amen* at the end of the short prayers in *Evening Prayer.* Since the brief prayers of *Evening Prayer* (and any other prayers which are introduced to it) have similar endings (like those of the Prayers for the Day), a pattern can be established so that the spoken *Amen* of the congregation will be firm and confident. When the worshiping assembly becomes accustomed to the inflection prior to the entry point, it will quite naturally grow in the meaningful custom of saying *Amen.*

The congregation is seated after the prayer. The service continues with *Let My Prayer Rise Before You* (from Psalm 141) on page 55.

An Alternate Beginning: The Service of Light

A second way to begin *Evening Prayer* is with the *Service of Light* (alternate beginning) (CW pp. 54,55). The *Service of Light* is a rendition of the ancient *Lucernarium* service (4:00 p.m.) and serves as a link between worship at the setting of the sun and at a time late in the evening. The *Service of Light* gives congregations an opportunity to add reflective and constructive ritual to their patterns of evening worship. It provides a thought-provoking meditation on God's creation ("Let there be light") and on Christ, the light of the world, who came to drive away sin and darkness.

Various uses

The *Service of Light* may be used in a variety of ways, some of which will depend on the architecture of the building and the musical gifts within a congregation. One way is to have the pastor sing or speak the opening verses at the altar and the congregation sing or speak the responses. The most effective way is to let the pastor sing these versicles without accompaniment (no stems on the notes indicates no accompaniment). The emphasis in the verses is on Jesus, the light of the world, the antithesis of all the powers of darkness. The words of the Emmaus disciples, "Stay with us, Lord, for it is evening, and the day is almost over," become the words of the worshiping New Testament congregation.

Another way to begin the *Service of Light* is with a procession carrying a large white candle, representing Christ, to a prominent place in the chancel area. The worship leaders make their way slowly down the aisle of the dimly lighted church while singing the verses and responses with the congregation. Handbell ringers may introduce each of the worship leader's lines.

A variation of this is to have a cantor sing the verses with either the congregation or a small group singing the responses. In yet another variation, the verses and responses are spoken by a reader with the congregation speaking the response as the procession heads toward the altar.

There are still other ways to utilize the *Service of Light*. The participating choir can divide into two groups and sing the verses responsively. The groups can do this from the balcony or from the two sides of the nave of the church. Or two readers or sets of readers can sing or speak the verses responsively from appropriate places in the church.

O Gracious Light

The responsorial prayer, "And hear our evening hymn of praise," ends the opening sentences and is followed directly by the Ordinary hymn sung by the congregation, *O Gracious Light, Lord Jesus Christ*. This hymn, *Phos Hilaron*, comes from the Greek church of the third century and is an integral part of *Lucernarium*. It was used in the ancient church during the lighting of the candles and was known as the *Candlelight Hymn*. The text for this hymn is the Bland Tucker translation as it appears in *The Hymnal 1982* (#261) and the name of the tune is *O Heilige Dreifaltigkeit*. As a visible manifestation of the words, "The lamps are lit to pierce the night," chancel candles may be lighted during the singing of this hymn of praise to Christ.

A Prayer

The *Service of Light* concludes with a prayer. The worship leader has a choice of prayers, something that will lend variety when *Evening Prayer* is used in successive weeks (Advent, Lent). The first prayer includes a historical reference from the Old Testament (the pillar of fire by night). The second prayer incorporates thoughts appropriate for the ending of the day and the beginning of worship. The prayer ends with an Amen spoken by the congregation. After the prayer, the congregation is seated to pause and think about the next part.

Psalms

Both openings continue with *Let My Prayer Rise Before You* (from Psalm 141) on page 55. Traditional Vesper versicles from Psalm 141 are set to music that congregations can readily learn and love to sing. The verses depict the believer's deep cry for God's help and deliverance. In the tradition of the hourly services, the minister reads a brief prayer following the sung portion of Psalm 141 and the congregation responds with a spoken *Amen.*

The second psalm is the *Psalm of the Day* or one chosen by the worship leader. (See CW pp.62-122 for Index to the Psalms and Psalm Selections.) As indicated elsewhere in this manual, the Psalm may be sung or spoken, or it may be a combination of the two. The preferable way is to sing it.

Glory Be to the Father

The Psalm concludes with the *Glory Be to the Father (Gloria Patri)*. The *Glory Be to the Father* reminds the church that it is singing the Old Testament psalms in the age of the New Testament. Here the church also bears witness to its belief in the Father, the Son, and the Holy Spirit.

Silence for Meditation

After the Psalm, provision is made for silence. The accent for silence in this part of *Evening Prayer* is on meditation. This may be a time span of up to thirty seconds for the believer to concentrate on certain thoughts or even a single thought of the foregoing psalm, apply them to one's personal life, and then to address a silent prayer to God. The worshiper will ask questions: "What does God want to say to ME here? How can I apply this psalm to my own life? What should I pray for?"

The presiding minister will have to introduce this practice if it is unknown to the congregation. If the atmosphere of unhurried contemplation is observed throughout the service, indicated even by the pace and voice of the pastor, meditation after the Psalm will seem natural and fitting.

Psalm Prayer

The minister signals the end of the silence by breaking into the appointed psalm prayer printed on pages 477-486 of this manual. If that is not available, the minister should read the brief prayer provided. Again, the congregation responds to the prayer with a spoken Amen. The Psalmody section has come to an end.

Lesson

As in *Morning Praise,* it is suggested that one Lesson be read. In selecting this Lesson, the worship leader is urged to pay attention to the church year calendar (CW pp. 157-160). Suggested Lessons as well as additional helps for all of the days listed in the calendar are found on pages 385-476 of this book. At the end of the Lesson the minister says, "This is the Word of the Lord."

Seasonal Responses

Following the reading of the Lesson, the appropriate Seasonal Response may be sung or spoken. This is to serve as a response to the Lesson. The best practice is to let a children's, youth, or adult choir of any size sing the appointed response. It is a good way to involve the choir in the actual process of singing portions of the liturgy. Musical settings of the Seasonal Responses have been prepared for *Morning Praise* and *Evening Prayer* and are available from Northwestern Publishing House.

Hymn

The major hymn of the service follows the response and precedes the Sermon. It should be chosen with care and be resplendent with the major thoughts of the season and the service. Please refer to comments on this hymn in the explanations of the other liturgies in this section of the manual.

Sermon

The Sermon may be based on all or part of the Lesson just read. When that is the case, it is not necessary to repeat the entire text. The Sermon will flow out of the Word and make application to the lives of the gathered congregation.

In most circumstances when *Evening Prayer* is used, there will be a Sermon. There may be times and circumstances, however, when *Evening Prayer* is used without a Sermon. At such times the hymn before the Sermon will be omitted. Where time may be limited to about thirty minutes, a service of hymns, canticles, psalms, a Lesson, and prayers is certainly worship and not incomplete. There may also be settings, other than that of the traditional church service, where a liturgical drama may be substituted for the Sermon.

Canticle

The *Song of Mary (Magnificat)* is the chief canticle (song from Scripture other than a Psalm) used historically in *Vespers*. Its words (Luke 1:46-55) are suitable for any season of the church year. However, it may fit best during the Advent and Christmas seasons. The tune for this canticle may be introduced by the choir and learned by the congregation.

For occasional variety the metrical version of this canticle (CW 274) may be chosen for use, or the choir might consider other renditions of the *Song of Mary,* or, as stated in the rubric, a hymn may be sung instead of the *Song of Mary.* The congregation stands for the canticle or hymn.

Offering

When choosing music for the gathering of the thankofferings, the organist or pianist will keep in mind the contemplative nature of *Evening Prayer.*

209

Lord, Have Mercy (Kyrie) and Prayers

A time for praying follows the presentation of the offering to the Lord. Prayers other than the suggested litany may be used. When this is done, the worship leader should plan them as a series of short prayers, with the congregation having opportunity to respond to each of them with a spoken *Amen*. The prayers always conclude with the Lord's Prayer followed by the Prayer for Peace.

The suggested prayer is a very short form of the classical litany and begins with the *Lord, Have Mercy*. It serves as a prayer of the church and includes petitions for various people. The minister may sing or speak his part. The congregation's responses ("Lord, have mercy" and "Lord, hear our prayer") are repetitious and easy to memorize since they have the same melodic line throughout. The Lord's Prayer and Prayer for Peace follow the litany (or any other prayer selected) and bring the prayer section to a close.

The timeless Prayer for Peace is judged by many to be one of the finest prayers from the early history of the church. Today's worshipers are privileged to be able to pray the same prayer thoughts as the generations of believers who preceded them.

Song of Simeon

The *Song of Simeon* (Luke 2:29-32) was the canticle associated historically with the *Compline* (late evening) service. However, it also fits well in *Evening Prayer. Christian Worship*'s setting begins with "In peace, Lord, you let your servant now depart," reflecting the thoughts of the Prayer for Peace just read. The new tune exudes the peace and love dwelling in the heart of Simeon after he saw the Christchild. It serves as a beautiful and memorable conclusion to *Evening Prayer.*

For variety, Martin Luther's metric version *In Peace and Joy I Now Depart* (CW 269), may be substituted. The prayerful compline office hymn, *Before the Ending of the Day* (CW 595), with its stark Benedictine plainsong tune, may also be used at this or another place in *Evening Prayer*, especially when nighttime terrors afflict the nation or a community.

210

Blessing

After hearing the Apostolic Blessing, the congregation, filled and renewed with the light and peace of Jesus Christ, departs with readiness to let that bright light shine in the darkness of this world of sin.

Christian Marriage

Background

The marriage service included in *Christian Worship* (pp. 140-143) is called *Christian Marriage*. While recognizing that marriage is not exclusively a Christian rite, the title *Christian Marriage* has been chosen for this service to emphasize that "the pattern for Christian marriage is the intimate union of Christ and his Church" (CW p. 141), which St. Paul describes in Ephesians chapter five.

This order of worship celebrates God's gracious gift of marriage. It invites participation by the congregation, relatives, and friends, all of whom share the joy of the bride and groom as they publicly promise lifelong love and faithfulness to each other. Using this order in the hymnal helps set a standard for marriage services in the congregation. It is also useful for pastors as a study and preparatory document in premarriage counseling.

Call to Worship

The Call to Worship helps to emphasize that the marriage liturgy is corporate worship. The worship leader should direct the wedding guests to the pages in the hymnal where the service is printed and give a few very brief instructions including indications for standing and sitting. After the trinitarian invocation, the minister welcomes the invited guests. The verses from the Psalms which may be spoken responsively, emphasize God's gracious love and care for all people. A brief prayer ends this introduction to the service.

Throughout the service the congregation is directed to speak the *Amens* to the prayers. In this way the worshipers express their agreement and their unity of heart with the one who prays. They are saying, "This is our prayer, too."

Hymns and Music

The general rubric appears at the bottom of page 140: "Congregational hymns or other music appropriate for worship may be sung here or at other places in the service." This emphasizes the importance of congregational singing in the marriage service. At the same time, it recognizes that the choice and placement of hymns and other music appropriate for worship will depend on differing circumstances and customs. The phrase "music appropriate for worship" includes instrumental as well as vocal and choir selections. A hymn may be placed at the beginning, at the bottom of page 140, after the Lessons, or after the Sermon.

Christian Worship has a section of hymns for Christian marriage services (CW 600-604). One is not limited to these choices, however. The following are additional hymns that might be considered from *Christian Worship:* 233, 236, 250, 262, 263, 275, 278, 360, 369, 422, 462, 478, 490, 491, 492, 494, 495, 500, 503, and 531.

Lessons and Sermon

One or more Lessons may be read. A list of appropriate samples is listed below. One should not be limited to this list, however. It may also serve as a helpful tool in premarriage counseling and service planning:

Genesis 1:26-31
Genesis 2:18-24
Psalm 23
Psalm 67
Psalm 127
Psalm 128
Isaiah 62:1-5
Matthew 19:4-6
John 2:1-10
John 15:9-12
1 Corinthians 12:31-13:13
Ephesians 5:21-33
Colossians 3:12-19
1 Peter 3:1-7
1 John 4:7-12
Revelation 19:6-9

The Sermon may be based on one of the Lessons. The use of the word "sermon" rather than "address" or some other term emphasizes the nature of this service. It does not, however, suggest a lengthy message.

Marriage Rite

The section Marriage Rite begins with an introduction to the promises that the groom and bride will be making. The first paragraph describes God's institution and the purpose of marriage. The second paragraph tells of sin, its consequences with respect to marriage, and its remedy in Christ. The third paragraph is based on 1 Corinthians 13 and reminds the couple that "marriage furnishes a unique opportunity to put this love into practice." The fourth paragraph quotes from Ephesians 5 and emphasizes that it is reverence for Christ that will motivate husband and wife to fulfill their responsibilities in marriage and so lay the foundation for a truly Christian marriage.

Marriage Promises

The groom and bride are each asked three questions by the minister. The first question is similar to the only question that Martin Luther proposed in the Order of Marriage he prepared in 1529.[4] The second question refers to the distinctive responsibilities that God has given to husband and wife, as earlier described in the quotation from Ephesians 5. The final question asks for a promise of enduring faithfulness and loving support in all situations of life. After the groom and bride have answered "I will" to the questions asked by the minister, they join their right hands and promise to be faithful to each other as long as they both shall live.

Exchange of Rings and Declaration of Marriage

The Marriage Promises are followed by the Exchange of Rings with the groom and bride speaking the same words in turn. The Declaration of Marriage is directed not to the couple but to the congregation. This declaration is followed by the Marriage Bless-

---

[4] See Luther's Works, American, Vol. 53, pp. 110-115.

ing of the couple. The groom and bride may kneel for this blessing and for what follows.

Hymn and Prayers

Two stanzas of the hymn *Now Thank We All Our God* are printed to be sung by the congregation, a choir, or solo voice. (Another
hymn may be substituted.) The printed prayer includes petitions
for both the newly married couple and for families in general. Other prayers may be said or substituted for the printed prayer. The
Lord's Prayer in two versions concludes the Prayer section.

Blessing

The final Blessing is intended for the entire congregation and
not only for the married couple.

Christian Funeral

Historical Background

Those who visit churches in different regions will discover a
variety of customs, forms, and orders relative to Christian buri-
als. Perhaps this is because Martin Luther did not write or authorize an order of worship for funerals. He detested the common
orders of his day, which gave the impression that they were in-
fluencing the fate of the dead. Instead of producing a funeral
liturgy. Luther was satisfied to write a few German and Latin
chorales for this purpose.

One should not conclude, however, that Luther was not concerned about proper funeral practices. He wrote: "It is meet and
right that we should conduct these funerals with proper decorum
in order to honor and praise that joyous article of faith, namely,
the resurrection of the dead, and in order to defy Death, that terri-
ble foe who so shamefully and in so many horrible ways goes on
to devour us."[5] For him the focal point of the service was not to
be the dead body but faith in the resurrection promised by the
Christ.

Luther's emphasis is certainly the theme of the funeral service
printed in *Christian Worship* (pp.144-147). The title of the service

---

[5] Luther's Works, American, Vol. 53, p. 326.

is *Christian Funeral* instead of *Christian Burial.* "Funeral" suggests observances held in a church or funeral home chapel for one who has died. "Burial" suggests graveside rites, which are not a part of the order printed in *Christian Worship.* Additional funeral forms and graveside rites may be found in various agendas.

In many funeral services of the past only the minister(s) spoke. There may be times and situations when this is necessary. *Christian Funeral,* however, invites participation by the congregation, friends, and relatives, those who are most deeply involved with the family at the time of death. This order is corporate worship for the congregation, which is a caring and supportive community united in worship under the cross of Christ.

The service seeks to lead this group from sorrow at the loss of one of its own toward the glad reaffirmation of the love of God in the gospel of Jesus Christ and his promised resurrection for all who die in faith. The service acknowledges the stark scriptural truth that the wages of sin is death. But it also gives clear and supportive witness to the resurrection and God's gift of eternal life through our Lord Jesus Christ.

It is natural and desirable that a service that bears witness to the resurrection be held in the church dedicated for corporate worship. The church is where the important events in the lives of God's people take place: baptisms, confirmations, weekly worship services and Bible classes, reception of the Lord's Supper, and Christian marriages. The church is also the natural place for a funeral or memorial service. Where local customs differ, however, this service may be utilized or adapted for use in funeral home chapels according to the discretion of the pastor.

Regional and congregational customs have many variations. The rubrics of *Christian Funeral* do not seek to prescribe new customs or interfere with practices outside of the service itself.

Processional

Although the customs vary, usually the family enters the sanctuary in procession before the start of the service. Some churches cover the coffin with a symbolical white pall to indicate that through baptism we have been clothed with the white robe of the Savior's righteousness (cf. Galatians 3:27), and to confess that, rich or poor, we are all ONE in Christ Jesus. The minister usually leads the procession, followed by the pallbearers with the coffin, and the family (if they have not been seated at an earlier time.) Informal announcements, instructions relative to the order of worship, and the reading of the obituary (if customary) may be given at this time.

Greeting and Prayer

Christian Funeral begins on a subdued note with the minister's greeting and word of empathy with the mourners. It acknowledges that sorrow at death is a natural and universal human emotion. The well known invitation of Christ, "Come unto me . . ." follows and directs those who are burdened by the sting of death to find their rest in him. The prayer guides the mourners from their sorrow to the uplifting thought of the resurrection, the theme to be emphasized for their comfort in this service.

Psalm and Hymn

The minister reads the printed text of the familiar Psalm 23, with its promise of God's guidance throughout life. There may be times when the minister invites the congregation to join him in the reading of this well-known psalm.

A hymn may follow Psalm 23. A choir or soloist may sing this hymn. Nevertheless, it is a good practice to encourage congregational singing at funerals. Singing serves as a natural way for the relatives and participants to express their faith. The first hymn is not the main one of the service. It should be one that is well-known and easily sung.

Resurrection Comfort

The service moves from the general thoughts of God's guidance in sorrow and sadness to the specific theme of the resurrection of Christ and the resurrection promised to his faithful people. This is the supreme comfort to be enjoyed and confessed. Participation by the mourners in the very words of these Scriptures can be healing and comforting. For that reason this section may be read responsively with the minister, as indicated in the service format. If the minister is adapting this service for special circum-

216

stances where the congregation has no printed text, he himself should read these comforting words.

Lessons

The minister may choose one or more readings at this point. Suggested psalms and Lessons from the Old and New Testaments are listed on pages 148-149 of *Christian Worship*. This list is to serve as a guide for the minister. He should not be limited to these choices, however. He may also select Lessons appropriate to the church year or to his prior visits with the one who has died.

The list of psalms and Lessons (CW pp. 148,149) is also designed for ministry to the sick, dying, and bereaved. The suggestions may be helpful to pastors, visitation committees, relatives, and friends as they care for those who are preparing for death or as they visit and encourage those who have recently experienced the loss of a loved one. Human words and expressions of sympathy and kindness are necessary and important. But nothing is as powerful and as comforting as a message from God's Word. It would be good for pastors to encourage their parishioners to make use of these readings for the above-mentioned purposes.

Hymns

The hymns before and after the Sermon are the primary ones for this service. They may be sung by a choir, soloist, or the congregation. Congregational singing of the hymns is to be encouraged. Luther promoted congregational singing at funerals. He did not want churches to be "houses of wailing or places of mourning" but "dormitories and resting places." He added these thoughts: "Nor do we sing any dirges or doleful songs over our dead and at the grave, but comforting hymns of the forgiveness of sins, of rest, sleep, life, and of the resurrection of departed Christians so that our faith may be strengthened and the people be moved to true devotion."[6]

Many of the hymns in *Christian Worship* are suitable for funerals. One should not limit choices to the Death and Burial section

---

[6] Luther's Works, American, Vol. 53, p. 326.

(CW 586-591). Hymns of the church year should receive consideration. The following are some numbers suitable for funerals in the various seasons.

ADVENT: 2,6-8,9,11,18,19,22,23,25,26,29
CHRISTMAS: 34,37,40,42,46,50
EPIPHANY: 79,84,86,90,93
LENT: 104,105,116,120,121,138,140
EASTER: 141,143-145,148,149,152,158,159,161,163,164,167,168
ASCENSION: 169-173
PENTECOST: 181,184,185,190,195,198,200,201
END TIME: 206-220

In addition, many hymns in other sections of *Christian Worship* may be considered.

Sermon

The minister may preach on one of the Lessons read previously, or he may choose an additional text. The Sermon will emphasize the comfort of the good news of Christ and his resurrection, what it meant in the life of the deceased, and what it means for all who have gathered for worship.

Apostles' Creed

Words that are familiar are important in a funeral service. The recitation of the Apostles' Creed testifies to the faith into which Christians have been baptized and by which they live.

A hymn follows the Creed. Hymn suggestions and comments are found in the paragraphs above.

Prayers

A responsive prayer involving the congregation is included as the standard. Since the congregation has just finished singing a hymn, the minister may have to instruct the people concerning this prayer and the page on which it is found. Toward the end of the prayer, a rubric states that a special intercession may be inserted by the minister.

The printed prayer seeks God's help for the future of those who have experienced the loss of a relative, friend, or associate. At its conclusion it leads the worshipers into the praying of the Lord's Prayer.

218

The minister is not limited to the use of this prayer. He may prefer to write his own or to select a different one from another source.

Blessing and Recessional

Christian Funeral concludes with the familiar and cherished words of the Aaronic Blessing. God's PEACE accompanies those who have resurrection faith through Jesus.

The recessional and dismissal should follow the customs of the local parish. Proper respect and decorum ought to be apparent to all who are present.

Devotions

The three devotions included in *Christian Worship* (pp. 150-153) are designed to enrich the worship of the family at home or various small groups in our churches and schools.

They may be used as printed, or adapted to the leader's wishes, the needs of the group, and the time available. In each of them, the group is actively participating, not only listening to a worship leader. Pastors, teachers, and congregational leaders will do well to encourage the use of these devotions in the home.

All three devotions have essentially the same pattern with some variations. Each begins with sentences spoken responsively by a leader and a group (or another individual). The *General Devotion* includes the Apostles' Creed, a responsive intercession that calls on the Lord to look with mercy on persons in need, and the Lord's Prayer. Those who use this devotion may wish to substitute one of the Prayers of the Church (CW pp.123-131) for the printed intercession. In the *Morning Devotion,* the Prayer for Grace from *Morning Praise* is used along with Luther's Morning Prayer. The Prayer for Peace from *Evening Prayer* and Luther's Evening Prayer are found in the *Evening Devotion.* The blessings in the three devotions are unique to each.

Various options are suggested for the Reading: a Scripture lesson, a devotional selection, or a portion of Luther's Small Catechism. Here is an opportunity for variety if these devotions are used regularly. The list of readings for the church year (CW pp.163-166) and the Daily Lectionary (pp. 516-527 in this manual) will be helpful in choosing appropriate selections from the Scriptures.

All three devotions suggest the singing or reading of a hymn or psalm. The Psalm Index (CW p. 62) and the various indices for the hymns (CW pp. 937-960 and pp. 528-572 of this manual) will be helpful in making these selections. Instructions for singing the psalms are found on page 63 of the hymnal. One or more of the Personal Prayers (CW pp. 134-139) may be used in place of the opening prayer in the *General Devotion* and before Luther's prayers in the *Morning* and *Evening Devotions.*

These devotions may be used for worship in Lutheran parish schools, Sunday schools, Lutheran high schools, and other educational institutions. They could also provide brief but meaty devotions for men's and women's groups, youth gatherings, choir rehearsals, and meetings of the church council and other committees. A wider use of the devotions would be at circuit meetings, conferences, and conventions. Finally, these devotions may serve the Christian family or individual in the home.

Private Confession

At several places in *The Book of Concord,* our Lutheran Confessions speak of the worth of confession, both the general confession made, for example, in the Lord's Prayer and the private or secret confession made before a single fellow Christian. Among the best of these statements is the one by Luther at the very end of the Large Catechism. Anyone who reads this should be quickly convinced of the usefulness of a simple order of *Private Confession* in the hymnal so that it is ready at hand when needed. Without some guidance in how to comfort a conscience-troubled sinner, it becomes difficult for Christians to serve one another in this vital matter that concerns spiritual well-being.

It is generally admitted and commiserated that private confession has fallen into great neglect among us, and that to our hurt. We are free from the coercion and intolerable burden once imposed upon Christians of enumerating their sins at specified intervals before a clerical judge. Everyone knows this and has learned it so well that our liberty has become a license, as if one never needs to make use of the comfort offered through private confession. Nevertheless, when a child of God deeply troubled by a particular sin makes a clean breast of it in confession before the minister or a trusted fellow Christian and hears that person's living voice forgiving the sin on the command and authority of the Lord Jesus Christ, this is heaven for the repentant believer. Pastors will do well in Bible class and various instruction classes to refer to this blessing.

Private confession is a precious gift that the Lord bestowed on his Church. It is there for Christians to use, not as an oppressive requirement but as a healing medicine to be sought out when a person feels the need for it. The service of *Private Confession* in *Christian Worship* was designed chiefly for this purpose.

Athanasian Creed

Our Lutheran Confessions declare that "next to the article of the holy Trinity," the greatest mystery in heaven and on earth is the personal union,[7] namely, that God and man are a single person in our Lord Jesus Christ. The safeguarding of the doctrine of the Trinity and the doctrine of Christ through many years of heated controversy is one of early Christianity's prized gifts to the church of the future.

The Athanasian Creed presents these two basic truths of Scripture in a manner that accentuates the mystery and does no violence to Scripture. This is its distinctive service to us. And although all early references to the creed point to its origin in the old Roman province of Gaul, far removed from where St. Athanasius lived in Egypt and where he died about one hundred years earlier, it is neither strange nor improper that the Creed should have been named after this church father. He was the foremost fighter for the full deity of the Son in the Godhead and for the absolute necessity of the Son's becoming fully human in the person of Jesus Christ.

The Athanasian Creed continued to serve the church at weekly monastic devotions throughout the thousand years after its appearance. That was how Luther learned to know and cherish it, as reflected in a treatise on the creeds that he wrote in 1538. Proba-

---

[7] Cf. Formula of Concord: Thorough Declaration, 8:33.

bly because of his influence, our Lutheran forefathers were persuaded to include also the Athanasian Creed, in addition to its better-known companions, with the rest of the Lutheran Confessions. Adding the heritage of the three creeds from the ancient church to the treasury of our confessions bears powerful witness to our continuing unity in faith with the early Christians and to genuine catholic ecumenicity.

In these gray and latter days of the world, the Athanasian Creed can serve us as it served God's people in the past. It can imprint on minds and hearts precisely those two central truths of Scripture that the winds of doctrinal laxity in contemporary Christendom treat with growing intensity as unimportant if not irrelevant. Of course, it is not necessary for salvation to know the Athanasian Creed nor to be conversant with its theology. On the other hand, anyone who is fully acquainted with its testimony yet denigrates or denies what it teaches about the Christian God and the Christian Savior has suffered shipwreck of the true Christian faith.

For our own benefit and in testimony to the world, we cannot make our confession too often that God—Father, Son, and Holy Spirit—is the only true God and that God's Son took our human nature to himself in the person of the God-man Jesus Christ so that by his death on the cross he might wash away the sins of the world.

The Athanasian Creed may be confessed in public worship at other times in the church calendar besides Trinity Sunday. It need not always be spoken in its entirety; it falls into two natural parts that may be used separately. The Creed may be spoken either in unison by the entire congregation or antiphonally by minister and congregation, the indented lines designating the congregation's parts.

Finally, it would be a distinct service to assembled worshipers if, on the Sundays when the *Athanasian Creed* is introduced, the church bulletin included some lines of explanation that, for the sake of better understanding, would put the message of the Creed into correct perspective.

Personal Preparation for Holy Communion

Christian Worship (p. 156) includes a form to help Christians prepare for the reception of the Lord's body and blood in Holy

Communion. Worship leaders ought to refer to this devotional tool in the weekly service folder and in Bible and instruction classes. It will assist those who desire guidance in proper preparation for Holy Communion. Pastors may also use this form when they have private consultation with members and encourage them toward regular use of the Lord's means of grace.

Personal Prayers

The apostle instructs, "Devote yourselves to prayer, being watchful and thankful" (Colossians 4:2). Watchfulness in praying is a hallmark of the people of God waiting for their Lord's return. Their prayers need not be long, but they will be voiced at every corner throughout their journey of life in the world's last days. And they will soar in daily thanksgiving to the God who gave his Son.

Christian Worship has two sections of personal prayers to exemplify such praying. The first set (CW pp.10,11) is to assist Christians in their meditation before, during, and after the hour of worship. The second set (CW pp.134-139) is an assortment of short prayers for various people and for common or difficult circumstances in life. These may serve as actual prayers or as prayer starters in preservice meditation, in private praying at any time, or for use with the three devotions (CW pp.150-153). The prayers on page 139 may be especially helpful when using *Morning, Evening,* or *General Devotion.*

SECTION THREE:

MUSIC IN CHRISTIAN WORSHIP

CHAPTER 12:

The Hymns of
the Worshiping Congregation

*Let the word of Christ dwell in you richly as you teach and admonish
one another with all wisdom, and as you sing psalms, hymns and
spiritual songs with gratitude in your heart to God.*

(Colossians 3:16,17)

Before Jesus ascended to his Father, he gave the command:
"Go and make disciples of all nations." His disciples did as Jesus
had said. Peter preached to his countrymen and to people from all
over the then-known world. He called them to account for their
sins, especially his countrymen, who had crucified the Savior. He
invited them to believe the good news and to be baptized for the
forgiveness of their sins. Other disciples went to the nations and
brought them the same good news.

The Apostle Paul took the gospel to the Greek and Latin world
and thereby became the link between us and the epoch-making
events that had taken place in the Holy Land.

Those ambassadors of Christ were filled with the gospel of salvation. With strong and convincing words, they brought those
who should be saved to the knowledge of Jesus Christ, the Lord
and Savior. Those who called and those who were called became
"tree[s] planted by streams of water" (Psalm 1:3). They yielded
fruit at the proper time. Their leaves did not wither, and the Lord
caused their life and work to prosper.

This compelling witness of God, sealed forever in the inspired
New Testament epistles, had a telling effect. It put the praises of
Israel: psalms, hymns, and spiritual songs, upon the lips of believers all over the world. With thankful hearts to God for his gift
of Jesus Christ, believers not only sang from the Psalter, but they
created their own creed-like hymns. They also sang solo songs
that expressed the joy that accompanied faith in Jesus Christ.

In his first letter to Timothy, Paul quoted a creed-like hymn:

> He appeared in a body,
>> was vindicated by the Spirit,
> was seen by angels
>> was preached among the nations,
> was believed on in the world,
>> was taken up in glory.
>
> (3:16)

Thus the psalms, hymns, and spiritual songs themselves became a compelling testimony to the saving acts of God in Christ Jesus. If the early believers had learned anything from the Old Testament, and from the Psalter in particular, they had learned that thanking and praising God in song means reciting before him and before each other his marvelous, saving acts. Gratitude was the theme of their song, and they sang it with faith created by the Holy Spirit. They sang for all they were worth.

Paul was also compelled to say that Christians' singing should be with "all wisdom." When you sing, the apostle urged, use your mind, which the Holy Spirit through his Word has turned toward God and filled with the gospel. Use your head.

During the first century, Philo of Alexandria, a contemporary of Jesus, asserted that God was not properly praised with words. Words, he said, belong to this sinful world and are produced by sinful people. Therefore, it would be much better to praise God in a "spiritual" way. This way avoided words and employed an ecstatic chain of meaningless syllables. Some scholars have suggested that Philo's thinking may well have influenced the Christian congregations to the north, across the Mediterranean, the congregation in Corinth in particular.

Paul, however, teaches believers to sing with wisdom, to remember what God has taught in the Scriptures of old (Psalm 16:7-11):

> I will praise the LORD, who counsels me;
>> even at night my heart instructs me.
> I have set the LORD always before me.
>> Because he is at my right hand,
>> I will not be shaken.

> Therefore my heart is glad and my tongue rejoices;
>> my body also will rest secure,
> because you will not abandon me to the grave,
>> nor will you let your Holy One see decay.
> You have made known to me the path of life;
>> you will fill me with joy in your presence,
>> with eternal pleasures at your right hand.

"Let the word of Christ dwell in your richly!" This is not a command. This beautiful passage is a prayer from the lips of Paul. It is a visionary prayer, because the answer to it was not yet at hand.

It is a prayer that God will bless the church with the gift of music in such a way that the gospel of Jesus Christ might sound forth freely to the joy and edifying of Christ's holy people. God answered the prayer of Paul with what we today call the history of western music. Hymn and chant, motet and mass, cantatas, symphonies of psalms, hymn preludes, preludes and fugues are words that only begin to describe how God, through the Holy Spirit, worked mightily in the church so that believers could sing psalms, hymns, and spiritual songs in all wisdom, with gratitude in their hearts to God.

It is difficult from their usage in the New Testament to apply modern generic definitions to the terms *psalms, hymns,* and *spiritual songs.* Contemporary use of these terms, on the other hand, is quite clear. *Psalms* usually refers to the contents of the Psalter. *Hymns* refers to the songs contained within the covers of the hymnal. Sometimes liturgical songs are also called hymns. *Spiritual songs* commonly refers to sacred choral and solo music.

The Lord has given his community of believers a treasury of psalms, hymns, and spiritual songs. A chapter in Section Two of this manual deals with the use of psalms in worship and psalm performance in connection with *Christian Worship.* The matter of "spiritual songs" is dealt with briefly in the chapter on the choir later in this section. In this chapter it is our intent to discuss Christian hymnody, considering both the qualities of excellence in hymns and the history of hymnody as it has unfolded from the days of the apostles to the production of *Christian Worship: A Lutheran Hymnal.*

Qualities of Excellence in Hymns

A *hymn* in our day is a generic term for any kind of song suitable for the congregation to sing in worship. Some years ago the Hymn Society of America defined a hymn as

> a lyric poem reverently and devotionally conceived, which is designed to be sung and which expresses the worshipers' attitude toward God or God's purpose in human life. It should be simple and metrical in form, genuinely emotional, poetic and literary in style, spiritual in quality and in its ideas so direct and so immediately apparent as to unify a congregation while singing it.[1]

To that definition we Lutheran Christians would no doubt add that our hymns are both a confession and a response to the gracious working of the triune God for us and in us. As we praise Father, Son, and Holy Spirit for his grace and mercy to us, we lay our offerings of praise before that Lord and also upon the hearts of our brothers and sisters in Christ. Young and old, men and women together encourage each other to place their faith in the triune God, who is the only source of salvation. Such a mutual ministry of strong encouragement requires discipline and good judgment in the choice of text and music. If the text of a hymn does not contain the message of salvation, there can be no strengthening of faith.

The music of a hymn, then, must convey the message, no more, no less. Anything else tends to blur and break communication from the heart of faith to the heart of faith. Hymnody at its very best helps the community of believers travel securely through this life and points their hearts to the glory that awaits them in eternity.

Several sources suggest the qualities of excellence in hymnody. The first of these is the poetry of the Old Testament, the psalms, Isaiah, Job, and other sources called canticles, which the church down through the ages has selected for use in its liturgies. The second source is the New Testament: the poetic prologue of St. Luke's Gospel; selected portions of St. Paul's epistles, particularly his Epistle to the Ephesians; and the Revelation

---

[1] *Singing with Understanding* (Nashville: broadman Press, 1980), p. 7.

230

to St. John. The third source is the hymnody of the New Testament church: from St. John Chrysostom to St. Ambrose, to Martin Luther and Paul Gerhardt and Martin Franzmann.

A careful study of these sources helps develop a set of qualities of excellence for which to look in evaluating hymnody. Not every good hymn, of course, will possess all of these qualities of excellence, and not all the qualities may be of equal importance. Furthermore, the Holy Spirit, who is the moving force behind all good hymnody, gives different gifts to different hymnwriters. They have different personalities, different training, different lives, and consequently divergent writing styles. Nevertheless, some or all of the identified qualities will be evident in the "great" hymns: the hymns that instruct, inspire, edify, and stand the test of time. Some of those qualities follow:

A good hymn is *liturgical.* It fits easily into the structure of the public worship. The Psalter is the best teacher of this quality, as it shows believers individually and corporately how to come before the true God with prayer and praise.

A good hymn is *doxological.* A doxology is a speech or song of praise. But true doxology is more than just a carelessly shouted, "Praise the Lord." Fruitful doxology praises God by giving him names that describe his saving activity in terms of the three articles of the Christian faith. It also praises God by reciting the great things he has done in terms of these three articles. Psalms 146-150 constitute a grand doxology of the Psalter.

A good hymn has *doctrinal content.* If the praise of God speaks of the great things God has done, this will almost always appear in a form that teaches. The chief doctrine Christian hymnody should proclaim is mankind's redemption from sin through Jesus Christ, Lord and Savior.

A good hymn *makes use of the Word of God.* It may quote the Scriptures directly, make use of word pictures from the Scriptures, or use Bible stories or biblical allusions to strengthen its message. It also *applies that message,* as Christians sing their hymns to and with each other or use their texts for private meditation.

A good hymn is *poetic,* with choices of words, thoughts, progressions, and word pictures drawn from experiences common to many people.

A good hymn has *emotional content* that supports the message. In much communication today the emotional impact of the communication IS the message. Think of the glut of sex and violence that flashes at us almost continually through the entertainment media. What is said in the pulpit, in a classroom, or in a hymnal, however, cannot be relegated to the position of servant of the emotions. But in good hymns, as in the psalms, the emotions grow from the message and reinforce it.

A good hymn is *influenced by the "year of our Lord."* The poet who lives in the Lord's year is moved to repeat the story of Jesus' birth, of his life, suffering, death, and resurrection. Furthermore, hymns influenced by the year of our Lord will speak of the salvation that Jesus' humiliation and exaltation have earned for all people and apply that salvation to individual lives.

Good hymns have *melodies that support the scriptural message and touch the heart of the worshiper.* It is not as easy to define what that means as it is to know it when one sees it. Simple and good tunes that do this are difficult to write. They require an innate sense of melody, supported by an intensive education in the craft of musical composition. The ability to write such tunes is a gracious gift of God.

Good hymnody is one of the truly special gifts of the Spirit to his Church. Of the several thousand hymns from a rich variety of sources that were considered for inclusion in *Christian Worship,* those chosen were perceived to excel in the above qualities of excellence. May our gracious Lord make their choice and their use a blessing to his Church.

Hymnody from the Apostles to *Christian Worship*

The 623 hymns that appear in *Christian Worship* represent a rich hymnic history and a marvelous confluence of sources, some reaching back over 3,000 years. The Christian church was born within the context of the temple and the synagogue, and its early worship bore the marks of its Jewish ancestry. From the Day of Pentecost, the Christian church had its own distinctive identity. But its worship tradition remained very much Jewish. For some time the first Christians in Jerusalem continued to gather at the temple. And the Apostle Paul always began his mission work in a new city in the Jewish synagogue, if one was located there.

Within that worship tradition hymns had their place. To what extent singing was used in early Christian worship is hard to tell, nor are we sure about the exact nature of the music itself. No document from the apostolic age gives us much information on the subject. But that the chant and song used in the temple and synagogue found their way into those early Christian groups is clear from Paul's encouragement to the first century Christians to "teach and admonish each other with psalms and hymns and spiritual songs," and to "sing with grace in your hearts to the Lord."

The psalms the early Christians used in their worship were undoubtedly many of the same psalms that had been well known and widely used in synagogue worship. Psalm singing dominated the New Testament church's praise for several centuries. The "hymn" that Jesus and his disciples sang at the conclusion of the Last Supper was part of the Hallel (Psalms 114-118). And the earliest inspired New Testament hymns, the *Magnificat (Song of Mary); the Benedictus (Song of Zechariah)* and the *Nunc Dimittis (Song of Simeon)* have a noticeable psalmlike character.

Modeled on the poetic form of the Old Testament psalms, those three New Testament lyrics may be representative of similar hymns composed by early Jewish Christians in Palestine before the Christian church was drawn more fully into the Gentile world. The form of those hymns was quite different from the hymns shaped as poetry and running in clearly marked verses as we know them today. They were, instead, rhythmic and poetic prose. Some familiar New Testament passages, such as Ephesians 1:3-14 and 1 Peter 1:3-12; 1 Timothy 3:16, quoted earlier in this essay; and portions of Revelation, particularly chapters 4 and 5, perhaps even passages like Philippians 2:6-11, might have been early Christian hymns quoted by the apostles or, conversely, apostolic quotes used by early Christians as hymns. These hymnlike passages all acclaim in poetic prose the saving works of God in Christ. Such rhythmic, poetic prose is also found in two classic writings of the early church, the *Didache* (ca. A.D. 90) and the *Epistle to Diognetus* (ca. 170).

233

As the early church extended its gospel proclamation beyond the borders of Palestine, Christian hymnody began to show the influence of Greek culture. John of Damascus and Synesius of Cyrene were early Greek hymnists. An early Greek hymn that has survived is an office hymn, *Joyful Light,* sung at the lighting of the lamps. A classic translation of this hymn is that of Robert Bridges, a former poet laureate of England (†1930):

> O gladsome light, O grace
> Of God the Father's face
> The eternal splendor wearing;
> Celestial, holy, blest,
> Our Savior, Jesus Christ
> Joyful in thine appearing.

Ignatius of Antioch (ca. A.D.110) is said to have used antiphonal singing of hymns among the Christians he served. Pliny the Younger, governor of Bithynia, wrote in secular literature of how Christians would gather before daybreak on a stated day and utter responsive songs of praise to Christ as to a God. About A.D.150, a group of 42 Greek hymns appeared in a collection called *Odes of Solomon.*

Most of the early Greek hymns stayed very close to Scripture's own words. Only a few writers tried free paraphrases of biblical texts and wrote hymns not based exclusively on Scripture. After the Gnostics and the Arians used their own original hymns and popular tunes to spread their false teachings early in the fourth century, the Council of Laodicea actually discouraged that kind of hymn writing, insisting that only the words of Scripture itself should be used for worship. The council, however, did not restrict the writing of poems for private use and circulation.

For the first five centuries of church history, the Eastern church proved to be more fertile ground than the Western for hymn writing. Poets, particularly in the monastic orders, invented forms like the "tri-paria," single stanza or short, one-sentence hymns. Gradually Greek poetic meters (anapestic, iambic) were also used in hymn writing. The early Greek hymns are characterized by fine, steel-like objectivity that rests in the revelation and attributes of God, particularly the personality and deity of Christ. They make little concession to human emotion. Though sometimes

234

born of controversy, the hymns that have survived are those that best give expression to the creedal truths that clearly set forth the universal Christian faith. A later Greek hymnwriter, Joseph the Hymnographer (†883) was probably the most prolific of all Greek writers of sacred song.

In the Western church the hymn was slower in finding its way, largely because of popular prejudice against any kind of praise that didn't directly quote the Scriptures. Not until the fourth century was hymn singing practiced in the West. It was probably during this period that the great hymn of praise, the *Te Deum Laudamus,* was written by an author believed to have been Bishop Necita of the remote Danubian province of Dacia. The *Te Deum* is thought to be an attempted "response in kind" to some of the false teachings being spread by the hymns of the Arians and Gnostics. The title of the first Latin hymnist is generally given to Hilary of Poitiers (ca. 350). The fragments of Hilary's hymns that have come down to us, however, indicate a rather dreary, dogmatic style. Perhaps that is why Hilary's hymns never really appealed to the common man of his day or became part of the church's lasting hymn treasury.

The greatest name and the greatest achievements in the history of fourth century Western hymnody belong to Ambrose of Milan. This venerable bishop is rightly called the "father of popular hymn singing in Western Europe." How many of the hundreds of hymns attributed to him Ambrose actually wrote may be disputed. But there is no question that he made his church in Milan a singing congregation.

At the time of the Arian heresy, Ambrose rallied the faithful to the orthodox cause with doctrinally powerful hymns composed in simple Latin meters. When Empress Justina, who favored the Arians, demanded that Ambrose open one of the churches in the diocese for the Arians' use, the bishop refused. When the soldiers of the empress arrived outside the church to try and enforce her decree, they found Ambrose and the congregation inside praying and singing. So great was the effect of the singing that the soldiers outside the sanctuary are said to have finally joined in with the well-known chants. Every effort to compel Ambrose to yield proved fruitless and the empress finally had to abandon her plans.

235

To Ambrose is attributed the development of the "long meter" versification still used in many of our hymns. The so-called Ambrosian hymns have a rugged solemnity about them. They use simple meters and forceful language to describe the majesty of God. The hymns of Ambrose have been adapted and readapted over the centuries for use in Christian worship. Two hymns ascribed to Ambrose that appear in *Christian Worship: A Lutheran Hymnal* are *Savior of the Nations, Come* (CW 2), an Advent hymn, and the morning hymn *O Splendor of God's Glory Bright* (CW 586).

Though Ambrose introduced hymn singing into the worship life of the Western church, the victory of the popular hymn was by no means universal. There was still uncertainty as to whether popular singing should be rejected, because heterodox groups like the Arians used it. Some still thought that popular singing should be restricted to the psalms and canticles found in the Scriptures themselves. Others thought it necessary to meet the Arians and others "on their own ground" with popular hymns that were doctrinally correct. After a number of contradictory decrees by various church councils, the Council of Toledo (ca. 600) decreed that no one should withhold hymns sung in the praise of God from the people.

There were other poets who, besides Ambrose, contributed to the growing treasury of Latin hymnody. Aurelius Clemens Prudentius (348-413) was a Spaniard. He beautifully wedded scholarship, poetry, and theology in his *Of the Father's Love Begotten* (CW 35), a "creedal" hymn in praise of Christ. The most prolific Latin poet of the sixth century was Venatius Fortunatus of Italy. Several late twentieth century hymnals, including *Christian Worship,* have included a text by Fortunatus with a modern tune by Carl Schalk in *Sing, My Tongue, the Glorious Battle,* a truly powerful and scriptural Lenten hymn (CW 122).

To the monasteries and the men associated with them, we owe the survival of hymnody from the seventh century to the time of Martin Luther. The so-called "Benedictine Rule" prescribed hymns for singing at the various "canonical hours," a cycle of prayer occurring eight times a day, every three hours. As the organized life of the church developed into the regular rhythm of the Christian year, various feast days and saints' days were also assigned appropriate hymns.

Many of those hymns were by writers who remained anonymous. Translations of a number of them appear in twentieth century hymnals, including *Christian Worship*. John M. Neale, a nineteenth century English scholar and translator, gave new life to many of these ancient texts by masterful translations. Some of the monastic hymns whose authors can be identified include: *Come, Holy Ghost, Creator Blest* (CW 177,178) by Rhabanus Maurus, abbot of Fulda in Germany (ca. 825); *All Glory, Laud, and Honor* (CW 131) by Theodulph of Orleans (ca. 750); *Jerusalem the Golden* (CW 214) by Bernard of Cluny (thirteenth century). *Oh, Come, Oh, Come Emmanuel* (CW 23) is an example of an anonymous monastic hymn that is still loved and used today. *Christian Worship* continues the Latin tradition by including a selection of these great hymns in its hymn corpus.

The monastic communities preserved the hymns and added to the church's hymn treasury. At the same time, however, they also contributed to taking those same hymns away from the people. The increasing complexity of the poetical and musical form of the hymns, together with the decreasing use of the Latin language by the common people resulted in the hymns becoming almost the exclusive possession of the monastic communities and no longer a vehicle for congregational expression.

The worshiping laity had to be satisfied with *tropes,* vernacular additions that clarified, expanded, or interpolated the prescribed liturgical texts. The music to which these tropes were sung was either borrowed from existing chant or newly composed in the style of the Gregorian chant. The Introit, Gradual, Alleluia, and Offertory were often subjected to troping. The sequence or prose that followed the Alleluia was a particularly important type of trope. In Germany, beginning about the eleventh century, vernacular responses after the *Kyrie eleison,* (called *leisen*) were tolerated, though not officially encouraged, particularly at special festivals. These *leisen* turned out to be an extremely important element in the return of the congregational hymn to the German congregations.

The Lutheran Reformation brought about the return of congregational hymn singing in Germany and eventually throughout

Christianity. Luther did not consider himself an innovator. But it was Luther who by encouragement and by personal work and example gave impetus to the revival of congregational hymn singing. Luther had learned to love music through his monastic training. His scholarly studies no doubt made him aware of how in earlier times Ambrose and Augustine had made use of congregational hymns.

Luther is also thought to have been influenced by the Hussite movement, which had taken place a century earlier in Bohemia. Jan Huss was condemned by the Council of Constance in 1415 and burned at the stake. His followers were sternly warned to stop teaching and singing the popular hymns he had taught and encouraged. But the desire for congregational singing never really died in Bohemia. The publication of a hymnal for the Bohemian Brethren in 1501 sparked a bit of a Hussite revival. Some of these hymns, especially the hymns of Michael Weisse, a contemporary of Luther, were included in early German Evangelical hymnals.

Luther's scriptural view of the universal priesthood of believers made it inevitable that the laity would be led to participate in the worship of the Evangelical church. Luther and the men around him also appreciated what a powerful ally popular hymn singing could be for disseminating Evangelical doctrine. Restoring congregational song, therefore, became a matter of high priority in the church that eventually bore Luther's name. Luther himself took the lead in finding, supplying, and publishing materials for popular congregational song. And he encouraged those who were skilled in music and the poetic arts to put God's Word into hymns with fitting music.

Luther's leadership and encouragement led to the development of the so-called "Lutheran chorale." The chorale was drawn from a wide variety of sources: the psalms; the chants of the medieval church; the pre-Reformation *Leisen* or *Kyrie songs*; Latin and German hymns from the church's earlier days; secular melodies to which sacred texts were added; and original works by Luther and men like Justus Jonas and Paul Speratus.

That the people were hungry for active participation in worship is testified to by the almost immediate success and remarkable popularity of the chorale. Chorale texts spoke clearly of sin and grace, law and gospel. They emphasized God's justification of sinners in the crucified and risen Christ. The congregation sang the chorale's melodies in unison and without accompaniment. They were vigorous and rhythmic.

This chorale heritage is a unique treasure of the Lutheran church. The Hymn of the Day plan (chapter 5) is designed to keep this treasure alive and on the lips of Lutheran worshipers of our generation and the generations to come. *Christian Worship* contains a generous selection of the historic Lutheran chorales. Let Lutherans continue to sing them with vigor and understanding. Learning the chorales does, it is true, take time and determination and practice. But it is time and practice well spent and determination that will pay rich dividends in the end.

Worshiping Lutherans center their congregational song in hymns of proclamation, prayer, and adoration. But Lutherans' hymns are not just general expressions of praise, loosely attached to the act of worship. They are a carefully selected element in a unified whole. From the beginning of the Reformation and the restoration of popular hymn singing, Luther desired that the hymns not disrupt the orderliness of the worship, but supplement the ancient liturgy of the church and provide a means of involving the congregation in that liturgy.

Yes, the Reformation hymn restoration brought new songs and new sounds into the church. But the end result was that the joy of the gospel was more easily and completely reflected in the people's worship. It remains true that when hymns for worship are well-chosen and hymnals are caringly and carefully produced as an aid to corporate worship, the Word of Christ will dwell richly among the community of believers gathered for worship. With such hymns believers will, until our Savior's return, continue to teach and admonish one another with wisdom, great jubilation, and hearts filled with gratitude to God.

More recently Lutherans have also been encouraged to sing the great "hymns" of the liturgy. In the various services included in *Christian Worship,* these hymns include hymns of praise (*Glory Be to God; O Lord, Our Lord*), arrangements of the *Sanctus* and the *Agnus Dei,* and the postcommunion canticles in the major services, as well as the hymns and canticles in the services entitled *Morning Praise* and *Evening Prayer.*

The wonderfully productive period of Reformation hymnody ended about 1580 when the *Book of Concord* was published. Several composers, however, during and immediately following this period, should not be overlooked, such as Nicholas Selnecker, Bartholamaus Ringwaldt, and Philip Nicolai. The latter (ca. 1600) wrote the so-called "king" and "queen" of chorales: *Wake, Awake, for Night Is Flying* (CW 206) and *How Lovely Shines the Morning Star* (CW 79).

In the seventeenth century, another outburst of German hymn writing took place during and after the Thirty Years' War. The anguish of the time was reflected by the hymnists who during this period wrote some of the church's greatest "Cross and Comfort" hymns. The privation and distress that affected so many people caught up in the Thirty Years' War was a significant factor in the development of a new kind of hymnody, more personal and subjective in nature. This hymnody gave poetic expression to the life situations in which believers of that day found themselves. It was also then that Martin Opitz reformed German poetry. The hymns of this period are rhythmically and poetically smoother, clearer, and softer.

Another important development of this period was the separation of the roles of poet and composer. Often during the time of the Reformation, a single writer would compose both text and tune. Now poets began writing only texts, and musicians crafted tunes to fit the texts. Johann Heermann, *O Dearest Jesus* (CW 117), was among the first to adopt this approach to sacred poetry. Martin Rinkart, *Now Thank We All Our God* (CW 610), and Johann Franck, *Soul, Adorn Yourself with Gladness* (CW 311), were others. Johann Crueger (1598-1662) on the other hand, wrote no hymn texts but composed 71 tunes that set the hymns of Heermann, Rinkart, and especially Paul Gerhardt to music. Rinkart's *Now Thank We All Our God,* a hymn of thanks written in the dark days of the Thirty Years' War, was sung at the signing of the Peace of Westphalia, which ended the war.

The one hymnwriter who stands above all other hymnists of this age is Paul Gerhardt (1607-1676), preacher and poet who

240

stood as a staunch representative of Lutheran orthodoxy. Gerhardt wrote over 120 hymns, many of which are still sung in translation by Evangelical Christians today. Some of Gerhardt's best-known hymns selected for *Christian Worship* include: *O Sacred Head, Now Wounded* (CW 105); *If God Himself Be for Me* (CW 419); *Awake, My Heart, with Gladness* (CW 156); and *Once Again My Heart Rejoices* (CW 37). Gerhardt's hymns are more personal and introspective than Luther's. But they beautifully turn the worshiper's attention to the saving love of God in Christ. Paul Gerhardt and Johann Crueger enjoyed a unique partnership as pastor and music director at the same church in Berlin. Crueger's choral collection of 1664 was an important one for Lutherans, filled with tunes that carried hymn texts like Gerhardt's in a manner truly expressive of the believing heart.

The Pietistic movement in the late seventeenth and early eighteenth centuries and its negative effect on the worship life of the Evangelical churches is described in greater detail in Section One of this manual. Pietism began as a reaction against what was viewed by many as "orthodox formalism," an outward adherence to correct doctrine and a participation for appearance sake in the outward ordinances of the church. Pietistic hymn texts were characterized by an almost mystical emphasis on the personal and subjective. Most were emotionally shallow and sentimental. Pietists regarded music as a means of stirring up feelings of devotion. Not surprisingly, the tunes of Pietism were florid and extremely sentimental. The stirring chorale melodies of the Reformation age were replaced with lighter melodies that often had waltzlike meters. They were sung in a slow, somber manner, again, with the intention of stirring up religious feeling.

Most of the hymns of Pietism have long since fallen out of use. Some, however, did survive. Examples of hymns from the age of Pietism included in *Christian Worship* are: *Baptized into Your Name Most Holy* (CW 294) and *My Maker, Be with Me* (CW 598) by Johann Rambach; *Awake, O Spirit, Who Inspired* (CW 567) by Karl von Bogatzky; and Adam Drese's tune *Seelenbräuetigam* (CW 422). German Reformed hymnists whose works, usually in edited and greatly shortened form, survived from this period and are found in *Christian Worship* include: Joachim Neander's

Praise to the Lord, the Almighty (CW 234); Nicolaus von Zinzen-dorf's *Jesus, Your Blood and Righteousness* (CW 376); Erdmann Neumeister's *Jesus Sinners Does Receive* (CW 304); and Ben-jamin Schmolck's *Open Now Thy Gates of Beauty* (CW 255).

Pietism's most significant hymnal was Johann Freyling-hausen's *Geistreiches Gesangbuch,* which originally appeared in 1704 and was republished a number of times. Freylinghausen's hymnal, a formidable tome of over 1,500 hymns and almost 900 melodies, was one of the first hymnals brought to America by German immigrants in the late eighteenth century.

Some Reformation hymns were still found in the Freyling-hausen hymnal but were generally lost among the pietistic hymns. Pietism's lack of intellectual strength and its emphasis on human feelings soon left the field open for the movement known as the Enlightenment, or Rationalism, in which hymns and liturgies were altered and rewritten to conform to purely human reason and in which the presentation of the gospel was all but abandoned.

A confessional revival led by Claus Harms in the nineteenth century sought to restore the unaltered texts of the Reformation chorales and give rhythmic form again to the chorale melodies. These reforms not only reflected a desire for greater faithfulness to the theological spirit of the Reformation, but reinvigorated congregational singing. The research of men like Wackernagel, Zahn, and Layritz helped to rediscover and repopularize the Re-formation chorales. Meanwhile, Mendelssohn was rediscovering and repopularizing the century-old hymn harmonizations of Jo-hann Sebastian Bach.

Good German hymnody in the nineteenth and twentieth cen-turies has been quite sparse, perhaps a sad reflection on the lack of spiritual life that today characterizes the "cradle of the Refor-mation." Among the best of twentieth century German composers is Heinz Werner Zimmermann (b.1930). Marjorie Jillson's *Have No Fear, Little Flock* (CW 442) is set to a contemporary Zimmer-mann tune.

The hymnody of Scandinavia also had its beginning in the Re-formation era. In Scandinavian churches hymns were led by choirs or a *precentor* a member of the congregation with a voice strong enough to lead the singing. Organs, when used, played only preludes or in alternation with the congregation's song. In the rural churches of Scandinavia, singing flourished as a purely vocal art. Imaginative precentors and other gifted singers embellished hymns that had been learned by rote, giving rise to a kind of "religious folk music." When they were published, Scandinavian hymnals were usually produced privately by individual pastors or organists. A few later received official sanction and were eventually used a bit more widely in churches.

Scandinavian hymnists whose contributions to Christian hymnody have flowed into *Christian Worship* include: Magnus Landstad, a nineteenth century Norwegian poet, *When Sinners See Their Lost Condition* (CW 32) and *Before You, God, the Judge of All* (CW 306); the nineteenth century Danish poet Nikolai Grundtvig, *God's Word Is Our Great Heritage* (CW 293) and *Built on the Rock* (CW 529); and Thomas Kingo, Denmark's first great hymnist (d. 1703). The latter's hymns include: *On My Heart Imprint Your Image* (CW 319,320), *Like the Golden Sun Ascending* (CW 147), and *Praise to You and Adoration* (CW 470). The tunes of Ludvig Lindeman, including *Fred Til Bod* (CW 153) and *Kirken Den Er Et Gammelt Hus* (CW 529), were said to have "taught the Norwegians to sing." *Children of the Heavenly Father* (CW 449), by the Swedish author Caroline Sandell Berg, reflects a spiritual revival that swept over Europe in the nineteenth century. *How Great Thou Art* (CW 256) by Carl Boberg (d. 1940), also a Swedish poet, is perhaps the most popular Scandinavian hymn in America, popularized in part by its use in the Billy Graham evangelistic crusades.

While hymnody flourished in post-Reformation Germany and Scandinavia, it suffered quite a different fate in nations influenced by Calvin and Zwingli. Their answer to "Let the people sing," was the metrical psalm. Congregational singing, they argued, must be biblical, disciplined, and dignified, with no allowance for human poetry and invention.

The result was the production of a series of gradually enlarged "psalters," beginning with Calvin's own "psalter" in 1737. Louis Bourgeois (d. 1561) provided many singable tunes for the psalms, including *Old Hundredth,* to which Christians today sing the long-meter doxology (CW 334), as well as a number of other hymns (CW 233,286,316,323). Bourgeois was also the chief musical contributor to the *Genevan Psalter,* published in 1562. This book contained all 150 psalms set to music, the Ten Commandments, and the *Nunc Dimittis. Genevan Psalter* melodies gained extensive use in the sixteenth and seventeenth centuries, not only in French-speaking countries, but in Germany, Holland, England, Scotland, and even the American colonies.

For 140 years, until the time of Isaac Watts, the Geneva pattern of metrical psalms dominated Reformed worship. Over 100 volumes of verses, or psalters were published between the early fifteenth and eighteenth centuries. When English protestants fled to Geneva, psalters were produced in English. Some of the tunes from the early English psalters, including *St. Anne* (CW 441) and *Dundee* (CW 324,356,420) are still in rather popular use today.

The sixteenth century English reformers chose to follow Calvin rather than Luther. This had great consequences for hymn writing in the Church of England. Some religious poetry flourished in the next two centuries, but few significant hymns for congregational use were produced because they weren't thought to be appropriate or necessary. Thomas Ken, author of *All Praise to Thee, My God, This Night* (CW 592), *Awake, My Soul, and with the Sun* (CW 582), and *Praise God, from Whom All Blessings Flow* (CW 334); and Samuel Crossman, author of *My Song Is Love Unknown* (CW 110), were two of the very few poets of the day who produced lasting hymn texts.

Isaac Watts (1647-1748), however, proved to be an important agent for change in English hymnody. A Congregational minister, he sought, with devotional lyric poetry, to amalgamate the two streams of paraphrasing Scripture and setting the exact words of Scripture to music. Watts believed that truly authentic praise for Christians could go beyond the words of Scripture to include original expressions of praise and thanksgiving. And, if the psalms were to be sung in Christian worship, Christian hymnists could summarize their thoughts, paraphrase, and "Christianize" them.

Watts' hymnal of 1709, which first introduced some of his own hymns, and especially his hymnal of 1719, *The Psalms of David Imitated,* marked the birth of modern hymnody in the English-speaking church. Despite some initial opposition, Watts began to regard hymns not simply as a non-official substitute for the psalms, but as a form in its own right, another medium for the piety and devotion of every worshiper. Watt's hymns are comprehensive in scope, scriptural in flavor, Calvinistic in theology, generally emphasizing the glory and the sovereignty of God. The English-speaking Lutheran church has also warmed to Watts' hymns. A representative sampling of them in *Christian Worship* includes: *From All that Dwell below the Skies* (CW 250); *We Sing the Almighty Power of God* (CW 261); *Joy to the World* (CW 62); *O God, Our Help in Ages Past* (CW 441); *When I Survey the Wondrous Cross* (CW 125); and *The Man Is Ever Blest* (CW 475).

The Methodist movement (ca. 1750) inspired a spiritual awakening in England. It also had a profound effect on English hymnody. The hymns of Charles Wesley (1707-1788) gave the movement both inspiration and education. Charles Wesley himself is thought to have written as many as 6,500 hymns. Most are intensely personal and appeal to the emotions. Many are also evangelistic, addressed to those who do not yet know Jesus as Savior. New tunes were also written to reflect the subjective character of the Wesleyian hymns. Charles Wesley's hymns were well-suited to the revival meetings that characterized the early Methodist movement. *Hark! The Herald Angels Sing* (CW 61); and *Jesus, Lover of My Soul* (CW 357) are among the hymns of Charles Wesley in *Christian Worship.*

Charles Wesley's brother John, though not himself a hymnist, collected and published hymns. During a mission journey to Georgia, John Wesley published *Collection of Psalms and Hymns,* one of the earliest English hymnals published in America. John Wesley was also a skilled translator, and his translations made it possible for English-speaking Christians to sing several German Moravian hymns, including *Jesus, Your Blood and Righteousness* (CW 376).

A number of gifted English hymnists soon followed the lead of Watts and Wesley. John Newton, William Cowper, and Augustus Toplady all produced hymns that are included in *Christian Worship.* Reginald Heber (d. 1826) produced one of the first English hymnals designed for corporate worship. It provided hymns for the church year and included both psalm settings and hymns together. The stated purpose of Heber's hymnal was to reinforce the teachings of the *Book of Common Prayer.*

Liturgical worship and good hymnody were emphasized by the Oxford Movement of the 1830s. The publication of *Hymns Ancient and Modern* in 1861 gave hymns an accepted and respected position in the Church of England. Building on the heritage of Watts and Heber, it brought the two main streams of congregational song, metrical psalmody, and free poetic expression, together in one book. *Hymns Ancient and Modern* was also richly eclectic. Its hymns included translations of German and Latin hymns and hymns with roots in different church bodies, much as the Christian hymnals being produced today are attempting to do. It also introduced many new tunes, including some folklike tunes printed without meter signature. *Hymns Ancient and Modern* was revised in 1950 and is still in print.

The English Hymnal of 1906 was notable for its harmonizations by Ralph Vaughn Williams. *The Church Hymnary* of 1927 brought enrichment to hymn literature by including a number of Celtic tunes, including *Slane* (CW 367) and *Kuortane* (CW 388,552). The twentieth century has produced several great English poets and hymnwriters whose works are included in most, if not all the hymnals produced in the last quarter of the twentieth century, including *Christian Worship.* These writers include F. Pratt Green, Brian Wren, Charles Bayly, Fred Kaan, and Timothy Dudley-Smith. In brilliant, contemporary poetry, their hymns address issues facing twentieth century Christians.

An eighteenth century Welsh poet, William Williams, produced over 800 hymn texts and published a number of hymnals. The greatest legacy of the Welsh to the hymnody of the church, however, is in the area of hymn tunes. The appealing, folklike character of the melodies, supported by sturdy harmonies, gives them the necessary qualities for congregational singing. *Hyfrydol* (CW 365,465,486,603), *Ebenezer* (CW 280), *Cwm Rhondda* (CW 237,523), and *Aberystwyth* (CW 357) are representative of the Welsh tunes included in *Christian Worship.*

Early American colonists brought their hymnals to the new world. From Lutherans and Moravians came the chorale treasury.

English, French, and Dutch settlers brought their metrical psalms. In 1640 a committee of New England clergy published the *Bay Psalm Book,* generally regarded as the first American hymnal. Later the hymns of Watts and other English poets made their way across the Atlantic to become part of the American hymn treasury. The hymns of Wesley and Watts were key elements in the eighteenth century spiritual revival known as the "Great Awakening." The oldest original American hymn tune is thought to be Oliver Holden's *Coronation* (CW 370).

After the Revolutionary War, hymn compiling in America began in earnest. Each denomination prepared its own collection of hymns. The Episcopal church had its prayer book with metrical psalms. Presbyterians, Baptists, and Congregationalists relied on the hymns of Watts. Methodists had Wesley. Early Lutheran immigrants used Freylinghausen's Pietistic hymnal of 1741, as well as hymn collections from Wuerttemberg and Marburg.

German Lutherans in Pennsylvania under Henry Melchior Muehlenberg prepared the first Lutheran hymnal in America in 1786, a hymnal that reflected the music and theology of Pietism. In 1795 Muehlenberg's son-in-law John Christopher Kunze published *A Hymn and Prayer-Book,* the first Lutheran hymnal in the English language to be published in America. Lutheran hymnody in America hit a low point in 1814, however, with a hymnal that appeared to thoroughly reject confessional Lutheranism and embrace the so-called Union Movement (a movement that sought to unite Lutherans and the Reformed) and the shallow American Lutheranism advocated by men like Samuel Schmucker. A backlash to this lack of confessionalism came in the 1870s, during the years of Walther and Loehe and the founding of the Synodical Conference. After the turn of the century, confessional Lutheran hymnals began to appear, first in the "mother tongues," then in English, as German and Scandinavian Americans responded to the need to pass down a confessional heritage to their children in teaching and in hymnody.

American poets began to publish their own hymns in the nineteenth century. *Christian Worship* contains a good representation of these hymns: *Hark! The Voice of Jesus Crying* (CW 573) is by a Presbyterian, Daniel March. *O Little Town of Bethlehem* (CW

65,66) and *O Christians, Haste* (CW 570) were written by Episcopal hymnists Phillips Brooks and Mary Ann Thompson. *Stand Up, Stand Up for Jesus* (CW 474) by George Duffield, Jr. first appeared in an American Presbyterian hymnal.

In the mid nineteenth century, another religious revival took place in America, spurred by a wave of frontier camp meetings. About this time the term *gospel song* entered the American hymn vocabulary. Gospel songs are generally folklike, narrative balladsongs emphasizing personal experiences, feelings, and emotions. Many of these hymns were collected by musicians like Ira Sankey, who worked with the evangelist Dwight Moody. A prolific author of gospel songs was Fanny Crosby (1820-1915). The tunes that carried the gospel songs were usually very simple, major key melodies, often with a refrain. These hymns continue to be fairly popular, perhaps because of their simplicity. *To God Be the Glory* (CW 399), *I Love to Tell the Story* (CW 562), and *God Be with You till We Meet Again* (CW 327,328) are examples of gospel songs selected for *Christian Worship*. Few new gospel songs have been produced in the last fifty years, perhaps because more recent evangelistic crusades have featured their own large choirs or soloists and audiences have become more passive.

American folk hymnody has both a written and an unwritten history. In its infancy folk hymnody existed only in oral tradition. The American folk hymns are mostly related to secular folk songs brought by early settlers, primarily from the British Isles.

The written history of the American folk hymn began when school teachers either notated them from oral tradition, took a hymn text and adapted a folk tune to it, or composed a melody themselves in a style identical to that of other folk hymns. An interesting development in the history of folk hymnody was the production of "shape-note hymnals." In an attempt to help those who did not read music learn tunes, different shapes were assigned to different tones on the scale. Fairly well-known folk hymnals like *Kentucky Harmony* (1816), *Southern Harmony* (1835), and *The Sacred Harp* (1844) are shape-note hymnals. Well-known American folk tunes included in *Christian Worship* include: *Nettleton* (CW 484), *Detroit* (CW 118,493), *New Britain* (CW 379), and *Wondrous Love* (CW 120).

Although American slaves were already singing spirituals in the pre-Civil War period, the first written collection, *Slave Songs of the United States* was published in 1869. These "spirituals" have been preserved and popularized by the many predominantly black churches in our nation, as well as by the vocal solos of great black singers like Mahalia Jackson. Many of these spirituals reflect the difficulty of the black experience in America. At the same time, however, most of them clearly articulate the gospel, Christ's vicarious atonement and the truth that those who rely on the Lord do not do so in vain. Black spirituals included in *Christian Worship* include: *Go, Tell It on the Mountain* (CW 57), *There Is a Balm in Gilead* (CW 564), and *Were You There* (CW 119). A hymnal that includes representative samplings of a wide variety of hymn sources may also be an important tool for evangelism and cross-cultural ministry. That is one reason for including these spirituals in *Christian Worship.*

Hymn writing in twentieth century America has not been particularly fruitful. Most twentieth century hymns included in *Christian Worship,* as well as many new tunes, originated in England rather than America. Most hymns written by American authors in the last half of the twentieth century reflect the secularization of American religion during that period. These often artless hymns encourage ecumenism, social justice, the addressing of urban problems, and the like.

Although few lasting hymns have been written by Americans, most American denominations have published hymnals during the last quarter of the twentieth century, a time that may well go down as the "golden age of American hymnal production." Notable Lutheran hymnal publications during this time have included *Lutheran Book of Worship* (1978) and *Lutheran Worship* (1982). Both books were thoroughly studied by the framers of *Christian Worship* and provided many resources for them.

Despite the general dearth of twentieth century confessional Lutheran hymns, there have been some noteworthy exceptions. Jaroslav Vajda, (b. 1919), a pastor, editor, and translator, has not only provided the church with translations of Slovak hymns, but has produced a number of beautiful original hymns, including the following in *Christian Worship: Up through Endless Ranks of Angels* (CW 172), an Ascension hymn; *Now the Silence* (CW 231), a hymn

249

whose imagery takes Christians on a journey through the worship service; *See This Wonder in the Making* (CW 300), a baptism hymn; *Where Shepherds Lately Knelt* (CW 54), a contemporary Christmas carol that has been set to music by Carl Schalk; and *Amid the World's Bleak Wilderness* (CW 342), a poetic commentary on Jesus' words in John 15:5: "I am the vine; you are the branches."

A history of the streams of hymnic tradition that have flowed together into *Christian Worship* would not be complete without mentioning two brothers raised in a Lutheran parsonage in Lake City, Minnesota: Martin and Werner Franzmann. Martin Franzmann (d. 1976) was a professor of classical studies and New Testament and a prolific author. His hymns are written in a lofty and elegant style, often using Elizabethan language. They are doctrinally and poetically strong and saturated with biblical pictures and allusion. Future generations may well judge Martin Franzmann to have been one of the most outstanding religious poets of the twentieth century. Examples of his work found in *Christian Worship* include: *Thy Strong Word* (CW 280), *In Adam We Have All Been One* (CW 396), *O God, O Lord of Heaven and Earth* (CW 400), and *O Kingly Love, that Faithfully* (CW 335).

The hymns of Werner Franzmann (b. 1905) proclaim his love of the Savior and his strong conviction that the birth, life, suffering, and death of Jesus are the answer to the struggles of the human condition and the problems of life. Werner Franzmann served as a parish pastor, a high school teacher, and a writer and editor of devotions for Christian homes. His hymns reflect his experience and touch hearts with dignified simplicity. He, too, has been a unique gift of God to the church on earth. Examples of his work found in *Christian Worship* include: *As Angels Joyed with One Accord* (CW 5), *Down from the Mount of Glory* (CW 97), *Triumphant from the Grave* (CW 151), *In Trembling Hands, Lord God, We Hold* (CW 199), and *For Years on Years of Matchless Grace* (CW 621).

Like most hymnals published during the generation it represents, *Christian Worship: A Lutheran Hymnal* is a hymnal whose hymns flow from different ages and diverse sources. It breaks new ground by offering worship materials contemporary with the time of its publication. But it is also firmly rooted in a hymnic tradition that goes back almost 3,000 years. May God bless its use.

CHAPTER 13:

The Organ and Instruments in Worship

"Therefore, with all the saints on earth and hosts of heaven, we praise your holy name and join their glorious song: 'Holy, holy, holy Lord God of heavenly hosts: heav'n and earth are full of your glory.'" The *Sanctus* with its preface indicates the size and diversity of the chorus that sings the praises of the Lord. Believers sing praises. They join the brothers and sisters in Christ who are with them. They sing with the entire community of believers on the planet. They sing with believers who have gone to their eternal rest. Angels and archangels join the song. The entire creation also joins in the magnificent chorus.

It is difficult to comprehend such a chorus, and it is particularly difficult to imagine how the creation can join in the praise of God. However, in many churches an instrument drawn from the creation leads worshipers as they join this chorus. This instrument is the pipe organ. The designer of the pipe organ draws together for the praise of God gold, silver, copper, brass, aluminum, lead, zinc, tin, steel, crude oil for plastic, wood, wool, and leather, and the basic forces of wind and electricity. All these components of nature under the laws of mathematics and physics are combined into a natural, marvelous sound.

Because of its natural sound, a pipe organ is an ideal choice for leading congregational worship. The real thing is always superior to an imitation. A pipe organ is also a long-term investment. With proper care it can last for many years and not lose its quality, effectiveness, or value. The great old organs in the cathedrals of Europe still function as a powerful testimony to that truth. Then, too, pipe organs are produced by craftsmen and artisans who retain a concern for the instrument. Each organ generally has an "opus" number, indicating the time in the organ builder's career during which the instrument was built, and putting the crafts-man's personal "stamp" on the instrument.

The pipe organ is ideal. But many of those who are reading this manual may never have the privilege of the use of a pipe organ in carrying out their music ministries. Many, perhaps even the majority, are working with electronic instruments. A word about such instruments is therefore also in place. Electronic organs may well serve a congregation's music needs satisfactorily, particularly if the congregation's worship building is small. The electronic instrument has the advantage that the building which houses it doesn't need the architectural supports necessary for a pipe organ or a ceiling high enough for the larger pipes. A speaker system, through which the electronic organ's sound is heard, doesn't require the space that a set of pipes requires. And in many cases the initial cost of the electronic organ is considerably less than the six-figure investment a congregation generally has to make to acquire a good pipe organ.

However, a congregation should keep in mind a number of considerations when contemplating the purchase of an electronic instrument for its church. If an electronic organ is going to be used for Lutheran worship, the congregation needs to purchase an instrument specifically designed for church use rather than for home use. The organist who is confronted with a small house organ without a full keyboard and with only pedal bars faces an almost insurmountable challenge as he or she prepares and plays music for congregational worship. Generally speaking, a piano may better serve a congregation's worship needs than an electronic organ designed only for home use.

Another problem that congregations getting an electronic organ should take care to prevent is poor installation due to inadequate speaker systems. Often one set of speakers is placed at only one end of the building. Consequently, loud sounds blast forth in the vicinity of the speakers, while the sound may be dying at the building's other end. This happens in part because, unlike a pipe organ, an electronic organ is not a custom designed instrument built for a specific church building. To insure proper installation of an electronic organ, a congregation should employ a reputable sound engineer and purchase the proper sound equipment. If this is done, however, and the congregation follows the engineer's advice, installing an electronic organ might prove more costly than was originally anticipated. In any case, a congregation is well-advised to call in a knowledgeable consultant before deciding on something as significant as the purchase of an organ.

It must also be said at this point that modern technology has made great strides in the area of sound production in the past several decades. And the possibilities for the future seem almost limitless. Sound production by means of computerization (MIDI systems, synthesizers, and the like) may offer congregations even more possibilities to consider when purchasing a worship instrument. On the other hand, the very rapidity with which technology is changing may make an instrument that was "state of the art" when it was first purchased obsolete in less than a generation.

Organists who are working with electronic instruments can best serve their congregations by paying close attention not so much to how many different kinds of sounds an electronic organ may be capable of producing as to how satisfactory the different possibilities that the organ offers for a "plenum" registration may be. The "plenum" or full registration (see also chapter 22 in this Section on "organ registration") is the registration used to accompany the hymns and the liturgies.

Organists who are forced to play instruments that have obviously limited or insufficient capability for leading the congregation's singing will simply have to improvise as best they can. If, for example, the organ has two incomplete manuals, a registration that best approximates a plenum registration can be used for both manuals, with the right hand playing the upper notes, and the left hand the lower, at least the tenor line, and the bass played by the pedal. The organist presiding for a worship service at an electronic organ should avoid the use of the tremolo and other coloristic effects intended for the playing of popular music.

Electronic and computer-generated sound technology has become a fascinating, and in many cases, promising field. Organists and worship committees will want to keep as watchful an eye as possible on new developments in this field, particularly through reading and study, so they might become as knowledgeable as possible on how new technologies might—or might not—be of benefit to the congregation's worship life.

A kind of "middle ground" between the choice of a larger pipe organ or an electronic instrument might be a small pipe organ with a single manual and pedal board. Such instruments can be built with only a few stops strongly emphasizing the pitches that are important in congregational singing. Organ builders can also divide the stops on a single manual organ so the sound is different above middle C. This makes it possible for the organist to play a solo voice with the right hand and an accompaniment with the left, thereby achieving a two-manual effect. The late 1980s and early 1990s witnessed a renewed interest in the small pipe organ, particularly in the United States. Its versatility is only beginning to be understood. The longevity and the quality of a well-built small pipe organ certainly make it a good value. Congregations looking to purchase a worship instrument should also consider this option.

The sound of the organ may be broadened with the addition of other instruments, traditionally bowed strings, flute and oboe, trumpet and trombone. At its best the Lutheran church has always welcomed the use of instruments as a particularly festive way of expressing the celebrative aspects of worship. A rich treasury of music for brass, strings, woodwinds, and percussion instruments in worship developed in the centuries after the Reformation. This literature includes instrumental pieces intended as postludes, preludes, interludes, chorale-based and free compositions for organ and solo instruments, as well as small-scale works for voices and instruments together. Instruments can also be used to support and enhance the congregation's song. Soprano instruments may double the melody. Instrumental choirs may play a solo stanza as part of a hymn sung alternately between congregation, instruments, and/or choir. Instrumental descants may also add to the joyful spirit of festival hymns. Likewise, many anthems intended for children's choirs contain descants that can be played on the flute, recorder, violin, or other quieter instruments.

The type of instruments and instrumental accompaniments used in the worship service is, to a certain extent, traditionally determined by the seasons of the year. Strings and woodwinds are particularly appropriate during the Advent and Christmas seasons. Brass instruments are also fitting to express the jubilation of Christmas and the joy of Epiphany. And they are certainly effective during the Easter season. Instruments, on the other hand, may remain silent or change moods in music as the worshiping community remembers the sufferings and death of the Lord. Thus the use of instruments in worship not only can call the community of believers to jubilant praise, it can highlight the major emphases of the annual church year calendar and bring a dimension to the congregation's praise that cannot be obtained in any other way. Instruments in worship are a valuable resource that should not be overlooked.

Instruments serve their highest purpose in the context of the Christian liturgies. Not only do they aid believers as they walk through the year of the Lord, but in connection with proclaiming the gospel and celebrating the suffering, death, and resurrection of Jesus Christ in the Lord's Supper, instruments call the community of believers to the loftiest heights of praise to God.

CHAPTER 14:

The Music of the Choir

After the pastor, organist, and/or minister of music, the most important force for effective congregational worship life is the choir. The worship life of a congregation with any choir at all will be enriched in many ways, and the possibilities for the worship life of a congregation with the strong musical leadership of a well-trained choir are almost limitless. The stronger the choir, the better the congregation will become at singing the hymns and liturgies. With the effective leadership of a choir or choirs, congregations will also more easily master new liturgies or hymns, and find real joy and satisfaction, both artistically and spiritually, in doing it.

In his treatise on the music of the choir, Carlos Messerli defines a church choir as simply "a group of dedicated people trained to sing in services of worship."[1] Dr. Arnold Lehmann expands a bit on Messerli's definition, calling a choir "A choral musical organization that helps support the musical portions of the worship service. It also presents independent choral selections."[2] The size of a congregation's choir may be large or small, its members young or old, their voices trained or untrained. But the key element is that this often-diverse group of people is united in the common purpose of praising the Lord through song, of glorifying God in the most artistic way possible in congregational worship.

Church choirs have a long and distinguished history. The Bible speaks of vocal music sung in praise of God already in Exodus 15, when it tells us that Moses and Miriam led the Israelites in an antiphonal song after God had delivered them from the Egyptians at the Red Sea. It may, of course, be argued that this and other

---

[1] Carlos Messerli, *A Handbook of Church Music* (St. Louis: Concordia Publishing House, 1978), p. 127.

[2] Arnold Lehmann, *Little Dictionary of Liturgical Terms* (Milwaukee: Northwestern Publishing House, 1980), p. 16.

"songs of the Israelites" recorded throughout the Old Testament were more congregational than choral. But the scriptural records of these songs and their singers don't rule out the possibility that some or all of them may have been sung by special groups of dedicated people trained to sing in services of worship.

Without a doubt, however it was King David who brought Old Testament choral singing to its greatest heights when he organized singers and instrumentalists into various groups for preparing and preserving music for worship. David's trained choir numbered 288 voices. 1 Chronicles 15 and 16 give detailed accounts of elaborate musical preparations for worship in the temple, which God promised that David's son, Solomon, would build. This choral musical activity begun by David was continued under Solomon (2 Chronicles 5:12,13; 9:11), Jehoshaphat (2 Chronicles 20:21,22), Josiah (2 Chronicles 35:15,25), and, after Judah's return from exile, by Ezra (Ezra 2:65; 3:11) and Nehemiah (Nehemiah 7:44; 10:28). That the "songs of Zion" were well known among the Israelites and even beyond seems evident from Psalm 137.

Choir music in the New Testament age can be dated from the angelic hosts that sang in concert from the skies over Bethlehem on the night of the Savior's birth. This singing will reach its glorious climax in the eternal chorus of all believers united in praise around God's heavenly throne.

As the worship life of the New Testament church began to take on its own identity, choirs took on an important role. This role became even more important, first as an overreaction to the use of popular, congregational song by the Gnostics and Arians to popularize their false teachings. And then because of the cultural (and spiritual) ignorance of the Middle Ages, the congregation became less and less active and finally almost completely passive participants in the worship services.

As the choir gained an ever more important role in the musical life of the church, *schola cantorum* or choir schools were organized throughout Europe for the specific purpose of training singers of liturgical music. Boys who were musically talented received training similar to that given to the boys enrolled in the monastery schools, but with greater emphasis on music. Some of the earliest of these *schola* were sponsored and encouraged by

257

early popes, including Sylvester (314-336) and Pope Gregory in the ninth century A.D. After the building of the Sistine Chapel in 473, the papal choirs and *schola* were moved to St. Peter's, and a significant era in the history of church choir music began. Monks and singers trained in the *schola* at Rome were often sent to other cities in Europe to open more schools. When Luther visited Rome before the Reformation began, he was much impressed by the quality of the music that had been developed there.

The history of church choirs in Germany unfolded in much the same way. The Benedictine monastery established at Fulda in 744 became known for its program of musical training. So did the Magdeburg Cathedral School, which Luther attended. Students in cathedral schools were expected to interrupt their studies to sing at weddings, funerals, and other church functions during the week. They also sang for Sunday services and other religious festivals. Often school choirs had students in their midst whose parents were too poor to pay for tuition, room, and board. These students, known as *kurrenden,* would sometimes walk the city streets singing and begging for food or money. Some of the students had the good fortune of being "adopted" and helped through school by local families. During his days at Magdeburg, Luther was a *kurrende.*

Princes and royal houses also became patrons of choirs, particularly in the later Middle Ages. Various courts would support entourages of musicians who performed liturgical worship music for services held at the court chapels. These singers were paid for their services and enjoyed good living conditions. Since many of the German princes became supporters of the Reformation, these court choirs were important forerunners of Evangelical church choirs. Frederick the Wise, Luther's prince, was a leading patron of court choirs.

After the Reformation and the formation of the Evangelical Church, Luther encouraged choirs both in towns and in the schools. He and Melanchthon developed a music program for Evangelical schools which involved all the students in the middle and upper grades. Singing by all students took place daily, because it was done to the praise and glory of God. The Evangelical school choirs carried on the tradition of the medieval cathedral schools by learning Gregorian chants and unison hymns. They also learned many of the new Evangelical hymns. Many towns also had select school choirs that specialized in the singing of polyphonic music. The church was particularly interested in educating students with the ability to sing and involving them in these types of choirs with the hope that many of them would become the church's future pastors and teachers.

The Evangelical school choirs benefited the church by creating an interest in music where there may not have been an interest before. Students who had been trained in the fundamentals of music in the schools could lead the congregation in the liturgical music of the church services, in which the lay members of the congregation were also now participating. The leading of the choir and the trained singers in the congregation inspired the congregations to more enthusiastic participation in the service.

Luther's *Deutsche Messe,* of course, could be sung without a choir, since all required singing was assigned to the congregation. This enabled smaller parishes without choirs to have complete services. But Luther's intent in providing the *Deutsche Messe* was not to do away with the music of the choir. Luther continued to consider the choir important for many reasons. The congregation could learn hymns and other parts of the service more quickly if a choir was present to lead. Various parts of the liturgies could be sung by the choir in a more artistic way. Latin mass and motet compositions were sometimes sung by the choir in place of the vernacular *Sanctus* and *Gloria in Excelsis.* German motets based on the use of the Propers written by early Lutheran composers and special settings of hymns prepared for alternate singing by the choir and the congregation also became part of the repertoire of those early Evangelical choirs. One year after the first popular Lutheran hymnal appeared, Johann Walter, under Luther's direction, published *Geistliche Gesangbuechlein,* a choir book for three, four, and five voices. The Lutheran church had now become a singing church. And the choir helped make it so. From its very beginnings Lutheran worship involved clergy, choir, and congregation.

What Luther began was continued in the seventeenth and eighteenth centuries by Lutheran church musicians, including Bach.

259

The position of *cantor,* or what we today might call *minister of music,* became an important one in Evangelical towns and cities. In a similar way the Church of England developed its choral heritage. Collegiate choirs and boys' choirs are still renowned for making English cathedrals ring with historic and contemporary worship music. The Lutheran church heading into the twenty-first century is heir to those rich choral traditions. And the church using *Christian Worship* as its worship book is still a liturgical church in which the choir has an important role to play.

Luther's views on the liturgical function of music, including the function of the choir, grew out of the general principle that everything in the worship service must serve the Word of God. The function of the choir in contemporary Lutheran worship has to be viewed in the same way. Messerli, in his article in *A Handbook of Church Music,* sees this taking place in three ways:

1. The choir encourages hearty and devout participation by the people in the liturgy and hymns that are assigned to the congregation.

2. The choir sings the texts of the liturgy assigned to it; it may also, upon occasion, sing the texts that are more usually given to the people or the pastor, but for which liturgical precedent makes choral provision.

3. The choir sings such music attendant to the liturgy as may be appropriate and possible.[3]

It is important that choirs and their directors understand that the most vital function of the choir in Lutheran worship is not just to provide "churchly musical entertainment," but liturgical leadership. The choir in Lutheran worship is a musically trained partner of the worshiping congregation, that "group of dedicated people" whose practiced efforts will serve to improve and intensify congregational participation in hymns and liturgies and provide leadership in singing that glorifies God and edifies his people.

A Lutheran church choir gives vocal leadership to the congregation both in singing hymns and the people's parts of the liturgy as well as in singing the parts of the liturgy specifically assigned to the choir. This happens, because, by virtue of its members'

---

[3] Messeerli, *Church Music,* p. 130.

training and practice, the choir is able to sing the people's parts of the service with clarity, vigor, and precision. This is always helpful. Even at worship services in which the choir does not participate per se, its members are scattered throughout the worshiping congregation. And the enthusiasm and vigor, as well as the clarity and precision with which the choir members sing the hymns and liturgies, will encourage those around them to better singing as well. This is certainly a good argument for taking a portion of the rehearsal time each week to sing through with the choir the hymns for the upcoming worship services.

Congregations with Lutheran elementary schools, too, can benefit from having the children, during music classes and choir periods in the school day, sing through the hymns scheduled for the weekly worship. Children in the lower grades will benefit from learning at least one of the scheduled hymns each month, so that, they, too, will be able to participate in congregational singing with excitement and joy.

The church choir will also provide the key leadership for successful introduction of new hymns, liturgies, and other worship materials that might be unfamiliar to the congregation. If there is careful planning and good communication between ministers and choir directors, new worship materials and the dates of their introduction and use can be given to the choir director months in advance, so that the choir may become thoroughly familiar with them and confident and precise in singing them. If a new liturgy is being introduced, the choir can be asked to sing the more difficult songs and chants for several weeks in the regular services, without congregational participation. And when the congregation begins to sing the new materials, the choir can serve as a steadying "backbone" for the congregation's song. Likewise, when a new hymn is introduced, the choir should be given at least several weeks' notice so its members can become familiar with the hymn. When the hymn is first introduced to the worshiping congregation, the choir may be assigned the first stanza or two, so the congregation has an opportunity to hear the melody before attempting to sing it. And even after the songs or hymns are learned by the congregation, the choir members will still be the leaders when these songs and hymns are sung.

The congregation blessed with a dedicated and well-trained choir will generally find the introduction of new worship materials considerably less traumatic than the congregation without a choir. Occasionally, particularly at festivals, the choir may replace the congregation's liturgical songs with purely choral settings of the text or with fitting alternate songs. So, by simply participating in an educated way in the congregation's song in both the hymns and the liturgy, the choir or choirs of a congregation can exercise their historic privilege of underscoring the theme for the day. And they can help the members of their congregation ponder anew what God has done for them.

Christian Worship also provides choirs with the opportunity for leadership in the singing of the psalms. The hymnlike refrains which begin and punctuate the psalm verses are intended for congregational singing. But the choir can certainly sing the refrain the first time it occurs, letting the congregation sing it all the other times. Or the refrain that introduces the psalm could be doubled, with the choir singing it first, followed by the congregation. It is anticipated that the choir or a cantor will sing the psalm verses themselves on the reciting tones. But congregations, too, can learn these tones rather easily. And the choir can provide leadership when the congregation sings them.

The Verse of the Day, which occurs between the Second Reading and the Gospel, is a part of the liturgy assigned to the choir. The verse helps direct the congregation's attention to the service theme and its place in the church year. When no choir is available, a general congregational verse replaces the seasonal verse.

The choir may provide additional enrichment for congregational hymn singing when choir and congregation engage in the historic practice of alternation. Following this practice, the congregation sings one stanza and the choir the next throughout the entire hymn. The choir may sing the stanzas assigned to it in unison or in simple or more elaborate choral settings, a cappella or accompanied. Alternation between choir and congregation is particularly encouraged for the singing of the Hymn of the Day, which will be discussed in a later chapter. As the choir sings its stanza and the congregation is silent, the congregation can meditate on the words the choir is singing. And since everyone does not have to sing every stanza of what might be a longer hymn, all the worshipers will be led to a greater appreciation of what the hymn has to say.

Yet another way in which the choir can enrich a congregation's worship is by the singing of carefully chosen "attendant music." This contribution of the choir to the service, however, should not be considered a "performance," drawing attention to itself simply for its own sake, but as an integral part of the whole of that day's worship. To that end the choir's attendant music should be both appropriate to the Sunday, festival, and season during which it is sung and appropriately placed in the liturgy, so as not to interrupt the smooth flow of the service. Some suggestions for the placement of an attendant anthem might be: as a choral prelude to the service; in place of the Verse of the Day (if not too lengthy); as a substitute for the Song of Praise in the major liturgies; as a response to the Sermon and Confession of Faith, which occurs after the Sermon in some of the services; during the Offering and during the Distribution. Occasionally even the Psalm may be replaced with a choir anthem, especially if the anthem is based on the Psalm for that day.

It stands to reason that all such attendant music must be within the musical capabilities of the choir. It is not necessary for every church choir to sing complicated anthems, even if they are popular ones. A well sung hymn, a cappella or even with accompaniment, is far more edifying than a poorly sung anthem. For small choirs with few gifted musicians, chanting the psalms or single voice line anthems will provide challenge enough, but at the same time be truly enriching to the congregation's worship life. Choirs with talented musicians should be challenged. But even then, difficult selections should not be offered until they have been thoroughly learned and polished. The music of the choir is an offering of praise to God. God's people simply do not want to present him with an offering that reflects less than their best.

When evaluating music for use as attendant music in the worship service, choir directors need to consider the text first of all. They need to examine the text's content, as well as its suitability for the time of the church year for which it is being chosen. No artistic experience in worship can be satisfying without an appropriate message. If the text is satisfactory, the director will then consider the anthem's musical quality, liturgical propriety, and its suitability for the choir for which it is being chosen.

The Lutheran church is the fortunate inheritor of a great musical legacy. In the Lutheran chorale and music based on the chorale, Lutherans have much literature that is of great significance spiritually and high quality musically. Lutheran church musicians will seek to reflect that heritage in the selection of attendant anthems, not simply because the music is Lutheran, but because it is vital and appropriate to Lutheran worship. Yes, musical variety is good and is appreciated by Lutheran Christians and musicians, too. But let us take care not to forsake our heritage, either. (Additional advice concerning the selection of appropriate attendant music is offered in Section One, chapter 8, "Planning for Worship," pp. 127-129.)

The leader of the church choir in many of our congregations is often a Lutheran elementary school teacher whose duties in the music department are additional to duties in the classroom. At other times the director may be a lay person who could best be described as a "gifted amateur." Ministers and congregations need to respect these people for their willingness to use their talents in the Lord's service, and strive to cooperate with them in ways that will enable them to carry out their music ministry with joy.

No doubt Carlos Messerli was thinking of the position of full-time minister of music when he suggested the following as qualifications for a church choir director. The part-time musician asked to serve in this capacity may not always possess all of these qualifications, but the suggestions provide food for thought. We quote once more from Messerli's article:

> The leader of the church choir should be the most qualified person available for the position. While it is not easy to identify the ideal director, certain qualifications suggest themselves as essential:
>
> 1. A strong Christian faith that expresses itself naturally in word and action.
>
> 2. A positive personality that enables easy working relationships with the church's pastor and members; that is optimistic and buoyant, yet modest and sincere; that inspires confidence by being friendly, yet fair and decisive; that reflects a sense of humor.

3. A sensitivity to the needs and limitations of the choir and the congregation, and to the requirements and possibilities of liturgical worship.

4. A thorough understanding of the art of choral directing and all that it entails, especially musical fundamentals, literature, history, analysis, interpretation, and vocal technique. The ability to perform acceptably on some solo instrument (preferably keyboard and voice) is most desirable.

5. A capacity to grow in knowledge and skill in all matters—liturgical, musical and personal—relating to choir leadership.[4]

A choir program, indeed, a multi-choir program, is attainable in almost every congregation. Just about any group of children, youth, and adults can be fashioned into a church choir that can serve a congregation and its worship as has been described in the previous pages. Yes, a sixty-voice choir that can sing a cappella or with ensembles of various kinds and can edify a congregation with flawlessly performed attendant music is laudable and a wonderful asset to any congregation. But so is a group of three or four "dedicated people," male or female, young or old, who are willing to work to learn to sing the psalms in unison and to help the congregation learn and better sing its liturgies and hymns. With hearts dedicated to serving the Lord by using the voices he has given them, such Christians and their choral leaders will work together in the spirit of Christian love to develop and maximize the abilities that God has given them. And the Lord of the church will make them a blessing to their congregations.

---

[4] Messerli, *Church Music,* p. 134.

CHAPTER 15:

The Music of the Chant: Pastor, Choir, and Congregation

For many pastors and congregations the question about chant is not *how* but, *why bother?* So this chapter begins with that question. St. Augustine's famous remark is a concise answer that leads to many reasons to chant: "He who sings prays twice." A more recent opinion elaborates: "The first prayer is the text that is sung—a prayer to God using the words; the second is the music, the singing itself, a prayer of praise from the soul."[1] In considering the place of chant in our worship we will look at several factors that can inform our choice. The elements most likely to be chanted are parts of the liturgy and the psalm.

Style

There may have once been a time when chant seemed to fit only certain denominational connotations. That time, at least for the most part, appears to be over. Chant even seems to appeal to some in our secular culture. Why, we wonder, would some people who listen to mostly pop music, find chant appealing? Is the appeal just novelty? Perhaps not. Perhaps it is either the beautiful simplicity of the chant itself, or the association of chant with the reverence of Christian worship that makes it appealing.

To consider this matter of style is to recognize that Christian worship is not the same as verbal events like Bible classes, speeches, talk shows, pep rallies, and the like. Some people may have expectations of worship as something akin to a Bible class or a talk show, but that doesn't change the fact that worship is different.

---

[1] Quentin and Mary Faulkner, "Good Music Is Good Prayer," *Liturgy,* Vol. 1, No. 4, p. 65.

One of Martin Luther's hymns encourages an element of worship that we can easily miss in our culture: "Let solemn awe possess us" (CW 574:3). Sung liturgy and psalms can heighten the often missing element of reverential awe, without causing an imbalance of too much solemnity. The sung *Service of Light* in *Evening Prayer* can help worshipers approach the following minutes with more reverence and less of the casual nonchalance that can so easily characterize worship.

As we consider the musical style(s) of the chant, we need to realize that there is a distinction between different *kinds* of music and their different purposes. Vigorous and exciting choral music accompanied by brass and organ can show the greatness of God. It can make spines tingle and spirits soar. Hearty congregational hymns put praise and prayer on the lips of every worshiper in a musical idiom within the reach of most people. Chant, however, is a musical style that shouldn't be tested by the same criteria used for choral music or hymns. While musical psalms can be exciting choral music, they can also be simple sung prayer using words God himself has given us. This kind of singing is not showy; it does not seek some powerful effect (neither powerfully penitential nor powerfully jubilant). It is simple music to enable sung prayer.

Dialogue

Another matter of style concerns dialogue in worship. The liturgist speaks, and the people respond. If we were not so accustomed to it, we might think it strange that one speaks and the other sings. If we could step back from our tradition, it might seem more natural for a sung response to follow something sung, not spoken. So, as a matter of style, pastors might aim for a more unified approach: spoken dialogue or sung dialogue—as the occasion determines. (This is an encouragement not only for sung dialogue, but also for spoken dialogue. After the richer experience of sung dialogue, a spoken dialogue—possibly for the Sundays in Lent—has its own impact.)

Worship Dynamic

The years preceding the publication of *Christian Worship* saw the restoration of greater portions of Scripture to our worship.

The three-year lectionary and greater use of the psalms bring more of God's Word to worshipers each week. God's Word can reach us not only through the cognitive means of hearing it read or preached; it can also reach us through the combined impact of words and music. This is valuable in at least three ways:

1. Some variety assists the worshiper in receiving God's Word. The impact of the Word, for many, can be diminished when all the elements of worship are read, or, for that matter, if they are all sung. One writer called a recited psalm a "dreary and boring exercise in devotional tennis."[2] While this judgment is unnecessarily harsh (and, for many, simply untrue) it does hint at an element that is missing when the Psalm is only read.

   The dynamic of worship is enhanced by alternating spoken and sung portions of the service. In a similar fashion the service overall may have a better balance when the pastor chants part of the liturgy. In a tradition that allows 18 to 22 minutes for a sermon, along with lessons and verbal prayers, the Word spoken will still remain most prominent. With so much time given to reading and teaching the Word, it may seem that worship is primarily a cognitive exercise: people gathering to *learn* God's Word. While that is true, Christians also gather to pray and offer praise to God. Prayer and praise will seem to most worshipers to be less of a cognitive exercise when offered in song rather than simply in prose.

   If the Psalm is sung rather than read, it will come across as a prayer or response rather than as another didactic element. The Psalm ought not to feel and function like a fourth lesson. It is a prayer, more intense when sung.

2. Musical settings of psalms can interpret or amplify the meaning of the psalm. A penitential psalm sung to a somber psalm-tone is more effective than the same words simply spoken or read. A serious refrain heightens the spiritual impact of the psalm. In the same way a jubilant refrain for a psalm of praise makes the words of praise more joyful and more personally felt and intended by each worshiper.

---

[2] James Hansen, *Cantor Basics* (Washington, D.C.: The Pastoral Press, 1991), p. 118.

3. The interplay of chanted psalm (by choir, pastor, or cantor) with congregation joining in a refrain is an effective way of involving many forces in an integrated and participatory way. Musical elements in worship are not mere decoration. They ought also to be functional. A chanted psalm can utilize any musical resources available: organ, brass, woodwinds, handbells, synthesizer, percussion. On the right occasion we can do what Psalm 150 encourages and join all the instruments with all the voices in a wonderful psalm of praise to God.

History

Another argument for chant always states that the psalms were sung, as were the great historical canticles of Christian worship, such as the *Gloria in Excelsis* or *Te Deum*. These were chanted in part because they are prose texts. While it is possible to write metrical versions, some historical continuity is lost when all liturgical songs are reduced to hymns in poetic meter.

While we appreciate the hymns (or the *idea* of hymnody) bequeathed to us by the Reformation, we appreciate and discuss far less, it seems, the continuity with the past that both Luther and the Confessions displayed. This continuity for them was not merely permissible (where it did not violate Scripture); it was also valuable and desirable. In this context, chanting has the value of placing our worship in the broad span of centuries and connects us with the earliest Christians as well as common Lutheran practice for centuries following the Reformation. The character of chant has for most people an unmistakable connection with "the church," things sacred, and worship. That is a good association, even though it has not always been so in every manifestation.

Scripture

God's Word offers its own input into the value of chant. St. Paul urges Christians to "sing psalms, hymns and spiritual songs" (Colossians 3:16). Isn't it a bit odd to respond, "Hymns, yes; psalms, no!"? Fifty-five psalms have the heading, "For the director of music." Other details speak to the musical rendition of the psalms, such as titles which seem to indicate the melody and that mysterious word, *Selah*.

Without being legalistic, one can say that the biblical norm is for psalms to be sung. One editor puts it this way: "The Holy Spirit and the various psalmists intended from the first that their psalms should be chanted in the corporate worship of God."[3]

Some Pointers

We move now from reasons to sing parts of the liturgy and the psalms to some practical guidelines for this practice. Good chant style exists within certain boundaries. The basic rule of thumb is that chant should follow the rhythm of careful speech. A variety of tempos is "right." But certain flaws should never fall within the boundaries of good chant. (1) A wooden approach is never good. (2) Careful articulation of *every* syllable is artificial. We do not talk that way; we shouldn't chant that way. (3) Do not rush words on the "reciting tone" or cause the notes at the end of a phrase to feel like a cadence in 4/4 time; we don't speak that way. These reminders are primarily for choir directors, the pastor, or cantor. It is not necessary to coach the congregation on subtle details. While choirs, pastors, and cantors should pursue a refined and expressive rendition, this is not possible with the congregation as a whole. Let them learn by hearing others rather than from detailed instructions and corrections.

As in public speaking, chant requires good ARTICULATION. Consonants communicate clearly. Be especially careful with final consonants. Certain consonants, such as *f* and *v*, need mild exaggerations when sung. The goal is good diction, so that the words can be clearly understood. Excessive articulation, however, will sound artificial.

Just as in spoken liturgy, some words will receive greater EMPHASIS. This should be slight and subtle, not a musical accent. A sensitive combination of speech rhythm, articulation, and emphasis will help chanted liturgy be expressive and effective.

Once you have decided to try chanting, don't hesitate to GET GOOD ADVICE. A few coaching sessions with a qualified choir director, organist, or voice teacher will pay happy dividends. The goal is not to turn pastors into soloists, but to assist them in find-

---

[3] Douglas Judisch, *Concordia Psalter* (Ft. Wayne, IN: Concordia Theological Seminary, 1980), p. 1.

ing a natural and comfortable singing style. In some cases the pastor who lacks the blessing of even a modest singing voice should seek help before leading a public service or consider not singing. But do not be discouraged by this caution. The average pastor who can sing a favorite hymn on pitch can do an acceptable job of singing parts of the liturgy, with or without some modest coaching.

Many descriptions of chant are available, but perhaps the most lasting benefits will come if you LEARN BY LISTENING. Give careful attention to good examples, wherever you can find them. Many recordings are available that do an excellent job of demonstrating a refined chanting style. Learn by listening as well as by reading.

ACCOMPANIMENT for chanting can serve several purposes. If a variety of instruments accompany a psalm refrain, accompaniment may be necessary to keep the pitch. Some people's first impressions may be more positive when chant is accompanied. As with many aspects of psalm singing, variety is valuable: rule out neither a cappella nor accompaniment. If accompaniment is used, it can serve its purpose even with the quietest volume that balances with the singer(s).

The pastor's voice in liturgy ought not to dominate the people. Find the "right" VOLUME that assists those who do not hear so well without overwhelming others' voices. The pastor's voice, when assisted by a microphone, ought not to sound like a soloist on stage amplified above the band. Be especially sensitive to the effect of amplification in large churches with a giant speaker suspended high above the congregation. A loud, disembodied voice from above does not communicate the character of sung prayer.

Introducing Chanting in a Congregation

Whatever the value the pastor may see in chant, he must proceed with care in introducing a new element into worship. But, as with any musical element, proper caution need not permanently postpone that new element.

Most worshipers are receptive to something new for a special season or occasion. Chanting psalms might be broadly perceived as lending a more solemn character to midweek worship during

Lent. The same people who welcome the new element on a Wednesday evening might not be as open to the introduction of that same element into a normal Sunday service. If you try psalm singing (by choirs or by the pastor), let the people know with an appropriate worship folder or verbal announcement.

A certain amount of understanding is useful before pastors chant liturgy or choirs sing psalms. Most people will never have thought through their preconceptions about these matters. Better for them to have a chance to discuss them or hear about them in a Bible class or an informal talk after a service than to have their first exposure during a service. Many approaches can help people think about the value of singing psalms. A Bible class with musical examples could demonstrate the remarkable variety of ways to sing psalms. Good recordings can demonstrate many styles.

A process of education recognizes that the use of chant will not "work" without some preparation and shared understanding. One author offers a useful reminder for any education process: "There is no doubt that chant has certain disadvantages: it is less familiar, it can have unfortunate associations, and it is not easy to learn quickly because its lack of meter means that important memory cues are missing. But its aesthetic compensations are inestimable. Its style can be as modern as one would wish, and yet chant will always have the weight of tradition behind it. It will never be confused with the secular; it always sounds sacred."[4]

In Conclusion

In 1967 *A Manual on Intoning,* forty-seven pages of practical help for singing the liturgy, was published. Its preface acknowledged that the editors of the *Service Book and Hymnal* (1958) had not expected many pastors to intone the liturgy. Interest turned out to be much higher than suspected, so the little volume was published to help all the interested pastors. The preface also touched on the "high-church" fear (or accusation) and said such a charge "is properly reduced to the ridiculous, when one considers those congregations of Danish, German, Norwegian and Slovak ancestry . . . where, utterly devoid of the trappings commonly as-

---

[4] Joseph Swain, "The Practicality of Chant," *The Diapason,* August, 1992.

sociated with that much maligned epithet [high church], services are, and have been conducted with dignity and simplicity by black-robed ministers who sing the liturgy."[5]

With a fair and balanced approach, the experience of those who read this manual might well turn out to be similar. Singing the liturgy need not have all kinds of connotations and accouterments. Black-robed pastors in small parishes can lead dignified worship, using the chant and other worship resources a gracious God has given us.

---

[5] Ulrich Leupold, *A Manual on Intoning* (Philadelphia: The Board of Publication of the Lutheran Church in America, 1967), p. V.

CHAPTER 16:

The Hymn of the Day and Its Use in *Christian Worship*

Together with the two other major Lutheran hymnals produced in the United States since 1978, *Christian Worship* includes and encourages a Hymn of the Day plan as a key element in the selection and use of hymns for corporate worship. Edward Klammer begins his essay on *de tempore hymn* by defining it as "The name given to the chief hymn in the service on every Sunday and festival, so called because it fits the specific day and season in the Church Year. It is the hymn that responds most intimately to the dominant theme of the day, which is usually contained in the Gospel for the day."[1]

The Hymn of the Day concept has a distinguished history in Lutheranism. Sixteenth century Lutheran hymnody grew out of liturgical understanding and use of hymns. Many early Lutheran hymns were written as substitutes for the Ordinary of the liturgical service. Luther himself wrote hymnic versions of the *Kyrie,* the Creed, the *Sanctus,* and the *Nunc Dimittis.*

Other of the early Lutheran hymns grew out of the *de tempore* idea of having hymns that reflected the themes of the various Sundays and festivals of the church year. In his Latin service, the *Formula Missae* of 1523, he retained the chanted Gradual as a solo sung by a cantor. But in his well-known German language service, the *Deutsche Messe* of 1526, Luther gave the Gradual to the congregation by suggesting that, after the reading of the Epistle, a German hymn should be sung and that this hymn should be

---

[1] Edward Klammer, *Key Words in Church Music* (St. Louis: Concordia, 1978), p. 162.

appropriate to the "character of the day," as determined by the day's Scripture lessons.

Many church orders during those early days of the Evangelical church followed Luther's lead in using hymns as gradual hymns. And so already in the sixteenth century, an order of hymns for every Sunday and festival of the church year was established. And for a century or more following the Reformation the practice of associating certain hymns with certain festivals and days continued.

When the Lutheran understanding and appreciation of the meaning of the liturgy declined during the ages of Pietism and Rationalism, appreciation for and use of the Hymn of the Day similarly declined. By the end of the eighteenth century it had been practically forgotten. A few attempts at reintroducing the plan by hymnological and liturgical scholars during the next century met with little success. The revival of the Hymn of the Day idea seems to have begun in the midtwentieth century in some of the Evangelical churches in Germany. About the same time similar plans also appeared in churches in Holland, Switzerland, and the Scandinavian countries. Lutheran liturgical scholars like Dr. Ralph Gehrke and Edward Klammer promoted the plan among Lutherans in the United States.

Dr. Gehrke's *Planning the Service: A Workbook for Organists, Pastors and Choir Masters*, published by Concordia Publishing House in 1961, was an especially useful tool in helping pastors and church musicians understand and implement the Hymn of the Day concept. *Planning the Service,* based on the one year "Standard" or "Ancient" lectionary, also strongly encouraged a unified service built around a single theme, with the verbal proclamation and confession of the Word surrounded by what Bach referred to as "well-ordered church music." Both *Lutheran Book of Worship* (Augsburg, 1978) and *Lutheran Worship* (Concordia, 1982) contain Hymn of the Day plans. Religious music publishers have produced choral settings and a wealth of attendant musical material for all the Hymns of the Day in both *Lutheran Worship* and Lutheran Book of Worship's listings. In all of *Christian Worship*'s major liturgies, the Hymn of the Day is placed before the sermon.

To properly understand the concept of the Hymn of the Day one must seek to understand the intimate relationship that exists between the Word read in the Scripture lessons, the Word preached in the sermon, and the Word sung by the congregation or congregation and choir in the Hymn of the Day. The Hymn of the Day is never merely a sermon hymn, though it certainly reinforces the message of liturgical preaching. Nor is it only a poetic paraphrase of the Gospel, though it is gospel related. But it is musical and poetic proclamation of, commentary on, and response to all the lessons, the confession of faith in the Creed, and the message communicated by the service as a whole. It is liturgical hymnody in the classic Lutheran sense, an integral part of the continual, reciprocal rhythm between God's Word and Christians' response to the Word that runs throughout the entire liturgy.

If the Hymn of the Day is regarded as the chief hymn of the service, it is natural that its importance should be celebrated with special musical treatment that helps its unique function and character become apparent. Alternation (see pp. 262, 263 of this manual) between the congregation and a partner—either the organ, instruments, or a choir—has been practiced in the Lutheran Church since the time of the Reformation. The use of alternation prevents a congregation from being "worn out" by singing every stanza, particularly of a longer and more difficult hymn.

The choral concertato includes singing in alternation, as well as a number of other elements that make the singing of the hymn a joyful and uplifting experience. Musicians serving in a church that employs a Hymn of the Day plan will also find many excellent concertatos based on Hymns of the Day. These special musical treatments provide the opportunity for the use of a wide variety of musical resources that will edify the congregation as it participates in this key liturgical hymn of the services. Time spent by church musicians and pastors in planning effective ways of presenting the Hymn of the Day will prove to be well spent. Such planning should be given high priority by the congregation's musical leaders. These great hymns, God's people who sing them, and the Lord they proclaim and glorify deserve no less.

Congregations can expect a number of practical results from a carefully planned and implemented Hymn of the Day program. Using the Hymn of the Day on a regular basis will help the congregation develop an increasing appreciation for the rhythm of the church year. It will keep alive in the congregation's consciousness the most important hymns in the hymnal. It may also add to the congregation's hymn vocabulary a number of great hymns that may not have been used or even tried before. It will help protect the congregation against subjectivism and poor taste in the regular choosing of hymns. It will help encourage liturgical preaching and planning of truly unified and thematic worship services. It will help church musicians plan their organ and choral music well in advance. And it will help make apparent to the congregation the unity that ought to exist in the service as the Word is read in the lessons, preached in the sermon, sung in the hymns, confessed in the Creed, and received in the "visible grace" of the Lord's Supper.

Christian Worship's Hymn of the Day plan is a graceful blending of some of the finest hymns of Christendom, both ancient and modern. It contains a good representation of Lutheran chorales, and it challenges congregations to learn and make use of newer hymns as well. There is a plan for both a three-year and one-year lectionary. As a general rule, hymns for all three years of the three-year series retain the same hymn during the festival weeks of the church year. This is usually the time of year when choirs are available to assist the congregation in the singing of these hymns. By repeating most of the same hymns during the festival half of each church year, the congregation will build up a strong repertoire of hymns for the festival seasons and will learn to sing them well and in a wide variety of satisfying ways. The hymns suggested for the non-festival half of the year often differ from one year to the next in the three-year lectionary. This reflects that the Sunday themes in the non-festival weeks, themes primarily concerned with the Christian life, may vary on given weeks from year to year.

An additional practical feature of *Christian Worship*'s Hymn of the Day series is the offering of alternate hymn choices for a number of Sundays. The alternate choices would appear to benefit particularly the smaller congregations or those with fewer musical resources at their disposal. If, for example, a congregation is unable to learn Luther's rather difficult *To Jordan Came the Christ, Our Lord* (CW 88) for Epiphany 1, an alternate hymn, *To Jordan's River Came Our Lord* (CW 89), which reflects the thought of the day but is musically somewhat less challenging, is offered.

So, the Hymn of the Day, with its roots deep in historical, liturgical Lutheran tradition, has been revived, renewed, and updated for the benefit of those who will use *Christian Worship* to sing our Lord's praise into the twenty-first century. May the Lord use this plan to his people's edification and great joy and to his own praise and glory.

CHAPTER 17:

Selecting Hymns For Worship

The hymn is certainly one of the greatest of all Lutheran contributions to public worship. The singing of hymns in the Lutheran service is one of the great joys and privileges afforded to the worshiping congregation. Consequently, the selection of hymns deserves deep interest, careful study, and determined commitment from Lutheran pastors or others who might be selecting them. When hymns are carefully selected to reflect the overall theme of the service and the thoughts of the day's Scripture lessons, a satisfying and edifying worship service results. When hymns are hastily selected at the last minute to "fill in" parts of the service that are "still missing," the results are considerably and understandably less satisfying.

In most congregations the pastor or pastors are responsible for selecting the hymns. That means that pastors, whether they consider themselves musically inclined or not, are cast in the role of church musicians. And they owe it to their congregations and to the Lord of the church to be familiar enough with the hymnal to provide their congregations with the opportunity to be taught and uplifted in their worship by means of well-chosen hymns. Likewise, by a careful and judicious use of a wide variety of hymns, a pastor can help the members of his congregation grow in their knowledge and familiarity with the best hymn literature of the Christian church.

The selection of hymns will quite naturally flow from the lectionary that is chosen for the church year. *Christian Worship* (pp. 163-166) contains both a three-year and one-year series of Scripture lessons (see Section Four of this manual). If a pastor chooses another lectionary for the church year, the organists and choir directors should by all means be informed and provided with the lesson selections for the entire church year. This will enable them better to plan their musical offerings for the church year.

Hymn of the Day

The framers of *Christian Worship* strongly urge the use of a Hymn of the Day plan as the starting point for the selection of hymns. If such a plan is followed, the pastor and the congregation's other church musicians should consider the Hymn of the Day the chief hymn of the service. The Hymn of the Day plan attempts to match the service theme and the read and preached lessons. (For a more thorough discussion of the Hymn of the Day, see chapter 16.)

A series of suggestions for the Hymn of the Day is included in Section Four of this manual. Pastors and church musicians are urged to study the lists of hymns together and determine which are fairly well-known by the congregation and which would require more time to be taught. That a list of Hymns of the Day is suggested, of course, does not exclude the possibility of changing or editing the list as the pastors and church musicians judge fitting. But the use of the best hymns of Christian hymnody as Hymns of the Day is strongly encouraged. And a mutual agreement on which hymns will be used as Hymns of the Day should be made at least a season or two, and ideally an entire church year, in advance. The Hymn of the Day will generally be the second major hymn of the service, the hymn immediately preceding the sermon.

The Opening Hymn

The opening hymn sets the tone or "mood" for worship. Historically the opening hymn is a replacement for the Introit or Entrance Hymn. The opening hymn should not be too long and should be well enough known by the congregation to enable the members to begin the week's worship with a vigorous and heartfelt expression of their faith and their joy at the privilege of coming before the Lord for instruction, prayer, and praise. The tune and the text should match the overall focus of the day.

The opening hymn can be a seasonal hymn, a hymn of invocation, or a general song of praise. *Christian Worship* contains Opening of Service, and Worship and Praise sections from which opening hymns may easily be chosen. But the careful selector of hymns will make use of many other sections of the hymnal as well in the search for an opening hymn that will turn the worshipers' thoughts away from the rush of the workaday world to an enthusiastic and meaningful worship of the Lord. The shorter seasonal hymns are very appropriate as opening hymns. Many seasonal hymns in *Christian Worship* have been revised to make them appropriate, not only for a festival day, but for the entire season to which they belong. Worship during Advent, Epiphany, Lent, and Easter can be beautifully begun by a judicious choice of a seasonal opening hymn. Worship on the Sunday after the Ascension can likewise be opened with one of the Ascension hymns for which no place could be found in the festival service the previous Thursday evening. During the non-festival half of the church year, hymns of invocation to the Holy Spirit, hymns to the Trinity, as well as shorter, familiar hymns that fit the day's theme and reflect the thoughts of the lectionary are also appropriate opening hymns.

This is the place in the service for singing hymns the congregation "likes." A few practical tips and cautions should also be given with regard to opening hymns. Even congregational (and pastoral) "favorite" hymns shouldn't simply be tossed into the service. The thoughts expressed in the hymns should at least in some way reflect the thoughts suggested by the lectionary for the day. The opposite extreme would be to select an opening hymn that, even though it might fit the thoughts of the service perfectly, might be too musically challenging for the congregation, or too long. The result will be that the congregation becomes weary and a bit discouraged even before the liturgy begins.

Occasionally, someone other than the pastor will be made responsible for selecting the hymns for a congregation. Or the pastor may choose the Hymn of the Day and perhaps also the sermon hymn, and the minister of music, an organist with gifts in the area of hymn selection, or perhaps even a Worship Committee might select the remaining hymns, particularly the opening and closing hymns. If this is the practice, however, those selecting the hymns must be provided with a list of Hymns of the Day, lessons, and service themes. And they, together with the pastor, must share a mutual understanding of the principles by which the service hymns are chosen.

The Sermon Hymn

The sermon hymn is a hymn that follows the Sermon and applies the sermon's message to the hearers. In *The Common Service* without communion and in the *Service of the Word* this hymn follows the Offering and the prayers. In *The Common Service* with communion, as well as in the *Service of Word and Sacrament,* the hymn most closely following the Sermon is the first hymn sung during the distribution of Holy Communion. The sermon hymn should also be rather well-known and may include emotional content. Its primary function is to help the worshipers apply the thoughts of the sermon to themselves.

Distribution Hymns

A hymn or hymns during the distribution of Holy Communion is not an absolute necessity. The worshipers may be offered a time of silence or quiet attendant music from the organ. The choir may also sing during the distribution. But distribution hymns, like all the other hymns during the service, can and should give the worshiping congregation the opportunity for meaningful participation in the service.

One section of hymns in *Christian Worship* contains hymns dealing directly with the Sacrament. But the selection of distribution hymns should not be restricted to that relatively small group of a dozen or so hymns. The time of distribution can also be an excellent opportunity to schedule hymns that focus the worshipers' attention once more on the key thoughts of the service. As indicated in the paragraph above, a sermon hymn is encouraged during the distribution.

Seasonal hymns also serve well as distribution hymns. Some of these hymns include *As Angels Joyed with One Accord* (CW 5) and *O Lord, How Shall I Meet You* (CW 18,19) for Advent; *From Heaven Above to Earth I Come* (CW 38) for Christmas; *How Lovely Shines the Morning Star* (CW 79) for Epiphany; *O Sacred Head, Now Wounded* (CW 105), *Upon the Cross Extended* (CW 113), and *O Dearest Jesus* (CW 117) for Lent; *Awake, My Heart, with Gladness* (CW 156) for the Easter season; and *Come, Oh, Come, Life-Giving Spirit* (CW 181) for Pentecost and the Pentecost season. *Dear Christians, One And*

All, Rejoice (CW 377) is a fitting distribution hymn for Reformation.

A common feature of these hymns is that they have five or more stanzas and would provide the congregation with the opportunity for singing during a longer distribution period. This same purpose can be achieved, however, by choosing more than one distribution hymn: a sermon hymn and a communion hymn, a sermon hymn and a seasonal hymn, two hymns that reflect the thought of the sermon or the season, or any number of other combinations. The possibilities for the use of hymns, choir contributions, and other attendant music during the distribution are almost endless and will be limited only by the amount of time available. Pastors and church musicians do well not to neglect this opportunity for congregational song. One final consideration: since part of the congregation is communing or preparing to approach the Lord's table during the time of distribution, the singing congregation will be somewhat diminished in numbers. Care should be taken that distribution hymns are fairly familiar, so that the reduced singing congregation will not have to struggle, but will continue to sing well.

Offering Hymn Stanzas

Though it is not in the rubrics for any of the *Christian Worship* services, many congregations have the custom of singing a hymn stanza or two as the offerings are brought forward. A good working knowledge of the hymns in *Christian Worship* will help pastors in congregations with this custom make judicious and meaningful stanza selections. Two stanzas of *We Give Thee But Thine Own* (CW 485), while entirely appropriate, can easily become tiresome. Some variety here could certainly enhance worship. *Christian Worship* includes a Stewardship section of hymns. Individual stanzas carefully selected from any of those hymns would serve well as offering stanzas.

Festival services and other special occasions cry out for joyous hymns and stanzas of thanksgiving as believers honor the Lord with their treasures. Congregations will quickly become accustomed to the practice of using many different stanzas as offering stanzas; and this practice will give them the opportunity to learn and sing additional hymns. Again, offering stanzas should be fairly familiar or easily learned, and not too lengthy.

Hymns of the Liturgy

Christian Worship also includes a section of hymns entitled Hymns of the Liturgy. While all of these hymns can stand on their own merits, each one of them is also suitable for substitution in the Ordinary. They have been placed together in a single section for the convenience of pastors and church musicians who might wish to make these hymnic substitutions from time to time for the sake of variety and freshness in worship. (For more complete discussion of Hymns of the liturgy, see Section Two, chapter 10.)

Under each hymn title in this section (CW 262-278) is a subtitle in small italics, indicating for which part of the Ordinary the hymn might serve as a suitable substitute. There is also a note at the bottom left corner of each page in the section indicating the exact pages in the various liturgies where these hymns can properly be substituted. Hymn 262 in *Christian Worship, All Glory Be to God Alone,* for example, is a hymnic version of the *Gloria in Excelsis; Isaiah, Mighty Seer in Days of Old* (CW 267) can be substituted for the *Sanctus* in the communion liturgies, and so on throughout the section.

Special events and festivals are a good time to make such substitutions. Changes of season can also be emphasized by substituting a hymn in this section for a part of the Ordinary. *This Is the Feast of Victory* (CW 265) is a particularly fitting substitute for the *Song of Praise* during the Easter Season. And the singing of *Lamb of God, Pure and Holy* (CW 268) in place of *O Christ, Lamb of God (Agnus Dei)* will be a solemn and effective reminder to the worshipers that they are in the season of Lent.

Occasionally a complete chorale service, in which appropriate hymns are substituted for all of the liturgical songs, will be a very uplifting experience for a congregation. Special services like that take some planning, but the planning is well worth the time when the worshipers are edified.

Closing Stanzas

Not all congregations are in the habit of singing a closing hymn or a closing stanza. Some feel strongly that the Benediction should be the last element in the service. If a closing hymn or stanza is used, however, the hymn should be relatively short and well-known. *Christian Worship* contains a Close of Service section. The pastor/hymn selector will use these hymns at times during the course of the year, but should take care not to overuse them. Individual stanzas of longer hymns also work well as closing stanzas. And the better the pastor learns to know the hymnal, the better he will be able to make meaningful stanza selections.

Related Matters of Hymn Selection

Several other related topics concerning hymns and hymn selection should be addressed here. Generally the congregation is seated during the singing of the hymns. Standing to sing can be helpful, both physically and emotionally. Standing, particularly for the final stanza of a powerful Hymn of the Day, certainly adds vigor and emotion to the singing of the hymn. Organists should be notified ahead of time that the pastor will rise and signal the congregation to rise as the second-to-last stanza of the hymn comes to an end. The organist can then repeat the final phrase of the hymn or provide a short interlude as the people are rising to their feet, then go on with the playing of the last stanza.

Many well-known hymns are available in choral concertato form. Here is an inspiring way to sing a hymn. The concertato generally includes a fairly elaborate introduction for organ and/or instruments; singing in alternation with the choir and congregation; unison stanzas for the congregation with both simple and more elaborate organ accompaniment; at least one stanza arranged for choir only; and often descants for choir and instruments. It may at first sound rather difficult and complicated. But musicians even in smaller congregations can, with a little imagination, tailor concertato arrangements to the ability levels of their congregations and choirs. Church musicians will want to get their names on the mailing lists of the major publishers of religious music in order to receive the most up-to-date information about the publication of choral concertatos.

A worthy feature of this manual is its topical index in Section Four. Those charged with hymn selection will want to use the topical index as a help in selecting hymns in keeping with the theme of the day. Care must be taken, however, to read the entire text of the hymn, and not make what could turn out to be an entirely inappropriate hymn choice on the basis of one word or one thought in a single stanza of a given hymn.

Alternate settings have been chosen for many tunes that appear more than once in *Christian Worship*. The hymn numbers for the alternate settings are found listed in small print on the lower right-hand side of the hymn page. The organist who struggles a bit with a difficult setting can check the other settings to find one with which he or she is more comfortable. And more accomplished organists can use more than one setting as they accompany hymns, especially longer and more familiar hymns. This provides musical variety both for the organist and the worshipers. Harmonic variations, even if available, may not be desired, however, when the congregation is not familiar with the hymn tune itself.

Careful and thorough planning is the key to good hymn selection and, in the end, edifying and joyful hymn singing. To that end, hymns should be provided to organists, choir directors, and Lutheran elementary school teachers at least a season, if not longer, in advance. Choir directors who have selected concertato music for use during the church year should request the pastor to schedule a certain hymn for a chosen date. The pastor will make every effort to accommodate choir director's expressed wishes for scheduling festival and concertato hymns, so there will be no conflicts or duplication. A typical memo or hymn chart provided by the pastor to the musicians and teachers should include the liturgy for the day, the Psalm, the lessons, the sermon text, and the hymns for the day. This assumes that all are aware of the lectionary chosen for the year and the Hymn of the Day program the pastor wishes to follow, if there is one. (See chapter 8 of this manual).

Periodical planning meetings between pastors and church musicians are desirable. They are absolutely essential in congregations with two or more pastors. In the multi-pastor parish, it may also be a good idea for one pastor or church musician to be authorized to take responsibility for hymn selection. This will avoid needless duplication and repetition of hymns. The careful hymn selector–planner will also develop some system of referencing the hymns that have been used during the course of a given church year. A good church secretary and/or computer can help. This practice will prevent the overuse of certain hymns that may be the pastor's favorites, and encourage the selection of a wider variety of hymns. There is certainly no absolute rule of thumb on how often a hymn can be used during a church year. But in a hymnal containing over 600 hymns, no hymn should have to be overused.

It's only logical that there is a tendency on the part of those who select hymns to choose hymns that are familiar to them or part of their own personal experience. "My congregation likes to sing this hymn" generally means, "I like this hymn, and, because I schedule it quite often, my congregation has learned it quite well." Members of a congregation should not be denied the pleasure of broadening their worship experience and their hymn vocabulary by learning new hymns and becoming more familiar with contemporary tunes and texts. Careful introduction of new hymns will prevent congregations from being "turned off" when such hymns are used for the first time in the worship services. There are practical suggestions for introducing new hymns in Section One of this manual, pages 134,135.

The exposure of congregations to new hymns can be an exciting and pleasurable experience that can bring joy and spiritual uplift to Christians. Many hymns are worthy of being learned, even if they aren't favorites the first few times they are introduced or sung. The real satisfaction comes later, when the "new" hymn, like the old favorites, can be sung with vigor and joy.

It would be well for all pastors and church musicians in congregations using it to learn the hymn contents of *Christian Worship* thoroughly, so that hymn selecting can be informed and edifying. (Additional information concerning hymn selection and service planning is offered in Section One, chapter 8, "Planning for Worship," pp. 123-127.)

CHAPTER 18:

The Hymn Section
of *Christian Worship*

In 1985 when the committee charged with preparing a new hymnal for the WELS began the work of selecting hymns for *Christian Worship,* they began their work with some specific directions from the members of the Wisconsin Evangelical Lutheran Synod. *The Lutheran Hymnal* of 1941 was to be a model for the new hymnal. The best-loved and most frequently used hymns in *The Lutheran Hymnal* were to reappear in a new hymnal, so that the rich hymnic heritage of the past would not be lost. This core of *The Lutheran Hymnal* hymns, in turn, could be supplemented by other hymns of the committee's choosing.

As the committee selected and arranged its hymn section, therefore, it began with a thorough review of each of the 660 hymns in *The Lutheran Hymnal,* considering the merits of each text and the frequency with which each hymn was being used. Early in the review process it appeared rather clear to the members of the Hymn Committee that a good mix of hymns from *The Lutheran Hymnal* and hymns that would be new to *Christian Worship,* assuming that there would be room for about 600 hymns in *Christian Worship,* would be about 400 hymns from *The Lutheran Hymnal* and 200 or so "new" hymns. As hymn selection progressed and was finally completed, that original goal proved realistic. About two-thirds of the hymns in *Christian Worship* are hymns that appeared in its predecessor, *The Lutheran Hymnal.* About one-third are hymns from other sources.

A long and careful process brought about the selection of the hymns that appear in *Christian Worship.* After reviewing each hymn in *The Lutheran Hymnal,* the committee studied thoroughly the other two Lutheran hymnals that had been produced in the two decades before work on *Christian Worship* began, *Lutheran*

Book of Worship (ELCA) and *Lutheran Worship* (LCMS), taking note especially of hymns selected for those books that were not in *The Lutheran Hymnal*. Then a wide variety of other hymnals and hymnal supplements was reviewed, several by the entire committee, many more by individual committee members. The committee also reviewed a number of original manuscripts from various poets and hymnists. The hymns finally selected for *Christian Worship*'s hymn section are hymns that clearly express the Christian faith and can best help God's people at worship in singing their "psalms, hymns and spiritual songs" with gratitude in their hearts to the Lord.

Two considerations were paramount in the shaping of *Christian Worship*'s hymn section. One was to give those who would be worshiping from this hymnal the opportunity to use the best of the hymns that were written by Christian hymnists in the half-century or so before *Christian Worship*'s publication, hymns that correctly express what the Scriptures teach and that encourage Christians in their faith and life. Hymn writers of the later twentieth century whose works appear in *Christian Worship* include Martin Franzmann, Werner Franzmann, Jaroslav Vajda, F. Pratt Green, Timothy Dudley-Smith, Henry Lettermann, Howard Edwards, and others. These "contemporary" hymns will no doubt make a significant contribution to the worship life of late twentieth and early twenty-first century Christians, even while they are still able to sing the sturdy chorales of Luther, Gerhardt, and other great Christian hymn writers of the past.

The second consideration follows quite naturally from the first. Though God's Word certainly does not change, nor does its message of sin and grace change, the world around Christians changes. The various areas of Christian life to which the Word needs to be applied change. And the type of temptations Christians face as they strive to practice their faith and live their lives for the Savior in the world change. Hymns that would strengthen Christians for their walk of life in today's world were sought for inclusion in *Christian Worship*. That emphasis is reflected in an enlarged Stewardship section, as well as in sections like Social Concern, Evangelism, Christian Love. Changes in the lectionary, most notably the shift to a widespread use of the three-year lectionary dictated a longer Epiphany hymn section, as well as the addition of the section End Time.

The "walk" through the hymn section of *Christian Worship* that follows is intended to illustrate some of the things mentioned above and help pastors and church musicians to better know and employ the hymns in *Christian Worship*.

Our journey through the hymn section of *Christian Worship* begins with hymns of the church year. That seasonal hymns are at the very beginning of the hymn section is a clear reminder that the Lutheran church is a liturgical church with a worship life built around the beautiful and regular rhythm of the Christian church year.

Advent

The Advent section in *Christian Worship* contains thirty-two hymns. This may at first seem like a large number of hymns for a four-week season, but the fact that many congregations conduct at least three midweek Advent services argued for a larger number of hymns in this section. Three hymns that are included in the Advent section in *Christian Worship* were found in other sections of *Christian Worship*'s predecessor, *The Lutheran Hymnal*. They are *Let the Earth Now Praise the Lord* (CW 28), *O Jesus, Lamb of God, You Are* (CW 27), and *When All the World Was Cursed* (CW 20).

The ancient Latin hymn *Hark! A Thrilling Voice Is Sounding* (CW 15) has been set to the nineteenth century English tune *Merton,* by William Monk. This hymn, incidentally, is the first of sixteen hymns in *Christian Worship* for which a descant is printed. Descants, especially for festival hymns, enable the choir or music readers in the congregation to soar above the regular melody line, adding additional interest to the singing of a hymn. Here is another opportunity for directors of adult and children's choirs to involve the choirs directly in the regular hymnody of the service.

Since a number of hymns have two melodies that both seem widely used, several hymns in *Christian Worship* are set to two tunes, in some cases an isometric and a rhythmic arrangement of the same melody. *Christian Worship*'s Advent section has two hymns with alternate melodies: *Lift Up Your Heads, You Mighty Gates* (CW 3,4); and *O Lord, How Shall I Meet You* (CW 18,19).

In the Advent section, as well as in other hymn sections, modernizing the language of a hymn may have resulted in a change of title from what might be familiar to those long accustomed to worshiping from *The Lutheran Hymnal.* To help find the revised hymns, the *The Lutheran Hymnal* title is listed alphabetically in the Index of Titles, indented to indicate that the title has been changed in *Christian Worship.*

Christmas/New Year/Presentation

The Christmas hymn section of Christian Worship has thirty-six hymns. There is no doubt that this is a great many hymns for a festival that includes basically Christmas Eve, Christmas Day, and one or two Sundays after Christmas. But the importance to our faith of the great events we celebrate at Christmas has moved Christian poets and hymn writers to produce a wealth of beautiful Christmas hymns that Christians love to sing.

Christian Worship's Christmas section offers a wide variety of hymns for the festival of our Savior's birth. These include powerful hymns with great doctrinal content, as well as a selection of "lighter" Christmas carols. The historical gems are well represented: *Once Again My Heart Rejoices* (CW 37); *From Heaven Above to Earth I Come* (CW 38); *O Jesus Christ, Your Manger Is* (CW 40). But to that ancient hymn treasury have been added a number of favorite carols, both ancient and modern. About fifteen of the hymns in this section would probably qualify under the loose designation of "carol." The benefits of including familiar carols in a hymnal are obvious. *Christian Worship*'s Christmas section can be used at the family altar and by families who have the custom of singing carols together at Christmas gatherings. Some congregations enjoy a pre-Christmas carol sing, perhaps after an Advent service. There are enough carols in Christian Worship to be able to have carol sings without having to reproduce carols from other sources or have extra carol booklets on hand. Many congregations also hold "midnight" Christmas Eve services during which traditional, favorite carols are sung. *Christian Worship* contains rich resources for all such services.

There is a single New Year section in *Christian Worship*, containing seven hymns suitable for both New Year's Eve and New Year's Day services. A contemporary melody has been furnished for *Now Let Us Come before Him* (CW 74), with the hope that the text of this hymn might be used more frequently. For those who use the "Name of Jesus" Gospel on New Year's Day, there is one hymn, *Jesus! Name of Wondrous Love* (CW 76). To encourage greater use of Isaac Watts' powerful, *O God, Our Help in Ages Past,* which is often associated with New Year's Eve or New Year, the hymn has been placed in the Trust section rather than in what might be considered a more "restricted" season section. Those who wish to sing this hymn over the New Year's holiday will find it there (CW 441).

There are two hymns in the tiny section Presentation. These hymns can be used on the Sunday after Christmas where the one-year lectionary is being read and in year B of the three-year lectionary.

Epiphany/Transfiguration

Because the three-year lectionary has lengthened the Epiphany season to as many as nine weeks, *Christian Worship* offers a rather substantial sixteen-hymn Epiphany section, with an additional three hymns for Transfiguration. Two of the section's hymns, *To Jordan Came the Christ, Our Lord* (CW 88) and *To Jordan's River Came Our Lord* (CW 89), reflect the Baptism of Jesus theme of the three-year lectionary for the first week after Epiphany. Other hymns in the section fit the various emphases of the season—missions: *Jesus Shall Reign Where'er the Sun* (CW 84); the divine majesty of the God-man: *How Lovely Shines the Morning Star* (CW 79); the revelation in the world of the promised Messiah: *Hail to the Lord's Anointed* (CW 93).

Hymns selected for congregational use during the Epiphany season, of course, need not be restricted to the hymnal's Epiphany section. Many of the Redeemer hymns contain thoughts very appropriate for the Epiphany season. Hymn of the Day selections, particularly those near the end of the nine-week season, include hymns from the Evangelism, Word of God, Worship and Praise, Justification, and Christian Love sections. The three Transfiguration hymns, including a powerful fifteenth century hymn rediscovered by our generation, *Oh, Wondrous Type! Oh, Vision Fair* (CW 96) and a late twentieth century hymn *Down from the Mount of Glory* (CW 97), conclude this section.

Lent/Palm Sunday/Maundy Thursday/Good Friday

Since many congregations hold midweek services in addition to regular, weekend services, here is another season in which a large number of hymns are used and sung. It is, in fact, usually during the midweek Lenten services that most of the seasonal hymns are used, since the Sundays have their own separate themes. Only Lent 5 has a Hymn of the Day selected from the Lent hymn section, although Lenten hymns are suitable as opening hymns during the Sundays of the season. Only four hymns are listed specifically for Good Friday, though Lenten hymns can certainly be used on Good Friday and vice versa.

The hymns in this section also come from a wide variety of sources and musical styles. There are many seventeenth, eighteenth, and nineteenth century hymns that believers have traditionally sung during the Lenten season. Among some interesting "new" features of *Christian Worship*'s Lenten section, Samuel Crossman's seventeenth century *My Song Is Love Unknown* (CW 110) is set to a hauntingly beautiful tune by a 20th century composer, John Ireland. Leland Sateren's *Marlee* is a contemporary tune that appears with two fairly recent texts, *Deep Were His Wounds* (CW 107) and *He Stood before the Court* (CW 115). *Oh, Come, My Soul* (CW 99) is a text and tune by a contemporary Lutheran composer, Kurt Eggert. *O Dearest Lord, Thy Sacred Head* (CW 118) and *What Wondrous Love Is This* (CW 120) are texts set to nineteenth century Appalachian tunes. *Were You There* (CW 119) is an African-American spiritual.

These "new" texts and tunes should add variety and freshness to a section of hymns that is loved, important, and thoroughly used. *O Bride of Christ, Rejoice* (CW 134) has been placed in the Palm Sunday section both to strengthen the section and with the hope that the hymn will be used more frequently. In the Good Friday section, what was formerly seven three-stanza hymns on the seven words from the cross has been reworked and reduced to a single, seven-stanza hymn, *Jesus, in Your Dying Woes* (CW 139).

Easter

That Easter is not only a one-day festival, but a six-week season is a key impression conveyed by *Christian Worship*'s hymns for the Easter season. Some text revising has been done to make a number of hymns more suitable for use not only on the Easter festival itself, but throughout the Easter season. A number of contemporary hymns supplement traditional Easter favorites. *His Battle Ended There* (CW 146) is a paraphrase of an African Chewa hymn set to African music. *Triumphant from the Grave* (CW 151)is a powerful twentieth century hymn with text by Werner Franzmann and tune by Bruce Backer.

Ascension/Pentecost/Trinity

Seven hymns are offered for the Festival of the Savior's Ascension. Two hymns that have at times been associated with the Ascension appear elsewhere in *Christian Worship*. *Jesus, My Great High Priest* (CW 359) is now found in the Redeemer section. *The Head that Once Was Crowned with Thorns* (CW 217) is found in the End Time section, specifically for use on the last Sunday of the church year, Christ the King.

Two hymns in the Pentecost section will be restricted to the Festival of Pentecost. *When God the Spirit Came* (CW 187) is a twentieth century hymn by Timothy Dudley-Smith with a melody unique to *Christian Worship*. *Hail Thee, Festival Day* (CW 179) is an ancient processional hymn that has been revised for use on the Day of Pentecost. Pastors and church musicians do well to keep in mind that the other hymns in this Pentecost section are actually "Holy Spirit" hymns and can be used at any time during the weeks after Pentecost as well as on the festival itself. Many are hymns of invocation to the Holy Spirit that serve well as opening hymns. It was originally hoped that this section could be larger, but good hymns reflecting clear, scriptural teachings about the Holy Spirit and his work through the means of grace are scarce.

Five hymns are offered for the festival of the Holy Trinity. The beautiful *Shades Mountain* tune by K. Lee Scott has been selected for *Father, Most Holy, Merciful, and Tender* (CW 191). Several "creedal" Trinitarian hymns, as well as Trinitarian hymns of praise are found in the Hymns of the Liturgy section.

St. Michael and All Angels/Reformation/End Time

The festival of St. Michael and All Angels falls on September 29th on the church calendar. When September 29th falls on a weekend, or in chapel services in schools on September 29th, an emphasis on God's blessings through the angels is certainly fitting. *Christian Worship* contains three "angel" hymns. *Around the Throne of God a Band* (CW 198), a nineteenth century text, is set to the rather well-known *Wareham*. *Lord God, to You We All Give Praise* (CW 196) is carried by *Deus Tuorum Militum,* an eighteenth century tune that has enjoyed a twentieth century revival. *They Leave Their Place on High* (CW 197) is a nineteenth century text set to a sixteenth century German folk melody.

Christian Worship's Reformation section has six hymns. Note that both rhythmic and isometric versions of *A Mighty Fortress Is Our God* (CW 200,201) are offered. *If God Had Not Been on Our Side* (CW 202), a Luther hymn, has been given a new tune, *Wächterlied,* with the hope that the livelier tune will help keep Luther's grand text alive. *In Trembling Hands, Lord God, We Hold* (CW 199) is a hymn written by two twentieth century Lutherans: Werner Franzmann (text) and Martin Albrecht (tune).

The hymn section End Time reflects the emphases of the last three Sundays of the church year in *Christian Worship*'s three-year lectionary: Last Judgment, Saints Triumphant, Christ the King. Here we find hymns that speak of the final judgment and of life everlasting. The last Sunday of the church year is Christ the King. Hymns in this section like *Saints, Behold! The Sight Is Glorious* (CW 216) and *The Head that Once Was Crowned* (CW 217), are fitting hymns for Christ the King Sunday. So are several hymns from the Redeemer section. The tune to *Jerusalem, My Happy Home* (CW 215) is an American folk tune, *Land of Rest.* And what was formerly the last stanza of the Lenten hymn *A Lamb Goes Uncomplaining Forth* (CW 100) has been given its own melody, *Wedding Glory,* and placed into this section as a separate hymn (CW 219).

Opening of Service

Following the hymns of the church year is the Opening of Service hymn section. This section contains both hymns specifically written for opening of worship services, as well as a number of praise hymns that can well serve and are frequently used to begin worship. *Come, Rejoice before Your Maker* (CW 228) is a contemporary paraphrase of Psalm 95, the "Venite Psalm." Jaroslav Vajda's *Now the Silence* (CW 231) is a beautifully crafted, thought provoking description of a communion service.

Worship and Praise

At the heart of every Christian hymnal is a strong Worship and Praise section. *Christian Worship* contains twenty-nine worship and praise hymns. The section includes some rather well-known contemporary favorites that will be a welcome addition to the hymn repertoire. These hymns include *Earth and All Stars,* (CW 247), *How Great Thou Art* (CW 256), and *Let All Things Now Living* (CW 260). More challenging, but rewarding contemporary hymns include *Sing a New Song to the Lord* (CW 245) and *The Stars Declare His Glory* (CW 246). Together with the favorite hymns of praise that generations of Christians have loved to sing, the newer hymns introduced in *Christian Worship*'s Worship and Praise section will continue to put songs and hymns of praise and thanksgiving on the lips and in the hearts of twenty-first century believers.

Hymns of the Liturgy

This section has already been mentioned in the chapter on selection of hymns. Each of the hymns in the Hymns of the Liturgy section can serve as a replacement for a part of the Ordinary in the various liturgies. To help determine which part of the Ordinary each hymn may replace, the Ordinary title is printed in bold italics just under the hymns title (e.g., hymn 262, *All Glory Be to God Alone* is a fitting hymn substitute for the *Gloria in Excelsis* or Song of Praise). There is also a notation at the bottom of the page referring to the exact page in the various liturgies that the substitutions may be made. Bringing all of these hymns together into a single, separate section should be a real service for pastors

296

and music directors who wish to vary the regular liturgies or set up special chorale services.

The use of the hymns in this section, however, certainly need not be restricted to that single use. Pastors and music directors should look this section over carefully, so that hymns that can be used well at specific times during the church year or as hymns of praise anytime during the year not be left "buried" or underused because they have been placed in this section. For example, a powerful hymn like *Holy God, We Praise Your Name* (CW 278) can be used as a substitute for the *Te Deum*. But it can certainly also stand very well on its own as a hymn to the Trinity.

Word of God

The hymn section Word of God includes well-known hymns about the law and the gospel and the Scriptures themselves. Martin Franzmann's powerful *Thy Strong Word* (CW 280) and George Briggs' *God Has Spoken by His Prophets* (CW 281) are notable twentieth century hymns that help Christians sing the truth that the Bible is God's verbally inspired and inerrant Word. A new translation of Luther's hymn on the Ten Commandments, *The Ten Commandments Are the Law* (CW 285), is very clear and understandable and deserves use. There is also a short, three-stanza summary of the commandments by a contemporary hymn writer, Daniel J. Meeter, *The Lord Is God; There Is No Other* (CW 292).

Baptism/Confession and Absolution/Holy Communion

Three contemporary Baptism hymns, *Baptized in Water* (CW 297), *See This Wonder in the Making* (CW 300), and *We Praise You, Lord* (CW 301) supplement familiar baptism hymns. These new hymns provide more variety in this section.

The Confession and Absolution section contains only seven hymns. Most have deep roots in Lutheran choral tradition, including hymns by Magnus Landstad, the great nineteenth century Norwegian poet (*Before You, God, the Judge of All*, CW 306), Martin Luther (*From Depths of Woe I Cry to You*, CW 305), and Johann Franck (*Lord, to You I Make Confession*, CW 302). *Wondrous Are Your Ways, O God* (CW 307) is a contemporary, two-stanza meditation on Psalm 139. It is set to the familiar Lenten tune, *Jesu Kreuz, Leiden Und Pein.*

Ten hymns in *Christian Worship* deal with the Sacrament of the Altar in the section Holy Communion. Several lengthy distribution hymns are retained. Horatius Bonar's *Here, O My Lord, I See You Face to Face* (CW 315), set to the tune *Farley Castle,* adds beauty and an opportunity to contemplate the blessings of the Sacrament. *Sent Forth by God's Blessing* (CW 318) by Omer Westendorf is an outstanding twentieth century post-Communion hymn. Further suggestions for selecting distribution hymns are given in chapter 17 in this section.

Close of Service

There are thirteen Close of Service hymns in *Christian Worship.* Congregations will enjoy having the opportunity to sing the rather well-known gospel hymn, *God Be with You till We Meet Again* (CW 327,328). *Go, My Children, with My Blessing* (CW 332) is set to the tune *Ar Hyd y Nos,* a familiar and loved eighteenth century Welsh melody. Pastors and church musicians are reminded again that a closing hymn or stanza is not always necessary. Selected verses of hymns that reflect and summarize the thoughts of the day's service may also serve well as a closing hymn or closing stanza.

Invitation

The Invitation section consists of mostly "old favorites," familiar tunes and texts from the nineteenth century, including texts by William Dix (*Come unto Me, Ye Weary,* CW 336), Horatius Bonar (*I Heard the Voice of Jesus Say,* CW 338), and Thomas Hastings (*Delay Not! Delay Not,* CW 337). A twentieth century addition to the section is Martin Franzmann's *O Kingly Love, that Faithfully* (CW 335). This is a powerfully written hymn with great spiritual depth, but it is quite difficult to sing. Congregations may learn it by having the choir or a small group sing the four stanzas, with the congregation joining in only on the refrain.

Redeemer/Justification/Faith

In the Redeemer and Justification sections are the hymns that express Scripture's central truths about the salvation of sinners. It is natural and proper, therefore, that both should be rather lengthy sections. *Christian Worship*'s Redeemer section has thirty-five hymns; its Justification section, thirty-two. These hymns, which honor the Savior and proclaim God's plan of salvation, are fitting for use during many different times of the church year, during both the festival and non-festival seasons. These hymns also work well for use at special services, such as weddings, funerals, anniversaries, and the like. The doctrine of justification by faith in Jesus Christ is the central teaching of Scripture. Christians encourage, instruct, and strengthen each other as they sing these hymns to and with each other.

As in other sections, the "Lutheran classics" and many traditional favorites are retained. Others, like *Amazing Grace—How Sweet the Sound* (CW 379) are already quite familiar.

Some "new" hymns, written during the quarter-century or so before *Christian Worship*'s publication, like *The King of Glory Comes* (CW 363) will be easily learned because of the nature of the tunes that carry them. Some hymns, such as *Jesus, Lover of My Soul* (CW 357), have been given new tunes, because most of Christendom is now singing that tune with that text.

A few "new" hymns in this section are quite challenging. Congregations, pastors, and church musicians need to remember that in a hymnal containing over 600 hymns, not all the hymns will— or have to—be learned and sung by all those who use the book. *Christian Worship*'s goal is to offer believers at worship the best of Christian hymnody; encourage the use of a strong core group of hymns through a Hymn of the Day plan (see chapter 16 in this section); and then let each congregation, according to its own preferences and abilities, make use of the hymns worshipers find most beneficial and desirable.

A particularly beautiful new hymn that is unique to *Christian Worship* is Kurt Eggert's *Not unto Us* (CW 392). Pastor Eggert was a Lutheran pastor and musician. Both the text, which is loosely based on Psalm 115, and the original tune clearly communicate the Christian's total dependence on God and his free and faithful grace. This hymn can be used at the close of the church year, as a worship and praise hymn, and for any number of special occasions, including church and church workers' anniversaries.

299

The hymns in the Faith section are hymns about faith. They speak, not so much about the contents of the faith Christians profess, but about the Spirit-wrought act of believing.

Prayer

The eight hymns in the Prayer section are, for the most part, not prayers themselves, but hymns about praying and the place of prayer in the Christian life. There are two summaries of the Lord's Prayer: Luther's longer, *Our Father, Who from Heaven Above* (CW 410); and Martin Franzmann's three-stanza, *O Lord, You Have in Your Pure Grace* (CW 407).

Trust

Hymns of cross and comfort, hymns describing Christians' struggles in the church militant, and hymns describing various aspects of the Christian's journey through life are brought together in this longer section under the general heading of Trust. The Christian makes his or her journey through life calmly and courageously, facing the dangers and fighting the battles, not in his or her own strength but the Lord's, trusting the Lord's loving promises each day, secure in those promises and blessed by God's love. Christians know from Scripture that the Lord is directing their lives in his wisdom as well as his love and leading them ever forward toward their real home in eternal glory.

These thirty-eight hymns proclaim the Christians' distinctive view of life. And Christians use these hymns to encourage and cheer one another in life's difficult days, as well as to praise God for his wise direction and unfailing love each day. This section is, not surprisingly, one of the longest in *Christian Worship*. Here, too, is material not only for weekend worship, but for home devotions, for weddings, funerals, confirmations, and all those occasions from the cradle to the grave when Christians need to be reminded that they have a secure refuge in the Lord and a sure foundation for their lives in his unfailing love. *Jesus, Shepherd of the Sheep* (CW 436) and *Lord, Take My Hand and Lead Me,* (CW 439) are hymns that have perhaps become familiar to Lutheran worshipers over the years through popular choral arrangements. A variety of hymn styles is also represented in this section. *On*

300

Eagles' Wings (CW 440) sets thoughts expressed in Isaiah 40 to an easily learned contemporary melody. *Precious Lord, Take My Hand* (CW 451) is a spiritual by Thomas Dorsey, which is deeply loved by black Christians and will no doubt be sung with vigor by Christians of all races.

Commitment

This is also a longer section with hymns that describe the Christian's life of sanctification, the believer's joyful response to all that God in love has done for us in Christ. Christians who know and love the Savior commit themselves and all they are and have to the Savior and his cause. They use his commandments as their guide and strive to make it evident that they belong to him who loved them and gave himself for them. The Christian life is not an easy one. There are constant struggles and temptations, daily spiritual enemies to face, and battles to fight. But Christians daily receive their spiritual strength from the Lord. Through his Word he arms them for the struggle and helps us overcome temptation and sin. One hymn in this section declares, "Forth in your name, O Lord, I go, My daily labor to pursue, Determined only you to know In all I think or speak or do" (CW 456). Worship leaders will find many hymns in this section for the non-festival half of the church year, hymns emphasizing Christian growth and sanctification in general. The sections that immediately follow touch on specific areas of Christian life.

Stewardship

Ten stewardship hymns have been selected for *Christian Worship*. All emphasize Christian stewardship principles: God is the owner of all things; we are managers of all the time, talents, and treasures he has entrusted to us. We are responsible to him for our management. And the motive for all stewardship is love for the Savior, who gave his all that we might be saved eternally. A number of interesting and easily learnable new tunes, including *Nettleton* (CW 484), *Sursum Corda* (CW 482), *Farley Castle* (CW 483), *Pleading Savior* (CW 489), and *Kingsfold* (CW 481), carry the texts well and will be enjoyed by congregations who learn them. Congregations who have the custom of singing an

301

"offering hymn" will also find a rich source of material in this section.

Christian Love

Pastors will no doubt appreciate the ten hymns in this section when looking for hymns to reinforce sermons based on texts from the Sermon on the Mount and 1 John, many of which are found in the three-year lectionary. All of these hymns are scriptural and speak to the needs of our age in contemporary language. Several of these hymns, including *Love in Christ Is Strong and Living* (CW 490) and *Though I May Speak with Bravest Fire* (CW 498), are suitable as congregational hymns or solos for weddings. We live in a selfish and impersonal age. As we speak to one another with our psalms, hymns, and spiritual songs, we need to encourage one another as our Savior encourages his disciples: "Love each another as I have loved you" (John 15:12). May the hymns in the Christian Love section of *Christian Worship* encourage us all in doing that.

Christian Home

The Christian Home section of *Christian Worship* supplies us with hymns that help us pray for Christian homes. Four nineteenth century hymns, including favorites like *Oh, Blest the House, Whate'er Befall* (CW 506), are supplemented by hymns from the pens of twentieth century authors, including F. Bland Tucker (*Our Father, by Whose Name*, CW 501) and Albert Bayly (*Lord of the Home*, CW 502). *Lord of Our Growing Years* (CW 507) by David Mowbray (b. 1938) is an excellent hymn that pictures Christians as they pass through every stage of earthly life surrounded by God's grace. A new tune for Magnus Landstad's nineteenth century text, *Oh, Blessed Home, Where Man and Wife* (CW 503) carries the text in a more pleasant and singable way.

Christian Education

The Christian Education hymns represent the works of Christian poets from about A.D. 200: Clement of Alexandria, (*Shepherd of Tender Youth*, CW 515); through the sixteenth century (*Lord, Help Us Ever to Retain*, CW 514); the seventeenth century, Isaac

302

Watts (*Let Children Hear the Mighty Deeds,* CW 512,and *How Shall the Young Secure Their Hearts,* CW 509) and Thomas Kingo (*I Pray You, Dear Lord Jesus,* CW 510); to the late twentieth century, Henry Lettermann (*Lord Jesus Christ, the Children's Friend,* CW 513) and Oliver Rupprecht (*O Lord, Our God, Your Gracious Hand,* CW 511). The latter two hymns give thanks for the blessings the Lord bestows on his Church not only through Christian education in general, but especially through Christian schools. The historical span represented by these hymns reminds us that Christian education will never stop being important.

Social Concern

The Lord has called believers living in what many regard as a post-Christian society to be that society's salt and light, to share his Word and reflect his love. This section contains eleven hymns that proclaim not a social gospel, but a God-pleasing, Christian concern for the society in which God has placed them. The texts range in content from a prayer for peace among nations adapted by Luther to twentieth century texts addressing the same subject. Other hymns deal with social concerns that Christians constantly face, including helping the less fortunate and putting aside racial and ethnic differences for the sake of Christian love. These are thought-provoking hymns that truly encourage Christians to reflect Christ's love in the society in which they live.

Church/Ministry/Saints and Martyrs

Scriptural truths about both the visible and invisible church are proclaimed in the fourteen hymns in *Christian Worship*'s Church section. The uplifting tune *Westminster Abbey* appears with the text *Christ Is Made the Sure Foundation* (CW 531). Nikolas Selnecker's sixteenth century classic, *Lord Jesus Christ, with Us Abide* (CW 541), is just as timely for our generation as it was over four centuries ago. *Our Fathers' God in Years Long Gone* (CW 535) is a compelling text with the powerful eighteenth century tune, *O Grosser Gott.* This hymn is also fitting for special occasions, particularly anniversaries.

To a number of familiar and regularly used hymns the Ministry section adds Martin Franzmann's *Preach You the Word* (CW 544).

303

Of special note in this rather short section is an excellent modernization of Christopher Wordsworth's, *Thou Who the Night in Prayer Didst Spend,* now entitled, *O Lord, in Prayer You Spent the Night* (CW 548). Worshipers' attention is directed to the ministry in several of the lessons in the three-year lectionary. Ministry hymns are also useful for installations and church workers' anniversaries. They help Christians focus their attention on the Lord's encouragement to pray for more workers in his harvest field.

Saints and Martyrs features hymns dealing with the Church triumphant. *By All Your Saints Still Striving* (CW 552) is a hymn that highlights the "saints' days" of the church year calendar. The hymn lists twenty-seven stanzas, but is really a three-stanza hymn in which the first and last stanzas stay the same and the stanza for the appropriate saint's day is inserted as stanza 2. Lutherans don't often pay much attention to saints' days. But Scripture itself urges us to remember those who have gone before us into eternity, to learn from and imitate their faith and lives. Schools of the church, particularly high schools and colleges at which chapel services are held each day, might wish to keep the entire church calendar in mind as devotions are planned. Many of the hymns in this section can also be used for comfort at Christian funerals.

Evangelism/Missions

History may well record the late twentieth century as the time when Lutheran Christians really began to understand how many people in our own nation and in our own communities are without Christ. Twelve hymns in *Christian Worship*'s Evangelism section focus on each Christian's call to share the Savior with others. The hymn styles range from the gospel hymn *There Is a Balm in Gilead* (CW 564), through the nineteenth century *Lord of the Living Harvest* (CW 559), to the contemporary text and tunes *Rise, Shine, You People* (CW 556) and *Christ High-Ascended* (CW 558). The entire section helps Christians focus on the Lord's great commission, which hasn't changed since the first century and will not change in the twenty-first century.

A living church must also be a church that desires to share the good news of the gospel in all the world. Thirteen stirring mission hymns remind us of our worldwide task. *Lift High the Cross*

(CW 579) has already become a favorite among many Christians. There are also old favorites like *From Greenland's Icy Mountains* (CW 571) by Reginald Heber (d. 1826), *May God Bestow on Us His Grace* (CW 574) by Luther, and *Awake, O Spirit, Who Inspired* (CW 567) by the Pietist Karl von Bogatzky. *Good News of God Above* (CW 568), a twentieth century mission hymn by Timothy Dudley-Smith, has been set to a melody unique to *Christian Worship, Dousman.* Many of the mission hymns are also suitable for use during certain weeks of Epiphany.

Morning/Evening

There are not many Morning and Evening hymns in *Christian Worship.* Since many of the evening services offered by congregations are identical to the weekend services or are seasonal services, as in Advent and Lent, hymns selected for those services would often not be evening hymns. Similarly, the number of morning hymns was kept at a minimum, to make room for more hymns in other sections.

Confirmation/Marriage/Death and Burial

These three sections mark the various rites of passage in Christians' lives. The Confirmation section is rather short. Commitment hymns, and even some seasonal hymns, are also fitting for use at confirmation.

Three of the five Marriage hymns are contemporary texts. All of the hymns in this section are suitable for congregational or solo singing at wedding services.

The Death and Burial section is also short, containing only four hymns. Gospel comfort for the bereaved can also be found in hymns from other sections of *Christian Worship:* Trust, Redeemer, Justification, seasonal hymns. A wonderful new Death and Burial hymn is Fred Pratt Green's three-stanza, *How Blest Are They* (CW 607). This hymn deserves widespread use, perhaps also for the end of the church year. It is set to the familiar tune *Winchester New.*

Thanksgiving/Nation/Church Anniversary

Eight familiar and easily singable hymns will assist users of *Christian Worship* in observing the national holiday of

Thanksgiving, as well as other special occasions of thanksgiving.

Four hymns help us carry out God's command to intercede with him for our nation.

Three hymns are especially suggested for use at church anniversaries, although there are many other hymns, throughout *Christian Worship,* suitable for use at anniversaries and special events.

In Conclusion

With a careful blend of classic, ancient hymns of Christianity, Reformation hymns, favorite hymns that appeared in *The Lutheran Hymnal,* and the best of hymnody in the half-century before *Christian Worship*'s production—with hymns drawn from many different cultures and traditions, all of which correctly reflecting scriptural teaching as confessed by the Lutheran church, the hymn section of *Christian Worship* offers the church the encouragement of the hymnist Fred Pratt Green in the hymn *When in Our Music God Is Glorified:*

> Let ev'ry instrument be tuned for praise;
> Let all rejoice that have a voice to raise,
> And may God give us faith to sing always:
> Alleluia!"   (CW 248, stanza 5)

CHAPTER 19:

Amens in *Christian Worship*

Amen is a word used frequently, and sometimes casually in our worship. It is part of the interaction of liturgical responses that identify Christians as a royal priesthood and a people set apart for God. The liturgical responses of believers in their worship here on earth in many ways mirror the joyful acclamations that the redeemed in heaven continually raise around God's eternal throne in thanksgiving for their salvation.

Amen is one of the most basic of the words we use in our liturgical responses. The word *Amen* is an Anglicized Hebrew word meaning, "firm, established, so be it." In using *Amen* as a liturgical response, Christians have taken their cue from Scripture itself, where *Amen* is a simple, yet firm and dramatic word spoken by the congregation at the end of a liturgical prayer. After a thanksgiving prayer that David first committed to Asaph and his associates, who probably sang it as a kind of liturgical prayer, we are told, "Then all the people said, 'Amen'" (1 Chronicles 16:36). Another example of the use of Amen in the Old Testament is found in Nehemiah 8:6, when, after a reading of Scripture and a word of praise from Ezra, "All the people lifted their hands and responded, 'Amen! Amen!'" The word occasionally also appears at the end of doxologies. In the Old Testament the 89th Psalm concludes, "Praise be to the Lord forever! Amen and Amen." And St. Paul several times ends doxologies in the New Testament, among them Romans 9:5 and Ephesians 3:21, with the joyful affirmation, *Amen*.

In the Gospels, *Amen* (usually translated "truly" in the NIV) appears at times at the beginning of Jesus' sayings. With that expression he who is God himself draws attention to the importance of what he is about to say and teach. He affirms that his every word is divinely true and proclaims himself to be the very heart of scriptural witness, God's great *Yes* and *Amen* to all the Old

Testament prophecies. The Book of Revelation refers to Jesus as the *Amen,* the faithful and true witness, the ruler of all creation. The congregation's *Amen* in corporate worship is likewise a testimony of faith and joy in the certainty of salvation in him who is God's great *Amen,* and the one through whom Christians can and do approach God in prayer and praise.

Given this background the questions naturally arise: "What is the proper use of the expression *Amen* in our hymns and liturgies? Should *Amen* be used only sometimes, or not at all? Can *Amen* be over-used?"

If we regard *Amen* as a congregational affirmation or expression of assent to prayer and praise, then it is obvious that its most fitting use is following a prayer, an expression of praise, a reading of Scripture, or a blessing spoken or sung. The congregation's *Amen* used in these settings emphatically declares, "This prayer, this expression of praise, this Scripture, this blessing is ours. We send it to God, or, in the case of the Scripture or the blessing, we receive it from God's spokesman with believing hearts." When a congregation sings or speaks *Amen,* the entire gathered body of worshipers subscribes to what those leading the worship have sung and/or said. *Amen* can also, however, serve as a congregational expression of unity of faith. It performs that function particularly well when spoken by the congregation after the creeds or prayers have been recited in unison by the entire worshiping assembly.

Those who subscribe to the above uses of the *Amen* also find that on occasion the use of *Amen* can be somewhat out of place and even unnecessary. The minister or worship leader who offers a prayer on behalf of the congregation, then speaks the *Amen* himself, is actually depriving the congregation of the opportunity to take ownership of that prayer for themselves. On the other hand, if the entire congregation has already sung its praise in a hymn as a body, an *Amen* at the end of the hymn becomes somewhat redundant. The congregation has already made the hymn its own by participating in singing it. Why should a further *Amen* be desirable or necessary?

It must be said, however, that there is a diversity of opinion on this point. Some liturgical scholars, while agreeing with the major premise that no affirmatory *Amen* is needed if a congregation has already made a hymn its own by singing it corporately still allow for an *Amen* as a joint confession of faith, particularly if the hymn is a prayer or a doxology. Obviously the choices and decisions on this particular point can become quite subjective.

Many contemporary liturgical scholars believe that the inclusion of the *Amens* at the ends of hymns in hymnals published early in the twentieth century was based on erroneous assumptions made by the music editors of that day. The practice of adding *Amen* to every hymn appears to have been unknown prior to the nineteenth century, when certain Anglican editors began the practice, incorrectly citing monastic hymns and antiphonal psalmody of the Middle Ages as models. In those cases a choir, a cantor, or some other worship leadership group or individual probably sang or chanted the body of the hymn or psalm, and the congregation responded to what they heard with the acclamation, *Amen,* thus making the prayer and praise of the leader(s) their own. Most modern hymnal editors, familiar with this contemporary view of worship history, are now omitting the *Amens* from the hymns, when the word itself is not part of the original poetry or text. *Christian Worship,* too, follows that pattern.

Christian Worship, however, does not force the issue of the *Amens* or make new liturgical laws for those who will worship from it. It recognizes that, in many congregations, entrenched customs and cherished worship traditions will, for the time being at least, carry more weight than the latest liturgical scholarship. And so, though the *Amens* are not printed with the hymns unless they are part of the actual text of the hymn or included as part of the melody line in those hymns that are chants, harmonizations for *Amens* are printed on a loose, laminated card that can be found in the organist's edition of *Christian Worship.* The *Amens* on the card cover the entire range of keys that are used in the hymns of *Christian Worship.* The accompanist can easily match the key of a hymn with the *Amen* of the same key. More accomplished organists need not even refer to the card, but can simply add a IV-I cadence to accompany the *Amen.* In this way an *Amen,* if desired, can easily be added to any of the hymns in *Christian Worship.*

CHAPTER 20:

Accompanying
the Hymns and the Liturgies

The organist serves the congregation within the worship service in several capacities. These include accompanying the hymns and liturgies, accompanying choirs, playing solo organ music, and accompanying various vocal and instrumental soloists and ensembles. All of these roles are important and appropriate to the worship service as we know it. Foremost among them, however, is the accompanying of the congregation's song in the hymns and liturgies.

Interpreting the congregation's song in a vital and musical way can be one of the most valuable contributions an organist makes to the worship life of a congregation. The accompanying of the hymns and liturgies need never be routine and something taken for granted. Rather, it should challenge the organist to play this music in the most convincing manner possible. If, in the planning of the worship service, first consideration is given to the careful preparation of the hymns and liturgies, the decisions regarding the remaining service music will be made more easily and naturally.

It is perhaps curious that the most important music-making in the worship service—that of the congregation—is normally not rehearsed. Accordingly, an even greater degree of musical acumen may be required on the part of the organist in his or her accompanying role. How often has it happened that the congregation's song has been marred by ill-chosen tempos, a disregard for the taking of breath, or the thoughtless projection of a musical line? In this area, as in others, it remains a truism that the organist, like any other musician, must always be a critical listener of his or her own playing.

Direct congregational participation in the hymns and liturgies has been historically a hallmark of Lutheran worship. Through the years ever more difficult music, such as Gregorian chants in free rhythm, Anglican chants in four-part harmony, or hymns in multimeter—all formerly the province of the trained choir—have become the congregation's song. And now a resurgent interest in psalm singing, reflected in *Christian Worship* and other contemporary hymnals, is making itself felt in congregational worship. Although the successful performance of this more difficult music may depend on the strong support of trained choirs, the organist will also need to possess a flexible keyboard technique and an understanding of a rather large range of musical styles in order to do them justice.

Some general and specific considerations regarding the organist's approach to the melodies of the congregation's songs will be discussed below. These include (1) the organist and the musical ear, (2) the nature of the organ as an accompanying instrument, (3) organ technique, (4) text and music, (5) tempo in metrical hymn settings, (6) accentuation, articulation, rubato, and shaping of phrases in metrical hymn settings, (7) hymn settings in free rhythm, (8) liturgical settings, (9) diversity of musical styles, and (10) unity and variety in the worship service. The suggestions given are sometimes advanced, and each organist will need to be selective according to his or her situation.

The Organist and the Musical Ear

Musicians often attest to the importance of critical listening in the playing of musical lines. Mechanical rote-playing is always the enemy of all truly expressive music-making where the musical ear is continuously engaged. Even in playing the simplest melody, each melodic interval should be heard by the inner ear before it is physically played. This "processing" of the melody through the inner ear must be rehearsed by the organist not only for the main melody, but for the secondary melodies as well. In the common four-part homophonic hymn or liturgical setting, this critical listening is thus extended to the alto, tenor, and bass lines. Frequently these lines are not heard as melodic in their own right, but merely as background components of a series of chords. The organist then would do well to practice the four lines simultaneously, but to listen selectively to each line in turn.

311

Accurate and note-perfect playing is often possible only by attending to the inner voices of hymn and liturgical settings. For example, even a good sight reader may have difficulty with the penultimate (second-last) phrase of *Schmücke dich* (CW 311, see Example 1). Admittedly other factors such as pedal and fingering techniques are involved here, but careful, focused attention to each of the lower three voices is essential. When all melodic lines of the homophonic setting are treated as if they were individual polyphonic lines, and recognized as such by the inner ear, a living and singing performance will result.

Example 1

The Nature of the Organ as an Accompanying Instrument

For historical and practical reasons the organ exists for us as the primary accompanying instrument for congregational worship. Although from time to time other instruments are rightfully employed in worship, the power, carrying quality, and "voice of leadership" exhibited by the organ is readily recognized. The organ, especially when specifically designed for the building in which it speaks, becomes an integral component—a "presence" as it were—of the worship space. When the piano is substituted for the organ as the chief accompanying instrument for worship, usually on a temporary basis, its inadequacy is immediately evident. While brass, woodwind, and string ensembles provide welcome variety from time to time, their exclusive accompanying of the hymns and liturgies is impractical.

The organ is basically a legato instrument capable of sustained tone beyond that of any other keyboard instrument. This feature can be a strength as well as a weakness. Its sustaining power can be an asset when the melodies of the congregation's song are played boldly and with authority. Unfortunately, its sustaining power becomes a liability when the organ fails to "breathe" naturally like other instruments. Although capable of unending sound, it must be made to clearly define the phrases of the congregation's song, sensitive to the breathing capacities of the human singer.

Because of the employment of the organ as the chief accompanying instrument in Lutheran worship over several centuries, a highly significant and extensive organ literature has developed and is now available to be used for the enhancement of the congregation's song. The rich chorale prelude literature includes some of the greatest music ever written. Fortunately, this repertory is being expanded today through the efforts of numerous composers.

Organ Technique

Having an adequate manual technique is basic for the playing of the hymns and liturgies. This includes the ability to play two or more legato polyphonic (many-voiced) lines characteristic of so much organ literature. Especially helpful is the ability to play with independence the soprano and alto voices simultaneously with the right hand. Various fingering techniques are used to achieve this, including playing occasional alto notes with the left hand, finger crossings, and finger substitutions.

Pedal technique includes alternate toe playing, toe-heel playing, alternate toe substitutions, some foot substitutions, slides, and crossings. As a general rule, toe-heel intervals of a third work well at the extremes of the pedal keyboard, but should be avoided in the pedal's center region. In this case alternate toe substitutions are frequently needed. One must be ready also to execute black key substitutions.

The normal legato touch involves neither overlapping nor separation of adjacent notes. It is used for virtually all *metrical* hymn and liturgical settings. This touch, however, is supplemented by a superlegato in which adjacent notes are slightly overlapped. This latter touch enhances hymns and liturgical settings which display *free rhythm*. If these chant settings are played with the normal legato, they will sound too fast. The superlegato playing will preserve the flowing character of chant and support a faster and more flexible declamation of the chant melody.

Most hymn and liturgy playing will be of the ensemble variety, where a single manual is employed for the soprano and alto (right hand) and tenor (left hand), together with the bass in the pedal. Even with psalm accompaniments in which manual only is often suggested, it will be easier to use pedal, but without 16-foot tone. A few times in every worship service the organist may want to "solo-out" the hymn melody on a more prominent or more colorful registration. Here the left hand alto and tenor as well as the pedal bass have background registrations (see chapter 22 on organ registration). This solo playing technique may be used to introduce the hymn, to highlight the stanzas of new or infrequently sung hymns, and to provide variety in hymns and liturgical settings.

The majority of the hymns in *Christian Worship* may be considered vocal settings where each syllable of the text is clearly notated in all four voices with a corresponding note, as in *Old Hundredth* (CW 323, see Example 2). With these hymns the organist need not play all of the repeated notes. In fact, in the interest of a more satisfactory accompaniment, it would be better if the organist makes an arrangement more suited to the organ. In Example 2 the opening repeated chord is problematic. If all the

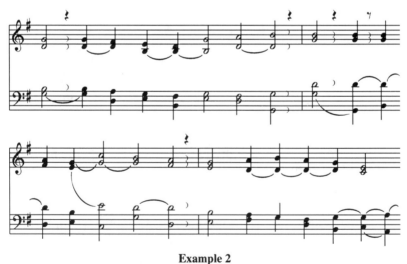

Example 2

notes are repeated as notated, the continuity of the setting is disturbed. If only the soprano and the bass notes are articulated, the decisive interval of the third in the tenor remains tied. In order to achieve proper accentuation as well as continuity, the solution given in Example 2 is offered as one possibility.

St. Thomas (CW 533), another vocal setting, will illustrate further the kinds of solutions that an organist may wish to employ (see Example 3). Here decisions regarding common notes between the soprano and alto voices frequently need to be made. Notice the tie between the soprano c and the c in chords 1 and 2 of phrase 1, where the initial rising interval of a fourth in the soprano is thereby kept legato. Notice, too, in chords 4 and 5 of phrase 3, where the articulated c in the alto allows for the soprano c to be given its proper accent. In addition to common note solutions that favor the clear playing of the soprano melody, alto and tenor repeated notes may be tied, as marked in Example 3. As an option, repeated notes in the bass may be tied.

Example 3

(In some hymns, like *O Durchbrecher aller Bande* (CW 87), *Coronae* (CW 216), and *Was frag ich nach der Welt* (CW 477), solutions regarding repeated notes have been made. The organist may find that some of the notated solutions can be handled in a different manner. A few *Christian Worship* hymns will prove to be especially challenging because of the profusion of their repeated notes and repeated chords. *O store gud* (CW 256), *God Be with You* (CW 327), *Precious Lord* (CW 451), and *Hankey* (CW 562) fall into this category.

Occasionally a hymn will have to be given its own special articulation, so that the text and music may be interpreted with greater excitement and vitality. Hymns such as *The King's Majesty* (CW 132), *Salve festa dies* (CW 179), or *Wojtkiewiecz* (CW 556) will profit from such treatment. Example 4 illustrates one possible organ arrangement of *Wojtkiewiecz*. Be aware that most of the articulations are eighth rests, with occasional sixteenth and quarter rests. The half notes at measure 3, beat 3, and at measure 9, beat 3, must be held their full value. Notice also that all soprano melody notes are to be kept legato. The kind of

Example 4

articulation as shown in Example 4 may also be used from time to time in any hymn when the singing becomes lackluster or lethargic and needs a more decisive accentuation.

Text and Music

A thorough and thoughtful reading of the individual texts of hymns and liturgical settings is essential for a meaningful musical interpretation of those texts on the part of the organist. Music is never merely a vehicle for the text. Rather, it communicates a meaning that simultaneously enhances and transcends the text. Having absorbed the mood and meaning of the text, the organist

Example 5

will respond in a convincing manner with appropriate musical gestures, articulations, tempos, and organ registrations.

Reading a poetic text aloud and singing such a text are two very different things. Perhaps the most powerful and elemental feature on the music side is the phrase ending that demands a breath following it, even though the poetic thought is incomplete. Example 5 presents *St. Anne* (CW 441), a hymn of four phrases. Recognition of each of the four cadences with articulation is needed, even though, in most of the stanzas, phrases 1 and 3 are poetically incomplete. A degree of continuity between phrases 1 and 2 and phrases 3 and 4 may be achieved by keeping the bass tied as illustrated. Nevertheless, articulation following each of the four phrases is mandatory.

When each stanza is completed poetically as well as musically, a pause of indeterminate length should follow. It is uncommon for a hymn to be rhythmically continuous from stanza to stanza, although *Alleluia No. 1* (CW 154) and *Engelberg* (CW 248) are among the exceptions. Normally, however, instead of maintaining a beat pattern while holding the final chord of the hymn, it would seem best if the organist would cease counting and treat the final chord with a fermata. Disregarding the notation of the final chord and leaving the length of this fermata to the musical instincts of the organist, the beat is resumed with the playing of the following stanza.

Tempo in Metrical Hymn Settings

It is a mark of a good musician to play a hymn or liturgical setting with integrity according to his or her musical instincts. We should expect diverse rather than uniform interpretations of the same music. And along with other musical elements, we should expect differing tempos.

Attitudes regarding tempo will become more flexible when it is recognized that some hymns are enhanced by a strict tempo, while others benefit from a more relaxed approach. Collegiate congregations may tend to sing hymns faster than those congregations comprising a rather wide age span. Reverberant worship spaces may not tolerate the faster pace appropriate to dry acoustics. Tempos suitable for trained choirs may be too fast for congregational singing.

When the organist is practicing a hymn in order to determine a proper tempo, it will be instructive to play the melody alone or in octaves, thus giving full attention to the melody itself. This procedure will allow for focusing on (1) the meter and the chosen beat, (2) the length of the phrases so that they may be sung in one breath, and (3) the faster note values so that they may be accommodated easily into the melody of each phrase.

In many contemporary hymnals, *Christian Worship* included, the time signature is sometimes omitted. Despite this omission, however, the organist must know exactly what the beat patterns are. In the discussion below the tempo markings are only suggestive.

With simple, duple meters in 4/4 a decision will have to be made as to whether a quarter-note beat or a half-note beat will best serve the given hymn. Hymns with the quarter-note beat are represented by *In Babilone* (CW 182, ♩=84[1]), *Winchester Old* (CW 259, ♩=80), *Es ist das Heil* (CW 390, ♩=112), *St. Anne* (CW 441, ♩=72), and *Cwm Rhondda* (CW 523, ♩=96). Hymns with the half-note beat are represented by *Mendelssohn* (CW 61, ♩=54), *Sonne der Gerechtigkeit* (CW 141, ♩=96), *Ellers* (CW 321, ♩=48), *Webb* (CW 474, ♩=56), and *Crucifer* (CW 579, ♩=69).

With simple triple meters in 3/4, the decision rests with either a quarter-note beat or a dotted half-note beat. Hymns with the quarter-note beat are represented by *The Ash Grove* (CW 260, ♩=112), *Hanover* (CW 243, ♩=108), *Slane* (CW 367, ♩=76), *Resignation* (CW 374, ♩=120), *Rockingham Old* (CW 549, ♩=100), and *Kremser* (CW 609, ♩=92). Hymns with dotted half-note beat are represented by *Westminster Abbey* (CW 77, ♩.=44), *Beatitudo* (CW 340, ♩.=40), and *Woodworth* (CW 397, ♩.=46). In a few cases triple meter hymns could receive either a quarter-note beat or a dotted half-note beat as in *Auf, auf, mein Herz* (CW 156, ♩=126 or ♩.=42), *Lobe den Herren* (CW 234, ♩=120 or ♩.=40), and *Nun lob, mein Seel* (CW 403, ♩=132 or ♩.=44)

Compound duple and triple meters in 6/8 and 9/8 require the dotted quarter note as the beat as in *Franklin* (CW 187, ♩.=56) and *Bunessan* (CW 297, ♩.=48). *Gabriel's Message* (CW 24, ♩.=66) and *Now* (CW 218, ♩.=60) are compound multimeter hymns. The

---

[1] These numerals represent metronome markings.

eighth-note beat in *Stille Nacht* (CW 60, ♪=92) is an exception. Some hymns given a 6/4 time signature are compound, as in *Puer Nobis Nascitur* (CW 5, ♩.=50).

Multimeter hymns that use quarter-note beats are those with alternating patterns of two and three beats. The following hymns are representative of this category: *Es ist genug* (CW 158, ♩=108), *Herr Jesu Christ, dich zu uns wend* (CW 230, ♩=116), *Mach's mit mir, Gott* (CW 453, ♩=104), and *Freu dich sehr* (CW 470, ♩=120).

In a fair number of simple duple meter hymns in which the half note is the beat, two shorter phrases may be sung as one longer phrase. Example 6 illustrates the first two phrases of *Valet will ich dir geben* (CW 94, ♩=60), which, because of the tempo, may be sung in one breath as one longer phrase. Other hymns in which this may happen include *St. Louis* and *Forest Green* (CW 65 and 66, ♩=48, *Gaudeamus pariter* (CW 142, ♩=56), *Lancashire* (CW 166, ♩=60), *Nicaea* (CW 195, ♩=52), *Es ist gewisslich* (CW 207, ♩=60), *Diademata* (CW 341, ♩=56), and *Aurelia* (CW 538, ♩=50).

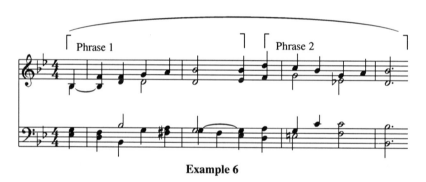

Example 6

Some hymns can become too hurried if their faster note values are not carefully assessed. The quarter-note beat of *Hyfrydol* (CW 465, ♩=112), for example, must be able to accommodate the four eighth notes in the hymn's second-last phrase. With *In Babilone* (CW 532, ♩=84), a moderate quarter-note beat must be chosen because of the hymn's frequent eighth-note motion. The dotted eighth and sixteenth-note rhythm on the word "victory" in *Festival Canticle* (CW 265, ♩=56) requires a carefully chosen slow half-note beat. Likewise with *Bryn Calfaria* (CW 352, ♩=69), attention must be given to the eighth notes within a moderately slow half-note beat in the hymns' second-last phrase.

Accentuation, Articulation, Rubato, and Shaping of Phrases in Metrical Hymns

The expressive and subtle control of sound and silence in music lies at the heart of all successful organ playing. The true meaning of such terms as *touch, accentuation, articulation, rubato, phrasing,* and *shaping* as applied to hymn playing can hardly be communicated properly in words. Rather, that meaning needs to be directly demonstrated on the organ by a good teacher in the presence of a receptive pupil. Faulty fingering techniques, overly tense hand positions, and extravagant gestures will have a detrimental effect on the often fine distinctions of touch.

Accentuation (emphasis on a note or chord) in music is obtained in a variety of ways, the most important of which are dynamics, articulation, and rubato. The first of these means of expression is basically unavailable on the organ. Although it is possible to achieve a dynamic accent of sorts with the swell pedal, individual notes within a phrase, for example, cannot be highlighted dynamically as is the case in virtually every other musical instrument.

Accentuation by means of articulation makes it possible to set one phrase apart from another. This type of articulation is most important for hymn playing, where the pause before the new phrase provides the congregation with the signal to take a breath and begin afresh with a new phrase. Articulation accents are also employed within the phrase in order to highlight repeated notes that coincide with a strong beat or with an expressive dissonance. The opening measures of *Aurelia* (CW 559) show this latter articulation. Following Example 7, notice how the second chord is given

Example 7

an accent by means of rests in soprano, alto, and tenor voices in the opening chord. Likewise the first chord of the second full measure, a dissonant chord, is preceded by similar articulation.

By far the most important accentuation is achieved by what is called *rubato:* the subtle modification of tempo for expressive purposes. The slight tempo fluctuations and give-and-take of rubato allow the organist (1) to distinguish between strong and weak beats, (2) to give shape to phrases and smaller melodic units, (3) to recognize expressive harmonic and melodic dissonances, and (4) to provide emphasis to a melodic climax within a hymn. These accents brought about by rubato are sometimes referred to as agogic accents.

It is essential that the organist shape each phrase or melodic unit of the hymn. This means that in addition to articulation, both the beginning and ending notes of the phrase are made intelligible to the listener by employing agogic accents. These accents are frequently subtle and may entail only "thinking the accent." In some cases they should be more direct and telling. Opening phrases of hymns beginning with a weak beat need special attention. Here the note or notes of the *upbeat* require emphasis, but even greater emphasis must be accorded the hymn's first *downbeat*. When this shaping is not done, as in certain problematic hymns like *Es ist das Heil* (CW 299) or *Werde munter* (CW 545), the organist is ahead of the singing, making it impossible for the congregation to sing the opening notes of the hymn.

Another problem concerns the seeming lack of breathing time at the end of phrases in some hymns. Here the organist is encouraged to "bend" the beat rather than employ a fermata in the interior phrases of the hymn. This "bending" will give the hymn stanza a degree of continuity which is unachievable when frequent fermatas are inserted. Two examples of hymns that benefit from this treatment include *Nun preiset alle* (CW 258, between measures 4 and 5, 8 and 9, 12 and 13, 16 and 17) and *O grosser Gott* (CW 85, between beats 3 and 4 of measures 4, 8, 12, and 15).

The various ways rubato and articulation may be employed are illustrated in *Grosser Gott, wir loben dich* (CW 278), Example 8. In the reading of this example, the following symbols will be encountered:

322

+ = Accent at beginning or ending of phrase or melodic unit
> = Accent on strong beat
— = Accent on expressive dissonance or melodic climax
) = Articulation or breath
‿ = Tying repeated notes or common notes; continuation of legato lines

Example 8

Hymn Settings in Free Rhythm

Christian Worship includes a number of hymns taken from the medieval and Renaissance musical traditions, some of which are best performed in a free rhythm, chanting style. In some cases this style can be recognized by the notation itself: the melody is

323

mostly written in eighth notes, and an organ accompaniment consisting of slower note values is provided. This notation—absent in *The Lutheran Hymnal,* but common to contemporary hymnals—may be found in *Christian Worship* (CW 31, 23, 35, 178, 266, 267, 271, 522, and 595). Other hymns in this category, but notated conventionally, include 39, 155, 177 and 534.

Characteristic of the flowing style of chant is a lack of metrical accentuation. A relaxed beginning and a tapered ending for each phrase (indicated with a + in the chant examples) and a super-legato touch will assure that the chant hymn does not sound rushed. *Divinum mysterium* (CW 35) is written in the usual chant notation. It has mainly stepwise movement with a pause at the close of each phrase. The rhythmic patterning shows a predominantly duple organization with an occasional triple organization at the close of phrases 2, 4, and 5. Although only one repeated note appears within the phrases of this hymn, repeated notes will call attention to themselves if they are articulated with the usual half-value rest. It would be well to perform repeated notes in this style with a stroking gesture which does not allow the key to completely surface (indicated by ↓ in the example). The careful control of two repeated notes may be seen in the opening phrase of *Veni, Emmanuel* (CW 23, see Example 9).

The indicated pauses are crucial, since they encourage natural breathing by the congregation. Unlike the articulation of repeated notes within the phrase, these pauses are not as tightly controlled.

Liturgical Settings

Free rhythm chant and metrical hymnody exist side by side in the liturgical settings of *Christian Worship.* For example, in the singing of the psalms (see CW pp. 64-122), the psalm verses and *Gloria Patri* in *chant* are interspersed with a *metrical refrain.* In order to determine the nature of a given liturgical setting, one may look for reciting tones and stepwise melodies of limited range in the case of chant, or melodies of wider range in the case of metrical hymnody. Sometimes, however, the notation may be misleading. The Offertory in *The Common Service* (CW p. 20), for example, is metrical despite its eighth-note "streamlining." It should sound virtually the same as it appeared in *The Lutheran*

Example 9

Hymnal. On the other hand, the Litany settings from *Evening Prayer* (CW pp. 59,60) are chants despite their predominant use of quarter notes. Here each of the congregational responses should follow the chant style initiated by the minister.

A careful reading of Tables 1 and 2, in which the liturgical settings are divided into chant and metrical hymnody, will alert the organist to examine each setting on its own merits. As with hymnody, one cannot approach the liturgies in a simplistic manner, expecting that the music is somehow unified and requires a common and self-evident style of playing.

Table 1

Liturgical Settings in *Christian Worship* Accompanied in Chant Style

Order	Setting	Page*
The Common Service	"Amen."	15,16,17,23,24,25; 5,7,11,12,13
	Glory Be to God	16,17;6
	"And also with you."	17;7
	Preface response	21;9
	Song of Simeon	24;12
	"And his mercy endures forever."	24;12
Service of Word and Sacrament	"Amen."	27,29,35,36; 16,18,22,23
	Lord, Have Mercy	27;16
	"And also with you."	33;20
	"We lift them up to the Lord."	33;20
	"It is right to give him thanks and praise."	33;20
Service of the Word	"Amen."	39,43;25,28
Morning Praise	"And my mouth shall declare your praise."	45;30
	"O Lord, come quickly to help me."	46;30
	Oh, Come, Let Us Sing to the Lord	46,47; 30,31
	We Praise You, O God	48,49;32,33
	Lord, Have Mercy	50;34
	"Thanks be to God."	51;34
Evening Prayer	"And my mouth shall declare your praise."	52;36
	"O Lord, come quickly to help me."	52;37
	"And also with you."	53;37
	Lord, Have Mercy	59,60;41,42

* The first cited page refers to the regular edition; the second cited page refers to the accompaniment edition.

Table 2

Liturgical Settings in *Christian Worship*
Accompanied in Metrical Hymn Style

Order	Setting	Page*
The Common Service	*Lord, Have Mercy*	15;5
	Alleluia	18;7
	Gospel responses	18;7
	Create in Me	20;8,9
	Holy, Holy, Holy	22;10
	O Christ, Lamb of God	23;11
	Three-fold *Amen*	25;13
Service of Word and Sacrament	*O Lord, Our Lord*	28;16,17
	Alleluia-Verse-Alleluia	30;18
	Gospel response	30;18
	Holy, Holy, Holy	34;21
	O Christ, Lamb of God	35;22
	Thank the Lord	36;23
	Three-fold *Amen*	37;23
Service of the Word	*Oh, Taste and See*	39;25
	Alleluia-Verse-Alleluia	40;26
	Gospel response	40;26
	Three-fold *Amen*	44;28
Morning Praise	*Father, We Praise You*	45;29
	"Amen."	51;34
Evening Prayer	*O Gracious Light*	54;38
	Let My Prayer Rise before You	55;38,39
	Song of Mary	57,58;40,41
	Song of Simeon	61;43
	"Amen."	61;43

---

* The first cited page refers to the regular edition; the second cited page refers to the accompaniment edition.

Diversity of Musical Styles

In *Christian Worship* the organist is confronted with a wider range of musical styles in hymn and liturgical settings than in *The Lutheran Hymnal*. These styles include Gregorian chant, European chorale, English hymn, African-American spiritual, gospel hymn, nineteenth century American spiritual folksong, world folksong, and contemporary hymn. Challenged by this diversity, the organist must be able to absorb and appreciate these styles and transcribe them for organ in a viable manner. No hymn should elude a sympathetic interpretation. In fact, each hymn—whatever its style or origin—should sound as if it were a favorite hymn. Even the most severe of German chorales like *Christ, Unser Herr zum Jordan Kam* (CW 88), with its labyrinthian melody, can become a favorite with convincing treatment and proper exposure.

The "new song" is generously represented in *Christian Worship,* reflecting our contemporary musical culture in both popular and art music sectors, and reflecting stylistic diversity. Although some contemporary hymns are completely tonal, a surprising number of them display elements of the modes in melody as well as harmony. Especially favored is the employment of the modal lowered seventh scale step. This and other modal elements often convey a feeling of vigor and power as may be encountered in the following hymns in *Christian Worship:* 122, 132, 140, 151, 172, 187, 219, 231, 245, 265, 335, 496, 527, and 602. Some of these modal hymns are also marked by a strong beat, melodic angularity, melodic and rhythmic ostinatos, heightened rhythmic character, syncopation, compound meter, multimeter, or folksong elements. Three contemporary tonal hymns that could have been composed only in our century because of their rhythmic vitality are 442, 363, and 556.

As the church musician deals with contemporary hymns that may have originally been accompanied by other instruments, such as guitar or piano, care must be given to the organ transcription. An example of such a contemporary hymn is the lyrical ballad, *On Eagle's Wings* (CW 440). It is a warm, expressive hymn in which a relaxed moderate quarter-note beat should be employed together with strong agogic accents. The opening *c-sharp*

328

of the melody is an expressive dissonance and rather difficult to sing; it must be given an expansive agogic accent. The left hand alto and tenor notes are for the most part easily accommodated, but in measures 3, 4 and 14 some alto notes will have to be reached on the Swell with the right hand.

Unity and Variety in the Worship Service

The organist is in a position to unify the worship service in several ways. Having read the Scripture lessons for the day, including the sermon text, and having assessed the function and reason for the chosen hymns, the organist will be able to respond to the mood and content of a given worship service with appropriate music. That the organist has viewed the service in its totality—not only texts, but music as well—is a unifying factor in its own right.

One of the unique features that has been included in *Christian Worship* is the use of two or more different harmonic settings for some hymn tunes that are used more than once. These alternate settings are noted on the bottom of the hymn page. Variety for a single hymn can be achieved by using these alternate settings for selected verses of the hymn.

Other ways of providing variation in playing hymns would include varying the registration both in strength and color, playing manuals alone or dropping the 16´ stop on the pedal, starting a stanza and then dropping out to let the congregation sing without accompaniment, and using instruments to double the melody or play appropriate descants.

For longer hymns, interludes between stanzas or even organ solos provide relief for the congregation. Also, the use of antiphonal singing between various groups provides interest during the singing of longer hymns. These groups could include congregation and choir, men and women, or even left and right sections of the congregation.

As the organist injects variety into the service in the form of alternate harmonizations, special organ registrations, and hymn intonations that depart from the hymnal setting, care must be given to the establishment of norms. These norms will include a standard plenum registration without reeds that will be used for a majority of the hymn stanzas and the liturgical settings. Likewise, a majority of the hymn stanzas will use the harmonizations as printed in the hymnal. Opportunities for repetition within the service are not to be missed. For example, the same solo cornet registration might be used for two different hymn introductions within the same service, or the same full plenum with reeds could highlight doxological stanzas in two different hymns. In the choice of music for preservice, voluntary, and postlude, it is important to relate these musics to the theme of the service by means of hymns already chosen or similar hymns, if this is deemed appropriate. Both hymn-based and free music might be chosen from one style of composition or unified by a common key or related keys.

Despite the diverse elements that make up a given service, the organist has the responsibility to convey through the music itself a mood or tone that underscores the dominant emotional meaning of the service. Even if this meaning is difficult to verbalize, it is important for the organist to be sensitive to these concerns for unity and balance within the service.

CHAPTER 21:

Organ Registration

The tonal resources of pipe organs, as well as those of their electronic counterparts, are most varied. The organ is not a standardized instrument like the piano, violin, flute, or oboe. With the exception of some "model" electronic instruments, there are very few organs having exactly the same tonal components. For that reason organists employ a general set of guidelines for selecting stops. These guidelines serve, in a general way, all instruments: large and small, wind-blown or electronically driven, Romantic or Baroque, old or new.

An analysis of a musical tone's individual components reveals the basis for organ registration. A vibrating body produces a complex tone that is comprised of a fundamental[1] and a number of upper partials also called overtones and harmonics, all present in varying degrees of intensity. Thus a vibrating air column

Diagram 1. Vibrating air columns depicting the first, second, and third partials.

---

[1] Some confusion results from the indiscriminate or incorrect interchange of the three terms: partial, harmonic, and overtone. The preferred term is partial; the fundamental is the first partial, the octave above that fundamental is the second partial, etc. When using the terms harmonic or overtone the fundamental is not numbered, thus the first overtone or harmonic is the octave.

within an organ pipe produces a complex tone having a fundamental and a number of upper partials. Diagram 1 illustrates the
presence of the first three partials of a vibrating air column in an
open cylindrical pipe.

In Diagram 2 the first twelve partials of a vibrating air column
within an open eight-foot pipe are notated.

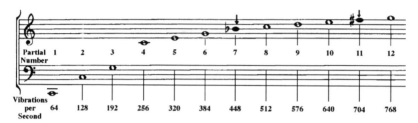

Diagram 2. Notation of the first twelve partials.

Although many individual partials are present and audible in a
musical tone, it is the first partial, the fundamental, that the human ear identifies as the pitch of the tone. Other partials color the
tone; their presence and strength relative to the fundamental determine its timbre.

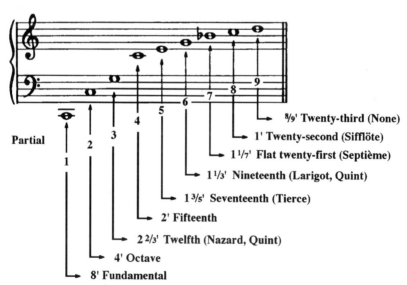

Diagram 3. Notation and pitch designations for the first nine partials.

The organ has sets (ranks) of pipes at various pitch levels. The pitch designation of an organ rank is determined by its longest pipe, which is the first and lowest-pitched pipe. An eight-foot (8') rank is considered a unison or standard-pitched rank; its pitch corresponds to that of the piano. Commonly, other ranks are pitched at 16'—an octave lower than unison; at 4'—an octave higher than unison; and at 2'—two octaves higher than unison. Diagram 3 indicates the first nine partials and the pitch designations.

Organists have at their disposal, therefore, a variety of pitch levels. By means of careful employment of them, ensembles of varying colors and intensities can be created. Until the advent of the synthesizer, the organ alone had the unique capacity to create, at the performer's will, a complex tonal structure based upon the natural harmonic series.

Mutations

Also following the harmonic series are sets of pipes called mutations. These are non-octave sounding ranks. The 2²/₃' produces the third partial (fifth or quint), the 1³/₅' produces the fifth partial (third or tierce), the 1¹/₃' produces the sixth partial (fifth or quint), the 1¹/₇' produces the seventh partial (seventh), and the ⁸/₉' produces the ninth partial (second). Stops having the latter two designations are quite rare. Diagram 4 provides information about the harmonic series and the mutational voices it is used to create.

Pitch Designation	Partial Number	Pitch Produced When Low "C" is Depressed	Interval Identify Name	Common Stop
2²/₃'	3	g	fifth, quint	Nasat, Nazard, Twelfth
2'	4	c'	unison, octave	Octave, Super Octave, Fifteenth
1³/₅'	5	e'	third	Terz, Tierce, Seventeenth
1¹/₃'	6	g'	fifth, quint	Klein Nasat, Larigot, Nineteenth
1¹/₇'	7	somewhat lowered b flat'	seventh	Septième

Pitch Designation	Partial Number	Pitch Produced When Low "C" is Depressed	Interval Identify Name	Common Stop
1'	8	c''	unison, octave	Twenty-second, Sifflöte
$^8/_9$'	9	d''	ninth	None

Diagram 4. Description of mutation voices. While the 2' and 1' pitches are not, strictly speaking, mutations they are included in the diagram because of their frequent inclusion with mutation voices in registration combinations.

As a general rule, flute (nonprincipal) pipes are used to serve as mutations. Mutations are used to create solo registrations.

Mixtures

A mixture is a compound stop that contains two or more ranks activated simultaneously. The individual ranks of a mixture are high-pitched; they usually consist of unison (octaves) and fifth-sounding pipes. The organ console stop indicates the number of individual ranks; thus a stop designated as Mixture III has three ranks of pipes which might speak at the 2' pitch, the 1 $^1/_3$' pitch, and the 1' pitch. The console stop control rarely indicates the pitch level of a mixture stop. Most mixture stops are placed into one of four basic categories. Diagram 5 illustrates the four mixture stop classifications.

Name	Usual Number of Ranks	Lowest Pitch	Usual Number of Segments
Rauschquint Rauschpfeife Grave Mixture	II	2 $^2/_3$'	1
Mixture Fourniture Plein Jeu	II-VII	usually 2' or 1 $^1/_3$'	3-4
Scharf	II-V	usually 1'	4-5
Zimbel Cymbal	II-III	usually $^2/_3$' or $^1/_2$'	5-6

Diagram 5. Mixture classifications and descriptions.

Mixture stops are added to a basic registration of 8' and 4' stops. The mixtures reinforce the upper partials. Mixture stops, generally, have a number of breaks, or segments. Thus a mixture stop that begins at 1 $^1/_3$' pitch will "fall back" several times throughout its compass; the uppermost segment, therefore, will most likely be at the 4' or 8' pitch. This practice provides clarity in the bass compass of the keyboard but supplies strength and gravity in the uppermost ranges. The pipes used to produce mixture stops are from the principal family.

Timbres

Historically and practically, four timbres of organ tone exist. They are (1) principals (diapasons), (2) flutes (nonprincipals, gedeckts), (3) strings, and (4) reeds. Pipes in the first three categories are known as flues, or labials, having the tone generated by an air stream passing from a windway (the flue) and striking a sharp edge or lip (the labial). Pipes in the latter category are known as reeds or linguals (tongues); the tone is generated by means of a vibrating reed with the resulting tone amplified and modified by a resonator.

Principals have a rather rich and full tonal spectrum and speak with a moderately strong intensity. The tone is produced in open cylindrical pipes having moderate diameters. A well-designed organ will have more than fifty percent of its pipes belonging to the principal family.

Flutes have a strong fundamental and a limited number of upper partials. Flutes have a somewhat dull sound. Generally, flutes speak with less intensity than principals. Flutes are found in a wide range of colors and a most varied nomenclature. The flute tone is produced in a variety of pipe shapes. Construction details include these characteristics: wide diameters; closed, capped, or half-closed pipes; rectangular wood as well as round metal pipe bodies; tapered pipes; and double-length, overblown pipes.

Strings have a weak fundamental but a full array of upper partials. Strings have a thin sound. Generally, strings speak with a light or moderate intensity. The string tone is produced in an open cylindrical pipe having a narrow diameter.

Reeds are very colorful and produce tones having moderate to strong intensities. The tone may imitate orchestral colors, both archaic and modern. Reed stops added to a principal chorus provide much color and strength. Reeds are colorful solo stops. The tone is produced by a reed set into vibration with the resulting tone amplified and modified by a resonator. The shape of the resonator does much to determine the strength and timbre of the tone. Some of the more common resonator shapes are conical, cylindrical, and half-length.

Ranks

Unfortunately, there is no standardized set of terms used to identify the various ranks of pipes or organ stops. The matter of stop names is influenced greatly by nationalistic as well as historical styles. Nevertheless, commonly used stop names can be placed into the four categories listed below:

Principals: Principal, Diapason, Open Diapason, Montre, Prestant, Choralbass. Also, most stop names denoting a number are principals: Octave, Super Octave, Quint, Twelfth, Fifteenth. All mixture stops are principals: Mixture, Plein Jeu, Fourniture, Scharf, Zimbel.

Flutes. **Open:** Concert Flute, Melodia, Nachthorn, Spitzflöte, Gemshorn, Hohlflöte, Harmonic Flute, Waldflöte, Piccolo, Flautino, Flachflöte.

    Fully or partly covered: Gedeckt (Gedackt), Stopped Flute, Quintadena, Quintade, Pommer, Bourdon, Subbass, Doppelflöte, Pommer, Spitzgedeckt, Konishgedeckt, Rohrflöte, Rohrpfeife, Rohrgedeckt, Spillflöte, Koppelflöte.

Strings: Salicional, Voix Celeste (tuned sharp), Unda Maris (tuned flat), Dulciana, Gamba, Viola, Violone, Cello, Aeoline.

Reeds. **Conical resonators:** Trumpet, Bombarde, Trombone, Posaune, Fagott, Oboe, English Horn.

    Cylindrical resonators: Krummhorn, Cromorne, Clarinet, Dulzian.

Basic Registrations

Organ registration, the combining of stops, involves the selection of available stops according to several general guidelines. All registration possibilities can be classified as one of the following four basic registrations: (1) plenum or principal chorus, (2) solo or foreground, (3) accompaniment or background, and (4) trio.

The Plenum Registration, the Principal Chorus

This type of registration is used for the hymns and liturgies, for much polyphonic literature, and for compositions in which both hands play on the same manual. A plenum registration consists of a minimum of two consecutive pitches with at least the upper pitch drawn from the principal family of tone. The plenum registration possibilities on well-designed instruments are many and they range from a modest combination of Principals 8' and 4' to full-bodied combinations of Principals 16', 8', 4', 2 $2/3'$, 2', and Mixtures. The plenum registration may substitute flute ranks for the lower pitches when principal ranks are missing in the organ design. When more color or intensity is needed, reed ranks may be added to any plenum registration—large or small. Reed ranks may also substitute for the 8' or 4' principal ranks. Chart A at the end of this chapter provides examples of the plenum registrations.

The Solo, Foreground Registration

This type of registration is used for a single-line melody played on one keyboard. The solo effect is produced through a use of reeds or a combination of mutations. All reeds work very well in both the soprano and tenor or bass range. The mutations drawn in various combinations work very well in the upper range. Chart B at the end of this chapter provides examples of solo registrations.

The Accompaniment, Background Registration

This type of registration fulfills three demands placed upon the organ: the accompaniment of vocal and instrumental solos, the accompaniment of choirs, and the accompaniment of organ solo registrations. The background effect is produced by the use of nonprincipal (flute or string) ranks at the 8' pitch or the 8' and 4' pitch. Ranks from the principal or reed family are rarely used for these purposes. Chart B also provides examples of background registrations.

The Trio Registration

This type of registration requires that each manual and the pedal produce tone of quite equal intensity but of contrasting colors. To achieve this type of registration each manual uses a registration quite different from that drawn on the other. The registration drawn for the pedal is also of a contrasting color. Chart C at the end of this chapter provides examples of trio registrations.

Choosing Registrations

To determine which of the four types of registrations, presented above, might be employed for a particular organ composition, it becomes necessary to study the piece, for the piece itself reveals the best registration to be used. Does it have a solo melody? Does it have full chords? Does it have a polyphonic texture in which all voices are of equal importance? These are some questions that provide clues for registration.

In addition to what has been suggested above, an appropriate registration might also be determined by considering the following: the suggested registration printed with the work, the resources available on the instrument, the setting in which the work will be heard, the acoustical properties of the room, and the music period to which the work belongs. Good musical sense as well as taste provides further guidance in the selection of a fitting registration.

Mechanical Devices

Organs contain a number of mechanical devices that assist in producing music on the instrument. Quite commonly the pipes of the Swell Organ are placed into a box or chamber with movable shutters on the front of it. The organist can, by means of a pedal, close or open the shutters and thereby control the dynamic level of the Swell Organ. When the organ or a portion of it has this capability, it is said to be "under expression."

The organ may have a device called a Tremulant. This device interrupts the flow of air into the pipe and produces a gentle vibrato. This effect is intended to be used with solo registrations particularly when the melody moves slowly. It is not intended for use in plenum registrations.

338

The Crescendo Pedal allows the organist to engage the stops of the organ, one after another, until all are drawn. Another device, called the Tutti, Full Organ, or Sforzando, turns on all stops instantly.

Preset pistons, or combination pistons, allow the organist to set registrations and save them. Thus registrations can be drawn instantly and conveniently by depressing the piston rather than by setting each stop individually. Preset pistons are found for the "thumb" as well as for the "toe."

Since the organ is not a standardized instrument, a wide variety of other mechanical devices, or accessories, are available. The size of the instrument, the budget, personal taste, and the organbuilder's style determine which devices are included on an instrument.

CHART A
Examples of the Plenum Registration, the Principal Chorus[2]

GREAT

		1	2	3	4	5	6	7	8	9	10	11	12	13	14
16'	Pommer			X						X					X
8'	Principal	X	X	X	X							X	X		X
8'	Rohrflöte					X	X	X	X	X	X				
4'	Octave	X	X	X	X	X	X		X			X	X	X	X
4'	Nachthorn							X		X	X				
2⅔' + 1⅗'	Sesquialtera														
2'	Octave	X	X	X		X	X	X	X	X	X	X	X	X	X
2'	Waldflöte														
1⅓'	Mixture III		X	X				X		X		X	X	X	
8'	Trumpet											X	X	X	X

SWELL

		1	2	3	4	5	6	7	8	9	10	11	12	13	14
8'	Holzgedackt	X		X											X
8'	Salicional		X												
4'	Spitzflöte	X	X	X	X										X
2'	Prinzipal	X	X	X	X										X
1⅓'	Klein Nasat														
8'	Krummhorn		X	X											

PEDAL

		1	2	3	4	5	6	7	8	9	10	11	12	13	14
16'	Subbass	X	X	X											X
8'	Flötenprinzipal	X	X	X	X	X									X
4'	Choralbass	X	X	X	X										X
16'	Fagott		X		X										X

COUPLERS

	1	2	3	4	5	6	7	8	9	10	11	12	13	14
Swell to Great														X
Great to Pedal														X
Swell to Pedal														X

---

[2] The registration examples given in Charts A, B, and C are based upon the tonal resources of the organ located in the Wisconsin Lutheran Seminary Chapel, Mequon, Wisconsin. The instrument was built by the Martin Ott Pipe Organ Company of St. Louis, Missouri. It employs mechanical action and is made up of 1109 pipes, 25 ranks, and 20 stops. It was dedicated in April 1991.

340

CHART B
Examples of the Solo, Foreground Registration, and Examples of the Accompaniment, Background Registration[3]

	1	2	3	4	5	6				1	2	3	4
GREAT													
16' Pommer													
8' Principal													
8' Rohrflöte	X	X	X	X	X					X	X		
4' Octave													
4' Nachthorn		X		X							X		
2⅔' + 1⅗' Sesquialtera	X	X	X	X									
2' Octave													
2' Waldflöte		X	X	X									
1⅓' Mixture III													
8' Trumpet						X							
SWELL													
8' Holzgedackt	X	X								X		X	
8' Salicional											X		X
4' Spitzflöte		X	X									X	X
2' Prinzipal													
1⅓' Klein Nasat	X	X	X										
8' Krummhorn			X										
PEDAL													
16' Subbass										X	X	X	
8' Flötenprinzipal										X			X
4' Choralbass	X												
16' Fagott													
COUPLERS													
Swell to Great												X	
Great to Pedal											X		
Swell to Pedal												X	

---

[3] Ibid.

CHART C
Examples of Trio Registrations[4]

GREAT

		1	2	3	4	5	6	7	8
16'	Pommer								
8'	Principal								
8'	Rohrflöte	X	X	X	X		X	X	X
4'	Octave								
4'	Nachthorn		X				X	X	
$2\frac{2}{3}' + 1\frac{3}{5}'$	Sesquialtera2'			X				X	X
2'	Octave								
2'	Waldflöte	X							X
$1\frac{1}{3}'$	Mixture III								
8'	Trumpet					X			

SWELL

		1	2	3	4	5	6	7	8
8'	Holzgedackt	X	X	X		X	X		
8'	Salicional				X				
4'	Spitzflöte	X	X	X		X			X
2'	Prinzipal								
$1\frac{1}{3}'$	Klein Nasat		X				X		
8'	Krummhorn							X	X

PEDAL

		1	2	3	4	5	6	7	8
16'	Subbass		X	X		X	X	X	X
8'	Flötenprinzipal	X	X	X	X	X	X	X	X
4'	Choralbass					X			
16'	Fagott								

COUPLERS
Swell to Great
Great to Pedal
Swell to Pedal

[4] Ibid.

CHAPTER 22:

Selecting Attendant
Organ Music for Worship

The organ has a fairly long history of use in the worship life of the church. As early as the 1400s the organ was used for the regular corporate worship service. During the past 350 years, the organ has acquired a prominent position in worship: (1) leading the congregation in singing liturgy and hymns; (2) accompanying choirs, soloists, and instrumentalists; and (3) providing attendant music to assist in the smooth flow of the service.

The term *attendant music* refers to music other than liturgy and hymns that the organist plays to bridge otherwise non-musical portions of the service: before and after the service, the Offering, and the Distribution. This chapter addresses the function of selecting and providing attendant music for the service.

Effectively leading the congregation in singing praises to its Lord and Savior is by far the first and most important function of the organ in worship. The Christian church on earth usually assembles for one short hour each week, and this is one of the few times when believers join together to praise God in anticipation of the glorious praises they will render to him eternally in heaven. If an organist struggles so much in the playing of a particular hymn (perhaps from lack of practice) that the congregation has great difficulty following along, the most well-prepared, beautiful musical selection played during the offering cannot compensate for the poor hymn playing. The organist's first priority is to be an effective leader of the congregation's singing. Practicing attendant music should not overshadow thorough hymn and liturgy preparation.

This priority may appear to reduce attendant music to mere "filler music" that needs little or no attention. Nothing, however could be further from the truth. Instead, once the organist realizes the place of attendant music in the worship service, then he or she can properly select it to fit the service.

Organists of today have many resources from which to draw. Not only can they draw from the many pieces and collections published every day by a host of publishing companies (Concordia, Augsburg-Fortress, and Morning Star being excellent examples), but they can also choose many classic pieces written over the last four hundred years or more. All these possibilities could seem to make music selection most difficult. How does an organist choose the best pieces to fit the season of the church year and the hymns chosen for a particular worship service? In addition, how does the organist find time to choose and to practice appropriate pieces? By following certain guidelines each time music is chosen for a service, the organist will develop a system that will, in time, make careful music selection much easier.

Guidelines for Choosing Attendant Music

Organists can follow four main guidelines when choosing attendant organ music for the worship service: the assigned Scripture readings for the day, the hymns chosen for the day, the time (season) of the church year, and the general "character" or prevailing mood of the service.

Scripture Readings

The focus of the Lutheran worship service is the gospel in Word and sacrament. Everything else in the service, from the hymns to the choir selections to the organ music, points to that precious Word. For centuries the Christian church has had assigned readings for each Sunday in the church year. Within the last twenty years, the Inter-Lutheran Commission on Worship (ILCW) expanded the ancient list of readings to a three-year series (or "Lectionary") so that the assembled congregation could hear a wider selection of Scripture readings over a three-year period.

Both a one-year and three-year series of lessons are listed in Section Four of this manual. Pastors are informed of these series of lessons during their seminary training and are encouraged to use the Lectionary in their congregations in order to insure adherence to the church year and a natural progression of Scripture lessons from week to week. Regardless of what Scripture reading series a pastor uses, the organist should request to be informed of these readings.

The first step in selecting attendant music for the service is to have in mind the theme for the day. The Old Testament reading, Psalm, Epistle, and Gospel for each Sunday are related to a certain extent (some Sundays more than others). A person can look up all of the readings and usually see a general theme or prevailing thought. As an example, the fifth Sunday of Epiphany in Series C has the following readings: Isaiah 6:1-8; 1 Corinthians 14:12b-20, and Luke 5:1-11. One can see a dominant theme running through all three lessons of "God calling us to serve." The next step, then, would be to have hymns based on that theme so the organist can begin selecting music.

Hymns

Certain principles govern hymn selection that are important to the conscientious musician and can make the task of music selection easier. (See chapter 17 of this manual for more information on selecting hymns.) First, the Hymn of the Day should be regarded as the focus hymn of the service, deserving special treatment (alternate accompaniment, choir, other instruments) wherever possible. This hymn should directly relate to the Scripture readings and prevailing theme for the day. A listing of the Hymn of the Day for each Sunday and festival of the church year in both one-year and three-year series of the Lectionary is also found in Section Four of this manual. The Hymn of the Day itself has been discussed in an earlier article in this section.

Second, the other hymns of the service should be coordinated with the Hymn of the Day and the service theme. As they work together, pastors and church musicians will want to make sure that they are on the "same page" when it comes to the principles of hymn selection. Generally, the pastor will select the hymns; but the church musicians should be given the opportunity to request that certain hymns be chosen for certain days, particularly if a Hymn of the Day plan is being followed.

The organist should locate the Hymn of the Day and the other selected hymns in the hymnal and find the tune name at the end

345

of each hymn. Then he or she can look for the tune names in the index of an organ music collection to find appropriate music based on those tunes. Most major publishers of organ and choral music for worship have excellent collections of attendant music based on the best-known hymn tunes.

An important consideration in hymn selection is that hymns should be chosen well in advance. This gives organists time to select and practice appropriate music and even expand their repertoire by learning new music. The organist can select music that helps the church-goer tune in to the general "train of thought" in the service instead of just playing "pretty music," or "selections I like."

Time (Season) of the Church Year

The Lutheran church is a liturgical church body that has a rich heritage of organized worship. The services are structured within the church year, which is centered around the three main Christian festivals: Christmas, Easter, and Pentecost. The church year begins about four weeks before Christmas and is divided into three cycles. The Time of Christmas includes Advent, Christmas, and Epiphany. It centers on Jesus' birth into the world as the Savior of the world. The Time of Easter begins with Lent and includes the Sundays after the Easter festival. Here attention is given to Jesus and his work of saving all people from their sins. The third and longest season is the Time of Pentecost, which begins on the day of Pentecost. The theme of these Sundays is sanctification (Christian growth). If the chosen readings for a particular service correspond with the current season, then the organist can also select attendant music based on hymns associated with that time of the church year.

General "Character" or "Mood" of the Service

This may seem to be a repetition of the first guideline, which refers to the theme of the service. "Mood" or "character," however, refers more to the type of service used in a particular congregation. This too should help decide what kind of music is chosen for a service.

Consider, for example, a Reformation service at an older, established congregation that often uses strong music from its

Lutheran heritage. Some of the hymns to be sung at this service might include *A Mighty Fortress Is Our God* (CW 200,201) and *Thy Strong Word* (CW 280), with choir and trumpets participating in concertatos. For such a service a pianistic arrangement of a Christian contemporary composition as preservice music might be somewhat out of place. The selection itself may be artistically beautiful. It might even be associated with an idea that would fit very well into the service theme. But because it comes from a totally different tradition, it simply would not fit well into a traditional service celebrating the historical principles of Lutheranism.

On the other hand, in a newly-established congregation in which many of the members may not be from Lutheran backgrounds, the occasional use of music in a more modern style (still in keeping with the theme and hymns for the day) would be very appropriate and would serve to keep the worshiper's thoughts directed to the theme of the service. Each organist must take into account his or her own particular situation.

Types of Attendant Music

Preservice Music

Preservice music is not a crucial element in the liturgy. Without it there is still an intact service. However, by playing music that is geared toward the main teaching that will be presented in the service, the organist takes the thoughts of the gathering worshipers away from their daily problems and prepares them to hear the saving gospel message. This is a challenge, because many worshipers are not trained to listen to or interpret a piece of music. Playing pieces that quote hymn tunes is one way to direct the worshipers' thoughts to the message of the day.

In some congregations all preservice music is played softly and postservice music loudly. That should not be a major consideration when choosing fitting music. Instead, the organist should try to prepare the listener for the "mood" of the service. To illustrate this point: on Easter morning and for a few Sundays after, the organist could play rather loud, triumphant pieces based on strong hymns of praise to the risen Savior (until the Scripture readings and hymns for the day shift in emphasis). Even during Lent, if the theme of the service is "Jesus' Cross Is My Victory over Sin," then a rousing, dynamic prelude based on *Lift High the Cross* would be in place.

If one or more of the hymns selected for the day's worship is perceived to be rather unfamiliar to the congregation, the organist would do well simply to play the hymnal settings of such hymns as preservice music. Another effective technique would be to play the hymn melody on a solo stop and the harmony on a softer manual.

There is one practice used in some churches that deserves mention here. Sometimes known as "the prelude," it is a piece played after the ringing of the bells but before the first hymn. This piece has the added advantage of being played after everyone is seated and quiet, thereby attracting and holding the worshipers' attention even more than a piece played before the service. This prelude should be based on the opening hymn (with the melody easily detectable) and should reflect the character of the hymn text. It should be rather short (generally, under two minutes), in order to effectively lead into the singing of the first hymn.

Offering Music

During an otherwise quiet time during the liturgy, the tradition of a solo organ piece has developed in most liturgical churches. The congregation here presents its offerings in grateful response to the Word just heard. The organist can do the same. Music based on the Hymn of the Day is ideal. If such music is not available, various selections can be used that quote other hymns in the service or a hymn with a similar theme. A nontune based composition that keeps to the mood of the service (joyful, somber, thankful, etc.) will also suffice. A type of English organ music, known as the "voluntary," is a good example.

Some congregations sing a hymn or hymn stanza during or toward the end of the offering. If this is the case, the organist could play music containing the melody of that hymn during the offering. If suitable music on the offering hymn is not available, a selection in a corresponding key can be used. Organists should take care to check the key even of attendant music based on the same hymn, because in more recent hymnals, including *Christian Worship,* some hymns have been lowered one whole or half-step to accommodate an overall decrease in the average range of congregational voices since the publication of *The Lutheran Hymnal*.

Distribution Music

The main source of music during Holy Communion is usually a congregational hymn or choir anthem. Often, however, this is not enough and the organist is called on to "fill in." Even at times like this, the organist can provide some fitting music to direct the listeners' thoughts either toward the theme of the day or to the focus of Holy Communion. Short, easy compositions having any of the following references can be chosen: hymn(s) sung during the Distribution, hymns sung elsewhere in the service, hymns relating to the Lord's Supper or the theme for the day. Appropriate, free compositions would also be suitable.

Postservice Music

The service is now over. God's people have heard the Word of life and have received forgiveness. Now it is time for them to return to the "outside world" and live the faith just strengthened. What can the organist do to give them a proper send-off? Play something that will "leave them humming"? That is a desired effect, but it is even more desirable that worshipers be left thinking of the service and its main thoughts. There are ways the organist can achieve this. As at all other times in the service the Gospel is to be the prevailing guideline. For example, if the sermon and main theme for the service was "Jesus, Savior of the World," (a typical Epiphany season theme), then Johann Sebastian Bach's *In Dir Ist Freude* would be very appropriate. If, in another instance, the service was centered on the amazing miracle of a tiny, precious baby born into the world to save the world, one might use Thomas Gieschen's rather quiet, expressive *Silent Night*. Postservice music need not always be loud. If it is fitting to the service and carefully chosen, then it will be appropriate.

Organizational Tools

Because there are a number of considerations to use when choosing attendant music, having a tool to organize selections would be helpful. Note such a help in Section One, page 122.

349

Included after this chapter is a listing of suggested organ pieces and collections that contain thoughtful, appropriate compositions. The list is by no means complete, since new music and new arrangements of existing classic works are constantly being produced. Pieces without an asterisk (*) are less challenging, while the pieces followed by an asterisk are more difficult.

A sample of a recipe card index or computer file is also included. This system enables an organist to find pieces quickly, without paging through a host of books. Notice that files should be arranged in two ways: (1) by tune name (for tune-based compositions), grouped into times of the church year and (2) by composer.

In Conclusion

It is hoped that with the presentation of *Christian Worship: A Lutheran Hymnal* the average worshiper can be raised to a higher level of mental and spiritual awareness in the worship service in order to foster spiritual growth. The organist can aid in this effort by, first of all, being a strong and effective leader in the playing of the liturgy and hymns. Then he or she should also provide well-chosen, theme-based attendant music to guide the worshiper into the thoughts of the service.

In all of his or her planning, preparing, and presenting music for the worship service, whether it be liturgies, hymns, choir accompaniments, or attendant music, the Christian organist dare never lose sight of that which gives dignity and value to everything he or she does. The Lutheran organist is not just someone with a certain degree of skill and training who has been "hired" by the congregation to "do a job." A Lutheran organist is a vital participant in the congregation's ministry of worship. As such he or she is using God-given talents as spiritual gifts to help build up the body of Christ, his Church.

Each time he or she presides at the organ during public worship, the Christian organist is presenting an offering of music to the Lord. Such an offering ought to draw attention not to the organist who is presenting the offering, but to the Lord to whom the offering is being presented and to the great things he has done for his believers in Christ Jesus. May all such offerings be given by us as the Lord desires: our very best; from sincere hearts; out of love for the Savior who has redeemed us and has given us our gifts; and entirely to his glory and praise.

If our music is offered to the Lord in this way, we will find joy and fulfillment in offering it. And our music will be pleasing and acceptable to our gracious God.

Appendix A
Suggested Basic Organ Repertoire

Selections marked * are more advanced.
Each listing contains the following information:

composer or editor, title of collection or piece, and publisher

The following abbreviations for frequently used publishers are:

APH: Augsburg Publishing House, Minneapolis, Minnesota
CPH: Concordia Publishing House, St. Louis, Missouri
MSM: Morning Star Music, St. Louis, Missouri

Collections from various composers:

Concordia Hymn Prelude Series, 42 volumes, ed. H. Gotsch/R. Hillert, CPH

Eighty Chorale Preludes, ed. Keller, Peeters

Hymn Preludes and Free Accompaniments, 20 volumes, APH

Old English Organ Music, 6 volumes, ed. Trevor, Oxford

Organ Music for the Communion Service, ed. Bunjes, CPH

The Parish Organist, 12 volumes, CPH

Wedding Music, 2 volumes, CPH

Wedding Music, 6 volumes, ed. Johnson, APH

Pieces and collections by a single composer:

*Timothy Albrecht,   Grace Notes, CPH

Johann Christoph Bach, Forty-four Chorale Preludes, Kalmus

Johann Sebastian Bach, Orgelbuchlein, Oliver Ditson Co.
                        Eight Little Preludes and Fugues, Peeters
                        Jesu, Joy of Man's Desiring, H.W. Gray

351

	Sheep May Safely Graze, H.W. Gray
	Now Thank We All Our God, H.W. Gray
Theodore Beck,	Forty-seven Hymn Intonations, CPH
	Fourteen Organ Chorale Preludes, CPH
Michael Bedford,	Seven Chorale Preludes for Ascension and Easter, Flammer Pub.
Jan Bender,	*Festival Preludes on Six Chorales, CPH
	Five Festive Preludes on Easter Hymns, CPH
	Hymn Introductions, 5 volumes, CPH
	O God, Our Help in Ages Past, APH
	Thirty Little Chorale Preludes, 3 volumes, Barenreiter
Michael Burkhardt,	Praise and Thanksgiving, 4 volumes, MSM
	Partita on "All Glory, Laud, and Honor," MSM
	Partita on "Awake, My Heart, with Gladness," MSM
Donald Busarow,	Processional on "Lift High the Cross," CPH
Dietrich Buxtehude,	*Preludes and Fugues, Peeters
	Chorale Preludes, Peeters
David Cherwein,	*Beautiful Savior, CPH
	Interpretations, 7 volumes, AMSI Publishers
	*Toccata on "In the Cross of Christ I Glory," CPH
Marcel DuPre,	Seventy-Nine Chorales, Novello
James Engel,	Eleven Chorale Preludes, Northwestern
	A Little Chaconne, CPH
	Organ Preludes for the Passion Season, D.M.L.C.
	Nineteen Chorale Preludes, Northwestern
	Twenty Chorale Preludes, Northwestern
	Variations on "In Dulci Jubilo," CPH
Thomas Gieschen,	Organ Pieces for Wedding and General Use, APH
	Prelude on "Silent Night," CPH
Raymond Haan,	Canonic Variations on "Infant Holy, Infant Lowly," CPH
	Festival Hymn Preludes, Sacred Music Press

	Partita on "In Dulci Jubilo", CPH
	Variations on "Sussex Carol", CPH
George Handel,	Six Processionals, CPH
Wilbur Held,	Hymn Preludes for the Autumn Festivals, CPH
	Hymn Preludes for the Pentecost Season, CPH
	Six Carol Settings, CPH
	Six Preludes on Easter Hymns, CPH
	A Suite of Passion Hymn Settings, CPH
Hal Hopson,	Five Preludes on Familiar Hymns, Flammer
David Johnson,	Deck Thyself, My Soul, with Gladness, APH
Paul Kickstat,	Five Christmas Chorales, MSM
	Six Advent Chorales, MSM
	Three Christmas Chorales, MSM
Gerhard Krapf,	Sing and Rejoice, 3 volumes, Sacred Music Press
	In Christian Love, Sacred Music Press
Paul Manz,	Chorale Improvisations, 10 volumes, MSM
	Aria, MSM
Charles Ore,	Eleven Compositions for Organ, 5 volumes, CPH
	*"A Mighty Fortress", CPH
	*"Veni, Creator, Spiritus", CPH
Johann Pachelbel,	Preludes, Kalmus
	Seven Partitas, Kalmus
Flor Peeters,	Aria,
	Hymn Preludes for the Liturgical Year, 24 volumes, Peeters
	Thirty Chorale Preludes, 3 volumes, Peeters
Piet Post,	Triptych for Organ, APH
Max Reger,	Thirty Short Chorale Preludes, Peeters
Samuel Scheidt,	Ausgewahlte Werke, Peeters
Frank Stoldt,	Hymn Settings, CPH
Helmut Walcha,	Chorale Preludes, 4 volumes, Peeters

353

Healy Willan,	Six Chorale Preludes, CPH
	Ten Hymn Preludes, 3 volumes, Peeters
Ralph Vaughan Williams,	Three Preludes on Welsh Hymn Tunes, Galaxy
S. Drummond Wolff,	Baroque Music for Manuals, 5 volumes, CPH
Dale Wood,	Brother James Air, Sacred Music Press

Appendix B
Suggested Music Filing System

Tune name file (cf. Section One, chapter 8, "Planning for Worship," pp. 130, 131.)

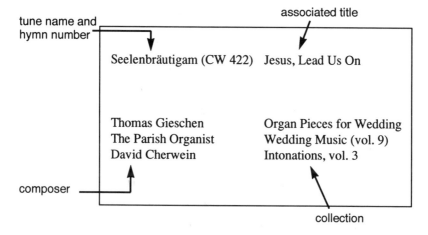

Composer file

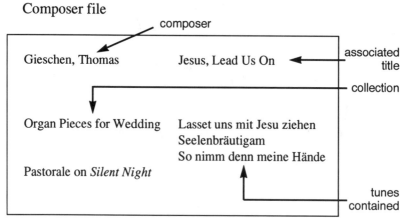

CHAPTER 23:

Mechanics of Music
in *Christian Worship*

As a musician pages through *Christian Worship,* any number of questions about the mechanics of the music might come to mind. As the music is put to use, no doubt more questions will arise. Why do some hymns have meter signatures and others do not? What was the rationale for the barring in the liturgical music? What is the significance of different types of closing bars in the liturgy? In some hymns only the melody is slurred while in others all voices are slurred—why the difference? Following are some answers to these and other questions.

Meter Signatures and Barring

In the Liturgy

Meter signatures have not been included in the liturgical music of *Christian Worship.* Because of the prose texts used in liturgical song, most of this music is irregular in meter. In cases where the music does follow a regular grouping of beats, the piece is barred to indicate the varying metrical groupings as in this excerpt from *Holy, Holy, Holy* (CW p. 34).

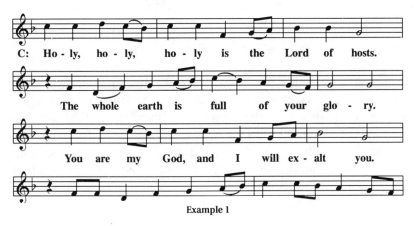

Example 1

In other instances, where there is no regular grouping, the music was barred according to phrases of the text. While these could have been barred in irregular measures, barring them by phrases gives a clean look to the score, makes the music easy to read, and clearly outlines the text. Bars appear only at the ends of phrases in this example from "O Lord, Our Lord." (CW p. 28)

Example 2

Three types of closing bars appear in the liturgical section: a single bar, a double bar, and a heavy double bar.

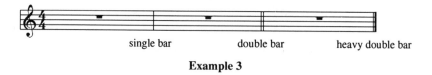

Example 3

The heavy double bar is used to end a liturgical section or to close a section of dialogue. The double bar is used to mark the end of a line or a song that is within a liturgical section. For example, The Prayer of the Day (CW p. 17) includes the Salutation ("The Lord be with you."), the Prayer of the Day, and the sung *Amen*. The Salutation closes with a double bar because it is part of this section but not the end. The *Amen* closes with a heavy double bar that marks the end of this section.

356

PRAYER OF THE DAY

M: The Lord be with you.

C: And al - so with you.

Example 4

M: Let us pray.

The minister says the Prayer of the Day.

C: A - men.

Example 5

The single bar at the close of a line appears only when there is sung dialogue between minister and congregation. This type of exchange appears only in *Morning Praise* and *Evening Prayer.* The minister's line ends with a single bar, the congregation's response ends with a double bar. The final couplet closes with a heavy double bar to mark the end of the section. The Service of Light from *Evening Prayer* (CW p. 54) provides an example of this type barring.

M: Jesus Christ is the light of the world,

C: the light no darkness can o - ver - come.

M: Stay with us, Lord, for it is eve-ning,

C: and the day is almost o - ver.

M: Be our light and scat - ter the dark-ness,

C: and hear our evening hymn of praise.

Example 6

357

In the Hymns

Meter signatures appear in the hymn section of *Christian Worship,* but not in every hymn. Meter signatures appear in those hymns where the entire hymn clearly falls into a regular, single meter. When metrical irregularities occur within the hymn, even in a single measure, the meter signature is omitted. A hymn that fluctuates between two or more meters is barred to indicate the metrical groupings but the changes in meter are not indicated with signatures. The hymn *Arise, My Soul, Arise* (CW 244) is barred in metrical groupings without meter signatures.

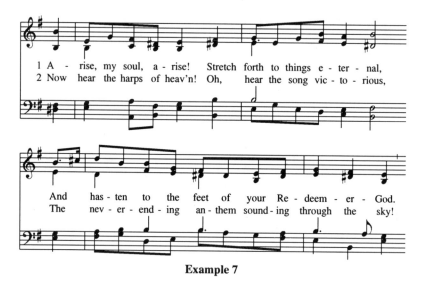

Example 7

Other hymns that do not fall into regular groups of beats are barred according to phrases of the text just as the prose texts in

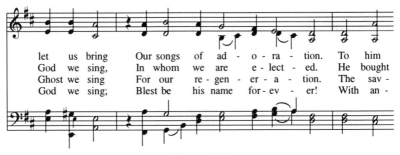

Example 8

the liturgy are barred according to phrases. Here is an example of this type of barring in Alleluia! Let Praises Ring (CW 241):

Breath Marks

Both in the liturgy and in the hymns breath marks, short vertical lines crossing the top line of the treble staff, are found in the music.

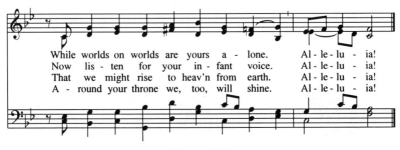

Example 9

Some hymnals use this mark in two ways. One is to mark the end of phrases. The other is to indicate a place in the music where the congregation needs time to catch a breath. *Christian Worship* uses this mark only as a breath mark. Bar lines are used to indicate the end of phrases in unmetered music.

Organists should be sensitive to the need for the people to catch a breath where these marks appear. Some compromise in the pulse should be made at these places. This is done by slightly lengthening the note before the breath mark, breaking, and then resuming the tempo with the note following the breath mark. The

359

lengthening of a note to accommodate a breath should not double the time value of the note. It should be just enough for the breath to be taken. The overall pulse of the hymn should not be destroyed. The best way to judge this is to sing the hymn without the keyboard to see how much time is needed to take the breath. Then sing it with the accompaniment. This should give an idea of what will work best when the congregation comes to this place in the hymn.

Slurs

In Melodies

Slurs are always included as needed in the soprano line. It should be noted that in the hymns, slurs are not used when a syllable is sung over a group of beamed notes (eighths or sixteenths). Here the beam serves as the slur.

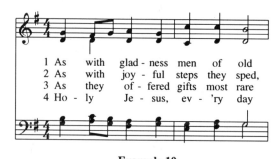

Example 10

There are a few hymns where slurs are used in conjunction with beamed notes.

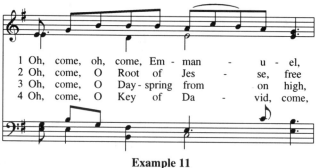

Example 11

In the liturgy, slurs are used in conjunction with beamed notes.

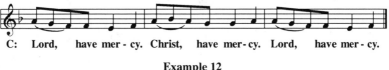

C: Lord, have mer - cy. Christ, have mer-cy. Lord, have mer - cy.

Example 12

In Other Voices

Slurs in the lower three voices (alto, tenor, bass) are used when the entire hymn appears in a blocked style. In these hymns, the parts can be sung by a choir. Each part has a note or notes for each syllable of the text and each part is slurred accordingly.

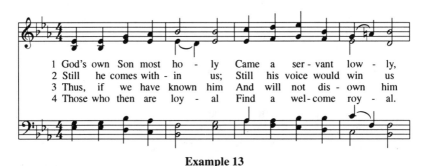

1 God's own Son most ho - ly   Came a ser - vant low - ly,
2 Still he comes with - in us;   Still his voice would win us
3 Thus, if we have known him   And will not dis - own him
4 Those who then are loy - al   Find a wel-come roy - al.

Example 13

Other hymn settings are oriented more toward the keyboard than toward the choir. In these harmonizations, the lower voices often move at a different rhythmic pace than the melody. These hymns do not have slurs for the lower voices since the number of notes and syllables do not match. Here is an excerpt from this type of hymn setting.

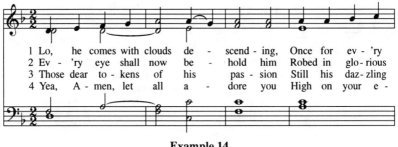

1 Lo, he comes with clouds de - scend - ing, Once for ev - 'ry
2 Ev - 'ry eye shall now be - hold him Robed in glo - rious
3 Those dear to - kens of his pas - sion Still his daz- zling
4 Yea, A - men, let all a - dore you High on your e -

Example 14

Rhythmic and Isometric Chorales

The terms *rhythmic* and *isometric* refer to the version of a tune. A rhythmic German chorale is a tune that appears in a version that closely reflects the original form of the tune. These tunes do not fit into a regular metrical structure. Consider the alternating between groups of 3 and 4 quarter note values in the first line of *A Mighty Fortress* (CW 200).

Example 15

Many of these rhythmic chorales have been "straightened out" somewhere in their lifetimes. Bach and others often made this type of adjustment when using the German chorale tunes. This "straightening out" changed the rhythmic structure of the tune by altering the melody in such a way that it fits into a regular meter. The contour of the melody remains recognizable, but the rhythm is drastically altered. In the case of A Mighty Fortress, the altered form of the tune fits into a straight 4\4 meter (CW 201).

This new form of the tune is called an isometric version of the tune, for it now falls into regular, equal-length measures. Either

362

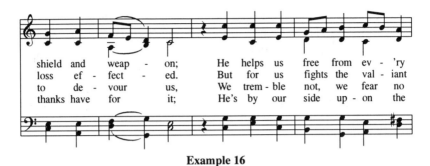

Example 16

form of the tune has been accepted and found use in worship. One is not necessarily superior to the other.

Helping Notes

There are a few places in the hymn settings where an accompanist, playing an instrument without pedals, will have difficulty reaching all the notes of a chord. In most of these instances, helping notes are included. These usually occur as bass notes printed an octave higher. The helping notes are smaller and are set off slightly to the right of the full chord. This excerpt includes a few helping notes.

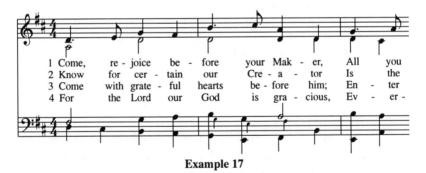

Example 17

Stemless Notes

In a very few places in the liturgy, stemless notes will be encountered, as in the *Service of Light* (CW p. 54).

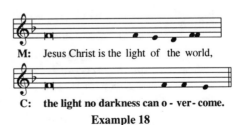

Example 18

363

These portions of the liturgy are parts that are sung without accompaniment. There is not harmony for these lines in *Christian Worship: Accompaniment for Liturgy and Psalms*. The music here is unaccompanied song, and the organ should not duplicate the melodic line. The stemless notes indicate this type of unaccompanied performance. All other lines of music with stemmed notes include harmony in the Accompaniment Edition.

Guitar Chords

A few hymns include chord designations for the guitar. These chord designations do not always match the keyboard harmony. Quite often the guitar chords move at a slower harmonic pace than the keyboard harmony. Because of this difference, the guitar and keyboard should not be used together. The hymns that include guitar chords are:

Amazing Grace	379
Away in a Manger	68
Children of the Heavenly Father	449
Glorious in Majesty	496
Go, My Children, with My Blessing	332
God of Love and God of Marriage	602
Jerusalem, My Happy Home	215
Love Is the Gracious Gift	505
My Shepherd Will Supply My Need	374
O Dearest Lord, Thy Sacred Head	118
Sing a New Song to the Lord	245
What Child Is This	67

Descants

Sixteen descants are found scattered throughout *Christian Worship*. These might be used by a choir, played on an instrument, or perhaps just used by individuals in the congregation. The hymns that include descants are:

A Hymn of Glory Let Us Sing	171
All Glory, Laud, and Honor	131
All Hail the Power of Jesus' Name	370
Crown Him with Many Crowns	341
Hark! A Thrilling Voice Is Sounding	15
Hark! The Herald Angels Sing	61

SECTION FOUR:

THE CHRISTIAN YEAR

CHAPTER 24:

The Calendar and Propers

The calendar of the Christian year is found on pages 157-159 of *Christian Worship: A Lutheran Hymnal* and on pages 385-476 of this manual. The calendar divides the Sundays and Major Festivals of the year into The Time of Christmas, The Time of Easter, and The Time of Pentecost. Tables listing the First Lesson, Second Lesson, and Gospel for Years A, B, and C of the three-year lectionary and the one-year readings are on pages 163-166 of the hymnal. The complete set of Propers (readings, Psalms, Prayer of the Day, Verse of the Day, Hymn of the Day, color) for the entire Christian year including Minor Festivals and Occasions is found in this manual beginning on page 385.

The Calendar of the Christian Year

"When the time had fully come, God sent his Son" (Galatians 4:4). It is the earthly time of God's Son—his birth, death, and resurrection—that sets the pattern for the Christian year. Year after year Christian worship celebrates the saving work of Jesus Christ.

In the first half of the Christian year (Advent to Pentecost), the focus is on the *time of Christ,* recalling the events of his life. The second half of the year constitutes the *time of the church,* the joyful response of the community of believers to God's grace in mission and service.

Though the basic pattern of the Christian year is established by events recorded in the Scriptures, the calendar included in *Christian Worship: A Lutheran Hymnal* is the result of a historical development going back to New Testament times. Various worship traditions from the East and the West, from Jerusalem, Antioch, Alexandria, Rome, Constantinople, North Africa, Spain, and Gaul, have contributed to the calendar as we have it today.

The calendar of the Christian year that we use today, however, has been influenced most by the practice of the church in Rome.

The reformers grew up with Rome's pattern of the Christian year. Article 24 of the Augsburg Confession makes the point that "no conspicuous changes have been made in the public ceremonies of the Mass, except that in certain places German hymns are sung in addition to the Latin responses."[1] Among these "public ceremonies" that have been retained by the Lutheran church was the pattern of the Christian year.

Sunday, the Day of the Resurrection

Sunday is the place to begin when describing the Christian year. The Scriptures tell us that it was on the morning of the first day of the week that the empty tomb of Jesus was discovered and the risen Lord appeared to various of his disciples. Christians continued to gather for worship on Sunday in remembrance of the Resurrection, the first day of the week (see John 20:26; Acts 20:7; 1 Corinthians 16:2). Sunday was also the first day of creation as Justin Martyr (d. 166) pointed out: "We assemble on the day of the sun because it is the first day, that on which God transformed the darkness and matter to create the world, and also because Jesus Christ our Savior rose from the dead on the same day."[2] Attendance at the weekly assembly was regarded as obligatory even in times of persecution. Each Sunday is a "little Easter."

Easter Sunday, the Festival of the Resurrection

Among the Sundays of the year, Easter Sunday has the place of prominence. On this day, the church celebrates the resurrection of Christ from death and the restoration of life to those dead in trespasses and sins. All who have been buried with Christ through baptism are united with him in his resurrection and walk in newness of life (Romans 6:4,5). Propers for both Easter Dawn and Easter Day are included in this manual.

By the second century, the feast of Easter had developed as an annual commemoration. The festival day was soon preceded by a time of fasting in preparation for the celebration followed by a fifty-day season of rejoicing concluded by Pentecost.

---

[1] Augsburg Confession, Art. 24:2 (Tappert, p. 56).

[2] Apology 1:67.

The date for Easter differs from year to year because it is established by the phases of the moon (as was the Jewish festival of Passover). The Festival of the Resurrection is celebrated annually on the first Sunday after the first full moon (14th of Nisan in the Jewish calendar) after the vernal equinox (see Calendar Dates for the Christian Church Year, CW p. 162).

Preparations for the celebration of the festival itself began already on Saturday night with the Easter vigil. One early Christian writing says: "Watch all night in prayers, supplications, the reading of the prophets, of the Gospel and of psalms in fear and trembling and continual supplication until three in the morning."[3] The church father Augustine (d. 430) called this "the mother of all vigils"[4] and no fewer than twenty-three of his sermons for the occasion have survived. From Hippolytus (d. ca 235) we learn how during the Easter vigil those persons who had completed a period of study for membership in the church were baptized.

The Easter Season and Pentecost

The fifty days of Easter constitute the oldest season of the Christian year. These fifty days correspond to the period in the Jewish year between the Passover and the Feast of Weeks. Tertullian (d. after 220) refers to this time of celebration several times, and Athanasius (d. 373) calls it "the great Sunday." Because of the importance of this season its Sundays are named "Sundays *of* Easter" rather than "Sundays *after* Easter."

The Festival of **Pentecost,** the Coming of the Holy Spirit, marks the close of the Easter season. The word *pentecost* (literally means "five ten times") was the Greek name for the Jewish Festival of Weeks.[5] On Pentecost the ascended Lord fulfilled his promise to baptize his disciples with the Holy Spirit (Acts 2:1-4).

Falling within the Easter season as an important event in the life of Jesus is his ascension into heaven on the fortieth day (Acts 1:1-11). The Festival of the **Ascension** emphasizes the truth that because of the resurrection of Jesus Christ, the members of his body will also share his heavenly glory.

---

[3] Didaskalia Apostoloram 21.

[4] Sermon 219.

[5] Tobit 2:1.

Holy Week

Holy Week came into existence as an intense period of preparation (prayer and fasting) for Easter. It begins with **Palm Sunday,** where in fourth century Jerusalem the distinctive feature was the palm procession from the Mount of Olives back into the city. The 1969 Roman calendar changed the title of the first day of Holy Week from Palm to Passion Sunday, a change that has been accepted by the calendars of a number of hymnals. *Christian Worship* retains the emphasis on the events of Palm Sunday.

Maundy Thursday (from the Latin *mandatum,* "command," John 13:34) recalls Christ's institution of Holy Communion at the Last Supper on the night in which he was betrayed. During the Passover meal, Jesus gave the disciples his body and blood together with the bread and wine. Each time we celebrate this sacrament we "proclaim the Lord's death until he comes" (1 Corinthians 11:26).

Good Friday is the solemn celebration of the Lord's suffering and death on the cross. Some congregations will remember the three hours of darkness from noon till three o'clock with a *tenebrae* (darkness) service. Augustine called the three days of Maundy Thursday, Good Friday, and Easter "the most holy *triduum* (three days) of the crucified, buried, and risen Lord."[6]

The Season of Lent

This season preceding Easter resulted from two elements: an extended fast in preparation for the celebration of the resurrection and a regulated period of preparation for baptism. In Egypt there was a post-Epiphany fast of forty days that followed the celebration of the baptism of our Lord and recalled his forty days of fasting and testing in the wilderness immediately following his baptism (Matthew 4:1,2). This pattern of a forty day fast affected the development of the Lenten fast in other areas of the church.

The Council of Nicea (A.D.325) mentions an undefined forty-day period, but the actual length of the season differed considerably in the various regions of the church depending on which days were included in the fast. It was not until the seventh century that

---

[6] Letter 55:24.

in Rome the Wednesday in the seventh week before Easter marked the beginning of the season. The Sundays in Lent were not counted as part of the forty days since they were not fast days but retained their significance as "little Easters." The season of Lent was somewhat obscured by the development of a season of pre-Lent which included the three Sundays before Ash Wednesday.

The custom of distributing ashes on **Ash Wednesday** was originally connected with entrance of public sinners into a period of repentance. It was not until 1091 that the imposition of ashes on the heads of all worshipers was made mandatory in Rome and thus giving this name to the first day of Lent.

Our word *lent* is from an Old English word for spring ("lengten," the time of the year when the days grow longer). For us the Lenten season is a time to meditate deeply on the meaning of Christ's suffering and death for our salvation as well as a time in which to concentrate on the continuing importance of amending our sinful lives.

For many Christians the preparation for Easter during the season of Lent seems of greater importance than the prolongation of the resurrection celebration throughout the fifty days of the Easter season. The entire Christian year will have its greatest significance, however, when the overriding importance of Easter and its season is emphasized.

Christmas and Epiphany

Whereas the Easter season has been termed "the cycle of life," the Christmas season is called "the cycle of light." Into a world of darkness came the Word made flesh, "the true light," Jesus Christ (John 1:9,14). Simeon sings of him as "a light for revelation to the Gentiles" (Luke 2:32). When Christ appeared, then was fulfilled Isaiah's word that "the people living in darkness have seen a great light; on those living in the land of the shadow of death a light has dawned" (Matthew 4:16). *Christian Worship* provides Propers for both Christmas Eve and Christmas Day.

The origins of the feasts of Christmas (December 25) and Epiphany (January 6) are elusive. The word *epiphany* comes from the Greek and means "appearance," referring to the appearance of Christ as the Savior (see Titus 3:4). It is almost certainly the older of the two festivals, with the written traces of an Epiphany celebration from Clement of Alexandria at the end of the second century. Other eastern writers confirm the identification of January 6th as the birth date of Jesus. At the same time in various regions of the east the coming of the Magi, the baptism of Christ, and his first miracle at Cana were celebrated on this day. As with the date for Christmas, various explanations have been advanced as to why January 6th was chosen as the Festival of the Epiphany.

December 25th as the day for the celebration of Christ's nativity had its origins in the West. Two theories have been advanced for this particular date. One holds that this date was chosen by the church to counter the pagan festival related to the winter solstice called *natalis solis invicti* (birth of the invincible sun), which had been established by the Roman emperor Aurelian in A.D. 274. The Christians celebrated the birth of their invincible *Son,* the Son of God.

The other suggestion for the selection of December 25th to celebrate Christ's birth resulted from an early computation that his death on the cross occurred on March 25th. There was a theological belief held by some that the death and birth dates of religiously significant persons is the same. By this reckoning, March 25th was not only the date of Jesus' death but also the day on which he was conceived in the womb of Mary, thereby establishing the birth date nine months later. There is evidence that the birth of Christ was celebrated on December 25th in North Africa even before the institution of the festival in Rome.

In the Western church, the Festival of the Epiphany was adopted as the day on which to recall the coming of the Magi to worship the infant King. The twelve days between Christmas and Epiphany came to be known as "the twelve days of Christmas." On the eighth day of Christmas, the naming and circumcision of our Lord is observed.

In distinction from Easter, whose date is established by the phases of the moon, the date for Christmas is based on solar computations. It occurs very near the time of the winter solstice, at that time of the year when in the Northern Hemisphere people experience the most darkness. At the darkest time of the year, we celebrate the coming of the light of the world.

374

The Season of Advent

The development of a season preparatory to Christmas is western in its origins and celebration. The first accounts of Advent (Latin word for "coming") are from Spain and Gaul. In fifth century Gaul, certain days were set aside for fasting in preparation for Christmas as early as St. Martin's Day (November 11th). In Gaul this season of preparation was penitential in nature.

In Rome there is also evidence of a pre-Christmas fast but of shorter duration. At the same time the days before Christmas had a more festive atmosphere in anticipation of the festival. From the seventh century come the *O Antiphons* (the basis of the Advent hymn *Oh, Come, Oh, Come, Emmanuel,* CW 23), which formed part of the psalmody from December 17th through 23rd. Pope Gregory the Great (d. A.D. 604) fixed the beginning of the Advent season as the fourth Sunday before Christmas, the Sunday nearest the Day of St. Andrew (November 30th).

Advent has come to have a threefold meaning: (1) the advent of our Lord in the flesh at Christmas, (2) the advent of the Lord in his Word, and (3) the advent of our Lord in glory at the end of time. Though Advent is a time for repentance, there is a note of joyful anticipation that runs through the season.

The custom of having an Advent wreath in churches and homes became popular in northern Europe. On each of the four Sundays of Advent, a new candle is lighted, dispelling the darkness, as the church moves forward to welcoming him who is the true light of the world.

Other Major Festivals

In the course of time certain other festivals came to be fixed as part of the Christian year. One of these is the **Baptism of our Lord,** which is observed each year on the Sunday after the Epiphany. This marks the beginning of Christ's public ministry and reminds worshipers of our cleansing in the water of baptism.

Another major festival is the **Transfiguration of our Lord.** In the Roman calendar, this event in Christ's life is celebrated on August 6th, but the Lutheran reformers moved the Propers for that day to the last Sunday after the Epiphany where it is observed no matter how many Sundays there might be in the

Epiphany season. It is particularly appropriate that the Transfiguration of our Lord be observed as the prelude for Lent, at the juncture between the seasons of Christmas and Easter.

Trinity Sunday is celebrated on the first Sunday after Pentecost. It is a festival that originated in northern Europe in the ninth and tenth centuries to honor the Holy Trinity: God the Father, God the Son, and God the Holy Spirit. It is a fitting summary of the first half of the Christian year.

The Season of End Time

Unique to *Christian Worship* is the designation of the last four Sundays of the Christian year as End Time. The first of these, **Reformation Sunday,** will fall either on the last Sunday in October or the first Sunday in November, depending on the start of the Advent season. This Sunday recalls Luther's nailing of the 95 Theses to the Wittenberg, Germany, church door on October 31, 1517. The second Sunday of End Time is the **Last Judgment.** The church is reminded of Christ's second coming to judge the living and the dead. Next is observed the Sunday of the **Saints Triumphant** when the eternal glory of the saints in heaven is emphasized. The Sunday of **Christ the King** closes out the Christian year. This is a modern addition to the Roman calendar (1925). This addition has been accepted in the calendars of a large number of newly published hymnals and has been included in the calendar of *Christian Worship*. This Sunday reminds us that the entire year of the church celebrates the rule of Christ over our hearts now and forever.

Sundays after the Epiphany and Pentecost

Each year, well over half the Sundays of the Christian year fall outside the seasons of Christmas and Easter. Because the date for Easter is movable (based on the lunar calendar) and the date for Christmas is fixed (based on the solar calendar), the number of Sundays between these two festivals will always vary. The lesser number will come after Epiphany whereas there are many Sundays after Pentecost (previous Lutheran calendars called these Sundays after Trinity).

Church year calendars have sought to deal with these Sundays in various ways. The modern Roman calendar simply titles them

Ordinary Sundays and numbers them beginning with the first Sunday after the Epiphany. The numbering continues for the Sundays till the beginning of Lent and then resumes after Pentecost for a total of 33 or 34 Ordinary Sundays each year. Many Protestant church calendars fix the Sundays after Pentecost according to the secular calendar year (e.g, the Sunday between September 18 and September 24 is called Proper 20).

The calendars of the various Lutheran hymnals have provided a full set of Propers for all the possible Sundays after the Epiphany and after Pentecost. As a result, depending on the date for Easter, not all Propers will be used each year. However, the calendar does specify that the Transfiguration of our Lord always be celebrated on the last Sunday after the Epiphany. And the season of End Time begins on the fourth-last Sunday of the Christian year.

Minor Festivals of the Christian Year

Some of the most ancient festivals of the church were the commemorations of its martyrs on the traditional day of their death. Several of these died already in New Testament times (e.g., James, Stephen). As the church spread and persecutions increased, each congregation kept a record of those of its number who had met death for their faith. The names of such martyrs, and in time also the names of some persons who were not martyrs, were added to the calendar.

The Lutheran church calendars generally retained only the festivals of those saints named in the Scriptures and of noteworthy events related to our faith. *Christian Worship* includes a total of thirty-three minor festivals. Of first rank are those related to Christ and his apostles. In addition the evangelists and other early Christian men and women are recalled. Among the Minor Festivals are included also the Presentation of the Augsburg Confession, Reformation Day, All Saints' Day, and New Year's Eve. When such Minor Festivals fall on a Sunday outside of the major seasons of the year, there is opportunity to use the Propers for that day. The Propers for the Minor Festivals may also be used for weekday worship and devotions on the appropriate date.

Occasions

It has become more common in recent times to observe "theme Sundays" often related to events in the secular calendar (Mother's Day, Independence Day, etc.). Some occasions in the life of our congregations, synod, and nation need to be observed. The calendar of *Christian Worship* provides for eighteen such occasions. The Propers for those days provide resources for such celebrations and observances.

The Propers of the Christian Year

The worship of the church has both variety and sameness. The sameness is provided by those parts of the service that do not vary from Sunday to Sunday. Many of the words spoken and sung by the minister and the people will be the same each week. There is value in such sameness. It gives people a sense of identity, a sense of belonging, a feeling of stability. Worshipers are able to participate when the words and songs of the liturgy are familiar. Those parts of the service that are the same each week are called the Ordinary. The **Ordinary** is explained on pages 41-43 of this manual.

But worshipers also need variety. If everything in the service were the same each Sunday, it would become boring and would fail to meet the spiritual needs of the worshiper. Variety in worship is provided by those items that vary from Sunday to Sunday. These variables are called the **Propers.** There is a proper set of readings for each Sunday of the year. This manual contains the Propers for each Sunday, Major Festival, Minor Festival, and Occasion included in the calendar of the Christian year. For the Sundays and Major Festivals there is additional variety because readings are listed for use over a three-year period (Year A, Year B, Year C) as well as for one year. For each of these years, a Scripture selection for the First Lesson, Second Lesson, and Gospel is given. For the Minor Festivals and Occasions only one set of Scripture readings has been selected. Other Propers are the Psalm of the Day, Prayer of the Day, Verse of the Day, and for Sundays and Major Festivals, a Hymn of the Day. In addition, the suggested color for the day is listed. The explanation of how to use these various Propers in the service will be found on pages 147-152 and 274-278 of this manual.

Lectionary (Lessons and Gospel)

The reading of the Scriptures was an important part of the worship of the Jewish synagogue. Two lessons were read in the service, one from the law (torah) and one from the prophets. Jesus read from Isaiah 61 in his home synagogue at Nazareth and applied the words to his own ministry (Luke 4:16-30).

The early Christians soon began to read from the Gospels and the letters of the apostles in addition to the Old Testament lessons. Justin Martyr (d. 166) tells us that "the memoirs of the apostles or the writings of the prophets are read as time permits."[7] During the early centuries of the church, it is quite obvious that a wide variety of practices prevailed as to which readings were used in the services, how many, and how they were selected. Tatian (d. 172) produced a harmony of the four Gospels which was no doubt intended for reading in public worship. In Syria in the fourth century, two lessons from the Old Testament and two from the New were read.

In many churches it seems that there was a continuous reading of Scripture, Sunday after Sunday, until an entire book was finished. However, this continuous reading was interrupted for the great festivals of the Lord such as Easter, Christmas, and Pentecost and for the feast days of the martyrs. On such days texts were selected to fit the occasion. Ambrose (d. 397) says the holy week readings are to include Job and Jonah. Augustine remarks that some persons were upset because he made changes in the accustomed readings that they expected to hear. In the course of time, the continuous reading of the Scripture was replaced by "proper" lessons for the various Sundays and Festivals.

Two lists of readings from the middle of the fifth century for part of the year are extant from Gaul. Both of these, however, were only for special seasons and not the whole year. A lectionary dating from 471 provides for three readings, one from the Old Testament, one from the Gospels, and one from other New Testament books. In time the continuous reading principle was abandoned as well as a reading from the Old Testament. This was

---

[7] Apology 1:67.

due mainly to the growing influence of the practices of the church of Rome. There the selected texts were shorter in general, with only two readings (letter, Gospel). The Roman system of readings was at first fixed only for the Advent, Christmas, Lent, and Easter seasons. Some areas of the church did set up Proper readings for all Sundays of the year, but these were not universally accepted.

The Reformers took various attitudes toward the lectionary they had inherited. Though Martin Luther favored retaining the Roman system of readings, he suggested that at some time a revision of the chosen texts was necessary. But he wrote in 1523 that "the time has not yet come to attempt" such a revision.[8] Luther never got around to making such a revision of the lectionary. Some efforts were made to establish a new system but without general acceptance. The Protestant reformers Zwingli, Calvin, and Bullinger all abolished the Roman lectionary in favor of some other pattern of Scripture readings.

During the age of Pietism and Rationalism, there was growing criticism of the lectionary system. In the middle of the nineteenth century, the criticism increased with the publication by Ernst Ranke of a historical study of the origins of the system. Efforts to remedy the situation were made in many areas. Many of these revised systems (14 series in all) are included in Paul Nesper's *Biblical Texts* (1921, 1951).

In America the early Lutherans made no great effort to retain the historic readings. However, as a result of the immigration of confessional Lutherans in the midnineteenth century and the influence of William Loehe (d. 1872) and Charles Porterfield Krauth (d. 1883), there developed a growing interest in preserving the historic readings. The *Common Service Book* of 1888 and 1917 was very influential in setting liturgical patterns among English speaking Lutherans. With the publication of *The Lutheran Hymnal* by the Synodical Conference in 1941, most Wisconsin Synod churches also began to read the historic lessons.

A new stimulus for a revision of the lectionary came from the Vatican Council II (1962-1965). It was stated that "the treasures of the Bible are to be opened up more lavishly, so that richer fare

---

[8] Luther's Works, American, Vol. 53, pp. 23f.

may be provided for the faithful at the table of God's Word. In this way a more representative portion of the Holy Scriptures will be read to the people over a set cycle of years."[9] The result was the *Lectionary for Mass* (1970) which set up a three-year cycle of readings and restored the Old Testament lesson.

The Inter-Lutheran Commission on Worship (ILCW) published The *Church Year Calendar and Lectionary* in 1973, which to a great extent followed the selections found in the *Lectionary for Mass*. The Wisconsin Evangelical Lutheran Synod was not a participant in the work of the ILCW but did appoint a special Lectionary Committee to study thoroughly the proposed lectionary in various pastoral conferences. The findings of this committee were reported to the synod in 1977. It was noted that "no doctrinal, pastoral, or liturgical reasons were found to stand in the way of the use of [the ILCW] series of texts" and that "no consideration would preclude the use of this series for worship."[10]

The three-year lectionary included in *Christian Worship: A Lutheran Hymnal* for the most part corresponds to the ILCW readings. The variations are primarily the result of a few changes in the calendar (Palm Sunday and season of End Time). Along with the three-year lectionary, a slightly revised version of the one-year historic series is included. Only a few of the standard readings from the letters and gospels were changed. A new set of Old Testament readings was selected so that three lessons might be read in the service when the one-year series is used.

Psalm of the Day

Jesus and the early Christians were well acquainted with the Psalter. In the New Testament, sixty different psalms are quoted. Among the sayings of Jesus in the Gospels, there are more quotations from the Psalms than from any other book of the Old Testament. Psalms were also used in the worship of the early church. They were read as lessons; they provided subjects for sermons; they were recited or sung at many points in worship.

---

[9] The Documents of the Vatican II, 155.
[10] WELS Proceedings 1977, p. 158.

381

An early use of the psalms was as a sung response to the first lesson. When the lessons were later reduced to two, the Psalmody and the Alleluia were combined and sung after the reading from a New Testament letter. In the Latin church this chant came to be called the Gradual since it was sung from the step (*gradus*) of the altar. In the course of time, psalms came to be used commonly at three other places in the service: during the entrance procession of the clergy (Introit), during the procession of people to bring their gifts to the altar (Offertory), and when the people came forward for communion. Gradually the Offertory and communion psalms disappeared, though a remnant of the offertory psalm is found with the singing of Psalm 51:10-12 and our practice of singing a hymn during the distribution of Holy Communion.

Martin Luther suggested that the German service begin with the singing of a hymn or psalm and that after the reading from a New Testament letter, a hymn be sung by the choir.[11] Luther turned psalms into "new songs" (e.g., Psalms 12,46,67, 124,130). Our hymns are an outgrowth of the singing of psalms in the early church.

Christian Worship includes a total of fifty-nine psalms for use in worship. An explanation of how to perform the psalms is found on pages 149-151 of this manual. The hymnal also makes suggestions of suitable psalms for various occasions on pages 62 and 148. In the three major services, the Psalm of the Day follows the reading of the First Lesson. A psalm is also included in the services of *Morning Praise* and *Evening Prayer.* The Propers included in this manual list psalm selections for all the Sundays, Festivals, and Occasions of the Christian year.

Prayer of the Day

This Proper is a brief prayer that follows the Song of Praise in the major services. In Latin it was known as the *collecta* which was translated into English as "collect." Many of these prayers come to us from the ninth century and before. They express in a terse manner the desires of God's people and tend to be general petitions, especially in the non-festival parts of the Christian year.

---

[11] Luther's Works, American, Vol. 53, pp. 74.

The prayers included in this manual come from various sources. Some are translations and slight alternations of ancient prayers; some are drawn from more modern sources; others are newly composed. All of them draw together the hearts and minds of the worshipers before the throne of God.

Verse of the Day

This Proper is an outgrowth of the psalm verses, called the Gradual, which were formerly sung between the reading of the letter and the Gospel. The joyful shout of "Alleluia", which was part of the Gradual except during the season of Lent, is retained in the Verse of the Day. These brief scriptural texts look ahead to the Gospel and are intended to be sung by a choir or solo voice. For an explanation of their use in the service see pages 151, 152 of this manual.

Hymn of the Day

This is a distinctively Lutheran addition to the Propers of the service. A yearly cycle of hymns for each Sunday of the year was set up in some parts of Germany following the Reformation. Johann Sebastian Bach composed cantatas in which he included hymn stanzas for many Sundays and Festivals of the Christian year. The Hymn of the Day as a Proper in the service has been revived in recent years and is included in *Christian Worship*. (See chapter 16, pp. 274-278 of this manual.)

Colors

The colors recommended for the paraments and vestments help to distinguish the various seasons and festivals of the Christian year and emphasize the significance of each. For more information of the colors of the church year, see Section One, pages 101, 102 of this manual.

When a special occasion is observed, it is appropriate to use red for a churchly celebration and the color of the season when the occasion is of a more general nature.

The Propers and Preaching

There is great value in making use of the Propers in sermon preparation. One of the lectionary selections may be used as the sermon text with the other Propers supplying complementary material. Following this practice will mean that all of biblical doctrine is adequately presented by the preacher in a given year, and the danger of dwelling on certain pet subjects will be lessened. Making use of the Propers in preaching will also edify the worshiper by relating the Sermon to the rest of the service. (See chapter 10, pp. 156-159 of this manual.)

The Propers and Worship Planning

The Propers provide a marvelous resource for worship planning and preparation not only for preachers but also for organists and choir directors. Lutheran elementary school teachers can help prepare their students for Sunday worship by utilizing the Propers in their devotions and lesson plans. Individual Christians will find added benefit from worship when they have prepared themselves by previously previewing the Propers for that day. (See chapter 8 of this manual.)

Daily Lectionary

Suggested Scripture readings for each day of the entire year are found on pages 516-527 of this manual. These selections will be helpful when one is called on to conduct devotions for church meetings, in schools, and for family and private use.

Major Festivals

Hymn of the Day selections listed in italics are alternates.

First Sunday in Advent

Lessons and Psalms

Year A
Isaiah 2:1-5
Romans 13:11-14
Matthew 24:37-44
Psalm 18

Year B
Isaiah 63:16b,17;64:1-8
1 Corinthians 1:3-9 *eagerly wait for J.C. to be revealed; he will keep you strong to the end*
Mark 13:32-37 *Day unknown - keep watch*
Psalm 24

Year C
Jeremiah 33:14-16
1 Thessalonians 3:9-13
Luke 21:25-36
Psalm 25

One Year
Jeremiah 33:14-18
Romans 13:11-14
Matthew 21:1-9
Psalm 24

Prayer of the Day

Stir up your power, O Lord, and come. Protect us by your strength and save us from the threatening dangers of our sins; for you live and reign with the Father and the Holy Spirit, one God, now and forever.

Verse of the Day

Alleluia. He who testifies to these things says, "Yes, I am coming soon." Amen. Come, Lord Jesus. Alleluia. (Revelation 22:20)

Hymn of the Day

Year ABC - Savior of the Nations, Come   (2)
One Year   - Savior of the Nations, Come   (2)

Color: Blue or Purple

Second Sunday in Advent
Lessons and Psalms

Year A
Isaiah 11:1-10
Romans 15:4-13
Matthew 3:1-12 *[handwritten: J.B. preaching repent]*
Psalm 130

Year B *[handwritten: prophecy of J.B.; prophecy of Jesus]*
Isaiah 40:1-11 *[handwritten: day of lord will come... new heaven new earth]*
2 Peter 3:8-14
Mark 1:1-8 *[handwritten: Is: I will send my messenger ahead of you; baptism of repentance for the forgiveness of sins; one more powerful than I]*
Psalm 85

Year C
Malachi 3:1-4
Philippians 1:3-11
Luke 3:1-6 *[handwritten: J.B. = baptism of repentance for forgiveness - prepare the way of the lord]*
Psalm 24

One Year
Malachi 4:1-6
Romans 15:4-13
Luke 21:25-36
Psalm 85

Prayer of the Day

Stir up our hearts, O Lord, to prepare the way for your only Son. By his coming give us strength in our conflicts and shed light on our path through the darkness of this world; through your Son, Jesus Christ our Lord, who lives and reigns with you and the Holy Spirit, one God, now and forever.

Verse of the Day

Alleluia. Prepare the way for the Lord, make straight paths for him. All mankind will see God's salvation. Alleluia. (Luke 3:4,6 cf. NIV)

Hymn of the Day

Year ABC - On Jordan's Bank the Baptist's Cry   (16)
One Year - The Bridegroom Soon Will Call Us   (10)

Color: Blue or Purple

Third Sunday in Advent
Lessons and Psalms

Year A
Isaiah 35:1-10
James 5:7-11
Matthew 11:2-11 *J.B. sends message to Jesus: are you the one?*
Psalm 146

Year B
Isaiah 61:1-3,10,11 *Messianic: Lord has appointed me to preach good news... proclaim freedom*
1 Thessalonians 5:16-24 *or kept blameless at J.C. coming*
John 1:6-8,19-28 *J.B.= witness to the light*
Psalm 71

Year C
Zephaniah 3:14-17
Philippians 4:4-7
Luke 3:7-18 *J.B. preaches*
Psalm 130

One Year
Isaiah 35:1-6
1 Corinthians 1:26-31
Matthew 11:2-10
Psalm 111

Prayer of the Day

Hear our prayers, Lord Jesus Christ, and come with the good news of your mighty deliverance. Drive the darkness from our hearts and fill us with your light; for you live and reign with the Father and the Holy Spirit, one God, now and forever.

Verse of the Day

Alleluia. I will send my messenger ahead of you, who will prepare your way before you. Alleluia. (Matthew 11:10 cf. NIV)

Hymn of the Day

Year ABC - Arise, O Christian People   (14)
One Year   - Arise, O Christian People   (14)

Color: Blue or Purple

Fourth Sunday in Advent

Lessons and Psalms

Year A
Isaiah 7:10-14
Romans 1:1-7
Matthew 1:18-25 *angel appears to Joseph; birth of Jesus*
Psalm 24

Year B
2 Samuel 7:8-16 *promise to David*
Romans 16:25-27 *Doxology: the revelation of the mystery hidden for long ages... now revealed... is that all might believe*
Luke 1:26-38 *the birth of Jesus foretold*
Psalm 89

Year C
Micah 5:2-5a
Hebrews 10:5-10
Luke 1:39-55 *Mary visits Elizabeth; Mary's Song*
Psalm 85

One Year
Isaiah 12:1-6
Philippians 4:4-7
Luke 1:46-55
Psalm 92

Prayer of the Day

Stir up your power, O Lord, and come. Take away the burden of our sins and make us ready for the celebration of your birth, that we may receive you in joy and serve you always; for you live and reign with the Father and the Holy Spirit, one God, now and forever.

Verse of the Day

Alleluia. The virgin will be with child and will give birth to a son, and they will call him Immanuel. Alleluia. (Matthew 1:23)

Hymn of the Day

Year ABC - Oh, Come, Oh, Come, Emmanuel   (23)
One Year   - Oh, Come, Oh, Come, Emmanuel   (23)

Color: Blue or Purple

The Nativity of Our Lord
Christmas Eve

Lessons and Psalms

Year A	*Year B*
Isaiah 9:2-7	Isaiah 9:2-7
Titus 2:11-14	Titus 2:11-14
Luke 2:1-20	Luke 2:1-20
Psalm 96	Psalm 96

Year C	*One Year*
Isaiah 9:2-7	Isaiah 9:2-7
Titus 2:11-14	Titus 2:11-14
Luke 2:1-20	Luke 2:1-20
Psalm 96	Psalm 8

Prayer of the Day

Almighty God, you made this holy night shine with the brightness of the true light. Grant that as we have known on earth the wonder of that light, we may also behold him in all his glory in the life to come; through your only Son, Jesus Christ our Lord, who lives and reigns with you and the Holy Spirit, one God, now and forever.

Verse of the Day

Alleluia. Today in the town of David a Savior has been born to you; he is Christ the Lord. Alleluia. (Luke 2:11)

Hymn of the Day

Year ABC	-	From Heaven Above to Earth I Come	(38)
	-	*Once Again My Heart Rejoices*	*(37)*
One Year	-	From Heaven Above to Earth I Come	(38)
	-	*Once Again My Heart Rejoices*	*(37)*

Color: White

389

The Nativity of Our Lord
Christmas Day

Lessons and Psalms

Year A	*Year B*
Isaiah 52:7-10	Isaiah 52:7-10
Hebrews 1:1-9	Hebrews 1:1-9
John 1:1-14	John 1:1-14
Psalm 98	Psalm 98

Year C	*One Year*
Isaiah 52:7-10	Micah 5:2-5a
Hebrews 1:1-9	Hebrews 1:1-9
John 1:1-14	John 1:1-14
Psalm 98	Psalm 98

Prayer of the Day

Almighty God, grant that the birth of your only Son in the flesh may set us free from our old bondage under the yoke of sin; through Jesus Christ our Lord, who lives and reigns with you and the Holy Spirit, one God, now and forever.

Verse of the Day

Alleluia. When the time had fully come, God sent his Son, born of a woman, born under law, to redeem those under law. Alleluia. (Galatians 4:4,5a)

Hymn of the Day

Year ABC	- Of the Father's Love Begotten	(35)
	- *All Praise to You, Eternal God*	*(33)*
One Year	- All Praise to You, Eternal God	(33)

Color: White

First Sunday after Christmas

Lessons and Psalms

Year A	*Year B*
Isaiah 63:7-9	Isaiah 45:20-25
Galatians 4:4-7	Colossians 3:12-17
Matthew 2:13-15,19-23	Luke 2:25-40
Psalm 2	Psalm 111

Year C	*One Year*
1 Samuel 2:18-20,26	Isaiah 42:1-4
Hebrews 2:10-18	Galatians 4:1-7
Luke 2:41-52	Luke 2:25-38
Psalm 111	Psalm 103

Prayer of the Day

Almighty God, in mercy you sent your one and only Son to take upon himself our human nature. By his gracious coming deliver us from the corruption of our sin and transform us into the likeness of his glory; through Jesus Christ our Lord, who lives and reigns with you and the Holy Spirit, one God, now and forever.

Verse of the Day

Alleluia. Let the peace of Christ rule in your hearts. Alleluia. (Colossians 3:15a)

Hymn of the Day

Year ABC	-	Let All Together Praise Our God	(41)
Year B	-	*In Peace and Joy I Now Depart*	*(269)*
One Year	-	Let All Together Praise Our God	(41)
	-	*In Peace and Joy I Now Depart*	*(269)*

Color: White

Second Sunday after Christmas
Lessons and Psalms

Year A	*Year B*
Isaiah 61:10—62:3	Micah 5:2-5a
Ephesians 1:3-6,15-18	Hebrews 2:10-18
John 1:14-18	John 7:40-43
Psalm 148	Psalm 148
Year C	*One Year*
Genesis 17:1-7	Jeremiah 31:15-20
Galatians 4:4-7	1 Peter 4:12-19
Luke 1:68-75	Matthew 2:13-23
Psalm 148	Psalm 18

Prayer of the Day

Almighty God, you have filled us with the new light of the Word who became flesh and lived among us. Let the light of our faith shine in all that we do; through your Son, Jesus Christ our Lord, who lives and reigns with you and the Holy Spirit, one God, now and forever.

Verse of the Day

Alleluia. All the ends of the earth have seen the salvation of our God. Alleluia. (Psalm 98:3b)

Hymn of the Day

Year ABC	-	Now Sing We, Now Rejoice	(34)
One Year	-	O Jesus Christ, Your Manger Is	(40)

Color: White

The Epiphany of Our Lord

Lessons and Psalms

Year A	*Year B*
Isaiah 60:1-6	Isaiah 60:1-6
Ephesians 3:2-12	Ephesians 3:2-12
Matthew 2:1-12	Matthew 2:1-12
Psalm 72	Psalm 72

Year C	*One Year*
Isaiah 60:1-6	Isaiah 60:1-6
Ephesians 3:2-12	Ephesians 3:2-12
Matthew 2:1-12	Matthew 2:1-12
Psalm 72	Psalm 72

Prayer of the Day

Lord God, by the leading of a star you once made known to the nations your one and only Son. Guide us, also, who know him now by faith, to come at last to the perfect joy of your heavenly glory; through Jesus Christ our Lord, who lives and reigns with you and the Holy Spirit, one God, now and forever.

Verse of the Day

Alleluia. We saw his star in the east and have come to worship him. Alleluia. (Matthew 2:2b)

Hymn of the Day

Year ABC - How Lovely Shines the Morning Star   (79)
One Year - How Lovely Shines the Morning Star   (79)

Color: White

First Sunday after the Epiphany

The Baptism of Our Lord

Lessons and Psalms

Year A	*Year B*
Isaiah 42:1-7	Isaiah 49:1-6
Acts 10:34-38	Acts 16:25-34
Matthew 3:13-17	Mark 1:4-11
Psalm 45	Psalm 2

Year C	*One Year*
1 Samuel 16:1-13	Isaiah 42:1-4
Titus 3:4-7	Acts 10:34-38
Luke 3:15-17,21,22	Matthew 3:13-17
Psalm 2	Psalm 89

Prayer of the Day

Father in heaven, at the baptism of Jesus in the River Jordan you proclaimed him your beloved Son and anointed him with the Holy Spirit. Keep us who are baptized into Christ faithful in our calling as your children and make us heirs with him of everlasting life; through your Son, Jesus Christ our Lord, who lives and reigns with you and the Holy Spirit, one God, now and forever.

Verse of the Day

Alleluia. You are my Son, whom I love; with you I am well pleased. Alleluia. (Mark 1:11b)

Hymn of the Day

Year ABC	-	To Jordan's River Came Our Lord	(89)
	-	*To Jordan Came the Christ, Our Lord*	(88)
One Year	-	To Jordan's River Came Our Lord	(89)
	-	*To Jordan Came the Christ, Our Lord*	(88)

Color: White

Second Sunday after the Epiphany

Lessons and Psalms

Year A
Isaiah 49:1-6
1 Corinthians 1:1-9
John 1:29-41
Psalm 89

Year B
1 Samuel 3:1-10
1 Corinthians 6:12-20
John 1:43-51
Psalm 67

Year C
Isaiah 62:1-5
1 Corinthians 12:1-11
John 2:1-11
Psalm 133-134

One Year
Isaiah 61:1-3
Romans 12:1-5
Luke 2:41-52
Psalm 84

Prayer of the Day

Almighty God, you gave your one and only Son to be the light of the world. Grant that your people, illumined by your Word and sacraments, may shine with the radiance of Christ's glory, that he may be known, worshiped, and believed to the ends of the earth; through Jesus Christ our Lord, who with you and the Holy Spirit lives and reigns, one God, now and forever.

Verse of the Day

Alleluia. He said to me, "You are my servant in whom I will display my splendor." Alleluia. (Isaiah 49:3 cf. NIV)

Hymn of the Day

Year AB   - The Only Son from Heaven   (86)
Year C   - Songs of Thankfulness and Praise   (82)
One Year   - Of the Father's Love Begotten   (35)

Color: Green

Third Sunday after the Epiphany

Lessons and Psalms

Year A
Isaiah 9:1-4
1 Corinthians 1:10-17
Matthew 4:12-23
Psalm 27

Year B
Jonah 3:1-5,10
1 Corinthians 7:29-31
Mark 1:14-20
Psalm 62

Year C
Isaiah 61:1-6
1 Corinthians 12:12-21,26,27
Luke 4:14-21
Psalm 19

One Year
Exodus 15:22-27
Romans 12:6-16a
John 2:1-11
Psalm 145

Prayer of the Day

Almighty God, you sent your Son to proclaim your kingdom and to teach with authority. Anoint us with the power of your Spirit that we, too, may bring good news to the afflicted, bind up the brokenhearted, and proclaim liberty to the captive; through Jesus Christ, your Son, our Lord, who lives and reigns with you and the Holy Spirit, one God, now and forever.

Verse of the Day

Alleluia. Jesus went throughout Galilee, teaching, preaching, and healing every disease. Alleluia. (Matthew 4:23 cf. NIV)

Hymn of the Day

Year ABC - O God from God, O Light from Light   (85)
One Year   - Songs of Thankfulness and Praise   (82)

Color: Green

Fourth Sunday after the Epiphany

Lessons and Psalms

Year A	*Year B*
Micah 6:1-8	Deuteronomy 18:15-20
1 Corinthians 1:26-31	1 Corinthians 8:1-13
Matthew 5:1-12	Mark 1:21-28
Psalm 1	Psalm 1

Year C	*One Year*
Jeremiah 1:4-10	2 Kings 5:1-15a
1 Corinthians 12:27—13:13	Romans 12:16b-21
Luke 4:20-32	Matthew 8:1-13
Psalm 78	Psalm 30

Prayer of the Day

Lord God, you know that we are surrounded by many dangers and that we often stumble and fall. Strengthen us in body and mind, and bring us safely through all temptations; through Jesus Christ, your Son, our Lord, who lives and reigns with you and the Holy Spirit, one God, now and forever.

Verse of the Day

Alleluia. The Spirit of the Lord is on me; he has anointed me to preach good news. Alleluia. (Luke 4:18a cf. NIV)

Hymn of the Day

Year ABC	-	Seek Where You May to Find a Way	(395)
	-	*Rise, Shine, You People*	*(556)*
One Year	-	O God from God, O Light from Light	(85)

Color: Green

Fifth Sunday after the Epiphany

Lessons and Psalms

Year A	*Year B*
Isaiah 58:5-9a	Job 7:1-7
1 Corinthians 2:1-5	1 Corinthians 9:16-23
Matthew 5:13-20	Mark 1:29-39
Psalm 111	Psalm 103

Year C	*One Year*
Isaiah 6:1-8	Exodus 14:13-22
1 Corinthians 14:12b-20	Romans 13:8-10
Luke 5:1-11	Matthew 8:23-27
Psalm 85	Psalm 33

Prayer of the Day

Almighty God, you sent your one and only Son as the Word of life for our eyes to see and our ears to hear. Help us believe what the Scriptures proclaim about him, and do the things that are pleasing in your sight; through Jesus Christ, your Son, our Lord, who lives and reigns with you and the Holy Spirit, one God, now and forever.

Verse of the Day

Alleluia. Jesus said, "I am the light of the world. Whoever follows me will never walk in darkness, but will have the light of life." Alleluia. (John 8:12 cf. NIV)

Hymn of the Day

Year A	- Thy Strong Word	(280)
Year BC	- Hail to the Lord's Anointed	(93)
One Year	- Seek Where You May to Find a Way	(395)

Color: Green

Sixth Sunday after the Epiphany

Lessons and Psalms

Year A
Deuteronomy 30:15-20
1 Corinthians 2:6-13
Matthew 5:21-37
Psalm 119a

Year B
2 Kings 5:1-14
1 Corinthians 9:24-27
Mark 1:40-45
Psalm 32

Year C
Jeremiah 17:5-8
1 Corinthians 15:12,16-20
Luke 6:17-26
Psalm 1

One Year
Exodus 34:5-10
1 Corinthians 9:24—10:5
Matthew 20:1-16
Psalm 46

Prayer of the Day

Lord God, in mercy receive the prayers of your people. Grant them the wisdom to know the things that please you and the grace and power always to accomplish them; through Jesus Christ, your Son, who lives and reigns with you and the Holy Spirit, one God, now and forever.

Verse of the Day

Alleluia. Lord, to whom shall we go? You have the words of eternal life. Alleluia. (John 6:68 cf. NIV)

Hymn of the Day

Year AC	-	Speak, O Savior; I Am Listening	(283)
Year B	-	Salvation unto Us Has Come	(390)
One Year	-	Salvation unto Us Has Come	(390)

Color: Green

399

Seventh Sunday after the Epiphany

Lessons and Psalms

Year A
Leviticus 19:1,2,17,18
1 Corinthians 3:10,11,16-23
Matthew 5:38-48
Psalm 103

Year B
Isaiah 43:18-25
2 Corinthians 1:18-22
Mark 2:1-12
Psalm 130

Year C
Genesis 45:3-8a,15
1 Corinthians 15:35-38a,42-49
Luke 6:27-38
Psalm 103

One Year
Isaiah 55:10-13
2 Corinthians 11:19—12:9
Luke 8:4-15
Psalm 1

Prayer of the Day

Gracious Father, keep your family, the Church, always faithful to you, that we may lean on the hope of your promises and be strong in the power of your love; through your Son, Jesus Christ our Lord, who lives and reigns with you and the Holy Spirit, one God, now and forever.

Verse of the Day

Alleluia. Be merciful, just as your Father is merciful. Alleluia. (Luke 6:36)

Hymn of the Day

Year AC	- Son of God, Eternal Savior	(492)
Year B	- I Know My Faith Is Founded	(403)
	- *My Faith Looks Up to Thee*	*(402)*
One Year	- Almighty God, Your Word Is Cast	(324)
	- *May God Bestow on Us His Grace*	*(574)*

Color: Green

Eighth Sunday after the Epiphany

Lessons and Psalms

Year A
Isaiah 49:13-18
1 Corinthians 4:1-13
Matthew 6:24-34
Psalm 119b

Year B
Hosea 2:14-16,19,20
2 Corinthians 3:1b-6
Mark 2:18-22
Psalm 133-134

Year C
Jeremiah 7:1-7
1 Corinthians 16:5-9,13,14
Luke 6:39-49
Psalm 92

One Year
Isaiah 42:5-9
1 Corinthians 13:1-13
Luke 18:31-43
Psalm 71

Prayer of the Day

Almighty and eternal God, you govern all things in heaven and on earth. In your mercy hear our prayers and grant us your peace all the days of our life; through Jesus Christ, your Son, our Lord, who lives and reigns with you and the Holy Spirit, one God, now and forever.

Verse of the Day

Alleluia. The steadfast love of the Lord never ceases, his mercies never come to an end. Alleluia. (Lamentations 3:22 cf. RSV)

Hymn of the Day

Year ABC - All Praise to God Who Reigns Above   (236)
One Year - In You, O Lord, I Put My Trust   (448)

Color: Green

Last Sunday after the Epiphany

The Transfiguration of Our Lord

Lessons and Psalms

Year A
Exodus 24:12,15-18
2 Peter 1:16-21
Matthew 17:1-9
Psalm 148

Year B
2 Kings 2:1-12a
2 Corinthians 3:12—4:2
Mark 9:2-9
Psalm 148

Year C
Exodus 34:29-35
2 Corinthians 4:3-6
Luke 9:28-36
Psalm 148

One Year
Deuteronomy 18:15-18
2 Peter 1:16-21
Matthew 17:1-9
Psalm 2

Prayer of the Day

Lord God, before the suffering and death of your one and only Son, you revealed his glory on the holy mountain. Grant that we who bear his cross on earth may behold by faith, the light of his heavenly glory and so be changed into his likeness; through Jesus Christ our Lord, who lives and reigns with you and the Holy Spirit, one God, now and forever.

Verse of the Day

Alleluia. A voice came from the cloud: "This is my Son, whom I love. Listen to him!" Alleluia. (Mark 9:7b)

Hymn of the Day

Year ABC - Down from the Mount of Glory (97)
One Year - Down from the Mount of Glory (97)

Color: White

Ash Wednesday
Lessons and Psalms

Year A
Isaiah 59:12-20
2 Corinthians 5:20b—6:2
Luke 18:9-14
Psalm 51a

Year B
Isaiah 59:12-20
2 Corinthians 5:20b—6:2
Luke 18:9-14
Psalm 51a

Year C
Isaiah 59:12-20
2 Corinthians 5:20b—6:2
Luke 18:9-14
Psalm 51a

One Year
Isaiah 59:12-20
2 Corinthians 5:17—6:2
Luke 7:36-50
Psalm 130

Prayer of the Day

Almighty and merciful God, you never despise what you have made and always forgive those who turn to you. Create in us such new and contrite hearts that we may truly repent of our sins and obtain your full and gracious pardon; through your Son, Jesus Christ our Lord, who lives and reigns with you and the Holy Spirit, one God, now and forever.

Verse of the Day

Return to the Lord, your God, for he is gracious and merciful, slow to anger, and abounding in steadfast love. (Joel 2:13 cf. RSV)

Hymn of the Day

Year ABC - In Adam We Have All Been One   (396)
Year One   - In Adam We Have All Been One   (396)

Color: Black or Purple

First Sunday in Lent
Lessons and Psalms

Year A	*Year B*
Genesis 2:7-9,15-17; 3:1-7	Genesis 22:1-18
Romans 5:12-19	Romans 8:31-39
Matthew 4:1-11	Mark 1:12-15
Psalm 130	Psalm 6

Year C	*One Year*
Deuteronomy 26:5-10	Genesis 3:1-15
Romans 10:8b-13	2 Corinthians 6:1-10
Luke 4:1-13	Matthew 4:1-11
Psalm 91	Psalm 91

Prayer of the Day

Lord our strength, the battle of good and evil rages within and around us, and our ancient foe tempts us with his deceits and empty promises. Keep us steadfast in your Word, and when we fall, raise us up again and restore us through your Son, Jesus Christ our Lord, who lives and reigns with you and the Holy Spirit, one God, now and forever.

Verse of the Day

It is written: "Worship the Lord your God, and serve him only." (Matthew 4:10b)

Hymn of the Day

Year ABC	-	A Mighty Fortress Is Our God	(200, 201)
One Year	-	A Mighty Fortress Is Our God	(200, 201)

Color: Purple

Second Sunday in Lent

Lessons and Psalms

Year A
Genesis 12:1-8
Romans 4:1-5,13-17
John 4:5-26
Psalm 121

Year B
Genesis 28:10-17
Romans 5:1-11
Mark 8:31-38
Psalm 73

Year C
Jeremiah 26:8-15
Philippians 3:17—4:1
Luke 13:31-35
Psalm 42-43

One Year
Isaiah 49:5-9a
1 Thessalonians 4:1-7
Matthew 15:21-28
Psalm 25

Prayer of the Day

Almighty God, you see that we have no power to defend ourselves. Guard and keep us both outwardly and inwardly from all adversities that may happen to the body and from all evil thoughts that may assault and hurt the soul; through Jesus Christ our Lord, who lives and reigns with you and the Holy Spirit, one God, now and forever.

Verse of the Day

Jesus humbled himself and became obedient to death, even death on a cross. (Philippians 2:8b cf. NIV)

Hymn of the Day

Year A   - God Loved the World So that He Gave (391)
Year BC   - Lord, You I Love with All My Heart   (434)
One Year - When in the Hour of Utmost Need   (413)

Color: Purple

405

Third Sunday in Lent

Lessons and Psalms

Year A
Isaiah 42:14-21
Ephesians 5:8-14
John 9:1-7,13-17,34-39
Psalm 143

Year B
Exodus 20:1-17
1 Corinthians 1:22-25
John 2:13-22
Psalm 19

Year C
Exodus 3:1-8b,10-15
1 Corinthians 10:1-13
Luke 13:1-9
Psalm 38

One Year
2 Samuel 22:1-7
Ephesians 5:1-9
Luke 11:14-28
Psalm 73

Prayer of the Day

Almighty God, look with favor on your humble servants and stretch out the right hand of your power to defend us against all our enemies; through Jesus Christ, your Son, our Lord, who lives and reigns with you and the Holy Spirit, one God, now and forever.

Verse of the Day

Just as Moses lifted up the snake in the desert, so the Son of Man must be lifted up, that everyone who believes in him may have eternal life. (John 3:14,15)

Hymn of the Day

Year A	- Christ Is the World's Light	(343)
Year B	- Forth in Your Name, O Lord, I Go	(456)
Year C	- Lord, to You I Make Confession	(302)
One Year	- Rise, My Soul, to Watch and Pray	(472)

Color: Purple

Fourth Sunday in Lent

Lessons and Psalms

Year A
Hosea 5:15—6:3
Romans 8:1-10
Matthew 20:17-28
Psalm 42-43

Year B
Numbers 21:4-9
Ephesians 2:4-10
John 3:14-21
Psalm 38

Year C
Isaiah 12:1-6
1 Corinthians 1:18-25
Luke 15:1-3,11b-32
Psalm 32

One Year
Exodus 16:11-17
Ephesians 3:14-20
John 6:1-15
Psalm 145

Prayer of the Day

Almighty God, we confess that we deserve to be punished for our evil deeds. But we ask you graciously to cleanse us from all sin and to comfort us with your salvation; through your Son, Jesus Christ our Lord, who lives and reigns with you and the Holy Spirit, one God, now and forever.

Verse of the Day

For God so loved the world that he gave his one and only Son, that whoever believes in him shall not perish but have eternal life. (John 3:16)

Hymn of the Day

Year A	- Lord of Glory, You Have Bought Us	(486)
	- *I Trust, O Christ, in You Alone*	*(437)*
Year B	- God Loved the World So that He Gave	(391)
Year C	- Jesus Sinners Does Receive	(304)
	- *I Trust, O Christ, in You Alone*	*(437)*
One Year	- Jesus, Priceless Treasure	(349)

Color: Purple

Fifth Sunday in Lent

Lessons and Psalms

Year A	*Year B*
Ezekiel 37:1-14	Jeremiah 31:31-34
Romans 8:11-19	Hebrews 5:7-9
John 11:17-27,38-45	John 12:20-33
Psalm 116	Psalm 143

Year C	*One Year*
Isaiah 43:16-21	Exodus 3:1-15
Philippians 3:8-14	Hebrews 9:11-15
Luke 20:9-19	John 8:46-59
Psalm 73	Psalm 45

Prayer of the Day

Eternal God and Father, help us to remember Jesus, who obeyed your will and bore the cross for our salvation that through his anguish, pain, and death we may receive forgiveness of sins and inherit eternal life; through your Son, Jesus Christ our Lord, who lives and reigns with you and the Holy Spirit, one God, now and forever.

Verse of the Day

The Son of Man did not come to be served, but to serve, and to give his life as a ransom for many. (Mark 10:45 cf. NIV)

Hymn of the Day

| Year ABC | - | My Song Is Love Unknown | (110) |
| One Year | - | My Song Is Love Unknown | (110) |

Color: Purple

Sixth Sunday in Lent

Palm Sunday

Lessons and Psalms

Year A	*Year B*
Zechariah 9:9,10	Zechariah 9:9,10
Philippians 2:5-11	Philippians 2:5-11
Matthew 21:1-11	Mark 11:1-10
Psalm 24	Psalm 24
Year C	*One Year*
Zechariah 9:9,10	Zechariah 9:9-12
Philippians 2:5-11	Philippians 2:5-11
Luke 19:28-40	Matthew 21:1-9
Psalm 24	Psalm 24

Prayer of the Day

We praise you, O God, for the great acts of love by which you have redeemed us through your Son, Jesus Christ. As he was acclaimed by those who scattered their garments and branches of palm in his path, so may we always hail him as our King and follow him with perfect confidence; who lives and reigns with you and the Holy Spirit, one God, now and forever.

Verse of the Day

The hour has come for the Son of Man to be glorified. (John 12:23 cf. NIV)

Hymn of the Day

Year ABC	- Ride On, Ride On in Majesty	(132, 133)
One Year	- Ride On, Ride On in Majesty	(132, 133)

Color: Purple

409

Maundy Thursday

Lessons and Psalms

Year A
Exodus 12:1-14
1 Corinthians 11:23-28
John 13:1-15,34
Psalm 116

Year B
Exodus 12:1-14
1 Corinthians 10:16,17
Mark 14:12-26
Psalm 116

Year C
Exodus 12:1-14
Hebrews 10:15-25
Luke 22:7-20
Psalm 116

One Year
Exodus 12:1-14
1 Corinthians 11:23-32
John 13:1-15
Psalm 111

Prayer of the Day

Lord Jesus Christ, in the sacrament of Holy Communion you give us your true body and blood as a remembrance of your suffering and death on the cross. Grant us so firmly to believe your words and promise that we may always partake of this sacrament to our eternal good; for you live and reign with the Father and the Holy Spirit, one God, now and forever.

Verse of the Day

As often as you eat this bread and drink the cup, you proclaim the Lord's death until he comes. (1 Corinthians 11:26 RSV)

Hymn of the Day

Year ABC - Jesus Christ, Our Blessed Savior   (313)
One Year   - Jesus Christ, Our Blessed Savior   (313)

Color: Purple or White

Good Friday
Lessons and Psalms

Year A
Isaiah 52:13—53:12
Hebrews 4:14-16; 5:7-9
John 19:17-30
Psalm 22

Year B
Isaiah 52:13—53:12
Hebrews 4:14-16; 5:7-9
John 19:17-30
Psalm 22

Year C
Isaiah 52:13—53:12
Hebrews 4:14-16; 5:7-9
John 19:17-30
Psalm 22

One Year
Isaiah 52:13—53:12
Hebrews 7:26-28
John 18:1—19:42
Psalm 22

Prayer of the Day

God Most Holy, look with mercy on this your family for whom our Lord Jesus Christ was willing to be betrayed, be given over into the hands of the wicked, and suffer death upon the cross. Keep us always faithful to him, our only Savior, who now lives and reigns with you and the Holy Spirit, one God, forever and ever.

Verse of the Day

Surely he took up our infirmities and carried our sorrows, yet we considered him stricken by God, smitten by him, and afflicted. (Isaiah 53:4)

Hymn of the Day

Year ABC - A Lamb Goes Uncomplaining Forth   (100)
          - *God Was There on Calvary*   *(140)*
One Year - A Lamb Goes Uncomplaining Forth   (100)
          - *God Was There on Calvary*   *(140)*

Color: Black

The Resurrection of Our Lord
Easter Dawn

Lessons and Psalms

Year A	*Year B*
Isaiah 12:1-6	Isaiah 12:1-6
1 Corinthians 15:51-57	1 Corinthians 15:51-57
John 20:1-18	John 20:1-18
Psalm 30	Psalm 30
Year C	*One Year*
Isaiah 12:1-6	Psalm 16
1 Corinthians 15:51-57	1 Corinthians 15:12-20
John 20:1-18	John 20:1-8
Psalm 30	Psalm 150

Prayer of the Day

O God, you made the dawn of this most holy day shine with the glory of our Lord's resurrection. Grant that we who have been raised from the death of sin by your life-giving Spirit may worship you in sincerity and truth; through Jesus Christ our Lord, who lives and reigns with you and the Holy Spirit, now and forever.

Verse of the Day

Alleluia. Alleluia. Christ is risen! He is risen indeed! Alleluia. For as in Adam all die, so in Christ all will be made alive. Alleluia. (1 Corinthians 15:22)

Hymn of the Day

Year ABC	- Christ Is Arisen	(144)
One Year	- Christ Is Arisen	(144)

Color: White or Gold

The Resurrection of Our Lord

Easter Day

Lessons and Psalms

Year A	*Year B*
Jonah 2:2-9	Isaiah 25:6-9
Colossians 3:1-4	1 Corinthians 15:19-26
Matthew 28:1-10	Mark 16:1-8
Psalm 118	Psalm 118

Year C	*One Year*
Exodus 15:1-11	Job 19:23-27a
1 Corinthians 15:1-11	1 Corinthians 5:6-8
Luke 24:1-12	Mark 16:1-8
Psalm 118	Psalm 118

Prayer of the Day

Almighty God, by the glorious resurrection of your Son Jesus Christ you conquered death and opened the gate to eternal life. Grant that we, who have been raised with him through baptism, may walk in newness of life and ever rejoice in the hope of sharing his glory; through Jesus Christ our Lord, to whom, with you and the Holy Spirit be dominion and praise now and forever.

Verse of the Day

Alleluia. Alleluia. Christ is risen! He is risen indeed! Alleluia. This is the day the Lord has made; let us rejoice and be glad in it. Alleluia. (Psalm 118:24 cf. NIV)

Hymn of the Day

Year ABC	-	Awake, My Heart, with Gladness	(156)
	-	*Christ Jesus Lay in Death's Strong Bands*	*(161)*
One Year	-	Awake, My Heart, with Gladness	(156)
	-	*Christ Jesus Lay in Death's Strong Bands*	*(161)*

Color: White or Gold

Second Sunday of Easter

Lessons and Psalms

Year A	*Year B*
Acts 2:14a,22-32	Acts 3:12-20
1 Peter 1:3-9	1 John 5:1-6
John 20:19-31	John 20:19-31
Psalm 16	Psalm 16

Year C	*One Year*
Acts 5:12,17-32	Genesis 15:1-6
Revelation 1:4-18	1 John 5:4-10
John 20:19-31	John 20:19-31
Psalm 16	Psalm 116

Prayer of the Day

O risen Lord, you came to your disciples and took away their fears with your word of peace. Come to us also by Word and sacrament, and banish our fears with the comforting assurance of your abiding presence; for you live and reign with the Father and the Holy Spirit, one God, now and forever.

Verse of the Day

Alleluia. Alleluia. Christ is risen! He is risen indeed! Alleluia. Blessed are those who have not seen and yet have believed. Alleluia. (John 20:29b)

Hymn of the Day

| Year ABC | - | O Sons and Daughters of the King | (165) |
| One Year | - | O Sons and Daughters of the King | (165) |

Color: White

Third Sunday of Easter

Lessons and Psalms

Year A
Acts 2:14a,36-47
1 Peter 1:17-21
Luke 24:13-35
Psalm 67

Year B
Acts 4:8-12
1 John 1:1—2:2
Luke 24:36-49
Psalm 118

Year C
Acts 9:1-19a
Revelation 5:11-14
John 21:1-14
Psalm 67

One Year
Lamentations 3:18-26
1 Peter 2:11-20
John 16:16-23a
Psalm 67

Prayer of the Day

O God, by the humiliation of your Son you lifted up this fallen world from the despair of death. By his resurrection to life, grant your faithful people gladness of heart and the hope of eternal joys; through your Son, Jesus Christ our Lord, who lives and reigns with you and the Holy Spirit, one God, now and forever.

Verse of the Day

Alleluia. Alleluia. Christ is risen! He is risen indeed! Alleluia. Our hearts were burning within us while he talked with us on the road and opened the Scriptures to us. Alleluia. (Luke 24:32 cf. NIV)

Hymn of the Day

Year ABC - This Joyful Eastertide   (160)
One Year   - Triumphant from the Grave   (151)

Color: White

415

Fourth Sunday of Easter

Lessons and Psalms

Year A	*Year B*
Acts 6:1-9; 7:2a,51-60	Acts 4:23-33
1 Peter 2:19-25	1 John 3:1,2
John 10:1-10	John 10:11-18
Psalm 23	Psalm 23

Year C	*One Year*
Acts 13:15,16a,26-33	Ezekiel 34:11-16
Revelation 7:9-17	1 Peter 2:21-25
John 10:22-30	John 10:11-16
Psalm 23	Psalm 23

Prayer of the Day

O Lord Jesus Christ, you are the Good Shepherd who laid down your life for the sheep. Lead us now to the still waters of your life-giving Word that we may abide in your Father's house forevermore; for you live and reign with him and the Holy Spirit, one God, now and forever.

Verse of the Day

Alleluia. Alleluia. Christ is risen! He is risen indeed! Alleluia. I am the good shepherd; I know my sheep and my sheep know me. Alleluia. (John 10:14)

Hymn of the Day

| Year ABC | - | The King of Love My Shepherd Is | (375) |
| One Year | - | The King of Love My Shepherd Is | (375) |

Color: White

Fifth Sunday of Easter

Lessons and Psalms

Year A	*Year B*
Acts 17:1-12	Acts 8:26-40
1 Peter 2:4-10	1 John 3:18-24
John 14:1-12	John 15:1-8
Psalm 33	Psalm 67

Year C	*One Year*
Acts 13:44-52	1 Chronicles 16:23-34
Revelation 21:1-6	James 1:16-21
John 13:31-35	John 16:5-15
Psalm 145	Psalm 66

Prayer of the Day

O God, you form the minds of your faithful people into a single will. Make us love what you command and desire what you promise, that among the many changes of this world, our hearts may ever yearn for the lasting joys of heaven; through your Son, Jesus Christ our Lord, who lives and reigns with you and the Holy Spirit, one God, now and forever.

Verse of the Day

Alleluia. Alleluia. Christ is risen! He is risen indeed! Alleluia. I am the way, the truth, and the life, says the Lord. Alleluia. (John 14:6 cf. NIV)

Hymn of the Day

Year AC	-	At the Lamb's High Feast We Sing	(141)
Year B	-	With High Delight Let Us Unite	(168)
One Year	-	Dear Christians, One and All, Rejoice	(377)

Color: White

417

Sixth Sunday of Easter

Lessons and Psalms

Year A
Acts 17:22-31
1 Peter 3:15-22
John 14:15-21
Psalm 66

Year B
Acts 11:19-26
1 John 4:1-11
John 15:9-17
Psalm 98

Year C
Acts 14:8-18
Revelation 21:10-14,22,23
John 14:23-29
Psalm 65

One Year
Jeremiah 29:11-14
James 1:22-27
John 16:23b-30
Psalm 85

Prayer of the Day

Father of lights, every good and perfect gift comes from you. Inspire us to think those things that are true and long for those things that are good, that we may always make our petitions according to your gracious will; through your Son, Jesus Christ our Lord, who lives and reigns with you and the Holy Spirit, one God, now and forever.

Verse of the Day

Alleluia. Alleluia. Christ is risen! He is risen indeed! Alleluia. If anyone loves me, he will obey my teaching. My Father will love him, and we will come to him and make our home with him. Alleluia. (John 14:23 cf. NIV)

Hymn of the Day

Year ABC - Dear Christians, One and All, Rejoice   (377)
One Year - Our Father, Who from Heaven Above   (410)

Color: White

The Ascension of Our Lord
Lessons and Psalms

Year A
Acts 1:1-11
Ephesians 1:16-23
Luke 24:44-53
Psalm 47

Year B
Acts 1:1-11
Ephesians 1:16-23
Luke 24:44-53
Psalm 47

Year C
Acts 1:1-11
Ephesians 1:16-23
Luke 24:44-53
Psalm 47

One Year
2 Kings 2:1-11
Acts 1:1-11
Luke 24:36-53
Psalm 47

Prayer of the Day

Lord Jesus, King of glory, on this day you ascended far above the heavens and at God's right hand you rule the nations. Leave us not alone, we pray, but grant us the Spirit of truth that at your command and by your power we may be your witnesses in all the world; for you live and reign with the Father and the Holy Spirit, one God, now and forever.

Verse of the Day

Alleluia. Alleluia. Christ is risen! He is risen indeed! Alleluia. Surely I will be with you always, to the very end of the age. Alleluia. (Matthew 28:20b cf. NIV)

Hymn of the Day

Year AC	- On Christ's Ascension I Now Build	(173)
Year B	- Crown Him with Many Crowns	(341)
One Year	- On Christ's Ascension I Now Build	(173)

Color: White

Seventh Sunday of Easter

Lessons and Psalms

Year A	*Year B*
Acts 1:1-14	Acts 1:15-26
1 Peter 4:12-17; 5:6-11	1 John 4:13-21
John 17:1-11a	John 17:11b-19
Psalm 8	Psalm 8
Year C	*One Year*
Acts 16:6-10	Ezekiel 36:24-28
Revelation 22:12-17,20	1 Peter 4:7-11
John 17:20-26	John 15:26—16:4
Psalm 8	Psalm 78

Prayer of the Day

Almighty God, your Son our Savior was taken up in glory and intercedes for us at your right hand. Through your living and abiding Word, give us hearts to know him and faith to follow where he has gone; who lives and reigns with you and the Holy Spirit, one God, now and forever.

Verse of the Day

Alleluia. Alleluia. Christ is risen! He is risen indeed! Alleluia. I will not leave you as orphans; I will come to you. Alleluia. (John 14:18)

Hymn of the Day

Year ABC	- Jesus, My Great High Priest	(359)
One Year	- If God Had Not Been on Our Side	(202)

Color: White

The Coming of the Holy Spirit

The Day of Pentecost

Lessons and Psalms

Year A	*Year B*
Joel 2:28,29	Ezekiel 37:1-14
Acts 2:1-21	Acts 2:1-21
John 16:5-11	John 14:25-27
Psalm 51b	Psalm 51b

Year C	*One Year*
Genesis 11:1-9	Joel 2:28-32
Acts 2:1-21	Acts 2:1-13
John 15:26,27	John 14:23-31
Psalm 51b	Psalm 51b

Prayer of the Day

Holy Spirit, God and Lord, come to us this joyful day (with your sevenfold gift of grace) Rekindle in our hearts the holy fire of your love that in a true and living faith we may tell abroad the glory of our Savior, Jesus Christ, who lives and reigns with you and the Father, one God, now and forever.

Verse of the Day

Alleluia. Come, Holy Spirit, fill the hearts of your faithful people, and kindle in them the fire of your love. Alleluia. (From the antiphon: Come, Holy Spirit)

Hymn of the Day

Year ABC	-	Come, Holy Ghost, God and Lord	(176)
One Year	-	Come, Holy Ghost, God and Lord	(176)

Color: Red

First Sunday after Pentecost

The Holy Trinity

Lessons and Psalms

Year A	*Year B*
Genesis 1:1—2:3	Isaiah 6:1-8
2 Corinthians 13:11-14	Romans 8:14-17
Matthew 28:16-20	John 3:1-17
Psalm 150	Psalm 150

Year C	*One Year*
Numbers 6:22-27	Isaiah 6:1-8
Romans 5:1-5	Romans 11:33-36
John 16:12-15	John 3:1-15
Psalm 150	Psalm 73

Prayer of the Day

Almighty God and Father, dwelling in majesty and mystery, filling and renewing all creation by your eternal Spirit, and manifesting your saving grace through our Lord Jesus Christ: in mercy cleanse our hearts and lips that, free from doubt and fear, we may ever worship you, one true immortal God, with your Son and the Holy Spirit, living and reigning, now and forever.

Verse of the Day

Alleluia. Holy, holy, holy is the Lord Almighty; the whole earth is full of his glory. Alleluia. (Isaiah 6:3b cf. NIV)

Hymn of the Day

Year ABC - Come, Holy Ghost, Creator Blest (177, 178)
One Year   - Come, Holy Ghost, Creator Blest (177, 178)

Color: White

Second Sunday after Pentecost

Lessons and Psalms

Year A	*Year B*
Deuteronomy 11:18-21,26-28	Deuteronomy 5:12-15
Romans 3:21-25a,27,28	2 Corinthians 4:5-12
Matthew 7:15-29	Mark 2:23-28
Psalm 78	Psalm 126
Year C	*One Year*
1 Kings 8:22,23,41-43	Deuteronomy 6:4-18
Galatians 1:1-10	1 John 4:16-21
Luke 7:1-10	Luke 16:19-31
Psalm 100	Psalm 143

Prayer of the Day

O God, you rule over all things in wisdom and kindness. Take away everything that may be harmful and give us whatever is good; through your Son, Jesus Christ our Lord, who lives and reigns with you and the Holy Spirit, one God, now and forever.

Verse of the Day

Alleluia. Your word is a lamp to my feet and a light for my path. Alleluia. (Psalm 119:105)

Hymn of the Day

Year ABC - We Now Implore God the Holy Ghost   (190)
One Year   - We Now Implore God the Holy Ghost   (190)

Color: Green

Third Sunday after Pentecost

Lessons and Psalms

Year A
Hosea 5:15—6:6
Romans 4:18-25
Matthew 9:9-13
Psalm 119c

Year B
Genesis 3:8-15
2 Corinthians 4:13-18
Mark 3:20-35
Psalm 51a

Year C
1 Kings 17:17-24
Galatians 1:11-24
Luke 7:11-17
Psalm 30

One Year
Isaiah 25:6-9
1 John 3:13-18
Luke 14:16-24
Psalm 100

Prayer of the Day

O God, the strength of all who trust in you, mercifully hear our prayers. Be gracious to us in our weakness and give us strength to keep your commandments in all we say and do; through Jesus Christ, your Son, our Lord, who lives and reigns with you and the Holy Spirit, one God, now and forever.

Verse of the Day

Alleluia. God was in Christ reconciling the world to himself, and entrusting to us the message of reconciliation. Alleluia. (2 Corinthians 5:19 cf. RSV)

Hymn of the Day

Year AB	- Let Me Be Yours Forever	(596)
Year C	- When in the Hour of Utmost Need	(413)
One Year	- Awake, O Spirit, Who Inspired	(567)

Color: Green

Fourth Sunday after Pentecost

Lessons and Psalms

Year A	*Year B*
Exodus 19:2-8a	Ezekiel 17:22-24
Romans 5:6-11	2 Corinthians 5:1-10
Matthew 9:35—10:8	Mark 4:26-34
Psalm 100	Psalm 92

Year C	*One Year*
2 Samuel 11:26—12:10,13-15	Deuteronomy 32:3-12
Galatians 2:11-21	1 Peter 5:6-11
Luke 7:36-50	Luke 15:1-10
Psalm 32	Psalm 103

Prayer of the Day

O God, protector of all the faithful, you alone make strong; you alone make holy. Show us your mercy and forgive our sins day by day. Guide us through our earthly lives that we do not lose the things you have prepared for us in heaven; through Jesus Christ our Lord, who lives and reigns with you and the Holy Spirit, one God, now and forever.

Verse of the Day

Alleluia. May your priests be clothed with righteousness; may your saints sing for joy. Alleluia. (Psalm 132:9)

Hymn of the Day

Year A	- In You Is Gladness	(346)
	- *Spread, Oh, Spread the Mighty Word*	*(576)*
Year B	- Creator Spirit, by Whose Aid	(188)
Year C	- Jesus, Your Boundless Love to Me	(479)
One Year	- Lord Jesus Christ, My Savior Blest	(362)
	- *I Trust, O Christ, in You Alone*	*(437)*

Color: Green

Fifth Sunday after Pentecost

Lessons and Psalms

Year A
Jeremiah 20:7-13
Romans 5:12-15
Matthew 10:24-33
Psalm 31

Year B
Job 38:1-11
2 Corinthians 5:14-21
Mark 4:35-41
Psalm 46

Year C
Zechariah 13:7-9
Galatians 3:23-29
Luke 9:18-24
Psalm 22

One Year
Isaiah 58:6-12
Romans 8:18-23
Luke 6:36-42
Psalm 133-134

Prayer of the Day

O Lord, our God, govern the nations on earth and direct the affairs of this world so that your Church may worship you in peace and joy; through your Son, Jesus Christ our Lord, who lives and reigns with you and the Holy Spirit, one God, now and forever.

Verse of the Day

Alleluia. Because we are his children, God has sent the Spirit of his Son into our hearts, crying, "Abba! Father!" Alleluia. (Galatians 4:6 cf. NIV)

Hymn of the Day

Year A	- Creator Spirit, by Whose Aid	(188)
Year B	- By Grace I'm Saved	(384)
	- *Amazing Grace—How Sweet the Sound*	*(379)*
Year C	- Lord Jesus Christ, the Church's Head	(536)
One Year	- Creator Spirit, by Whose Aid	(188)

Color: Green

Sixth Sunday after Pentecost

Lessons and Psalms

Year A	*Year B*
Jeremiah 28:5-9	Lamentations 3:22-33
Romans 6:1b-11	2 Corinthians 8:1-9,13,14
Matthew 10:34-42	Mark 5:21-24a,35-43
Psalm 89	Psalm 30

Year C	*One Year*
1 Kings 19:14-21	Jeremiah 1:4-10
Galatians 5:1,13-25	1 Peter 3:8-15
Luke 9:51-62	Luke 5:1-11
Psalm 62	Psalm 67

Prayer of the Day

O God, you have prepared joys beyond understanding for those who love you. Pour into our hearts such love for you that, loving you above all things, we may obtain your promises, which exceed all that we can desire; through your Son, Jesus Christ our Lord, who lives and reigns with you and the Holy Spirit, one God, now and forever.

Verse of the Day

Alleluia. If anyone would come after me, he must deny himself and take up his cross and follow me. Alleluia. (Mark 8:34b)

Hymn of the Day

Year A	- Come, Follow Me, the Savior Spoke	(453)
Year B	- In the Midst of Earthly Life	(534)
	- *In You, O Lord, I Put My Trust*	*(448)*
Year C	- Jesus, I My Cross Have Taken	(465)
One Year	- Come, Follow Me, the Savior Spoke	(453)

Color: Green

Seventh Sunday after Pentecost

Lessons and Psalms

Year A	*Year B*
Exodus 33:12-23	Ezekiel 2:1-5
Romans 7:15-25a	2 Corinthians 12:7-10
Matthew 11:25-30	Mark 6:1-6
Psalm 145	Psalm 143

Year C	*One Year*
Isaiah 66:10-14	Genesis 13:5-11
Galatians 6:1-10,14-16	Romans 6:3-11
Luke 10:1-12,16-20	Matthew 5:20-26
Psalm 66	Psalm 19

Prayer of the Day

God of all power and might, you are the giver of all that is good. Help us love you with all our heart, strengthen us in true faith, provide us with all we need, and keep us safe in your care; through Jesus Christ, your Son, our Lord, who lives and reigns with you and the Holy Spirit, one God, now and forever.

Verse of the Day

Alleluia. Happy are they who hear the Word, hold it fast in an honest and good heart, and bring forth fruit with patience. Alleluia. (Luke 8:15 cf. RSV)

Hymn of the Day

Year A	- If God Himself Be for Me	(419)
Year B	- Preach You the Word	(544)
	- *Lord Jesus Christ, the Church's Head*	*(536)*
Year C	- O Christians, Haste	(570)
One Year	- All Mankind Fell in Adam's Fall	(378)

Color: Green

Eighth Sunday after Pentecost
Lessons and Psalms

Year A
Isaiah 55:10,11
Romans 8:18-25
Matthew 13:1-9,18-23
Psalm 65

Year B
Amos 7:10-15
Ephesians 1:3-14
Mark 6:7-13
Psalm 78

Year C
Deuteronomy 30:9-14
Colossians 1:1-14
Luke 10:25-37
Psalm 25

One Year
Psalm 107:1-9
Romans 6:19-23
Mark 8:1-9
Psalm 146

Prayer of the Day

Almighty God, we thank you for planting in us the seed of your Word. By your Holy Spirit help us to receive it with joy and to bring forth fruits in faith and hope and love; through your Son, Jesus Christ our Lord, who lives and reigns with you and the Holy Spirit, one God, now and forever.

Verse of the Day

Alleluia. The Word is very near you; it is in your mouth and in your heart so you may obey it. Alleluia. (Deuteronomy 30:14 cf. NIV)

Hymn of the Day

Year A	- May God Bestow on Us His Grace	(574)
	- *Almighty God, Your Word Is Cast*	*(324)*
Year B	- The Son of God, Our Christ	(525)
Year C	- Forth in Your Name, O Lord, I Go	(456)
One Year	- All Praise to God Who Reigns Above	(236)

Color: Green

Ninth Sunday after Pentecost

Lessons and Psalms

Year A
Joel 3:12-16
Romans 8:26,27
Matthew 13:24-30,36-43
Psalm 18

Year B
Jeremiah 23:1-6
Ephesians 2:13-22
Mark 6:30-34
Psalm 23

Year C
Genesis 18:1-14
Colossians 1:21-29
Luke 10:38-42
Psalm 119a

One Year
Jeremiah 23:16-24
Romans 8:12-17
Matthew 7:15-23
Psalm 1

Prayer of the Day

Grant us, Lord, the spirit to think and do what is right that we, who cannot do anything that is good without you, may by your help be enabled to live according to your will; through Jesus Christ, your Son, our Lord, who lives and reigns with you and the Holy Spirit, one God, now and forever.

Verse of the Day

Alleluia. My Word will not return to me empty, but will accomplish what I desire and achieve the purpose for which I sent it. Alleluia. (Isaiah 55:11b cf. NIV)

Hymn of the Day

Year A	- Lord Jesus Christ, with Us Abide	(541)
Year B	- Lord Jesus Christ, My Savior Blest	(362)
Year C	- One Thing's Needful	(290)
One Year	- Come, Oh, Come, Life-Giving Spirit	(181)

Color: Green

430

Tenth Sunday after Pentecost

Lessons and Psalms

Year A
1 Kings 3:5-12
Romans 8:28-30
Matthew 13:44-52
Psalm 119b

Year B
Exodus 24:3-11
Ephesians 4:1-7,11-16
John 6:1-15
Psalm 84

Year C
Genesis 18:20-32
Colossians 2:6-15
Luke 11:1-13
Psalm 6

One Year
Genesis 39:1-6a
1 Corinthians 10:6-13
Luke 16:1-9
Psalm 92

Prayer of the Day

O Lord, your ears are always open to the prayers of your humble servants, who come to you in Jesus' name. Teach us always to ask according to your will that we may never fail to obtain the blessings you have promised; through Jesus Christ, your Son, our Lord, who lives and reigns with you and the Holy Spirit, one God, now and forever. *Amen*

Verse of the Day

Alleluia. Lord, to whom shall we go? You have the words of eternal life. Alleluia. (John 6:68 cf. NIV)

Hymn of the Day

Year A	- My God Will Never Leave Me	(418)
Year B	- Jesus, Priceless Treasure	(349)
Year C	- Our Father, Who from Heaven Above	(410)
One Year	- One Thing's Needful	(290)

Color: Green

Eleventh Sunday after Pentecost

Lessons and Psalms

Year A
Isaiah 55:1-5
Romans 8:35-39
Matthew 14:13-21
Psalm 42-43

Year B
Exodus 16:2-15
Ephesians 4:17-24
John 6:24-35
Psalm 145

Year C
Ecclesiastes 1:2; 2:18-26
Colossians 3:1-11
Luke 12:13-21
Psalm 34

One Year
Daniel 9:15-18
1 Corinthians 12:1-11
Luke 19:41-48
Psalm 51a

Prayer of the Day

O God, you reveal your mighty power chiefly in showing mercy and kindness. Grant us the full measure of your grace that we may obtain your promises and become partakers of your heavenly glory; through Jesus Christ, your Son, our Lord, who lives and reigns with you and the Holy Spirit, one God, now and forever.

Verse of the Day

Alleluia. Jesus replied, "If anyone loves me, he will obey my teaching. My Father will love him, and we will come to him and make our home with him." Alleluia. (John 14:23)

Hymn of the Day

Year A	- Jesus, Priceless Treasure	(349)
Year B	- I Know My Faith Is Founded	(403)
	- *My Faith Looks Up to Thee*	*(402)*
Year C	- Brothers, Sisters, Let Us Gladly	(484)
One Year	- Lord, to You I Make Confession	(302)

Color: Green

Twelfth Sunday after Pentecost

Lessons and Psalms

Year A
1 Kings 19:9-18
Romans 9:1-5
Matthew 14:22-33
Psalm 73

Year B
1 Kings 19:3-8
Ephesians 4:30—5:2
John 6:41-51
Psalm 34

Year C
Genesis 15:1-6
Hebrews 11:1-3,8-16
Luke 12:32-40
Psalm 33

One Year
2 Samuel 12:1-13
1 Corinthians 15:1-10
Luke 18:9-14
Psalm 6

Prayer of the Day

Almighty and everlasting God, you are always more ready to hear than we to pray, and to give more than we either desire or deserve. Pour upon us the abundance of your mercy, forgiving us those things of which our conscience is afraid, and giving us those good things for which we are not worthy to ask, except through the merits and mediation of your Son, Jesus Christ our Lord, who lives and reigns with you and the Holy Spirit, one God, now and forever.

Verse of the Day

Alleluia. Now faith is being sure of what we hope for and certain of what we do not see. Alleluia. (Hebrews 11:1)

Hymn of the Day

Year A	-	By Grace I'm Saved	(384)
	-	*Amazing Grace—How Sweet the Sound*	*(379)*
Year B	-	Lord, Enthroned in Heavenly Splendor	(352)
Year C	-	Rise, My Soul, to Watch and Pray	(472)
	-	*Have No Fear, Little Flock*	*(442)*
One Year	-	From Depths of Woe I Cry to You	(305)
	-	*Now I Have Found the Firm Foundation*	*(386)*

Color: Green

433

Thirteenth Sunday after Pentecost

Lessons and Psalms

Year A	*Year B*
Isaiah 56:1,6-8	Proverbs 9:1-6
Romans 11:13-15,28-32	Ephesians 5:15-20
Matthew 15:21-28	John 6:51-58
Psalm 133-134	Psalm 1

Year C	*One Year*
Jeremiah 23:23-29	Micah 7:18-20
Hebrews 12:1-13	2 Corinthians 3:4-11
Luke 12:49-53	Mark 7:31-37
Psalm 139a	Psalm 34

Prayer of the Day

Almighty and merciful God, it is only by your gift of grace that we come into your presence and offer true and faithful service. Grant that our worship on earth may always be pleasing to you, and in the life to come give us the fulfillment of what you have promised; through Jesus Christ, your Son, our Lord, who lives and reigns with you and the Holy Spirit, one God, now and forever.

Verse of the Day

Alleluia. The Word of God is living and active, sharper than any two-edged sword, discerning the thoughts and intentions of the heart. Alleluia. (Hebrews 4:12 cf. RSV)

Hymn of the Day

Year AC	- When in the Hour of Utmost Need	(413)
Year B	- O Holy Spirit, Grant Us Grace	(185)
One Year	- Praise to the Lord, the Almighty	(234)

Color: Green

Fourteenth Sunday after Pentecost

Lessons and Psalms

Year A
Exodus 6:2-8
Romans 11:33-36
Matthew 16:13-20
Psalm 34

Year B
Joshua 24:1,2a,14-18
Ephesians 5:21-31
John 6:60-69
Psalm 71

Year C
Isaiah 66:18-24
Hebrews 12:18-24
Luke 13:22-30
Psalm 72

One Year
Leviticus 19:9-18
Galatians 3:15-22
Luke 10:23-37
Psalm 133-134

Prayer of the Day

Almighty and everlasting God, give us an increase of faith, hope, and love; and, that we may obtain what you promise, make us love what you command; through Jesus Christ, your Son, our Lord, who lives and reigns with you and the Holy Spirit, one God, now and forever.

Verse of the Day

Alleluia. Jesus Christ has destroyed death and brought life and immortality to light through the gospel. Alleluia. (1 Timothy 1:10b cf. NIV)

Hymn of the Day

Year A   - Lord Jesus Christ, the Church's Head   (536)
Year B   - Rise, Shine, You People   (556)
Year C   - I Walk in Danger All the Way   (431)
One Year   - Lord of Glory, You Have Bought Us   (486)

Color: Green

Fifteenth Sunday after Pentecost

Lessons and Psalms

Year A
Jeremiah 15:15-21
Romans 12:1-8
Matthew 16:21-26
Psalm 121

Year B
Deuteronomy 4:1,2,6-8
Ephesians 6:10-20
Mark 7:1-8,14,15,21-23
Psalm 119c

Year C
Proverbs 25:6,7
Hebrews 13:1-8
Luke 14:1,7-14
Psalm 119a

One Year
Deuteronomy 8:10-18
Galatians 5:16-24
Luke 17:11-19
Psalm 116

Prayer of the Day

O Lord Jesus Christ, preserve the congregation of believers with your never-failing mercy. Help us avoid whatever is wicked and harmful, and guide us in the way that leads to our salvation; for you live and reign with the Father and the Holy Spirit, one God, now and forever.

Verse of the Day

Alleluia. Your words became a joy to me, and the delight of my heart. Alleluia. (Jeremiah 15:16 cf. RSV)

Hymn of the Day

Year A	- Jesus, I My Cross Have Taken	(465)
Year B	- O God, My Faithful God	(459)
Year C	- O Fount of Good, for All Your Love	(524)
One Year	- Your Hand, O Lord, in Days of Old	(520)

Color: Green

436

Sixteenth Sunday after Pentecost

Lessons and Psalms

Year A
Ezekiel 33:7-11
Romans 13:1-10
Matthew 18:15-20
Psalm 51a

Year B
Isaiah 35:4-7a
James 1:17-27
Mark 7:31-37
Psalm 146

Year C
Proverbs 9:8-12
Philemon 1:1,10-21
Luke 14:25-33
Psalm 19

One Year
1 Kings 17:8-16
Galatians 5:25—6:10
Matthew 6:24-34
Psalm 62

Prayer of the Day

Let your continual mercy, O Lord, cleanse and defend your Church; and because it cannot continue in safety without your help, protect and govern it always by your goodness; for you live and reign with the Father and the Holy Spirit, one God, now and forever.

Verse of the Day

Alleluia. Rejoice in the Lord always; again I will say, Rejoice. Alleluia. (Philippians 4:4 RSV)

Hymn of the Day

Year A	- Jesus Sinners Does Receive	(304)
	- *Lord of All Nations, Grant Me Grace*	*(521)*
Year B	- Praise the Almighty; My Soul, Adore Him	(235)
Year C	- I Trust, O Christ, in You Alone	(437)
	- *Jesus Christ, My Pride and Glory*	*(464)*
One Year	- In God, My Faithful God	(438)

Color: Green

437

Seventeenth Sunday after Pentecost

Lessons and Psalms

Year A
Genesis 50:15-21
Romans 14:5-9
Matthew 18:21-35
Psalm 103

Year B
Isaiah 50:4-10
James 2:1-5,8-10,14-18
Mark 8:27-35
Psalm 116

Year C
Exodus 32:7-14
1 Timothy 1:12-17
Luke 15:1-10
Psalm 51a

One Year
1 Kings 17:17-24
Ephesians 3:13-21
Luke 7:11-17
Psalm 126

Prayer of the Day

Lord, we pray that your mercy and grace may always go before and follow after us that loving you with undivided hearts, we may be ready for every good and useful work; through your Son, Jesus Christ our Lord, who lives and reigns with you and the Holy Spirit, one God, now and forever.

Verse of the Day

Alleluia. Everything that was written in the past was written to teach us, so that through endurance and the encouragement of the Scriptures we might have hope. Alleluia. (Romans 15:4 cf. NIV)

Hymn of the Day

Year A	- Forgive Our Sins as We Forgive	(493)
Year B	- Come, Follow Me, the Savior Spoke	(453)
Year C	- Jesus Sinners Does Receive	(304)
One Year	- The Will of God Is Always Best	(435)

Color: Green

Eighteenth Sunday after Pentecost

Lessons and Psalms

Year A
Isaiah 55:6-9
Philippians 1:18b-27
Matthew 20:1-16
Psalm 27

Year B
Jeremiah 11:18-20
James 3:13-18
Mark 9:30-37
Psalm 31

Year C
Amos 8:4-7
1 Timothy 2:1-8
Luke 16:1-13
Psalm 38

One Year
Micah 6:6-8
Ephesians 4:1-6
Luke 14:1-11
Psalm 143

Prayer of the Day

Lord God, you call us to work in your kingdom and leave no one standing idle. Help us to order our lives by your wisdom and to serve you in willing obedience; through Jesus Christ, your Son, our Lord, who lives and reigns with you and the Holy Spirit, one God, now and forever.

Verse of the Day

Alleluia. My grace is sufficient for you, for my power is made perfect in weakness. Alleluia. (2 Corinthians 12:9a)

Hymn of the Day

Year A	- Salvation unto Us Has Come	(390)
Year B	- Lord of Glory, You Have Bought Us	(486)
Year C	- All Depends on Our Possessing	(421)
One Year	- The Church's One Foundation	(538)

Color: Green

439

Nineteenth Sunday after Pentecost

Lessons and Psalms

Year A	*Year B*
Ezekiel 18:1-4,25-32	Numbers 11:16,24-29
Philippians 2:1-11	James 4:7-12
Matthew 21:28-32	Mark 9:38-50
Psalm 25	Psalm 51b

Year C	*One Year*
Amos 6:1-7	Deuteronomy 10:12-21
1 Timothy 6:6-16	1 Corinthians 1:4-9
Luke 16:19-31	Matthew 22:34-46
Psalm 146	Psalm 2

Prayer of the Day

Mercifully grant, O God, that your Holy Spirit may in all things direct and rule our hearts, for without your help we are unable to please you; through Jesus Christ, your Son, our Lord, who lives and reigns with you and the Holy Spirit, one God, now and forever.

Verse of the Day

Alleluia. At the name of Jesus every knee should bow, and every tongue confess that Jesus Christ is Lord, to the glory of God the Father. Alleluia. (Philippians 2:10,11 cf. NIV)

Hymn of the Day

Year A	- Before You, God, the Judge of All	(306)
Year B	- Triune God, Oh, Be Our Stay	(192)
Year C	- We Now Implore God the Holy Ghost	(190)
One Year	- Lord, You I Love with All My Heart	(434)

Color: Green

Twentieth Sunday after Pentecost

Lessons and Psalms

Year A
Isaiah 5:1-7
Philippians 3:12-21
Matthew 21:33-43
Psalm 118

Year B
Genesis 2:18-24
Hebrews 2:9-11
Mark 10:2-16
Psalm 139b

Year C
Habakkuk 1:1-3; 2:1-4
2 Timothy 1:3-14
Luke 17:1-10
Psalm 27

One Year
Exodus 15:22-26
Ephesians 4:22-28
Matthew 9:1-8
Psalm 139a

Prayer of the Day

Almighty God, in your bountiful goodness keep us safe from every evil of body and soul. Make us ready, with cheerful hearts, to do whatever pleases you; through Jesus Christ, your Son, our Lord, who lives and reigns with you and the Holy Spirit, one God, now and forever.

Verse of the Day

Alleluia. I will proclaim your name to my people; in the midst of the congregation I will praise you. Alleluia. (Hebrews 2:12 cf. RSV)

Hymn of the Day

Year A	- Lord, Keep Us Steadfast in Your Word	(203)
Year B	- Oh, Blessed Home, Where Man and Wife	(503)
Year C	- Come, Oh, Come, Life-Giving Spirit	(181)
One Year	- Praise the Almighty; My Soul, Adore Him	(235)

Color: Green

Twenty-first Sunday after Pentecost

Lessons and Psalms

Year A	*Year B*
Isaiah 25:6-9	Amos 5:6,7,10-15
Philippians 4:4-13	Hebrews 3:1-6
Matthew 22:1-14	Mark 10:17-27
Psalm 23	Psalm 90

Year C	*One Year*
Ruth 1:1-19a	Hosea 1:2-11
2 Timothy 2:8-13	Ephesians 5:15-21
Luke 17:11-19	Matthew 22:1-14
Psalm 111	Psalm 27

Prayer of the Day

Grant, O merciful Lord, to your faithful people pardon and peace that they may be cleansed from all their sins and serve you with a quiet mind; through Jesus Christ, your Son, our Lord, who lives and reigns with you and the Holy Spirit, one God, now and forever.

Verse of the Day

Alleluia. This is the Lord, we trusted in him; let us rejoice and be glad in his salvation. Alleluia. (Isaiah 25:9b cf. NIV)

Hymn of the Day

Year A	- Jesus, Your Blood and Righteousness	(376)
	- *O Kingly Love, that Faithfully*	*(335)*
Year B	- Your Works, Not Mine, O Christ	(401)
Year C	- Your Hand, O Lord, in Days of Old	(520)
One Year	- Jesus, Your Blood and Righteousness	(376)
	- *O Kingly Love, that Faithfully*	*(335)*

Color: Green

Twenty-second Sunday after Pentecost

Lessons and Psalms

Year A	*Year B*
Isaiah 45:1-7	Isaiah 53:10-12
1 Thessalonians 1:1-5a	Hebrews 4:9-16
Matthew 22:15-21	Mark 10:35-45
Psalm 96	Psalm 22

Year C	*One Year*
Genesis 32:22-30	Deuteronomy 1:26-36
2 Timothy 3:14—4:5	Ephesians 6:10-17
Luke 18:1-8a	John 4:46-54
Psalm 121	Psalm 139b

Prayer of the Day

Lord, keep your household, the Church, in continual godliness and set us free from all adversities that, under your protection, we may serve you with true devotion and holy deeds; through Jesus Christ, your Son, our Lord, who lives and reigns with you and the Holy Spirit, one God, now and forever.

Verse of the Day

Alleluia. For we are God's workmanship, created in Christ Jesus to do good works. Alleluia. (Ephesians 2:10a)

Hymn of the Day

Year A	- All Depends on Our Possessing	(421)
Year B	- Come, Oh, Come, Life-Giving Spirit	(181)
Year C	- In You, O Lord, I Put My Trust	(448)
One Year	- Lord, Keep Us Steadfast in Your Word	(203)

Color: Green

Twenty-third Sunday after Pentecost

Lessons and Psalms

Year A
Leviticus 19:1,2,15-18
1 Thessalonians 1:5b-10
Matthew 22:34-46
Psalm 33

Year B
Jeremiah 31:7-9
Hebrews 5:1-10
Mark 10:46-52
Psalm 126

Year C
Deuteronomy 10:12-22
2 Timothy 4:6-8,16-18
Luke 18:18-27
Psalm 119b

One Year
Genesis 50:15-21
Philippians 1:3-11
Matthew 18:23-35
Psalm 38

Prayer of the Day

God, our refuge and strength, have mercy on your Church, as we come in prayer before you. Answer us not in judgment on our sins, but in peace and forgiveness; through Jesus Christ, your Son, our Lord, who lives and reigns with you and the Holy Spirit, one God, now and forever.

Verse of the Day

Alleluia. The Lord will rescue me from every evil and will bring me safely to his heavenly kingdom. Alleluia. (2 Timothy 4:18 cf. NIV)

Hymn of the Day

Year A	- Lord, You I Love with All My Heart	(434)
Year B	- In God, My Faithful God	(438)
Year C	- Before You, God, the Judge of All	(306)
One Year	- Lord Jesus Christ, the Church's Head	(536)

Color: Green

Twenty-fourth Sunday after Pentecost

Lessons and Psalms

Year A
Malachi 3:14-18
1 Thessalonians 3:7-13
Matthew 25:14-30
Psalm 92

Year B
Deuteronomy 6:1-9
Hebrews 7:23-28
Mark 12:28-34
Psalm 119a

Year C
Exodus 34:5-9
2 Thessalonians 1:1-5,11,12
Luke 19:1-10
Psalm 145

One Year
Deuteronomy 10:12-20
Philippians 3:17-21
Matthew 22:15-22
Psalm 89

Prayer of the Day

Lord God, forgive the wrongdoing of your people and be gentle with us in our weakness. Deliver us from the bondage of our sin and direct us to the path of righteousness; through Jesus Christ, your Son, our Lord, who lives and reigns with you and the Holy Spirit, one God, now and forever.

Verse of the Day

Alleluia. Grow in the grace and knowledge of our Lord and Savior Jesus Christ. Alleluia. (2 Peter 3:18a cf. NIV)

Hymn of the Day

Year A	-	Brothers, Sisters, Let Us Gladly	(484)
Year B	-	O God of Mercy, God of Might	(499)
Year C	-	God Loved the World So that He Gave	(391)
One Year	-	All Depends on Our Possessing	(421)

Color: Green

First Sunday of End Time
Reformation Sunday

Lessons and Psalms

Year A
Daniel 6:10-12,16-23
Galatians 5:1-6
Matthew 10:16-23
Psalm 46

Year B
Jeremiah 18:1-11
Revelation 14:6,7
Mark 13:5-11
Psalm 46

Year C
Jeremiah 31:31-34
Romans 3:19-28
John 8:31-36
Psalm 46

One Year
Isaiah 43:1-7
Romans 3:19-28
John 17:6-19
Psalm 46

Prayer of the Day

Gracious Lord, our refuge and strength, pour out your Holy Spirit on your faithful people. Keep them steadfast in your Word, protect and comfort them in all temptations, defend them against all their enemies, and bestow on the Church your saving peace; through your Son, Jesus Christ our Lord, who lives and reigns with you and the Holy Spirit, one God, now and forever.

Verse of the Day

Alleluia. If you continue in my Word, you are truly my disciples, and you will know the truth, and the truth will make you free. Alleluia. (John 8:31,32 cf. RSV)

Hymn of the Day

Year A   - A Mighty Fortress Is Our God   (200, 201)
Year B   - O God, Our Lord, Your Holy Word   (204)
Year C   - Salvation unto Us Has Come   (390)
One Year - Come, Holy Ghost, God and Lord   (176)

Color: Red

Second Sunday of End Time

Last Judgment

Lessons and Psalms

Year A	*Year B*
Daniel 7:9,10	Malachi 4:1,2a
1 Thessalonians 5:1-11	Hebrews 9:24-28
Matthew 25:31-46	John 5:19-24
Psalm 90	Psalm 90

Year C	*One Year*
Jeremiah 26:1-6	Jeremiah 8:4-7
2 Thessalonians 1:5-10	1 Thessalonians 4:13-18
Luke 19:11-27	Matthew 25:31-46
Psalm 90	Psalm 16

Prayer of the Day

Lord God Almighty, so rule and govern our hearts and minds by your Holy Spirit that we may always look forward to the end of this present evil age and to the day of your righteous judgment. Keep us steadfast in true and living faith and present us at last holy and blameless before you; through your Son, Jesus Christ our Lord, who lives and reigns with you and the Holy Spirit, one God, now and forever.

Verse of the Day

Alleluia. Watch therefore, for you do not know on what day your Lord is coming. Alleluia. (Matthew 24:42 RSV)

Hymn of the Day

Year A	- Day of Wrath, Oh, Day of Mourning	(209)
Year B	- My Hope Is Built on Nothing Less	(382)
Year C	- Forth in Your Name, O Lord, I Go	(456)
One Year	- The Day Is Surely Drawing Near	(207)

Color: Red

Third Sunday of End Time
Saints Triumphant

Lessons and Psalms

Year A
Isaiah 52:1-6
1 Thessalonians 4:13-18
Matthew 25:1-13
Psalm 84

Year B
Daniel 12:1-3
Hebrews 10:11-18
John 5:25-29
Psalm 118

Year C
Isaiah 65:17-25
2 Thessalonians 2:13—3:5
Luke 20:27-38
Psalm 150

One Year
Isaiah 65:17-25
1 Thessalonians 5:1-11
Matthew 25:1-13
Psalm 121

Prayer of the Day

Almighty God and Savior, you have set the final day and hour when we shall be delivered from this world of sin and death. Keep us ever watchful for the coming of your Son that we may sit with him and all your holy ones at the marriage feast in heaven; through Jesus Christ, your Son, our Lord, who lives and reigns with you and the Holy Spirit, one God, now and forever.

Verse of the Day

Alleluia. They are before the throne of God and serve him day and night in his temple. Alleluia. (Revelation 7:15a)

Hymn of the Day

Year A	-	Wake, Awake, for Night Is Flying	(206)
Year BC	-	The Day Is Surely Drawing Near	(207)
One Year	-	Wake, Awake, for Night Is Flying	(206)

Color: White

Last Sunday of End Time

Christ the King

Lessons and Psalms

Year A
Ezekiel 34:11-16,23,24
1 Corinthians 15:20-28
Matthew 27:27-31
Psalm 47

Year B
Daniel 7:13,14
Revelation 1:4b-8
John 18:33-37
Psalm 45

Year C
Jeremiah 23:2-6
Colossians 1:13-20
Luke 23:35-43
Psalm 98

One Year
Isaiah 51:4-8
Revelation 1:9-18
John 18:33-37
Psalm 45

Prayer of the Day

Lord Jesus Christ, by your victory you have broken the power of the evil one. Fill our hearts with joy and peace as we look with hope to that day when every creature in heaven and earth will acclaim you King of kings and Lord of lords to your unending praise and glory; for you live and reign with the Father and the Holy Spirit, one God, now and forever.

Verse of the Day

Alleluia. I am the Alpha and the Omega, the First and the Last, the Beginning and the End. Alleluia. (Revelation 22:13)

Hymn of the Day

Year AB   - The Head that Once Was Crowned   (217)
Year C   - Not unto Us   (392)
One Year   - The Head that Once Was Crowned   (217)

Color: White

Minor Festivals and Occasions

Minor Festivals

The Name of Jesus

New Year's Day
January 1

Lessons and Psalm

Numbers 6:22-27
Philippians 2:9-13
Luke 2:21
Psalm 8

Prayer of the Day

Eternal Son of God, on this day you were called Jesus, a name that proclaims you to be the Savior of all people. Give us strength in the new year to live each day to the honor of your name; for you live and reign with the Father and the Holy Spirit, one God, now and forever.

Verse of the Day

Alleluia. At the name of Jesus every knee should bow, and every tongue confess that Jesus Christ is Lord, to the glory of God the Father. Alleluia. (Philippians 2:10,11 cf. NIV)

Color: White

The Confession of St. Peter

January 18

Lessons and Psalm

Acts 4:8-13
2 Peter 1:1-4
Matthew 16:13-19
Psalm 18

Prayer of the Day

Almighty God, you inspired Simon Peter to confess Jesus as the Messiah and Son of the living God. Keep your Church firm on the rock of this faith that in unity and peace it may proclaim one truth and follow one Lord, your Son, our Savior Jesus Christ, who lives and reigns with you and the Holy Spirit, one God, now and forever.

Verse of the Day

Alleluia. You will be my witnesses in Jerusalem, and in all Judea and Samaria, and to the ends of the earth. Alleluia. (Acts 1:8b)

Color: White

St. Timothy, Pastor and Confessor	The Conversion of St. Paul
January 24	January 25

Lessons and Psalm

Acts 16:1-5
2 Timothy 1:1-7
John 21:15-17
Psalm 84

Lessons and Psalm

Acts 9:1-19a
Galatians 1:11-24
Luke 21:10-19
Psalm 67

Prayer of the Day

O almighty God, you have always given your Church faithful shepherds to feed and nourish your flock. Grant that all pastors may rightly preach your Word and administer your sacraments that your people may be guided in the way that leads to eternal life: through our Lord Jesus Christ, who lives and reigns with you and the Holy Spirit, one God, now and forever.

Prayer of the Day

Lord God, through the conversion of your apostle Paul you caused the light of the gospel to shine in all the world. Grant that we may follow his example and be witnesses to the truth that is in your Son, Jesus Christ our Lord, who lives and reigns with you and the Holy Spirit, one God, now and forever.

Verse of the Day

Alleluia. My mouth will tell of your righteousness, of your salvation all day long. Alleluia. (Psalm 71:15a)

Color: White

Verse of the Day

Alleluia. God has raised this Jesus to life, and we are all witnesses of the fact. Alleluia. (Acts 2:32)

Color: White

St. Titus,
Pastor and Confessor

January 26

The Presentation
of Our Lord

February 2

Lessons and Psalm

Acts 20:28-35
Titus 1:1-9
Matthew 24:42-47
Psalm 84

Lessons and Psalm

1 Samuel 1:21-28
Hebrews 2:14-18
Luke 2:22-40
Psalm 84

Prayer of the Day

O almighty God, you have always given your Church faithful shepherds to feed and nourish your flock. Grant that all pastors may rightly preach your Word and administer your sacraments that your people may be guided in the way that leads to eternal life; through our Lord Jesus Christ, who lives and reigns with you and the Holy Spirit, one God, now and forever.

Prayer of the Day

Almighty and ever-living God, grant that like Simeon and Anna of old, we may see with the eyes of faith him who is the glory of Israel and the light for all nations, your Son, Jesus Christ our Lord, whom with you and the Holy Spirit, we adore, now and forever.

Verse of the Day

Alleluia. My mouth will tell of your righteousness, of your salvation all day long. Alleluia. (Psalm 71:15a)

Color: White

Verse of the Day

Alleluia. My eyes have seen your salvation. Alleluia. (Luke 2:30)

Color: White

453

St. Matthias, Apostle
February 24

St. Joseph
March 19

Lessons and Psalm
Isaiah 66:1,2
Acts 1:15-26
Luke 6:12-16
Psalm 133-134

Lessons and Psalm
2 Samuel 7:4,8-16
Romans 4:13-18
Matthew 2:13-15,19-23
Psalm 89

Prayer of the Day

Almighty God, you chose your faithful servant Matthias to be numbered among the Twelve. Grant that your Church, being delivered from false apostles, may always be taught and guided by faithful and true pastors; through your Son, Jesus Christ our Lord, who lives and reigns with you and the Holy Spirit, one God, now and forever.

Prayer of the Day

O God, you raised up Joseph from the family of your servant David to be the guardian of your incarnate Son and the spouse of his virgin mother. Give us grace to imitate his uprightness of life and his obedience to your commands; through Jesus Christ our Lord, who lives and reigns with you and the Holy Spirit, one God, now and forever.

Verse of the Day

Alleluia. My Father will honor the one who serves me. Alleluia. (John 12:26c)

Verse of the Day

Alleluia. Joseph did what the angel had commanded and took Mary home as his wife. Alleluia. (Matthew 1:24 cf. NIV)

Color: Red

Color: White

454

*The Annunciation
of Our Lord*

March 25

St. Mark, Evangelist

April 25

Lessons and Psalm

Isaiah 7:10-14
Hebrews 10:5-10
Luke 1:26-38
Psalm 45

Lessons and Psalm

Isaiah 52:7-10
2 Timothy 4:6-11,18
Mark 1:1-15
Psalm 146

Prayer of the Day

Pour your grace into our hearts, O Lord, that we, who have known the incarnation of your Son, Jesus Christ, announced by an angel, may by his cross and passion be brought to the glory of his resurrection; who lives and reigns with you and the Holy Spirit, one God, now and forever.

Prayer of the Day

O almighty God, as you have enriched your Church with the precious gospel proclaimed by the evangelist Mark, grant us firmly to believe your good news of salvation and daily to walk according to your Word; through Jesus Christ, your Son, our Lord, who lives and reigns with you and the Holy Spirit, one God, now and forever.

Verse of the Day

Alleluia. The Mighty One has done great things for me. Alleluia. (Luke 1:49a)

Verse of the Day

Alleluia. God has raised this Jesus to life, and we are all witnesses of the fact. Alleluia. (Acts 2:32)

Color: White

Color: Red

455

*St. Philip and
St. James, Apostles*

May 1

The Visitation

May 31

Lessons and Psalm

Isaiah 30:18-21
2 Corinthians 4:1-6
John 14:8-14
Psalm 119b

Lessons and Psalm

Isaiah 11:1-5
Romans 12:9-16
Luke 1:39-47
Psalm 139b

Prayer of the Day

Almighty God, your Son, Jesus Christ, revealed himself to the Apostles Philip and James as the way, the truth, and the life. Grant that we also may know that truth, and find in him the way that leads to eternal life; for he lives and reigns with you and the Holy Spirit, one God, now and for- ever.

Prayer of the Day

Almighty God, in choosing the virgin Mary to be the mother of your Son, you made known your gracious regard for the poor, the lowly, and the despised. Grant us grace to re- ceive your Word in humility and so be made one with your Son, Jesus Christ our Lord, who lives and reigns with you and the Holy Spirit, one God, now and forever.

Verse of the Day

Alleluia. You will be my witnesses in Jerusalem, and in all Judea and Samaria, and to the ends of the earth. Alleluia. (Acts 1:8b)

Verse of the Day

Alleluia. My eyes have seen your salvation. Alleluia. (Luke 2:30)

Color: Red

Color: White

456

St. Barnabas, Apostle

June 11

The Nativity of
St. John the Baptist

June 24

Lessons and Psalm

Isaiah 42:5-12
Acts 11:19-30; 13:1-3
Matthew 11:25-30
Psalm 85

Lessons and Psalm

Isaiah 40:1-5
Acts 13:16-26
Luke 1:57-67
Psalm 85

Prayer of the Day

Grant, almighty God, that we may follow the example of your faithful servant Barnabas, who, seeking not his own renown but the well-being of your Church, gave generously of his life and possessions for the relief of the poor and the spread of the gospel; through Jesus Christ our Lord, who lives and reigns with you and the Holy Spirit, one God, now and forever.

Prayer of the Day

Almighty God, you gave your servant John the Baptist to be the forerunner of our Savior Jesus Christ. Grant us grace to repent of our sins, to boldly rebuke vice, and to patiently suffer for the truth's sake; through Jesus Christ our Lord, who lives and reigns with you and the Holy Spirit, one God, now and forever.

Verse of the Day

Alleluia. God has raised this Jesus to life, and we are all witnesses of the fact. Alleluia. (Acts 2:32)

Verse of the Day

Alleluia. John came as a witness to testify concerning the light. Alleluia. (John 1:7a cf. NIV)

Color: Red

Color: White

457

Presentation of
the Augsburg Confession

June 25

St. Peter and
St. Paul, Apostles

June 29

Lessons and Psalm

Isaiah 55:6-11
Romans 10:5-17
Matthew 10:32-39
Psalm 46

Lessons and Psalm

Ezekiel 34:11-16
1 Corinthians 3:16-23
Mark 8:27-35
Psalm 18

Prayer of the Day

O Lord, favorably receive the prayers of your Church, that being instructed by the doctrine of the blessed apostles, we may always make a pure confession of your saving truth; through Jesus Christ, your Son, our Lord, who lives and reigns with you and the Holy Spirit, one God, now and forever.

Prayer of the Day

Almighty God, you gave the Apostles Peter and Paul courage to lay down their lives for the sake of your Son. Grant that like them we may boldly confess your saving truth, and be ready at all times to lay down our lives for him who laid down his life for us; even Jesus Christ our Lord, who lives and reigns with you and the Holy Spirit, one God, now and forever.

Verse of the Day

Alleluia. Sanctify them by the truth; your word is truth. Alleluia. (John 17:17)

Verse of the Day

Alleluia. God has raised this Jesus to life, and we are all witnesses of the fact. Alleluia. (Acts 2:32)

Color: White

Color: Red

| St. Mary Magdalene | St. James the Elder, Apostle |
| July 22 | July 25 |

Lessons and Psalm

Exodus 2:1-10
Philippians 4:1-7
John 20:1,2,11-18
Psalm 73

Lessons and Psalm

1 Kings 19:9-18
Acts 11:27—12:3a
Mark 10:35-45
Psalm 103

Prayer of the Day

Almighty God, your Son, Jesus Christ, restored Mary Magdalene to health of body and mind, and called her to be a witness to his resurrection. Mercifully grant that we may be healed from our infirmities and gladly witness to you all the days of our life; through Jesus Christ our Lord, who lives and reigns with you and the Holy Spirit, one God, now and forever.

Prayer of the Day

O gracious God, we remember today your servant James, who readily followed the calling of your Son, Jesus Christ, and was first among the Twelve to suffer martyrdom for his name. Enable the leaders of your Church to forsake all false and passing allurements and follow him alone, who lives and reigns with you and the Holy Spirit, one God, now and forever.

Verse of the Day

Alleluia. My Father will honor the one who serves me. Alleluia. (John 12:26c)

Verse of the Day

Alleluia. Blessed are those who are persecuted because of righteousness, for theirs is the kingdom of heaven. Alleluia. (Matthew 5:10)

Color: White

Color: Red

459

St. Mary,
Mother of Our Lord

August 15

St. Bartholomew, Apostle

August 24

Lessons and Psalm

Isaiah 61:7-11
Galatians 4:4-7
Luke 1:46-55
Psalm 45

Lessons and Psalm

Exodus 19:1-6
1 Corinthians 4:9-15
John 1:43-51
Psalm 121

Prayer of the Day

Almighty God, you chose the blessed virgin Mary to be the mother of your incarnate Son. Grant that we, who have been redeemed by his blood, may with Mary and all the saints share in the glory of your eternal kingdom; through Jesus Christ our Lord, who lives and reigns with you and the Holy Spirit, one God, now and forever.

Prayer of the Day

Almighty God, your Son, Jesus, chose Bartholomew to be an apostle to preach the blessed gospel of salvation. Grant to your Church also in our time faithful pastors and teachers to proclaim the glory of your name; through Jesus Christ our Lord, who lives and reigns with you and the Holy Spirit, one God, now and forever.

Verse of the Day

Alleluia. The Mighty One has done great things for me. Alleluia. (Luke 1:49a)

Verse of the Day

Alleluia. How beautiful on the mountains are the feet of those who bring good news, who proclaim salvation. Alleluia. (Isaiah 52:7 cf. NIV)

Color: White

Color: Red

St. Matthew, Apostle
September 21

St. Michael and All Angels
September 29

Lessons and Psalm

Ezekiel 2:8—3:11
Ephesians 2:4-10
Matthew 9:9-13
Psalm 1

Lessons and Psalm

Daniel 10:10-14; 12:1-3
Revelation 12:7-12
Luke 10:17-20
Psalm 91

Prayer of the Day

Almighty God, your Son, our Savior, called a despised collector of taxes to become his apostle. Help us, like Saint Matthew, to forsake all covetous desires and love of riches, and so follow our Lord Jesus Christ; who lives and reigns with you and the Holy Spirit, one God, now and forever.

Prayer of the Day

Everlasting God, you have ordained and constituted in a wonderful order the ministries of angels and mortals. Mercifully grant that, as your holy angels always serve and worship you in heaven, so by your direction they may help and defend us here on earth; through your Son, Jesus Christ our Lord, who lives and reigns with you and the Holy Spirit, one God, now and forever.

Verse of the Day

Alleluia. You will be my witnesses in Jerusalem, and in all Judea and Samaria, and to the ends of the earth. Alleluia. (Acts 1:8b)

Verse of the Day

Alleluia. Praise the Lord, you his angels, who obey his word. Alleluia. (Psalm 103:20 cf. NIV)

Color: Red

Color: White

461

St. Luke, Evangelist
October 18

St. James of Jerusalem
October 23

Lessons and Psalm

Isaiah 43:8-13
2 Timothy 4:5-11
Luke 1:1-4; 24:44-53
Psalm 139b

Lessons and Psalm

Acts 15:12-22a
James 1:1-12
Matthew 13:54-58
Psalm 1

Prayer of the Day

Almighty God, you called Saint Luke the physician to reveal in his gospel the love and healing power of your Son. Grant that by hearing and believing your Word we may be healed of all sin and serve you with willing hearts; through Jesus Christ our Lord, who lives and reigns with you and the Holy Spirit, one God, now and forever.

Prayer of the Day

Grant, O God, that following the example of your servant James of Jerusalem, brother of our Lord, your Church may give itself to fervent prayer and to the healing of strife and discord; through Jesus Christ our Lord, who lives and reigns with you and the Holy Spirit, one God, now and forever.

Verse of the Day

Alleluia. How beautiful on the mountains are the feet of those who bring good news, who proclaim salvation. Alleluia. (Isaiah 52:7 cf. NIV)

Verse of the Day

Alleluia. Every good and perfect gift is from above, coming down from the Father of the heavenly lights. Alleluia. (James 1:17 cf. NIV)

Color: Red

Color: Red

462

St. Simon and
St. Jude, Apostles

October 28

Lessons and Psalm

Jeremiah 26:7-16
Jude 1-4,17-23
John 14:21-27
Psalm 119c

Prayer of the Day

O God, we thank you for the glorious company of the apostles and, especially for Saint Simon and Saint Jude. We pray that, as they were faithful and zealous in their mission, so may we with ardent devotion make known the love and mercy of our Lord and Savior Jesus Christ, who lives and reigns with you and the Holy Spirit, one God, now and forever.

Verse of the Day

Alleluia. You did not choose me, but I chose you to go and bear fruit. Alleluia. (John 15:16a cf. NIV)

Color: Red

Reformation Day

October 31

Lessons and Psalm

Isaiah 55:1-11
Galatians 3:17-22
John 6:29-35
Psalm 46

Prayer of the Day

Almighty God, through the preaching of your servants, the blessed Reformers, you caused the light of the gospel to shine forth. Grant that we may faithfully defend it against all enemies and joyfully proclaim it to the salvation of people everywhere to the glory of your holy name; through your Son, Jesus Christ our Lord, who lives and reigns with you and the Holy Spirit, one God, now and forever.

Verse of the Day

Alleluia. If you continue in my Word, you are truly my disciples, and you will know the truth, and the truth will make you free. Alleluia. (John 8:31,32 cf. RSV)

Color: Red

463

All Saints' Day

November 1

Lessons and Psalm

Isaiah 26:1-4,8,9,12,13,
19-21
Revelation 7:9-17
Matthew 5:1-12
Psalm 34

Prayer of the Day

Almighty God, you have knit your people together in one holy Church, the body of Christ our Lord. Grant us grace to follow the example of your blessed saints in lives of faith and willing service and with them at last inherit the inexpressible joys that you have prepared for those who love you; through your Son, Jesus Christ our Lord, who lives and reigns with you and the Holy Spirit, one God, now and forever.

Verse of the Day

Alleluia. They are before the throne of God and serve him day and night in his temple. Alleluia. (Revelation 7:15a)

Color: White

St. Andrew, Apostle

November 30

Lessons and Psalm

Ezekiel 3:16-21
Romans 10:10-18
John 1:35-42
Psalm 19

Prayer of the Day

Lord Jesus Christ, your apostle Saint Andrew obeyed your call without delay. Grant that we who have been called by your holy Word may likewise follow with joyful heart and life; for you live and reign with the Father and the Holy Spirit, one God, now and forever.

Verse of the Day

Alleluia. You will be my witnesses in Jerusalem, and in all Judea and Samaria, and to the ends of the earth. Alleluia. (Acts 1:8b)

Color: Red

St. Thomas, Apostle

December 21

Lessons and Psalm

Judges 6:36-40
Ephesians 4:11-16
John 20:24-29
Psalm 25

Prayer of the Day

Our Savior Jesus Christ, after your resurrection from the dead, you strengthened the faith of your apostle Saint Thomas, and he acknowledged you as Lord and God. We pray that you would also keep us steadfast in this true and saving faith and by your Word and sacrament banish every doubt; for you live and reign with the Father and the Holy Spirit, one God, now and forever.

Verse of the Day

Alleluia. You will be my witnesses in Jerusalem, and in all Judea and Samaria, and to the ends of the earth. Alleluia. (Acts 1:8b)

Color: Red

St. Stephen, Deacon and Martyr

December 26

Lessons and Psalm

Jeremiah 26:1-9,12-15
Acts 6:8—7:2a,51-60
Matthew 23:34-39
Psalm 31

Prayer of the Day

Eternal Son of God, accompany us with your grace, that whenever we suffer for your Word, we may follow the example of Saint Stephen, your first martyr, and like him, commending our cause to you, be ready to pray for those who would do us harm; for you live and reign with the Father and the Holy Spirit, one God, now and forever.

Verse of the Day

Alleluia. Blessed are those who are persecuted because of righteousness, for theirs is the kingdom of heaven. Alleluia. (Matthew 5:10)

Color: Red

St. John, Apostle and Evangelist

December 27
Lessons and Psalm
Genesis 1:1-5,26-31
1 John 1:1—2:2
John 21:20-25
Psalm 8

The Holy Innocents, Martyrs

December 28
Lessons and Psalm
Jeremiah 31:15-17
1 Peter 4:12-19
Matthew 2:13-18
Psalm 130

Prayer of the Day

Merciful Lord, cast the bright beams of your light on the whole Christian Church, that, being instructed by the teachings of your blessed apostle and evangelist John, we may always walk in the light of your saving truth, until at last we inherit the gift of eternal life; through your Son, Jesus Christ, who lives and reigns with you and the Holy Spirit, one God, now and forever.

Prayer of the Day

We remember today, O God, the slaughter of the holy innocents of Bethlehem by order of King Herod. Receive into the arms of your mercy all who lay down their lives for your sake, and prepare us by your grace to be ready at all times to live and die for you; through your Son, Jesus Christ our Lord, who lives and reigns with you and the Holy Spirit, one God, now and forever.

Verse of the Day

Alleluia. The message of the cross is the power of God to us who are being saved. Alleluia. (1 Corinthians 1:18 cf. NIV)

Verse of the Day

Alleluia. Blessed are those who are persecuted because of righteousness, for theirs is the kingdom of heaven. Alleluia. (Matthew 5:10)

Color: White

Color: Red

466

New Year's Eve

December 31

Lessons and Psalm

Isaiah 51:1-6
1 Peter 1:22-25
Luke 13:6-9
Psalm 90

Prayer of the Day

Eternal Father, before whom all generations rise and fall, teach us to think earnestly on the brevity of our lives and on the immensity of your goodness. Help us to enter the new year trusting in the name of your Son and walking in the way of his peace; through Jesus Christ our Lord, who lives and reigns with you and the Holy Spirit, one God, now and forever.

Verse of the Day

Alleluia. Your word is a lamp to my feet and a light for my path. Alleluia. (Psalm 119:105)

Color: White

Occasions

Christian Education

Church Anniversary

Lessons and Psalm

Deuteronomy 11:1-7,16-21
2 Timothy 3:14-17
Matthew 7:24-27
Psalm 78

Lessons and Psalm

Deuteronomy 7:6-9
Revelation 3:7-13
John 17:1,13-26
Psalm 100

Prayer of the Day

Almighty God, you have committed to your Church the task of making disciples of all nations. Enlighten with your wisdom those who teach and those who learn, that, rejoicing in the knowledge of your truth, they may worship and serve you from generation to generation; through Jesus Christ our Lord.

Prayer of the Day

O God, you have promised to be with your Church forever. We thank you for those who founded this community of believers and for the signs of your favor over these past years. Increase our faith, knit us together in the bonds of love, and make our fellowship an example to all people; through Jesus Christ our Lord.

Verse of the Day

Alleluia. The Lord gives wisdom, and from his mouth come knowledge and understanding. Alleluia. (Proverbs 2:6 cf. NIV)

Verse of the Day

Alleluia. Not to us, O Lord, not to us but to your name be the glory, because of your love and faithfulness. Alleluia. (Psalm 115:1 cf. NIV)

Color: Color of the Season

Color: Red

Church Dedication

Lessons and Psalm

1 Kings 8:54-63
Ephesians 2:8-10,19-22
Matthew 16:13-19
Psalm 84

Prayer of the Day

O almighty, everlasting God, you have joined together all believers into one spiritual temple in Christ. Look with favor on this church, which we have built to be a dwelling place for your glorious name and a house of prayer for your people. Accept it, O Lord, and bless our coming in and our going out from this time forth even forevermore; through Jesus Christ our Lord.

Verse of the Day

Alleluia. I rejoiced with those who said to me, "Let us go to the house of the Lord." Alleluia. (Psalm 122:1 cf. NIV)

Color: Red

Environment

Lessons and Psalm

Genesis 1:26-31a
Romans 8:18-23
Matthew 6:25-34
Psalm 65

Prayer of the Day

Almighty God, in giving us dominion over things on earth, you made us fellow workers in your creation. Give us wisdom and reverence to use the resources of nature, so that no one may suffer from our abuse of them, and that generations yet to come may continue to praise you for your bounty; through your Son, Jesus Christ our Lord.

Verse of the Day

Alleluia. The earth is the Lord's, and everything in it, the world, and all who live in it. Alleluia. (Psalm 24:1 cf. NIV)

Color: Color of the Season

469

Evangelism

Family

Lessons and Psalm

Acts 8:26-39
1 Peter 3:8-18a
John 1:35-42
Psalm 51b

Lessons and Psalm

Joshua 24:14-18
Colossians 3:12-21
Mark 3:31-35
Psalm 145

Prayer of the Day

Lord God of our salvation, you have called us to be witnesses of the good news that in Christ the world has been reconciled to yourself. Inspire our witness that all may know the power of his forgiveness and the hope of his resurrection; through your Son, Jesus Christ our Lord.

Prayer of the Day

Almighty God, our heavenly Father, we commend to your care all the homes where your people live. Fill them with faith, virtue, knowledge, moderation, patience, and godliness. Bind together in enduring affection those who have become one in marriage. Let children and parents have full respect and affection for one another; through Jesus Christ our Lord.

Verse of the Day

Alleluia. Those who had been scattered preached the Word wherever they went. Alleluia. (Acts 8:4 cf. NIV)

Verse of the Day

Alleluia. Be imitators of God as dearly loved children and live a life of love. Alleluia. (Ephesians 5:1,2a cf. NIV)

Color: Color of the Season

Color: Color of the Season

470

Home Missions

Installation/Ordination

Lessons and Psalm

Jonah 3:1-10
Romans 10:8-15
Matthew 9:35-38
Psalm 96

Lessons and Psalm

Joshua 1:1-9
1 Peter 5:1-7
Matthew 9:35—10:4
Psalm 46

Prayer of the Day

Merciful Father, your kindness caused the light of the gospel to shine among us. Use us now as instruments of your love to reach out with the message of salvation to all people. Bless those who labor in the mission fields of our nation and grant success to their witness that many may be freed from sin; through Jesus Christ our Lord.

Prayer of the Day

Almighty God, look with favor on those whom you have called to minister to your people. Fill them with faithfulness to your doctrine and clothe them with holiness of life that they may joyfully serve to the glory of your name and for the benefit of your Church; through your Son, Jesus Christ our Lord.

Verse of the Day

Alleluia. How beautiful on the mountains are the feet of those who bring good news, who proclaim salvation. Alleluia. (Isaiah 52:7 cf. NIV)

Verse of the Day

Alleluia. Let the one who has my word speak it faithfully. Alleluia. (Jeremiah 23:28 cf. NIV)

Color: Red

Color: Red

Nation   *Organ Dedication*

Lessons and Psalm

Deuteronomy 6:4-7,17
Romans 13:1-7
Matthew 22:15-22
Psalm 148

Lessons and Psalm

Exodus 15:1-13
Revelation 5:6-14
Luke 19:37-40
Psalm 150

Prayer of the Day

Lord, keep this nation under your care. Bless the leaders of our land that we may be people at peace among ourselves and a blessing to other nations of the earth. Help us elect trustworthy leaders, contribute to wise decisions for the general welfare, and serve you faithfully in our generation to the honor of your holy name; through Jesus Christ our Lord.

Prayer of the Day

God of majesty, saints and angels delight to worship you in heaven. Accept our earthly sacrifices of praise and grant that the organ we today dedicate may serve to glorify your holy name and lead the songs of your thankful people; through Jesus Christ our Lord, who lives with you and the Holy Spirit, one God, now and forever.

Verse of the Day

Alleluia. Righteousness exalts a nation, but sin is a disgrace to any people. Alleluia. (Proverbs 14:34)

Verse of the Day

Alleluia. How good it is to sing praises to our God, how pleasant and fitting to praise him! Alleluia. (Psalm 147:1 cf. NIV)

Color: Color of the Season

Color: Red

School Dedication

Lessons and Psalm

Deuteronomy 6:1-9
Ephesians 4:7-15
Mark 10:13-16
Psalm 119c

Prayer of the Day

O Almighty, Everlasting God, you have granted us grace to erect this place of learning. Come and be present in this building by your Word that it may be a workshop of your Spirit in which our youth will be made wise for salvation and be trained for useful service in this life to the glory of your holy name; through your Son, Jesus Christ our Lord.

Verse of the Day

Alleluia. Train a child in the way he should go, and when he is old he will not turn from it. Alleluia. (Proverbs 22:6)

Color: Red

Social Concern

Lessons and Psalm

Leviticus 19:9-16
James 2:14-26
Luke 6:20-36
Psalm 103

Prayer of the Day

Lord God, your Son came among us to serve and not to be served, and to give his life for the sins of the world. Lead us by his love to serve those to whom the world offers no comfort and little help. Through us give hope to the hopeless, love to the unloved, peace to the troubled, and rest to the weary; through your Son, Jesus Christ our Lord.

Verse of the Day

Alleluia. As we have opportunity, let us do good to all people, especially to those who belong to the family of believers. Alleluia. (Galatians 6:10 cf. NIV)

Color: Color of the Season

473

Stewardship	*Synod*
Lessons and Psalm	**Lessons and Psalm**
Proverbs 3:1-10	Isaiah 49:1-6
2 Corinthians 8:1-9	Philippians 1:3-11
Matthew 25:14-30	John 17:13-21
Psalm 62	Psalm 133-134

Prayer of the Day

O merciful Creator, your hand is open wide to satisfy the needs of every living creature. Make us always thankful for your loving providence; and grant that we, remembering the richness of your grace, may be faithful stewards of all your good gifts; through your Son, Jesus Christ our Lord.

Prayer of the Day

Lord of the Church, you have united us in faith and worship to make disciples of all nations and to nurture believers for lives of Christian service. Guide our leaders and help them fulfill their responsibilities with patience and understanding. Keep the congregations of the synod faithful to your Word and give them a willingness to support the worldwide mission of your Church to the glory of God; through Jesus Christ our Lord.

Verse of the Day

Alleluia. I live by faith in the Son of God, who loved me and gave himself for me. Alleluia. (Galatians 2:20 cf. NIV)

Verse of the Day

Alleluia. How good and pleasant it is when brothers live together in unity! Alleluia. (Psalm 133:1)

Color: Color of the Season

Color: Red

Thanksgiving Day

Lessons and Psalm

> Deuteronomy 8:10-18
> Philippians 4:10-20
> Luke 17:11-19
> Psalm 100

Prayer of the Day

Almighty God our Father, your generous goodness comes to us new every day. By the work of your Spirit lead us to acknowledge your goodness, give thanks for your benefits, and serve you in willing obedience; through your Son, Jesus Christ our Lord.

Verse of the Day

Alleluia. Give thanks to the Lord, for he is good. His love endures forever. Alleluia. (Psalm 136:1 cf. NIV)

Color: White

Time of Crisis

Lessons and Psalm

1 Jn 5:1-9

> Nehemiah 1:4-11a
> 2 Corinthians 1:3-7
> Luke 12:22-34
> Psalm 91

Prayer of the Day

Lord God, accept our humble confession of the wrongs we have done, the injustice to which we have been party, and the countless denials of your mercy we have expressed. Cleanse us by your grace, deliver us from this time of crisis, and turn us toward your love; through your Son, Jesus Christ our Lord.

Verse of the Day

Alleluia. God is our refuge and strength, an ever-present help in trouble. Alleluia. (Psalm 46:1)

Color: Color of the Season

Worker Training	*World Missions*

Lessons and Psalm

1 Kings 19:9-21
Romans 12:1-8
Matthew 20:1-16
Psalm 119a

Lessons and Psalm

Isaiah 60:1-6
Romans 15:23-33
Matthew 28:18-20
Psalm 67

Prayer of the Day

Lord of the harvest, inspire the hearts of many to offer themselves for the public ministry of your church. Look with favor on our schools, blessing those who teach and those who learn that they may apply themselves diligently to your will and faithfully to your service; through Jesus Christ our Lord.

Prayer of the Day

O God, you have made of one blood all the peoples of the earth and have sent your messengers to preach peace to those who are far off and to those who are near. Grant that by the witness of your Church many may be brought into your kingdom and worship you, the only true God; through your Son, Jesus Christ our Lord.

Verse of the Day

Alleluia. He gave some to be pastors and teachers, to prepare God's people for works of service. Alleluia. (Ephesians 4:11,12a cf. NIV)

Verse of the Day

Alleluia. Declare his glory among the nations, his marvelous deeds among all peoples. Alleluia. (Psalm 96:3)

Color: Color of the Season

Color: Red

Psalm Prayers

Psalm 1

Lord God, you have planted us like trees beside streams of water. Grant that we may ever delight in your Word and yield abundant fruit in our lives; through Jesus Christ, your Son, our Lord.

Psalm 2

Lord God, you anointed your Son to be king for the sake of your Church. Help us, as members of his kingdom, to serve him faithfully and to come to the full knowledge of his grace and glory, who lives and reigns with you and the Holy Spirit, one God, now and forever.

Psalm 6

Lord God, you are merciful and tenderhearted, abounding in love and faithfulness. Turn to us in our anguish over sin and hear our cry for mercy that we may be at peace; through your Son, Jesus Christ our Lord.

Psalm 8

Almighty God, by the coming of your Son into the world, you have rescued us from sin and death. Grant that with joyful hearts we may ever serve him whom you have made ruler over all things to the praise of his glorious name, who lives and reigns with you and the Holy Spirit, one God, now and forever.

Psalm 16

Lord Jesus, keep our minds fixed on your precious Word and our thoughts on your glorious victory over death so that we may know the joy of your resurrection and share the pleasures of the saints at your right hand, where you live and reign with the Father and the Holy Spirit, one God, now and forever.

Psalm 18

Lord God, our mighty Rock of salvation, give us such strength of faith that we may cling to you in every trouble and, armed with your strong Word, be preserved from every assault of Satan and his forces of evil; through your Son, Jesus Christ our Lord.

Psalm 19

O Lord, you speak to us in the wonders of your creation and in the words of your precious book. Give us ears to hear your voice and eyes to see your goodness that we may joyfully serve you all our days; through Jesus Christ, your Son, our Lord.

Psalm 22

Father, when your Son hung on the cross, he cried out to you in agony and grief. You gave him the strength to endure so that death might be destroyed and life restored. Have mercy on us all our days and preserve us in true faith unto life everlasting; through your Son, Jesus Christ our Lord.

Psalm 23

Lord Jesus Christ, Shepherd of the Church, in the waters of baptism you have given us new life and at your table you nourish us with the food of salvation. Lead us along safe paths through the darkness of this world, dispel the terrors of death, and bring us at last to your house, where you dwell with the Father and the Holy Spirit, one God, now and forever.

Psalm 24

Lord God, Ruler of heaven and earth, cleanse our lives and purify our hearts so that your Son, the King of glory, may come in and lead us rejoicing to your heavenly city, where with the Holy Spirit you live and reign, one God, now and forever.

Psalm 25

O God, compassionate Father and Friend, remember not our sins but rather remember your love and mercy. Relieve our distress and satisfy us with eternal peace through your Son, Jesus Christ our Lord.

Psalm 27

Gracious Father, you have been the light and salvation of your people in every age. Bring us, we pray, through the troubles of this present life that we may see your goodness in eternity; through your Son, Jesus Christ our Lord.

Psalm 30

God our Father, you work all things for the good of those who love you. Be not deaf to our cry for mercy but rather turn our mourning into joy that our hearts may sing your praise; through your Son, Jesus Christ our Lord.

Psalm 31

God, our Rock and Fortress, protect your people, who confess your name, and strengthen the hearts of those who trust your mercy that they may proclaim your goodness and praise your unfailing love; through your Son, Jesus Christ our Lord.

Psalm 32

Gracious Father in heaven, in countless ways we have transgressed against you. But you have been merciful to us and have forgiven the guilt of our sin. Surround us with your unfailing love that we may rejoice in your great goodness now and forever; through your Son, Jesus Christ our Lord.

Psalm 33

Lord God, through your Son you made the heavens and the earth; through him you continue to rule over all things. Make us, your chosen people, witnesses of your power and heralds of your glory to the praise of your unfailing love; through your Son, Jesus Christ our Lord.

Psalm 34

Dearest Lord, helper of the weary and the brokenhearted, we have tasted and seen that you are good and ready to help in time of trouble. Calm our minds with peace and make us radiant with joy; through your Son, Jesus Christ our Lord.

479

Psalm 38

Lord our God, you did not forget the pierced body of your Son and his sighing was not hidden from you. In your kindness look also on us, your children, weighed down with sins, and grant us the fullness of your mercy; through Jesus Christ, your Son, our Lord.

Psalms 42-43

God of hope, send the Holy Spirit to fill us with all joy and peace in believing, so that we may throw off the cares that disturb us and come into your presence to praise you with our whole being; through your Son, Jesus Christ our Lord.

Psalm 45

Lord God, you called the Church to be the bride of Christ and to listen always to the voice of the Bridegroom. Anoint our hearts with the oil of joy that we may serve you in righteousness and sing your praises now and forever; through your Son, Jesus Christ our Lord.

Psalm 46

Lord God, our refuge and strength, when the restless powers of this world and the fury of Satan rise up against your holy city, watch over it and keep it safe. Be with us in every time of trouble and bring us to the new Jerusalem where you live and reign, one God, now and forever.

Psalm 47

Lord Jesus, your Father raised you on high, seated you at his right hand, and appointed you to be head over everything for the sake of the Church. Gather the elect from all nations into your Church and make them a holy people to praise and adore you, who lives and reigns with the Father and the Holy Spirit, one God, now and forever.

Psalm 51a

Almighty and merciful Father, you freely forgive those who, as David of old, acknowledge and confess their sins. Create in us

480

pure hearts, and wash away all our sins in the blood of your dear Son, Jesus Christ our Lord.

Psalm 51b

Lord God, with contrite hearts and afflicted spirits we come to you for healing and help. Restore to us the joy of your salvation and refresh us with your Holy Spirit that we may declare your praise and teach your saving ways; through Jesus Christ, your Son, our Lord.

Psalm 62

Lord God, in this changing world we look to you as our unchanging rock of refuge and hope. Hear us as we plead for your mercy, and grant us your saving grace and protection; through your Son, Jesus Christ our Lord.

Psalm 65

Bountiful Lord God, your presence fills our hearts with joy and your blessing nourishes our souls with peace. Enlighten us by your Holy Spirit that we may see and appreciate these gifts as tokens of your amazing love to your glory and praise; through Jesus Christ, your Son, our Lord.

Psalm 66

Almighty Father, by the waters of baptism you have clothed us in the robe of your Son's righteousness and have given us a new heart to hate sin. Preserve us in this saving faith and hear us as we lift our voices in songs of praise for your unfailing power and love; through your Son, Jesus Christ our Lord.

Psalm 67

Gracious and merciful God, fill our hearts with joy and confidence so that with all boldness we may proclaim the story of your salvation among all the peoples of the earth to the praise of your great name; through Jesus Christ, your Son, our Lord.

Psalm 71

Lord God, support us all the years of our lives that we may follow your gracious will both in good times and bad, that our lives may be an unending testimony to your love and faithfulness; through your Son, Jesus Christ our Lord.

Psalm 72

Almighty God, we praise you for the gracious rule of your Son, Jesus Christ. Let his kingdom come to us and to all people so that the whole earth may know his saving help and be filled with his glory, who with you and the Holy Spirit lives and reigns, one God, now and forever.

Psalm 73

Father, your Son endured the agony of the cross so that by his death and resurrection we might become heirs of eternal life. Fill us with the joy and peace of believing as you guide us on the way that leads to the heavenly country where you live and reign with your Son and the Holy Spirit, one God, now and forever.

Psalm 78

Let your Word, loving Father, be a lamp for our feet and a light to our path so that we and our children may understand what you would have us know and believe, as we walk on the way that leads to eternal life; through Jesus Christ, your Son, our Lord.

Psalm 84

Almighty God, grant that during our earthly pilgrimage we may so treasure your Word and sacraments that being nourished in faith we may one day dwell in the courts of heaven to praise you forever; through your Son, Jesus Christ our Lord.

Psalm 85

God of love and faithfulness, you showed favor to your people by sending your one and only Son to be our Savior. Help us to trust in him as our gracious Redeemer and so enjoy the peace he came to bring, who lives and reigns with you and the Holy Spirit, one God, now and forever.

Psalm 89

Lord, we rejoice in you and acclaim your love and faithfulness. Grant that as we have sung your praises here on earth, so we may proclaim your wonders with all your saints in eternity; through Jesus Christ, your Son, our Lord.

Psalm 90

Eternal God and Father, keep us mindful of the shortness and frailty of this present life. Give us hearts of wisdom that we may cling in faith to Jesus, our Savior, and use the time of our pilgrimage on earth to serve him with joyful hearts, who lives and reigns with you and the Holy Spirit, one God, now and forever.

Psalm 91

Father in heaven, teach us by the perfect obedience of your Son to find in your strong Word a weapon for resisting the temptations of the evil one. Shield us from harm and danger by commanding your angels to guard us in all our ways; through Jesus Christ, your Son, our Lord.

Psalm 92

O Lord, spare us from the folly of wickedness and the pursuit of evil. Make us rejoice in your saving acts that we who have been redeemed by your Son may abound in works of faith, hope, and love; through Jesus Christ, your Son, our Lord.

Psalm 96

Lord Jesus Christ, eternal Word of the Father, when you became flesh and made your home among us, the heavens were glad and the earth rejoiced. In hope and love we await your return. Help us to proclaim your glory to those who do not know you, until the whole earth sings a new song to you and the Father and the Holy Spirit, one God, now and forever.

Psalm 98

Lord Jesus, by your gracious coming into the world you destroyed death and made all things new. Grant that we may never tire of proclaiming your salvation to the ends of the earth; for you live and reign with the Father and the Holy Spirit, one God, now and forever.

Psalm 100

God our Father, you made us, and we belong to you. Keep us mindful of your goodness that with thankful hearts we may sing your praise who alone is worthy of honor and glory together with your Son and the Holy Spirit, one God, now and forever.

Psalm 103

Good and gracious God, you have compassion for the sinner, as a father has compassion for his children. Forgive the sins of your people, heal our weaknesses, and crown our lives with your love, that with all the saints and angels we may glorify you, Father, Son, and Holy Spirit, now and forever.

Psalm 111

God of majesty and power, the works of your hands are gracious and glorious, worthy of praise. Fill us with awe and reverence for your mighty deeds that we may follow your precepts all our days; through Jesus Christ, your Son, our Lord.

Psalm 116

God of mercy and might, through the resurrection of your Son you have freed us from the anguish of guilt and the bonds of death. Be with us on our pilgrimage and help us glorify you in the presence of all your people; through Jesus Christ our Lord.

Psalm 118

Lord Jesus, when you rose victorious from death, you gave us a day of great rejoicing. The stone that the builders rejected has become the cornerstone of our faith. Let cries of joy and exultation ring out to celebrate the good news of your resurrection, for you live and reign with the Father and the Holy Spirit, one God, now and forever.

Psalm 119a,b,c

O Lord, your Word is useful for teaching, for reproof, for correction, and for training in righteousness. Guide our footsteps by your Word so that we may remain steadfast in faith, love you with all our hearts, and love our neighbor as ourselves; through Jesus Christ, your Son, our Lord.

Psalm 121

Lord God, you never slumber nor sleep, but your eyes are always open to our needs. Watch over our welfare on this perilous journey, shade us from the dangers that surround us, and keep us safe from harm; through Jesus Christ, your Son, our Lord.

Psalm 126

Lord Jesus, in this world we experience pain and sorrow. But you promise that our tears, like seed sown in the earth, will bring a rich harvest of joy. Sustain us by this hope and keep us watchful for your coming, for you live and reign with the Father and the Holy Spirit, one God, now and forever.

Psalm 130

God of might and compassion, open your ears to the prayers of your people, who wait for you. Do not leave us in the depths of our sins, but listen to your Church pleading for the fullness of your redemption; through Jesus Christ our Lord.

Psalm 133-134

Lord Jesus, where two or three gather in your name, you promised to be with them and share their fellowship. Look on us, your family, and graciously bless us with unity and harmony; for you live and reign with the Father and the Holy Spirit, one God, now and forever.

Psalm 139a

Eternal Father, ruler of wind and wave, comfort our hearts with the assurance that wherever we might be, your right hand holds us fast and your Spirit guides our way; through Jesus Christ, your Son, our Lord.

Psalm 139b

Almighty Father, your creation is beyond description and your power beyond measuring. In your wisdom and love you knit us together in our mothers' wombs and counted out days for our use. May our praise answer for your goodness; through Jesus Christ, your Son, our Lord.

Psalm 143

Lord Jesus, you bring light to those who dwell in darkness and make your love known to them. Enter not into judgment with your servants, but strengthen us in the saving faith and guide us into the land of perfect peace where with the Father and the Holy Spirit you live and reign, one God, now and forever.

Psalm 145

Loving Father, you are faithful in your promises and tender in your compassion. Hear the cries of all who call on you for mercy, and satisfy their needs according to your gracious purpose; through Jesus Christ, your Son, our Lord.

Psalm 146

God of glory and power, happy indeed are all who trust in you and not in human wisdom. Grant that casting all our care on you, we may enjoy your gracious favor and sing your praises now and forever; through Jesus Christ, your Son, our Lord.

Psalm 148

God Most High, by your Word you created a wondrous universe, and through your Spirit you breathed into it the breath of life. Accept creation's hymn of praise from our lips, and let the praise that is sung in heaven resound in the heart of every creature on earth, to the glory of the Father, and the Son, and the Holy Spirit, now and forever.

Psalm 150

Lord God, unite our voices with the praise of all creation, that we may worthily magnify your excellent greatness; through your Son, Jesus Christ our Lord, who lives and reigns with you and the Holy Spirit, one God, now and forever.

Copyright Information

Prayer of the Day—Sundays and Major Festivals

First Sunday in Advent: Adapted and reprinted from *Lutheran Book of Worship,* copyright © 1978, by permission of Augsburg Fortress.

Second Sunday in Advent: Adapted and reprinted from *Lutheran Book of Worship,* copyright © 1978, by permission of Augsburg Fortress.

Third Sunday in Advent: © 1993 Northwestern Publishing House.

Fourth Sunday in Advent: Adapted and reprinted from *Lutheran Book of Worship,* copyright © 1978, by permission of Augsburg Fortress.

The Nativity of Our Lord—Christmas Eve: © 1993 Northwestern Publishing House.

The Nativity of Our Lord—Christmas Day: © 1993 Northwestern Publishing House.

First Sunday after Christmas: © 1993 Northwestern Publishing House.

Second Sunday after Christmas: Adapted and reprinted from *Lutheran Book of Worship,* copyright © 1978, by permission of Augsburg Fortress.

The Epiphany of Our Lord: © 1993 Northwestern Publishing House.

First Sunday after the Epiphany—The Baptism of Our Lord: Adapted and reprinted from *Lutheran Book of Worship,* copyright © 1978, by permission of Augsburg Fortress.

Second Sunday after the Epiphany: public domain.

Third Sunday after the Epiphany: Adapted and reprinted from *Lutheran Book of Worship,* copyright © 1978, by permission of Augsburg Fortress.

Fourth Sunday after the Epiphany: © 1993 Northwestern Publishing House.

Fifth Sunday after the Epiphany: Adapted and reprinted from *Lutheran Book of Worship,* copyright © 1978, by permission of Augsburg Fortress.

Sixth Sunday after the Epiphany: © 1993 Northwestern Publishing House.

Seventh Sunday after the Epiphany: © 1993 Northwestern Publishing House.

Eighth Sunday after the Epiphany: © 1993 Northwestern Publishing House.

Last Sunday after the Epiphany—The Transfiguration of Our Lord: public domain.

Ash Wednesday: © 1993 Northwestern Publishing House.

First Sunday in Lent: Adapted and reprinted from *Lutheran Book of Worship,* copyright © 1978, by permission of Augsburg Fortress.

Second Sunday in Lent: public domain.

Third Sunday in Lent: © 1993 Northwestern Publishing House.

Fourth Sunday in Lent: © 1993 Northwestern Publishing House.

Fifth Sunday in Lent: From *Lutheran Worship* © 1982 Concordia Publishing House. Reprinted by permission.

Sixth Sunday in Lent—Palm Sunday: Adapted and reprinted from *Lutheran Book of Worship,* copyright © 1978, by permission of Augsburg Fortress.

Maundy Thursday: © 1993 Northwestern Publishing House.

Good Friday: Adapted and reprinted from *Lutheran Book of Worship,* copyright © 1978, by permission of Augsburg Fortress.

The Resurrection of Our Lord—Easter Dawn: public domain.

The Resurrection of Our Lord—Easter Day: © 1993 Northwestern Publishing House.

Second Sunday of Easter: © 1993 Northwestern Publishing House.

Third Sunday of Easter: Adapted and reprinted from *Lutheran Book of Worship,* copyright © 1978, by permission of Augsburg Fortress.

Fourth Sunday of Easter: © 1993 Northwestern Publishing House.

Fifth Sunday of Easter: Adapted and reprinted from *Lutheran Book of Worship,* copyright © 1978, by permission of Augsburg Fortress.

Sixth Sunday of Easter: © 1993 Northwestern Publishing House.

The Ascension of Our Lord: © 1993 Northwestern Publishing House.

Seventh Sunday of Easter: © 1993 Northwestern Publishing House.

The Coming of the Holy Spirit—The Day of Pentecost: © 1993 Northwestern Publishing House.

First Sunday after Pentecost—The Holy Trinity: © 1993 Northwestern Publishing House.

Second Sunday after Pentecost: © 1993 Northwestern Publishing House.

Third Sunday after Pentecost: © 1993 Northwestern Publishing House.

Fourth Sunday after Pentecost: © 1993 Northwestern Publishing House.

Fifth Sunday after Pentecost: © 1993 Northwestern Publishing House.

Sixth Sunday after Pentecost: Reprinted from *Lutheran Book of Worship,* copyright © 1978, by permission of Augsburg Fortress.

Seventh Sunday after Pentecost: © 1993 Northwestern Publishing House.

Eighth Sunday after Pentecost: Adapted and reprinted from *Lutheran Book of Worship,* copyright © 1978, by permission of Augsburg Fortress.

Ninth Sunday after Pentecost: From *Lutheran Worship* © 1982 Concordia Publishing House. Reprinted by permission.

Tenth Sunday after Pentecost: © 1993 Northwestern Publishing House.

Eleventh Sunday after Pentecost: © 1993 Northwestern Publishing House.

Twelfth Sunday after Pentecost: Adapted and reprinted from *Lutheran Book of Worship,* copyright © 1978, by permission of Augsburg Fortress.

Thirteenth Sunday after Pentecost: © 1993 Northwestern Publishing House.

Fourteenth Sunday after Pentecost: From *The Lutheran Hymnal* © 1941 Concordia Publishing House. Reprinted by permission.

Fifteenth Sunday after Pentecost: © 1993 Northwestern Publishing House.

Sixteenth Sunday after Pentecost: From *The Lutheran Hymnal* © 1941 Concordia Publishing House. Reprinted by permission.

Seventeenth Sunday after Pentecost: © 1993 Northwestern Publishing House.

Eighteenth Sunday after Pentecost: © 1993 Northwestern Publishing House.

Nineteenth Sunday after Pentecost: © 1993 Northwestern Publishing House.

Twentieth Sunday after Pentecost: © 1993 Northwestern Publishing House.

Twenty-first Sunday after Pentecost: From *The Lutheran Hymnal* © 1941 Concordia Publishing House. Reprinted by permission.

Twenty-second Sunday after Pentecost: © 1993 Northwestern Publishing House.

Twenty-third Sunday after Pentecost: © 1993 Northwestern Publishing House.

Twenty-fourth Sunday after Pentecost: © 1993 Northwestern Publishing House.

First Sunday of End Time—Reformation Sunday: Reprinted from *Service Book and Hymnal,* copyright © 1958, by permission of Augsburg Fortress.

Second Sunday of End Time—Last Judgment: © 1993 Northwestern Publishing House.

Third Sunday of End Time—Saints Triumphant: © 1993 Northwestern Publishing House.

Last Sunday of End Time—Christ the King: © 1993 Northwestern Publishing House.

Prayer of the Day—Minor Festivals

The Name of Jesus/New Year's Day: © 1993 Northwestern Publishing House.

The Confession of St. Peter: Adapted and reprinted from *Lutheran Book of Worship,* copyright © 1978, by permission of Augsburg Fortress.

St. Timothy, Pastor and Confessor: From *Lutheran Worship* © 1982 Concordia Publishing House. Reprinted by permission.

The Conversion of St. Paul: © 1993 Northwestern Publishing House.

St. Titus, Pastor and Confessor: From *Lutheran Worship* © 1982 Concordia Publishing House. Reprinted by permission.

The Presentation of Our Lord: © 1993 Northwestern Publishing House.

St. Matthias, Apostle: Adapted and reprinted from *Lutheran Book of Worship,* copyright © 1978, by permission of Augsburg Fortress.

St. Joseph: public domain.

The Annunciation of Our Lord: Adapted and reprinted from *Lutheran Book of Worship,* copyright © 1978, by permission of Augsburg Fortress.

St. Mark, Evangelist: © 1993 Northwestern Publishing House.

St. Philip and St. James, Apostles: © 1993 Northwestern Publishing House.

The Visitation: Adapted and reprinted from *Lutheran Book of Worship,* copyright © 1978, by permission of Augsburg Fortress.

St. Barnabas, Apostle: Adapted and reprinted from *Lutheran Book of Worship,* copyright © 1978, by permission of Augsburg Fortress.

The Nativity of St. John the Baptist: public domain.

Presentation of the Augsburg Confession: © 1993 Northwestern Publishing House.

St. Peter and St. Paul, Apostles: From *Lutheran Worship* © 1982 Concordia Publishing House. Reprinted by permission.

St. Mary Magdalene: Reprinted from *Lutheran Book of Worship,* copyright © 1978, by permission of Augsburg Fortress.

St. James the Elder, Apostle: From *Lutheran Worship* © 1982 Concordia Publishing House. Reprinted by permission.

St. Mary, Mother of Our Lord: Adapted and reprinted from *Lutheran Book of Worship,* copyright © 1978, by permission of Augsburg Fortress.

St. Bartholomew, Apostle: From *Lutheran Worship* © 1982 Concordia Publishing House. Reprinted by permission.

St. Matthew, Apostle: © 1993 Northwestern Publishing House.

St. Michael and All Angels: Adapted and reprinted from *Lutheran Book of Worship,* copyright © 1978, by permission of Augsburg Fortress.

St. Luke, Evangelist: From *Lutheran Worship* © 1982 Concordia Publishing House. Reprinted by permission.

St. James of Jerusalem: public domain.

St. Simon and St. Jude, Apostles: Adapted and reprinted from *Lutheran Book of Worship,* copyright © 1978, by permission of Augsburg Fortress.

Reformation Day: Reprinted from *Service Book and Hymnal,* copyright © 1978, by permission of Augsburg Fortress.

All Saints' Day: Adapted and reprinted from *Lutheran Book of Worship,* copyright © 1978, by permission of Augsburg Fortress.

St. Andrew, Apostle: © 1993 Northwestern Publishing House.

St. Thomas, Apostle: From *Lutheran Worship* © 1982 Concordia Publishing House. Reprinted by permission.

St. Stephen, Deacon and Martyr: From *Lutheran Worship* © 1982 Concordia Publishing House. Reprinted by permission.

St. John, Apostle and Evangelist: © 1993 Northwestern Publishing House.

The Holy Innocents, Martyrs: © 1993 Northwestern Publishing House.

New Year's Eve: © 1993 Northwestern Publishing House.

Prayer of the Day—Occasions

Christian Education: public domain.

Church Anniversary: © 1993 Northwestern Publishing House.

Church Dedication: From *The Lutheran Agenda* © 1966 Concordia Publishing House. Reprinted by permission.

Environment: Adapted and reprinted from *Lutheran Book of Worship,* copyright © 1978, by permission of Augsburg Fortress.

Evangelism: © 1993 Northwestern Publishing House.

Family: Adapted and reprinted from *Lutheran Book of Worship,* copyright © 1978, by permission of Augsburg Fortress.

Home Missions: © 1993 Northwestern Publishing House.

Installation/Ordination: public domain.

Nation: Reprinted from *Lutheran Book of Worship,* copyright © 1978, by permission of Augsburg Fortress.

Organ Dedication: © 1993 Northwestern Publishing House.

School Dedication: From *The Lutheran Agenda* © 1966 Concordia Publishing House. Reprinted by permission.

493

Social Concern: Adapted and reprinted from *Lutheran Book of Worship,* copyright © 1978, by permission of Augsburg Fortress.

Stewardship: Adapted and reprinted from *Lutheran Book of Worship,* copyright © 1978, by permission of Augsburg Fortress.

Synod: © 1993 Northwestern Publishing House.

Thanksgiving Day: © 1993 Northwestern Publishing House.

Time of Crisis: Adapted and reprinted from *Lutheran Book of Worship,* copyright © 1978, by permission of Augsburg Fortress.

Worker Training: From *Lutheran Worship* © 1982 Concordia Publishing House. Reprinted by permission.

World Missions: public domain.

Psalm Prayers

Psalm 1: © 1993 Northwestern Publishing House.

Psalm 2: © 1993 Northwestern Publishing House.

Psalm 6: © 1993 Northwestern Publishing House.

Psalm 8: © 1993 Northwestern Publishing House.

Psalm 16: Adapted and reprinted from *Lutheran Book of Worship: Minister's Desk Edition,* copyright © 1978, by permission of Augsburg Fortress.

Psalm 18: © 1993 Northwestern Publishing House.

Psalm 19: © 1993 Northwestern Publishing House.

Psalm 22: © 1993 Northwestern Publishing House.

Psalm 23: © 1993 Northwestern Publishing House.

Psalm 24: © 1993 Northwestern Publishing House.

Psalm 25: © 1993 Northwestern Publishing House.

Psalm 27: © 1993 Northwestern Publishing House.

Psalm 30: © 1993 Northwestern Publishing House.

Psalm 31: © 1993 Northwestern Publishing House.

Psalm 32: © 1993 Northwestern Publishing House.

Psalm 33: Adapted and reprinted from *Lutheran Book of Worship: Minister's Desk Edition,* copyright © 1978, by permission of Augsburg Fortress.

Psalm 34: © 1993 Northwestern Publishing House.

Psalm 38: Adapted and reprinted from *Lutheran Book of Worship: Minister's Desk Edition,* copyright © 1978, by permission of Augsburg Fortress.

Psalms 42-43: © 1993 Northwestern Publishing House.

Psalm 45: © 1993 Northwestern Publishing House.

Psalm 46: Adapted and reprinted from *Lutheran Book of Worship: Minister's Desk Edition,* copyright © 1978, by permission of Augsburg Fortress.

Psalm 47: © 1993 Northwestern Publishing House.

Psalm 51a: Adapted and reprinted from *Lutheran Book of Worship: Minister's Desk Edition,* copyright © 1978, by permission of Augsburg Fortress.

Psalm 51b: © 1993 Northwestern Publishing House.

Psalm 62: Adapted and reprinted from *Lutheran Book of Worship: Minister's Desk Edition,* copyright © 1978, by permission of Augsburg Fortress.

Psalm 65: © 1993 Northwestern Publishing House.

Psalm 66: © 1993 Northwestern Publishing House.

Psalm 67: © 1993 Northwestern Publishing House.

Psalm 71: © 1993 Northwestern Publishing House.

Psalm 72: © 1993 Northwestern Publishing House.

Psalm 73: © 1993 Northwestern Publishing House.

Psalm 78: © 1993 Northwestern Publishing House.

Psalm 84: © 1993 Northwestern Publishing House.

Psalm 85: © 1993 Northwestern Publishing House.

Psalm 89: © 1993 Northwestern Publishing House.

Psalm 90: © 1993 Northwestern Publishing House.

Psalm 91: © 1993 Northwestern Publishing House.

497

Index to the Lectionary

Key: **A** — Year A of the three-year lectionary
B — Year B of the three-year lectionary
C — Year C of the three-year lectionary
O — One-year lectionary

499

501

INDEX

503

505

Index to the Psalms

Key: **A** — Year A of the three-year lectionary
B — Year B of the three-year lectionary
C — Year C of the three-year lectionary
O — One-year lectionary

510

511

Index to the Verses

515

Daily Lectionary

Week of Advent 1

M	2 Corinthians 1:15-22	Habakkuk 2:1-4
T	Micah 2:1,2,9,12,13	Colossians 1:9-14
W	2 Samuel 7:4-9,11-14a,16	Genesis 49:8-10
T	Isaiah 64:1-3	Numbers 24:15-18
F	Hebrews 10:19-25	John 18:33-37
S	Revelation 22:12-14,16,17,20,21	Zephaniah 3:14-17

Week of Advent 2

M	Luke 12:35-40	Isaiah 26:1-12
T	2 Thessalonians 3:1-5	2 Peter 1:3-11
W	Revelation 2:1-5,7	Zechariah 2:10-13
T	Mark 13:5-13	Haggai 2:1-9
F	Luke 17:20-25	Revelation 1:4-8
S	Revelation 3:14-22	Isaiah 35:1-7

Week of Advent 3

M	Matthew 11:11-15	Luke 1:5-25
T	Matthew 3:1-11	Luke 1:57-70
W	Luke 3:10-20	John 5:31-36
T	John 1:6-9,15,16	Hosea 14:5-9
F	John 1:29-34	2 Timothy 4:5-8
S	Luke 7:29-35	Isaiah 62:1-3,10-12

Week of Advent 4

M	Isaiah 45:1-8	Luke 1:39-56
T	1 Corinthians 2:6-10	Jeremiah 31:2-6,14
W	Mark 3:31-35	Isaiah 7:10-16
T	Romans 1:1-7	Isaiah 40:9-11
F	John 1:29-34	2 Timothy 4:5-8
S	John 19:25b-27	Isaiah 52:5—53:5

Christmas Eve (Dec. 24)

516

Christmas Day (Dec. 25)
St. Stephen (Dec. 26)
St. John (Dec. 27)
Holy Innocents (Dec. 28)

D 29   John 12:35-43 .... Isaiah 49:7-13
D 30   John 12:44-50 .... 2 Corinthians 5:1-8

New Year's Eve (Dec. 31)
The Name of Jesus (Jan. 1)

J 2   Luke 4:16-21 .... Deuteronomy 33:26-29
J 3   Isaiah 43:16-19 .... Acts 4:8-12
J 4   Joshua 1:1-9 .... Romans 14:7-9
J 5   James 4:13-17 .... Micah 7:7-10a,18-20

The Epiphany of Our Lord (Jan. 6)
Week of Epiphany (as needed)

M   1 Thessalonians 5:5-1 .... 1 John 8:12-20
T   Ephesians 5:8-14 .... Acts 11:1-18
W   1 John 2:7-11 .... John 9:1-12
T   1 John 1:5-10 .... John 9:24-39
F   John 3:16-21 .... Matthew 5:13-16
S   1 John 2:12-17 .... Revelation 21:9-12,21-27

Week of Epiphany 1

M   Mark 1:1-8 .... 1 John 4:9-16a
T   Mark 1:9-15 .... Mark 1:21-28
W   John 1:35-42 .... John 1:43-51
T   Matthew 4:12-17............................. Matthew 4:18-25
F   Hebrews 2:14-18 .... John 10:31-38
S   John 5:19-24 .... Luke 10:21-24

Week of Epiphany 2

M   Mark 2:18-22 .... Isaiah 61:10,11
T   Mark 3:1-6 .... Exodus 20:1-17
W   Matthew 19:3-9 .... Deuteronomy 4:5-13
T   Matthew 5:17-26 .... Deuteronomy 32:45-47; 33:1-4
F   John 1:15-18 .... Hebrews 12:18-24
S   Acts 7:35-40,51-53 .... Micah 6:6-9

518

Week of Epiphany 8

M	Exodus 34:29-35	2 Corinthians 3:12-18
T	2 Corinthians 4:3-6	2 Corinthians 4:7-12
W	2 Corinthians 4:13-18	1 Peter 2:9-10
T	Galatians 1:11-24	Acts 26:4-20
F	Matthew 16:24-28	Colossians 1:24-29
S	Philippians 3:20—4:1	Revelation 1:9-18

Week of Transfiguration

M	Luke 13:31-35	Genesis 13:7-18
T	Luke 9:18-23	Luke 9:51-56

Ash Wednesday

T	Luke 9:57b-62	Genesis 15:1-6
F	Isaiah 58:5-12	Matthew 6:1-8
S	Mark 9:14-29	Mark 6:45-52

Week of Lent 1

M	James 4:1-10	Job 1:6-22
T	James 1:13-18	Deuteronomy 8:2-5,11-18a
W	Hebrews 4:14-16	Exodus 24:12-18
T	Hebrews 12:1-7	John 2:13-22
F	Matthew 16:21-28	Hebrews 2:9-18
S	Matthew 12:38-42	Revelation 20:1-6

Week of Lent 2

M	John 7:14-18	Hebrews 11:8-12,17-19
T	Acts 5:17-29	Acts 5:34-42
W	1 Samuel 3:1-18	Matthew 21:28-32
T	Jeremiah 20:7-13	Acts 16:8-15
F	Hebrews 5:4-10	Isaiah 41:8-13
S	Matthew 21:33-46	Isaiah 49:7-13

Week of Lent 3

M	1 Peter 1:13-21	John 1:29-37
T	Mark 6:7-13	Acts 8:1-8
W	Luke 22:24-30	John 10:17-25
T	Luke 4:38-44	Acts 18:1-11
F	1 Corinthians 4:9-16	Jeremiah 11:18-20
S	Isaiah 49:1-6	Revelation 5:11-14

Week of Lent 4

M	John 6:22-29	Exodus 16:2-7a,13-15
T	1 Kings 19:1-8	John 6:30-35
W	Mark 12:28-34	Mark 12:41-44
T	John 6:47-59	John 6:60-65
F	John 12:20-26	2 Corinthians 4:7-14
S	John 8:21-30	John 11:17-45

Week of Lent 5

M	Hebrews 7:23-27	Hebrews 8:1-4,6-13
T	John 7:1-13	Hebrews 9:15-22
W	John 13:31-35	Hebrews 9:24-28
T	Hebrews 10:1-10	Hebrews 10:11-18
F	John 11:47-55	2 Corinthians 1:3-11
S	Exodus 32:30-34	Hebrews 10:19-23

Week of Lent 6

M	1 Peter 2:21-24	John 12:1-36
T	1 Timothy 6:12-14	John 12:37-50
W	Jeremiah 15:15-21	Luke 22:1-6

Maundy Thursday
Good Friday

S	1 Peter 3:17-22	Matthew 27:57-66

Week of Easter

M	Acts 10:34-43	Luke 24:13-35
T	Acts 13:16a,26-33	Luke 24:36-47
W	Acts 3:12-20	John 21:1-14
T	Acts 8:26-40	Matthew 28:16-20
F	1 Peter 3:18-22	John 20:11-18
S	1 Peter 2:1-10	John 20:1-9

Week of Easter 2

M	2 Timothy 1:6-10	Ezekiel 36:22-27
T	2 Timothy 2:1-5	Colossians 2:9-15
W	1 Peter 1:22-25	John 5:1-14
T	1 Timothy 1:12-17	2 Kings 5:1-19a
F	1 Peter 1:3-9	Romans 6:3-11
S	John 2:1-10	1 John 2:12-17

Week of Easter 3

M	Ephesians 4:17-24	Job 38:1-11
T	Ephesians 4:25-32	Job 42:1-10
W	1 John 4:7-14	Isaiah 65:17-19,23-25
T	Acts 17:22-32	Colossians 1:15-18
F	2 Corinthians 5:16-21	Romans 8:18-23
S	Romans 1:18-25	Revelation 21:1-5

Week of Easter 4

M	Ephesians 2:4-10	John 10:1-11
T	Matthew 26:31-35	Matthew 14:23-33
W	John 21:15-19	Matthew 18:10-14
T	1 Peter 5:1-4	Ezekiel 34:23-31
F	John 18:1-9	Hebrews 13:12-21
S	Acts 20:28-32	John 10:27-30

Week of Easter 5

M	Ephesians 5:8-14	1 Timothy 3:16
T	John 6:66-69	Acts 16:25-34
W	Colossians 3:16-24	Luke 19:29-40
T	Matthew 21:12-17	Exodus 14:10-14,24—15:3
F	2 Timothy 2:8-13	1 Corinthians 2:6-10
S	1 Samuel 16:14-23	Revelation 4:2-11

Week of Easter 6

M	Mark 1:35-39	Mark 11:22-26
T	Colossians 4:2-6	James 5:13-18
W	1 Timothy 2:1-8	John 17:11-26

Ascension Day

F	Colossians 3:1-4	Colossians 1:18-23
S	Luke 18:1-8a	Ephesians 1:15-23

Week of Easter 7

M	John 14:15-21	Jeremiah 29:11-14a
T	John 15:17-21	Luke 12:8-12
W	1 Corinthians 2:12-16	1 John 2:24-29
T	John 7:37-39	Numbers 20:2-12
F	Hebrews 11:32-40	Ezekiel 11:14-20
S	Isaiah 41:17-20	Genesis 11:1-9

521

Week of Pentecost

M	Isaiah 44:1-8	John 3:16-21
T	Acts 2:42-47	John 6:44-51
W	Acts 3:1-10	Acts 3:11-21
T	Acts 4:5-22	Acts 4:23-31
F	Ephesians 2:17-22	Ephesians 4:11-16
S	Acts 8:14-25	John 20:19-23

Week of Holy Trinity

M	Deuteronomy 6:4-13	Ephesians 3:14-21
T	Colossians 2:1-9	1 Kings 8:6-14,22,23,26-30
W	Ephesians 4:1-6	2 Corinthians 13:11-13
T	1 Timothy 3:14-16	Numbers 6:22-27
F	Ephesians 1:3-14	1 Corinthians 12:1-6
S	John 5:17-23	Ezekiel 1:4-6,22-28

Week of Pentecost 2

M	2 Timothy 3:14-17	2 Peter 1:16a,19-21
T	Ezekiel 2:1-7	Jeremiah 15:15-21
W	Acts 8:26-35	John 5:41-47
T	Luke 10:1-11	Ephesians 4:11-16
F	Ezekiel 3:22-27	Luke 24:44-49
S	Isaiah 5:1-7	Luke 13:22-28

Week of Pentecost 3

M	Acts 6:1-7	John 4:4-14
T	Ecclesiastes 5:1-6	Jeremiah 3:14-17
W	Matthew 11:25-30	1 Corinthians 14:26-33
T	Luke 14:12-15	1 Corinthians 14:1-4,23-25
F	1 Corinthians 1:20-25	Isaiah 45:22-25
S	James 2:1-9	Revelation 7:9,10,13-17

Week of Pentecost 4

M	Mark 2:1-12	Jeremiah 14:7-9
T	Judges 10:6-16	Luke 7:36-50
W	Mark 2:13-17	Luke 15:11-32
T	Romans 4:1-8	Romans 4:16-25
F	Romans 5:1-5	Romans 5:6-11
S	1 John 2:1-6	Isaiah 43:22-28

Week of Pentecost 5

M	John 8:1-11	Colossians 3:12-15
T	2 Corinthians 2:5-11	1 Samuel 24:2-20
W	Matthew 5:43-48	Ephesians 4:30—5:2
T	Matthew 18:15-20	Philippians 2:1-4
F	Romans 15:1-7	Acts 7:54-59
S	Galatians 6:1-5	Revelation 22:1-5

Week of Pentecost 6

M	Luke 9:57b-62	Mark 9:38-41
T	1 Kings 19:15-21	Philippians 3:12-16
W	Luke 9:51-57a	Matthew 19:27-30
T	2 Timothy 4:1-5	Ezekiel 13:17-23
F	Luke 9:18-26	1 Thessalonians 2:13-20
S	Luke 14:25-35	Matthew 13:47-52

Week of Pentecost 7

M	Titus 3:3-7	Isaiah 45:9-13
T	1 Peter 3:18-22	1 Corinthians 6:9-11
W	Galatians 3:26-29	Mark 10:13-16
T	Mark 16:14-18	Acts 10:34-48a
F	Matthew 3:13-17	Colossians 2:6-10a,12,13a
S	Ephesians 3:14-21	Revelation 3:1-6

Week of Pentecost 8

M	Mark 8:13-21	Colossians 3:18-23
T	James 3:1-10	Romans 6:12-18
W	1 Corinthians 6:19,20	Luke 11:34-36
T	Mark 9:43-50	Galatians 4:12-20
F	Romans 12:1,2	Matthew 10:26-33
S	1 Corinthians 9:24-27	1 Corinthians 15:35-45

Week of Pentecost 9

M	Matthew 5:13-16	John 8:31-36
T	Galatians 6:7-10	Matthew 12:33-37
W	James 2:14-17	Colossians 1:3-11
T	1 Corinthians 12:12-26	1 Corinthians 12:27—13:3
F	Philippians 1:6-11	Philippians 2:12-18
S	Matthew 21:18-22	Revelation 14:14-20

523

Week of Pentecost 15

M	Mark 1:40-45	Isaiah 40:25-31
T	1 Timothy 1:12-17	1 Thessalonians 5:16-24
W	2 Corinthians 9:10-15	1 Chronicles 17:16-27
T	1 Thessalonians 1:2-10	2 Thessalonians 2:13-17
F	Philippians 1:12-18	Mark 14:3-9
S	Philippians 1:19-26	Revelation 4:1-11

Week of Pentecost 16

M	Proverbs 30:4-9	1 Timothy 4:4-8
T	1 Timothy 6:6-12a	Luke 16:9-13
W	1 Corinthians 7:20-24	Acts 27:20-37
T	1 Kings 17:1-6	1 Thessalonians 2:9-12
F	John 4:31-38	2 Thessalonians 3:6-12
S	Luke 6:20-26	Revelation 22:1-5

Week of Pentecost 17

M	Lamentations 3:22-33	2 Samuel 12:19-23
T	Hebrews 12:4-11	James 1:2-12
W	Job 2:1-10	James 5:7-11
T	Ephesians 6:18-20	Mark 6:14-29
F	Hebrews 10:35-39	Isaiah 49:14-21
S	Luke 21:10-19	Revelation 2:8-11

Week of Pentecost 18

M	Romans 13:8-10	Matthew 12:1-8
T	Matthew 15:1-9	Matthew 15:10-20
W	Matthew 17:24-27	Isaiah 1:10-17
T	1 Corinthians 9:19-23	Galatians 2:11-21
F	Galatians 5:1,4-6,13-15	Galatians 6:14-18
S	Amos 5:10-15	Hebrews 4:9-13

Week of Pentecost 19

M	1 Thessalonians 4:9-12	John 15:9-17
T	Genesis 4:2b-15	1 John 3:11-18
W	1 John 4:7-16a	Ephesians 5:21-33
T	Deuteronomy 30:11-14	Ephesians 6:1-9
F	2 Corinthians 8:1-9	2 Corinthians 8:10-15
S	Acts 5:1-11	1 John 4:16b-21

Week of Reformation Sunday

M	Matthew 7:1-5	Exodus 34:1-9
T	Luke 17:1-4	1 Samuel 26:5-25
W	Matthew 6:9-15	Genesis 33:1-16
T	1 John 3:18-22	Lamentations 3:37-44,49,50
F	1 Corinthians 5:9-13	Genesis 18:20-23
S	2 Peter 3:13-18	Isaiah 64:5-11

Week of the Last Judgment

M	John 5:19-24	Daniel 5:1-30
T	Hebrews 10:26-31	Genesis 19:15-29
W	Luke 13:1-9	Romans 2:1-11
T	Luke 21:11-19	Ezekiel 14:12-23
F	Revelation 2:1-5,7	Revelation 2:8-11
S	1 Peter 4:1-7	Revelation 20:11-15

Week of the Saints Triumphant

M	Hebrews 11:1-7	Hebrews 11:8-16
T	2 Timothy 1:6-12	John 3:16-21
W	Matthew 22:23-33	1 Corinthians 15:35-43
T	2 Corinthians 2:14-17	2 Corinthians 5:1-10
F	Hebrews 11:17-22	Hebrews 11:23-31
S	Revelation 2:12-17	Revelation 21:1-7

Week of Christ the King

M	Philippians 2:6-11	Luke 12:35-40
T	Hebrews 12:12-18	Isaiah 54:11-17
W	Mark 13:33-37	Revelation 3:7-13
T	Matthew 25:14-30	Luke 13:22-30
F	Hebrews 10:32-39	Isaiah 49:14-21
S	Hebrews 12:22-29	Revelation 21:9-14,18-27

Hymn of the Day Index

Key: **A** — Year A of the three-year lectionary
B — Year B of the three-year lectionary
C — Year C of the three-year lectionary
O — One-year lectionary
Italics indicate alternate selections

Hymn Title	Hymn Number	Day	Lectionary Series
A Lamb Goes Uncomplaining Forth	100	Good Friday	ABCO
A Mighty Fortress Is Our God	200, 201	Lent 1	ABCO
		Reformation Sunday	A
All Depends on Our Possessing	421	Pentecost 18	C
		Pentecost 22	A
		Pentecost 24	O
All Mankind Fell in Adam's Fall	378	Pentecost 7	O
All Praise to God Who Reigns Above	236	Epiphany 8	ABC
		Pentecost 8	O
All Praise to You, Eternal God	33	Christmas Day	O
		Christmas Day	*ABC*
Almighty God, Your Word Is Cast	324	Epiphany 7	O
		Pentecost 8	*A*
Amazing Grace—How Sweet the Sound	379	*Pentecost 5*	*B*
		Pentecost 12	*A*
Arise, O Christian People	14	Advent 3	ABCO
At the Lamb's High Feast We Sing	141	Easter 5	AC
Awake, My Heart, with Gladness	156	Easter Day	ABCO
Awake, O Spirit, Who Inspired	567	Pentecost 3	O
Before You, God, the Judge of All	306	Pentecost 19	A
		Pentecost 23	C
Brothers, Sisters, Let Us Gladly	484	Pentecost 11	C
		Pentecost 24	A
By Grace I'm Saved	384	Pentecost 5	B
		Pentecost 12	A

528

INDEX

Hymn Title	Hymn Number	Day
Christ Is Arisen	144	Easter Dawn
Christ Is the World's Light	343	Lent 3
Christ Jesus Lay in Death's Strong Bands	161	*Easter Day*
Come, Follow Me, the Savior Spoke	453	Pentecost 6
		Pentecost 17
Come, Holy Ghost, Creator Blest	177, 178	Holy Trinity
Come, Holy Ghost, God and Lord	176	Pentecost Sunday
		Reformation Sunday
Come, Oh, Come, Life-Giving Spirit	181	Pentecost 9
		Pentecost 20
		Pentecost 22
Creator Spirit, by Whose Aid	188	Pentecost 4
		Pentecost 5
Crown Him with Many Crowns	341	Ascension
Day of Wrath, Oh, Day of Mourning	209	Last Judgment
Dear Christians, One and All, Rejoice	377	Easter 5
		Easter 6
Down from the Mount of Glory	97	Transfiguration
Forgive Our Sins as We Forgive	493	Pentecost 17
Forth in Your Name, O Lord, I Go	456	Lent 3
		Pentecost 8
		Last Judgment
From Depths of Woe I Cry to You	305	Pentecost 12
From Heaven Above to Earth I Come	38	Christmas Eve
God Loved the World So that He Gave	391	Lent 2
		Lent 4
		Pentecost 24
God Was There on Calvary	140	*Good Friday*
Hail to the Lord's Anointed	93	Epiphany 5
Have No Fear, Little Flock	442	*Pentecost 12*
How Lovely Shines the Morning Star	79	Epiphany
I Know My Faith Is Founded	403	Epiphany 7
		Pentecost 11
I Trust, O Christ, in You Alone	437	*Lent 4*
		Pentecost 4
		Pentecost 16
I Walk in Danger All the Way	431	Pentecost 14
If God Had Not Been on Our Side	202	Easter 7
If God Himself Be for Me	419	Pentecost 7

Hymn Title	Hymn Number	Day	Lectionary Series
Lord, to You I Make Confession	302	Lent 3	C
		Pentecost 11	O
Lord, You I Love with All My Heart	434	Lent 2	BC
		Pentecost 19	O
		Pentecost 23	A
May God Bestow on Us His Grace	574	*Epiphany 7*	*O*
		Pentecost 8	A
My Faith Looks Up to Thee	402	*Epiphany 7*	*B*
		Pentecost 11	*B*
My God Will Never Leave Me	418	Pentecost 10	A
My Hope Is Built on Nothing Less	382	Last Judgment	B
My Song Is Love Unknown	110	Lent 5	ABCO
Not unto Us	392	Christ the King	C
Now I Have Found the Firm Foundation	86	*Pentecost 12*	*O*
Now Sing We, Now Rejoice	34	Christmas 2	ABC
O Christians, Haste	570	Pentecost 7	C
O Fount of Good, for All Your Love	524	Pentecost 15	C
O God from God, O Light from Light	85	Epiphany 3	ABC
		Epiphany 4	O
O God, My Faithful God	459	Pentecost 15	B
O God of Mercy, God of Might	499	Pentecost 24	B
O God, Our Lord Your Holy Word	204	Reformation Sunday	B
O Holy Spirit, Grant Us Grace	185	Pentecost 13	B
O Jesus Christ, Your Manger Is	40	Christmas 2	O
O Kingly Love, that Faithfully	335	*Pentecost 21*	*AO*
O Sons and Daughters of the King	165	Easter 2	ABCO
Of the Father's Love Begotten	35	Christmas Day	ABC
		Epiphany 2	O
Oh, Blessed Home, Where Man and Wife	503	Pentecost 20	B
Oh, Come, Oh, Come, Emmanuel	23	Advent 4	ABCO
On Christ's Ascension I Now Build	173	Ascension	ACO
On Jordan's Bank the Baptist's Cry	16	Advent 2	ABC
Once Again My Heart Rejoices	37	*Christmas Eve*	*ABCO*
One Thing's Needful	290	Pentecost 9	C
		Pentecost 10	O
Our Father, Who from Heaven Above	410	Easter 6	O
		Pentecost 10	C

531

Hymn Title	Hymn Number	Day	Lectionary Series
When in the Hour of Utmost Need	413	Lent 2	O
		Pentecost 3	C
		Pentecost 13	AC
With High Delight Let Us Unite	168	Easter 5	B
Your Hand, O Lord, in Days of Old	520	Pentecost 15	O
		Pentecost 21	C
Your Works, Not Mine, O Christ	401	Pentecost 21	B

Hymns with Reduced Vocabulary

For some years now the Special Ministries Board of the Wisconsin Evangelical Lutheran Synod has been reaching out to the developmentally disabled in our own congregations and beyond. Various materials have been produced for this ministry, including a simplified catechism and some simple Bible story lessons. After reviewing the hymn texts of *Christian Worship,* the Special Education Services Committee of the Special Ministries Board has selected the following list of hymn stanzas as being suitable for use with and for teaching persons with severe learning disabilities or mental retardation. The simple vocabulary of these hymns also makes them well suited for use in mission outreach to those for whom English is a relatively new or a second language. These hymn stanzas are certainly also suitable for use with young children. The hymns are listed by section and number as they appear in *Christian Worship.*

Hymn Number	Title	Suggested stanzas
	Advent	
12	Hark the Glad Sound! The Savior Comes	1–4
27	O Jesus, Lamb of God, You Are	4
31	O Lord of Light, Who Made the Stars	6
16	On Jordan's Bank the Baptist's Cry	5
2	Savior of the Nations, Come	5*
1	The Advent of Our King	6
	Christmas	
37	Once Again My Heart Rejoices	1–6

*suitable for persons with severe mental retardation

534

Hymn Number	Title	Suggested stanzas
63	Angels We Have Heard on High	1*,3
68	Away in a Manger	1–3*
42	Come, Your Hearts and Voices Raising	5
38	From Heaven Above to Earth I Come	1,2,7
57	Go, Tell It on the Mountain	1–3
51	I Am So Glad When Christmas Comes	1*,2*,5*
55	Oh, Come, All Ye Faithful	1*
50	Once in Royal David's City	1,2
60	Silent Night! Holy Night	1–3
43	To Thee My Heart I Offer	1–3
48	When Christmas Morn Is Dawning	1,3

Lent and Holy Week

103	Glory Be to Jesus	1,6
118	O Dearest Lord, Thy Sacred Head	1–4*
119	Were You There	1–3*
120	What Wondrous Love Is This	3,4
138	Oh, Perfect Life of Love	1,5
140	God Was There on Calvary	1*,2,3*,4*,6*

Easter

154	Alleluia, Alleluia, Give Thanks	1*,2*,3,4,5*
152	I Know that My Redeemer Lives	1,2,6,8

Opening of Service

230	Lord Jesus Christ, Be Present Now	4

Worship and Praise

239	Glory Be to God the Father	1–4
259	When All Your Mercies, O My God	4

Baptism

297	Baptized in Water	3

Close of Service

326	May the Grace of Christ, Our Savior	3
334	Praise God, from Whom All Blessings Flow	1*

535

Topical Index of Hymns

Topic	Hymn Title	Hymn Number
Absent Ones	Almighty Father, Strong to Save	517
	Bless Our Loved Ones, Holy Father	504
	Now Let Us Come before Him	74
	Savior, Thy Dying Love	488 st. 3
	We Give Thee but Thine Own	485
Absolution	(*See* Confession and Absolution; Sin—Consequences of)	
Adoration	(*See* Worship and Praise)	
ADVENT (1-32)	Let All Mortal Flesh Keep Silence	361
	My Soul Now Magnifies the Lord	274
	The King of Glory Comes	363
Affliction	(*See* Comfort and Consolation; Trouble, rescue from; Trust)	
Aging	Abide with Me	588
	Lord of Our Growing Years	507 st. 3-5
All Saints	(*See* Saints and Martyrs)	
Angels	(*See also* St. Michael and All Angels)	
	As Angels Joyed with One Accord	5
	At the Name of Jesus	344
	I Walk in Danger All the Way	431 st. 4
	Isaiah, Mighty Seer in Days of Old	267
	Let All Mortal Flesh Keep Silence	361
	Lord, You I Love with All My Heart	434 st. 3
	Now the Day Is Over	589 st. 4
	Oh, Sing, My Soul, Your Maker's Praise	425
	Songs of Praise the Angels Sang	222
	The Angel Gabriel from Heaven Came	24
	We Thank You for Your Blessings	615 st. 2

Topic	Hymn Title	Hymn Number
Annunciation	(*See also* Advent)	
	Jesus! Name of Wondrous Love	76 st. 2
	The Angel Gabriel from Heaven Came	24
ASCENSION		
(169-175)	Christ High-Ascended	558
	Dear Christians, One and All, Rejoice	377 st. 9, 10
	Holy Spirit, God of Love	180
	Lord, Enthroned in Heavenly Splendor	352
	Lord Jesus Christ, You Have Prepared	312
	Saints, Behold! The Sight Is Glorious	216
Ash Wednesday	(*See* Lent)	
Assurance	(*See* Comfort and Consolation; Trust)	
Atonement of Christ	(*See also* Justification; Lent; Redeemer)	
	A Lamb Goes Uncomplaining Forth	100
	Glory Be to Jesus	103
	Hail, O Once-Despised Jesus	351
	In the Midst of Earthly Life	534
	Jesus, My Great High Priest	359
	Jesus, Your Blood and Righteousness	376
	Let All Together Praise Our God	41
	Not All the Blood of Beasts	128
	O Dearest Jesus	117
	O Dearest Lord, Thy Sacred Head	118
	Oh, Perfect Life of Love	138
	Once Again My Heart Rejoices	37
	Rock of Ages, Cleft for Me	389
	To God Be the Glory	399
	To Jordan's River Came Our Lord	89
	When All the World Was Cursed	20
	Your Works, Not Mine, O Christ	401
Awe and Wonder	God Himself Is Present	224
	How Great Thou Art	256
	Isaiah, Mighty Seer in Days of Old	267
	My Song Is Love Unknown	110
	Oh, Love, How Deep	371
	Soul, Adorn Yourself with Gladness	311

Topic	Hymn Title	Hymn Number
	To Your Temple I Draw Near	226 st. 5
	What Wondrous Love Is This	120
	When All Your Mercies, O My God	259
BAPTISM		
(294-301)	As Angels Joyed with One Accord	5
	Lord, Help Us Ever to Retain	514
	Our Lord and God, Oh, Bless This Day	599
	To Jordan Came the Christ, Our Lord	88
Beginning of Service	(*See* Morning; Opening of Service)	
Belief	(*See* Faith)	
Benediction	Christians, While on Earth Abiding	408
	God Be with You till We Meet Again	327, 328
	Hail the Day that Sees Him Rise	175 st. 4
	May God the Father of Our Lord	597
	Now Let Us Come before Him	74
	O Love that Casts Out Fear	604
	See, the Conqueror Mounts in Triumph	174 st. 3
Bible	(*See* Word of God)	
Birth of Christ	(*See* Christmas; Incarnation)	
Blessings from God	(*See also* Stewardship; Thanksgiving)	
	I Know that My Redeemer Lives	152
	May God Bestow on Us His Grace	574
	My Shepherd Will Supply My Need	374
	Now, the Hour of Worship O'er	330
	O Lord, Our God, Your Gracious Hand	511
	Oh, that I Had a Thousand Voices	194
	Praise to God, Immortal Praise	612
	To God the Anthem Raising	73
	We Thank You for Your Blessings	615
Burial	(*See* Death and Burial; Death and Resurrection)	
Call to Worship	(*See* Invocation; Opening of Service; Worship and Praise)	
Care and Concern —God's for Us	(*See also* Evening; Love—God's for Us; Trust)	
	Evening and Morning	430

539

Topic	Hymn Title	Hymn Number
	The Ten Commandments Are the Law	285 st. 5-11
	We Thank You for Your Blessings	615 st. 2
Christian Life	(*See* Christian Love; Commitment; Love–Ours for God and Neighbor; Sanctification; Walk with God)	
CHRISTIAN LOVE (490-499)	(*See also* Fellowship; Love–Ours for God and Neighbor; Marriage)	
	Forgive Us, Lord	482
	Lord of All Nations, Grant Me Grace	521
	Lord of Glory, You Have Bought Us	486
	Love Is the Gracious Gift	505
	May We Your Precepts, Lord, Fulfill	458
	O Holy Spirit, Enter In	184
	Savior, Thy Dying Love	488
	The Ten Commandments Are the Law	285 st. 5-10
	We Give Thee but Thine Own	485
	We Now Implore God the Holy Ghost	190
Christian Warfare	(*See* Church Militant)	
CHRISTMAS (33-68)	Angels from the Realms of Glory	80
	Dear Christians, One and All, Rejoice	377
	O Jesus So Sweet, O Jesus So Mild	366
	The Angel Gabriel from Heaven Came	24
CHURCH (528-541)	(*See also* God's House)	
	Alleluia! Let Praises Ring	241
	Have No Fear, Little Flock	442
	When God the Spirit Came	187
CHURCH ANNIVERSARY (621-623)	Built on the Rock	529
	God's Word Is Our Great Heritage	293
	O God, Our Help in Ages Past	441
	Our Fathers' God in Years Long Gone	535

541

Topic	Hymn Title	Hymn Number
	Lord of My Life, Whose Tender Care	232
	Lord, You Love the Cheerful Giver	489
	Oh, Blest the House, Whate'er Befall	506
	To Thee My Heart I Offer	43
	We Are the Lord's	427
Communion	(*See* Holy Communion)	
Communion of Saints	(*See* Christian Love; Fellowship)	
CONFESSION AND ABSOLUTION (302-308)	Blessed Are They, Forever Blest	383
	Chief of Sinners Though I Be	385
	Comfort, Comfort All My People	11
	Forgive Our Sins as We Forgive	493
	I Lay My Sins on Jesus	372
	I Trust, O Christ, in You Alone	437
	Jesus, I Will Ponder Now	98
	Just As I Am, without One Plea	397
	Lord Jesus, You Are Going Forth	126
	Lord, We Confess Our Numerous Faults	398
	O Jesus, Lamb of God, You Are	27
	Rejoice, My Heart, Be Glad and Sing	443 st. 4
	Savior, When in Dust to You	124
	Speak, O Savior; I Am Listening	283
	The Ten Commandments Are the Law	285
	To Your Temple I Draw Near	226
	When O'er My Sins I Sorrow	109
	When Sinners See Their Lost Condition	32
Confession of Faith	(*See* Creed and Confession)	
Confidence	(*See also* Faith)	
	I Know that My Redeemer Lives	152
	Jesus Christ, My Sure Defense	167
	Jesus Lives! The Victory's Won	145
	This Is the Threefold Truth	406
	To Shepherds as They Watched by Night	53
	We Are the Lord's	427

Topic	Hymn Title	Hymn Number
CONFIRMATION		
(596-599)	(*See* Pentecost)	
Cornerstone-Laying	(*See* God's House)	
Creation	(*See also* God the Father)	
	A Great and Mighty Wonder	36 st. 3
	Almighty Father, Heaven and Earth	480
	Angels We Have Heard on High	63 st. 1
	At the Name of Jesus	344
	Beautiful Savior	369
	Creator Spirit, by Whose Aid	188 st. 1
	Earth and All Stars	247
	God, Who Made the Earth and Heaven	590
	How Great Thou Art	256
	Jesus, Savior, Pilot Me	433
	Joy to the World	62
	Let All Things Now Living	260
	Lord of Lords, the Sparkling Heavens	237
	Now Rest Beneath Night's Shadow	587
	O God, Your Hand the Heavens Made	481
	O Jesus Christ, Your Manger Is	40 st. 2
	O Lord of Heaven and Earth and Sea	487
	Oh, that I Had a Thousand Voices	242
	Oh, Worship the King	243
	Songs of Praise the Angels Sang	222 st. 1,3
	The Stars Declare His Glory	246
	This Day at Your Creating Word	229
	Thy Strong Word	280
	We Sing the Almighty Power of God	261
	When All Your Mercies, O My God	259
	When Morning Gilds the Skies	251
Creed and Confession	(*See also* Hymns of the Liturgy)	
	At the Name of Jesus	344
	Christ the Lord is Risen Again	155
	Come, Holy Ghost, Creator Blest	177, 178
	Father Most Holy, Merciful, and Tender	191
	For All the Saints	551

Topic	Hymn Title	Hymn Number
	For Years on Years of Matchless Grace	621 st. 3
	God, We Praise You	277
	Jesus! and Shall It Ever Be	347
	Jesus Christ, Our Blessed Savior	313 st. 8
	Lord Jesus Christ, the Church's Head	536
	O Christ, Our True and Only Light	569
	O Holy Spirit, Enter In	184
	O Jesus, King Most Wonderful	373
	O Jesus, King of Glory	94
	O Savior, Precious Savior	368
Cross-Bearing	(*See also* Trust)	
	Be Still, My Soul	415
	Come, Follow Me, the Savior Spoke	453
	Come, Oh, Come, Life-Giving Spirit	181
	Father, Let Me Dedicate	75
	I Walk in Danger All the Way	431 st. 2
	Jerusalem, Thou City Fair and High	212
	Jesus, I My Cross Have Taken	465
	Jesus, I Will Ponder Now	98 st. 6
	Lord Jesus Christ, You Set Us Free	123
Cross of Christ	(*See also* Lent)	
	Christ, the Life of All the Living	114
	Drawn to the Cross	387
	How Great Thou Art	256 st. 3
	In the Cross of Christ I Glory	345
	Oh, Darkest Woe	137
	The Head that Once Was Crowned	217
	When I Survey the Wondrous Cross	125
Day of Worship	(*See also* Opening of Service)	
	God Is Here! As We His People	532
	The Ten Commandments Are the Law	285 st. 4
DEATH AND BURIAL (**605-608**)	(*See also* Death and Resurrection; Easter)	
	Abide with Me	588
	For All the Saints	551
	I Am Jesus' Little Lamb	432

Topic	Hymn Title	Hymn Number
Entrance/ Procession	(*See also* Opening of Service)	
	All Glory, Laud, and Honor	131
	Come, Rejoice before Your Maker	228
	Oh, Sing to the Lord	252
	Open Now Thy Gates of Beauty	255
	The King of Glory Comes	363
Environment	(*See* Ecology)	
EPIPHANY (79-94)	Gentle Mary Laid Her Child	56
	Oh, Rejoice, All Christians, Loudly	45
Eternal Life	(*See* Life Everlasting)	
Eucharist	(*See* Holy Communion)	
EVANGELISM (556-566)	(*See also* Great Commission; Ministry; Missions; Planting the Seed)	
	Alleluia, Alleluia, Give Thanks	154
	Built on the Rock	529
	Christ, the Lord Is Risen Again	155
	Dear Lord, to Your True Servants Give	542
	Go, Tell It on the Mountain	57
	God's Word Is Our Great Heritage	293
	In Trembling Hands, Lord God, We Hold	199
	Jesus! and Shall It Ever Be	347
	Saints, Behold! The Sight is Glorious	216
	Not unto Us	392
	O Kingly Love, that Faithfully	335
	Oh, Rejoice, All Christians, Loudly	45
	Oh, that I Had a Thousand Voices	194
	Oh, that I Had a Thousand Voices	242
	Oh, Worship the King	243
	The Day of Resurrection	166
	There's a Voice in the Wilderness Crying	13
	With High Delight Let Us Unite	168
EVENING (587-595)	Lord Jesus Christ, with Us Abide	541
	When Morning Gilds the Skies	251

Topic	Hymn Title	Hymn Number
	My Song Is Love Unknown	110
	O God, My Faithful God	459
	O Master of the Loving Heart	491
	This Is My Will	497
	What a Friend We Have in Jesus	411
Fruits of Faith	Amid the World's Bleak Wilderness	342
	O Holy Spirit, Enter In	184 st. 3
	O Holy Spirit, Grant Us Grace	185
	Sent Forth by God's Blessing	318
	Speak, O Savior; I Am Listening	283
	This Is My Will	497
Gifts of the Spirit	Come, Now, Almighty King	193
	Come, Oh, Come, Life-Giving Spirit	181 st. 5
	Holy Spirit, Ever Dwelling	182 st. 2
Gladness	(See Joy/Gladness)	
Glory	Christ Is the World's Light	343
	Glory Be to God the Father	239
	I Love to Tell the Story	562
	Lord, When Your Glory I Shall See	219
	Then the Glory	218
	To God Be the Glory	399
God	(See also Holy Trinity)	
	Abide with Me	588
	All Glory Be to God on High	263
	Father Most Holy, Merciful and Tender	191
	Holy, Holy, Holy, Lord God Almighty	195
	How Firm a Foundation	416
	How Lovely Shines the Morning Star	79
	Immortal, Invisible, God Only Wise	240
God—the Father	(See also Creation)	
	Children of the Heavenly Father	449
	Evening and Morning	430
	Father, Let Me Dedicate	75
	We All Believe in One True God	271 st. 1
God— the Holy Spirit	(See Pentecost; Sanctification)	
	Dear Christians, One and All, Rejoice	377 st. 9

549

Topic	Hymn Title	Hymn Number
	Jesus, Refuge of the Weary	108
	Lord of Our Growing Years	507
	Lord, 'Tis Not that I Did Choose You	380
	On Christmas Night All Christians Sing	52
Great Commission	(*See also* Evangelism; Missions)	
	As Surely As I Live, God Said	308
	Christ High-Ascended	558
	Go, Tell It on the Mountain	57
	Good News of God Above	568
	Hail Thee, Festival Day	179
	Spread, Oh, Spread the Mighty Word	576
	To Jordan Came the Christ, Our Lord	88
	We All Are One in Mission	566
	When God the Spirit Came	187
Great Exchange	(*See also* Atonement of Christ)	
	Dear Christians, One and All, Rejoice	377
	If Your Beloved Son, O God	393
	Let All Together Praise Our God	41
	Once Again My Heart Rejoices	37
	Triumphant from the Grave	151
	Your Works, Not Mine, O Christ	401
Guidance	Come, My Soul, with Every Care	409
	Guide Me, O Thou Great Jehovah	331
	Jesus, Lead Us On	422
	Lord, Take My Hand and Lead Me	439
	My Faith Looks Up to Thee	402
	O Word of God Incarnate	279
	Oh, that the Lord Would Guide My Ways	462
Heaven	(*See* Life Everlasting)	
Holiness	(*See also* Justification; Pentecost; Trust)	
	Holy, Holy, Holy, Lord God Almighty	195
Holy Baptism	(*See* Baptism)	
HOLY COMMUNION (309-318)	As Angels Joyed with One Accord	5
	Now the Silence	231

Topic	Hymn Title	Hymn Number
Humiliation and Exaltation of Christ	(*See also* Ascension; Incarnation)	
	At the Name of Jesus	344
	Crown Him with Many Crowns	341
	Dear Christians, One and All, Rejoice	377
	Down from the Mount of Glory	97
	Hail, O Once-Despised Jesus	351
	O Jesus, King of Glory	94
	See in Yonder Manger Low	58
Humility	Love in Christ Is Strong and Living	490
	Savior, When in Dust to You	124

HYMNS OF THE LITURGY (262-278)

Topic	Hymn Title	Hymn Number
Idolatry	All Mankind Fell in Adam's Fall	378
	All Praise to God Who Reigns Above	236 st. 5
	From Greenland's Icy Mountains	571
	Holy Spirit, Light Divine	183
	Jesus Calls Us O'er the Tumult	463
	The Ten Commandments Are the Law	285
Image of God	Jesus, Jesus, Only Jesus	348
	O Jesus, King Most Wonderful	373
Imitation of Christ	O Master of the Loving Heart	491
Immortality	(*See* Hope; Life Everlasting)	
Incarnation	(*See also* Christmas; God—the Son)	
	A Great and Mighty Wonder	36
	All Praise to You, Eternal God	33
	Hark! The Herald Angels Sing	61
	Oh, Love, How Deep	371
	Savior of the Nations, Come	2
Installation	(*See* Ministry)	

INVITATION (335-339)

Topic	Hymn Title	Hymn Number
	(*See also* Commitment)	
	All Praise to God Who Reigns Above	236 st. 5

Topic	Hymn Title	Hymn Number
	May the Grace of Christ Our Savior	326
	Oh, Blessed Home, Where Man and Wife	503
	The Lord Is God; There Is No Other	292
	The Ten Commandments Are the Law	285 st. 7
Materialism	(*See also* Stewardship)	
	Forgive Us, Lord	482
	Jesus, Priceless Treasure	349
	O Jesus Christ, Your Manger Is	40 st. 5
	Son of God, Eternal Savior	492
	Take the World, but Give Me Jesus	355
	The Ten Commandments Are the Law	285 st. 8,10
	What Is the World to Me	477
	When I Survey the Wondrous Cross	125
MAUNDY THURSDAY (135-136)	(*See also* Lent)	
	This Is My Will	497
Means of Grace	(*See also* Baptism; Holy Communion; Word of God)	
	Built on the Rock	529
	Faith Is a Living Power from Heaven	404
	God Is Here! As We His People	532
	Lord Jesus Christ, with Us Abide	541
	Lord, We Confess Our Numerous Faults	398
	O Lord of Heaven and Earth and Sea	487
Mercy	Christ Is Arisen	144
	In the Midst of Earthly Life	534
	Kyrie, God Father in Heaven Above	266
	Lamb of God, Pure and Holy	268
	Now I Have Found the Firm Foundation	386
	We Now Implore God the Holy Ghost	190
	With Broken Heart and Contrite Sigh	303
MINISTRY (542-548)	(*See also* Personal Ministry)	
	Awake, O Spirit, Who Inspired	567
	Dear Christians, One and All, Rejoice	377 st. 10
	Send Forth, O Lord, to Every Place	572
	To Your Temple I Draw Near	226

Topic	Hymn Title	Hymn Number
Prayers (Individual Stanzas)	Arise, O Christian People	14 st. 4
	Away in a Manger	68 st. 3
	Christians, While on Earth Abiding	408 st. 2
	Come, O Precious Ransom, Come	8 st. 2
	Come, Your Hearts and Voices Raising	42 st. 5
	From Heaven Above to Earth I Come	38 st. 13
	Jesus, in Your Dying Woes	139 st. 1-7
	Let the Earth Now Praise the Lord	28 st. 4-6
	Lift Up Your Heads, You Mighty Gates	3, 4 st. 5
	Like the Golden Sun Ascending	147 st. 5
	Now Rest Beneath Night's Shadow	587 st. 3
	Now Sing We, Now Rejoice	34 st. 2
	Now, the Hour of Worship O'er	330 st. 3
	Now the Light Has Gone Away	593
	O Little Town of Bethlehem	65, 66 st. 4
	Oh, Blessed Home, Where Man and Wife	503 st. 3
	To Thee My Heart I Offer	43 st. 4
	Triune God, Oh, Be Our Stay	192
	Up Through Endless Ranks of Angels	172 st. 3,4
	We Thank You for Your Blessings	615
Predestination	(*See* Election)	
Prejudice	(*See* Races and Cultures)	
Preparation/ Readiness	Great God, What Do I See and Hear	208
	Lord, Dismiss Us with Your Blessing	329
	O'er the Distant Mountains Breaking	220
	Wake, Awake, for Night Is Flying	206
Presence of God	(*See also* Trust)	
	Abide, O Dearest Jesus	333
	Abide with Me	588
	Alleluia! Sing to Jesus	169
	Evening and Morning	430
	God Himself Is Present	224
	Here, O My Lord, I See You Face to Face	315
	Lord Jesus Christ, Be Present Now	230
	Lord Jesus Christ, You Have Prepared	312

Topic	Hymn Title	Hymn Number
	Lord Jesus Christ, the Church's Head	536
	Lord Jesus Christ, with Us Abide	541
	Who Knows When Death	210
Sadness	(*See* Sorrow and Sadness, deliverance from)	
ST. MICHAEL AND ALL ANGELS (196-198)	(*See* Angels; Christmas)	
SAINTS AND MARTYRS (549-555)	By All Your Saints Still Striving	552
	God, We Praise You	277
Salvation	(*See also* Justification; Redeemer)	
	All Mankind Fell in Adam's Fall	378
	All Praise Be Yours	350
	Dear Christians, One and All, Rejoice	377
	From Heaven Above to Earth I Come	38
	God Was There on Calvary	140
	I Love to Tell the Story	562
	Jesus Christ, Our Blessed Savior	313
	Rejoice, Rejoice This Happy Morn	49
	Salvation unto Us has Come	390
	The Day Full of Grace	254
Sanctification	(*See also* Walk with God)	
	From Eternity, O God	461
	Love Divine, All Love Excelling	365
	O God, My Faithful God	459
	O Holy Spirit, Enter In	184
	Redeemed, Restored, Forgiven	388
	Sent Forth by God's Blessing	318
	Songs of Thankfulness and Praise	82
Sanctity of Life	(*See also* Baptism)	
	By All Your Saints Still Striving	552 st. 27
	I Will Sing My Maker's Praises	253
	Let All Things Now Living	260
	Lord of Our Growing Years	507

565

Topic	Hymn Title	Hymn Number
	Forgive Us, Lord	482
	How Can I Thank You, Lord	460
	Let All Things Now Living	260
	Like the Golden Sun Ascending	147 st. 2,5
	O Lord, Our Father, Thanks and Praise	72
	Oh, that I Had a Thousand Voices	242
	To God the Anthem Raising	73
	When All Your Mercies, O My God	259
The Fall	All Mankind Fell in Adam's Fall	378
	Come to Calvary's Holy Mountain	106
	In Adam We Have All Been One	396
	Joy to the World	62
	Lord God, to You We All Give Praise	196
	The Bridegroom Soon Will Call Us	10
	To Jordan's River Came Our Lord	89
Time of Grace	Amazing Grace—How Sweet the Sound	379
	Delay Not! Delay Not	337
	I Hear the Savior Calling	560
	There Still Is Room	565

**TRANSFIGURA-
TION (95-97)**

Topic	Hymn Title	Hymn Number
Travelers	Almighty Father, Strong to Save	517
Trial and Tribulation	(*See* Comfort and Consolation; Sorrow and Sadness, deliverance from; Trouble, rescue from; Trust)	
Trinity	(*See* Holy Trinity)	
Trouble, rescue from	(*See also* Trust)	
	Lord Jesus Christ, My Savior Blest	362
	Now Let Us Come before Him	74
	Oh, for a Faith that Will Not Shrink	405
	What a Friend We Have in Jesus	411
	When in the Hour of Utmost Need	413
	Why Should Cross and Trial Grieve Me	428

INDEX